Tocqueville's *Democracy in America* i
perhaps the most important book—i
ety. John D. Wilsey's abridgment suc
magnum opus in the hands of studei... ... general readers, while his introduction provides a clear guide for understanding the work. By sharing Tocqueville's ideas broadly, Wilsey has contributed to educating the American democracy.

Jonathan Den Hartog, associate professor of history,
University of Northwestern—St. Paul, St. Paul, Minnesota

Alexis de Tocqueville is the greatest political theorist of democracy, and *Democracy in America* is his greatest writing. Editor John Wilsey provides an excellent introduction to Tocqueville's thought and a judicious abridgment of the book that trims it down to half its original size while retaining Tocqueville's most important thoughts on issues such as democracy, liberty, religion, and race. Highly recommended.

Bruce Ashford, provost and professor of theology and culture,
Southeastern Baptist Theological Seminary

John Wilsey's edition of *Democracy in America* brings Tocqueville's essential text into the classroom. Focusing on democracy, liberty, and racial prejudice, Wilsey draws attention to the important themes that have made Tocqueville's work required reading as both a historical artifact and a statement of political philosophy. With careful abridgment and an approachable introduction, Wilsey helps faculty and students alike understand the meaning of *Democracy in America* in its own time and today.

Emily Conroy-Krutz, assistant professor of history, Michigan State University

Framed by a thoughtful introduction to *Democracy in America*'s historical context and its core philosophical and social concerns, this volume deftly balances reader accessibility with coverage of essential elements of the original text.

Lloyd Benson, W. K. Mattison Professor of History, Furman University

Wilsey's marvelous editing of Alexis de Tocqueville's classic *Democracy in America* is both timely and instructive, given our current political context and racial climate in 21st-century America. Students, professors, and the general reader will benefit from a renewed edition of Tocqueville's prescient 19th-century observations of our still-burgeoning republic as well as from Wilsey's skillful teasing out of Tocqueville's views on race and slavery in a fresh, thoughtful, and insightful introduction. This book will be a benefit to American classrooms and a "must have" for educators' libraries for decades to come.

Otis W. Pickett, assistant professor of history, Mississippi College

John D. Wilsey has achieved something near impossible—the abridgment of Alexis de Tocqueville's masterpiece *Democracy in America* while retaining its core contributions to our understanding of Jacksonian America up to the present. In his introduction, Wilsey provides readers an excellent guide for understanding Tocqueville's treatment of equality, democracy, liberty, and especially slavery. This volume is perfect for high school and college students, but any curious reader could pick up a copy to start his or her study of this classic text.

James M. Patterson, assistant professor of politics, Ave Maria University

Democracy in America has always been essential reading for students of American history and of the history of political and social thought. But teachers on the secondary-school and undergraduate levels who might otherwise make generous use of Tocqueville's luminous text have often been daunted by the length and expense entailed in assigning the whole book. For such teachers and their students, this careful abridgment of the *Democracy*, trimmed to half its original length and framed by the editor's thoughtful introductory essay, will prove to be just what the doctor ordered.

Wilfred M. McClay, G. T. and Libby Blankenship Chair in the History of Liberty, and director of the Center for the History of Liberty, University of Oklahoma

Tocqueville's unparalleled analysis of the American experiment—his praise of it, and his prescient warnings about a people detached from virtue and religion—should be required reading for every American citizen. This superb abridgment communicates the power of the original in a way that makes thinking with Tocqueville easier than ever. Recommended!

C. C. Pecknold, associate professor of theology, The Catholic University of America

Wilsey's volume on Tocqueville's notoriously complex *Democracy in America* does an excellent job of contextualizing for the modern reader. He reminds readers of the importance of reading Tocqueville in a historically critical manner that takes into account Tocqueville's own views of democracy, as well as the fact that his writings should be properly understood as a "window into Jacksonian America." Wilsey's consideration of Tocqueville's predictions on what slavery and racial inequality might mean for the United States are another important contribution this volume makes to the considerable scholarship on Tocqueville.

Jessica M. Parr, adjunct professor and project coordinator for public history, UNH-Manchester

Democracy in America

A New Abridgment for Students

Democracy in America

A New Abridgment for Students

Alexis de Tocqueville

Edited and abridged with an introduction

by John D. Wilsey

LEXHAM PRESS

To the memory of my grandfather

Jasper Newton Dorsey

Christian, Husband, Father, Grandfather,
Churchman, Servant, Soldier, Citizen

1913 – 1990

Contents

---★---

Introduction

The gradual development of the equality of conditions is therefore a providential fact, and it possesses all the characteristics of a divine decree: it is universal, it is durable, it constantly eludes all human interference, and all events as well as all men contribute to its progress.

Alexis de Tocqueville, 1835

O n the night of November 26, 1831, a steamship traveling down the Ohio River on her way to Cincinnati struck a reef in the middle of the river known as Burlington Bar, just upstream from Wheeling, Virginia.[1] The steamship was the *Fourth of July*, and immediately after striking the obstruction, she began to sink in the freezing water. The river is about a half mile wide at that point, but the sound of the ship striking Burlington Bar could easily be heard on both shores. There were 200 passengers aboard the *Fourth of July*, but only enough skiffs for about a dozen people. A great tragedy seemed imminent until the ship suddenly stopped sinking—it became hung up on Burlington Bar, which ironically saved the ship after dealing her a fatal blow. After several hours, the steamship *William Parsons* rescued the stranded passengers of the crippled *Fourth of July* and no one was lost.[2]

---

1. Today, Wheeling is in West Virginia, which became a state in 1863 during the Civil War.
2. George Wilson Pierson described this adventure in his work, originally titled *Tocqueville and Beaumont in America*. The specific details of the *Fourth of July* accident are a bit hazy, because Tocqueville described them in his now lost

This might seem a rather obscure, though propitious, event. But there were two important foreign visitors aboard the *Fourth of July* who likely would have perished had the ship foundered in the middle of the icy river: Alexis de Tocqueville (1805–1859) and Gustave de Beaumont (1802–1866), commissioners from France traveling through America to study prisons. The two travelers survived the accident, completed their mission, and produced an award-winning book on American prisons, titled *Du système pénitentiaire aux Étas-Unis et de son application en France*. And in addition to fulfilling their mission in America, both authors completed separate projects of their own. Beaumont wrote a novel based on his observations of racial prejudice in antebellum America, titled *Marie, or Slavery in the United States* (*Marie, ou l'esclavage aux Etats-Unis*). Tocqueville wrote a study of American political and social institutions and culture, titled *Democracy in America* (*De la Démocratie en Amérique*). Tocqueville's work went on to become one of the most celebrated works in modern political theory and arguably the most articulate and prescient firsthand analysis of American politics and society ever written. If the *Fourth of July* had succumbed to the frigid waters of the Ohio River in November 1831, subsequent generations including our own likely would have been denied one of the shrewdest and most influential observers of nineteenth-century American polity.

Tocqueville and Beaumont arrived in the United States on May 9, 1831,[3] and returned to France on February 20, 1832, spending about nine months traveling throughout Jacksonian America. Tocqueville took copious notes, carried on continuous correspondence, and built numerous relationships with Americans in preparation for writing what became *Democracy in America*. He completed the first volume of the work in 1835 and the second in 1840.

---

correspondence with his wife, Marie Mottley. After Tocqueville died in 1859, Marie destroyed the letters her husband wrote her while he was in America. What details are available about the accident are taken from Beaumont's recollections and a small contemporary newspaper account. See George Wilson Pierson, *Tocqueville in America* (1938; repr., Baltimore: Johns Hopkins University Press, 1996), 545–47.

3. Their ship's intended destination was New York, but they landed in Newport, Rhode Island on May 9 due to unfavorable winds off Long Island. They arrived in New York by a separate steamer two days later, on May 11.

Tocqueville's idea to come to America originally was the product of a desire to flee the Revolution of 1830 and the July Monarchy under King Louis-Philippe. He was a young lawyer at the time, and his family was closely associated with Charles X, France's last king in the Bourbon line. Louis-Philippe, a cousin of Charles seeking to establish a constitutional monarchy, deposed him in 1830. After Louis-Philippe's rise to power and the establishment of the July Monarchy, all public officials were required to take an oath of loyalty to the new government, which Tocqueville reluctantly—but out of necessity—took.

Taking the oath was something of a no-win situation for Tocqueville. The new government was untried, Tocqueville's family was opposed to Louis-Philippe, and his own prospects for advancement in France's legal profession after the revolution were uncertain. Still, Tocqueville was among many in France who were interested in prison reform, and the work undertaken in this area—especially by the Quakers in the American state of Pennsylvania—intrigued Tocqueville. Taking an extended trip to the United States to study prisons on behalf of the French government seemed a plausible way to advance his career and escape the pressure on him at home. Tocqueville and his colleague Beaumont were able to secure their official commissions from the Ministry of the Interior by February 1831, and they departed for America on April 2 aboard the ship *Havre* for a thirty-eight day trip across the Atlantic.

While prison reform was of interest to the two travelers, it is no secret that Tocqueville's primary interest was to study the republican example that America presented to the world and, in particular, to France. Prison reform was the pretext—a cynic would call it an excuse—for Tocqueville to leave France for a time to observe firsthand how democracy was unfolding in the young United States. His ultimate goal was to write a book not to celebrate America or even democracy, but to identify lessons derived from the Americans' experience of democratic revolution for the benefit of his own countrymen. In August 1830, Tocqueville wrote to his old schoolmate, Charles Stoffels, "I have long had the greatest desire to visit North America: I shall go see there what a great republic is like; my only fear is lest, during that time, they establish one in France."[4] And in his introduc-

---

4. Alexis de Tocqueville to Charles Stoffels, August 26, 1830, quoted in Pierson, *Tocqueville in America*, 31.

tion to *Democracy*, Tocqueville sought immediately to dismiss suspicions that he was writing an uncritical work of democratic institutions in America. Rather, he accepted democracy as an objective fact and wanted to address positive and negative lessons the French people could learn from the American example. He wrote, "I sought there the image of democracy itself, with its inclinations, its character, its prejudices, and its passions, in order to learn what we have to fear or to hope from its progress."[5] Thus, at least two realities are important for modern readers to keep in mind when approaching Tocqueville's *Democracy*. First, Tocqueville wrote for a French audience, not an American one. Second, Tocqueville was an aristocrat, and therefore was an outsider to democracy. He believed that democracy would inevitably grow and displace hierarchical social and political structures, but he was not convinced that democracy was an unmitigated good for society. He wanted to acquaint himself with democracy's assets as well as its liabilities, and to consider ways that Frenchmen might benefit from democracy while avoiding its dangers.

Tocqueville's first volume opens with what is perhaps the work's most important chapter—the introduction. Immediately, Tocqueville explains his purpose for the book, which was to analyze the nature of "equality of condition" as he observed it in America. He writes, "I observed that equality of condition, though it has not there [that is, in Europe] reached the extreme limit which it seems to have attained in the United States, is constantly approaching it; and that the democracy which governs the American communities appears to be rapidly rising into power in Europe. Hence I conceived the idea of the book which is now before the reader."[6] Although equality of condition had taken hold in the United States and seemed to Tocqueville to be destined by Providence to overspread all of human civilization, he thought it was necessary to control the effects of equality. Later in his introduction, he writes, "The first of the duties which are at this time imposed upon those who direct our affairs, is to educate the democracy; to renovate, if possible, its religious belief; to purify its morals; to regulate its movements; to substitute by degrees a knowledge of business for its inexperience, and an acquaintance with its

---

5. I.Introduction, 42.
6. I.Introduction, 30.

true interests for its blind instincts; to adapt its government to time and place, and to make it conform to the occurrences and the men of the times."[7] Tocqueville's book, *Democracy in America*, was both the product of his observations about equality of condition in America and his prescription for how to prevent such equality from degrading into what he called "democratic despotism."[8]

Some Tocqueville scholars have noted that *Democracy in America* is not an easy read.[9] To the modern American reader, this might well be true. Tocqueville wrote in the style of an early nineteenth-century French aristocrat. But more importantly, Tocqueville's *Democracy* is actually two books in one. The first volume is based on Tocqueville's concrete observations of American democracy. The second volume is more philosophical, focusing on democracy as an idea. Tocqueville finished the second volume almost ten years after returning from America, so his writings there are clearly distinguishable from those of the first volume, which show evidence of fresher impressions. Alan Ryan remarks that the first volume "focuses on what everyone would conventionally describe as the features of democratic government."[10] Olivier Zunz and Alan Kahan write of the second volume, that it "focused on how the principle of equality affected society and culture."[11] Part of the struggle modern readers face results from this difference in style between volumes 1 and 2, but if the reader can appreciate these distinctions beforehand, the difficulties can be mitigated.

Almost immediately after the first volume appeared in print, it was received as a work of genius. Tocqueville's publisher said, "I see you have written a masterpiece."[12] Tocqueville's mentor, Pierre-Paul Royer-Collard, a member of the French parliament under the July Monarchy, called *Democracy* "the most remarkable political work

---

7. I.Introduction, 34.

8. II.iv.6, 463.

9. For example, in his introduction to the 1994 Everyman's Library edition, Alan Ryan wrote, "*Democracy in America* is not an entirely easy book to describe and analyse." Alan Ryan, introduction to *Democracy in America* by Alexis de Tocqueville (New York: Knopf, 1994), xxix.

10. Ibid.

11. Olivier Zunz and Alan S. Kahan, eds., *The Tocqueville Reader: A Life in Letters and Politics* (Oxford: Blackwell, 2002), 19.

12. Ryan, "Introduction," xxvi.

which has appeared in thirty years." He went on to pay Tocqueville the ultimate compliment for a nineteenth-century French political thinker: "Since Montesquieu, there has been nothing like it."[13] George Wilson Pierson surveyed twenty-three articles reviewing volume 1 of *Democracy* within a year of its publication, and only one stood out as a negative outlier.[14] One of the most enthusiastic readers of *Democracy* was John Stuart Mill (1806–1873), the great English political and social theorist. Ryan writes that Mill helped the work to become a success in the English-speaking world.[15]

Volume 1 brought Tocqueville immediate fame. In 1835, the year volume 1 was published, he was inducted into the prestigious Académie des Sciences Morales et Politiques. He celebrated the book's success by marrying Marie Mottley, and in 1836 the couple took possession of the family estate at Tocqueville in Normandy upon the death of Alexis' mother. He also entered politics. He ran for a seat in the Chamber of Deputies as the representative of the town of Valognes, which lay adjacent to the Tocqueville estate. His busy personal and professional life explains why volume 2, published in 1840, took a long time to write, and it may explain the more philosophical nature of the work. Volume 2 was not as well received as the first, but the combined work's success as a groundbreaking and enduring work in political science and sociology speaks for itself.

But why should Americans continue to read Tocqueville's *Democracy* in today's technology-saturated, selfie-obsessed culture, defined by an attention span measured in seconds and a distaste for anything theoretical? The United States is not the same country it was in 1840. Voluntary associations—like churches—do not occupy the central position of influence in American social and political life as they once did. Most citizens of the United States—who are vastly more culturally diverse today—no longer accept the Protestant Christian religion and morality as normative like they did in the early republican period. And the America encountered by Tocqueville was at the threshold of the Industrial Revolution, whereas our own America is grappling

---

13. Pierson, *Tocqueville in America*, 4.
14. Ibid. The negative review appeared in the *Gazette de France*, which Pierson described as "ultra-royalist."
15. Ryan, "Introduction," xxvii.

with the effects of industrialism and post-industrialism. Furthermore, what Tocqueville observed about the American obsession with the pursuit of wealth pales in comparison with today's ethos. That is the nature of history, after all; the past is indeed, as L. P. Hartley famously said, a foreign country. Is *Democracy* now more of a historical artifact from Jacksonian America than a relevant political theory for our own times?

It is both. *Democracy* represents one consideration of a moment early in the career of the United States. For that reason, Tocqueville's work is of great interest to historians and laypersons alike, because it is an open window facing the world of Jacksonian America. And Tocqueville was observing early republican society from the perspective of someone who had personally experienced the destruction of liberty in a great revolution in his native France. He offered his nineteenth-century readers, just as he offers his readers of today, wisdom on how to control the Phaethonian chariot of democracy, to keep it from becoming the instrument of tyranny rather than of liberty. Contemporary readers must be cautious about receiving Tocqueville in a historically uncritical manner. We must think historically about *Democracy in America*.[16] But Tocqueville's work still speaks to legitimately timeless elements in human beings as "political animals," as Aristotle famously said, and for that reason we can continue to learn from him.

Alexis-Charles-Henri Clèrel (Tocqueville's family name) was born on July 29, 1805, to an ancient Norman aristocratic family. His father, Hervé, was a civil servant for the post-revolutionary, pre-Napoleonic restored Bourbon monarchy. Hervé's line was not exceedingly wealthy, but it was of the *noblesse d'épeé*—that is, the family had achieved its noble rank through military service.[17] His mother, Louise-Madeleine Le Peletier de Rosanbo, also was of noble birth. Her family was of the *noblesse de robe*; they received their title from services rendered in the

---

16. See John Fea, *Why Study History: Reflecting on the Importance of the Past* (Grand Rapids: Baker, 2013) and Nathan A. Finn, *History: A Student's Guide* (Wheaton: Crossway, 2016).

17. Tocqueville could claim an ancestor who had fought for William the Conqueror against the Anglo-Saxons at Hastings in 1066.

judicial bureaucracy. Before Alexis was born, the French Revolution nearly destroyed his family during the 1790s. Tocqueville's maternal great-grandfather, Chrétien Malesherbes (1721–1794), and his daughter were beheaded during the Terror in 1794 for his role as Louis XVI's defense attorney.[18] Hervé and Louise-Madeleine were imprisoned and marked for execution that same year, but the arrest and beheading of Maximilien Robespierre ended the Reign of Terror and their imprisonment.

Tocqueville grew up fully aware of his social position as a member of the aristocracy. Zunz and Kahan write that Tocqueville "never forgot" his aristocratic position and "always knew himself to be of a class born apart."[19] However, as is clear from Tocqueville's introduction to volume 1 of *Democracy*, he knew that the aristocratic hierarchies of feudal Europe were being steadily usurped by egalitarian forces and ultimately would disappear. Tocqueville writes, "The gradual development of the principle of equality is, therefore, a Providential fact. It has all the chief characteristics of such a fact: it is universal, it is durable, it constantly eludes all human interference, and all events as well as all men contribute to its progress."[20] His belief in the inevitable decline of feudalism was formed in his early education as a teenager, reading the books in his father's rich library. He was most deeply influenced by Montesquieu, Guizot, Rousseau, and Pascal, to name a few political and moral philosophers whose volumes graced his father's ample library.

What of Tocqueville's faith? In his early years, he was a devoted Catholic. He admired Pascal, and was particularly compelled by Pascal's famous wager theory.[21] But as a young adult, he became interested in the writings of the *philosophes* and the Romantics, like Chateaubriand and Rousseau. These thinkers were suspicious, not only of feudal

---

18. Malsherbes was forced to witness his daughter's execution on the guillotine before going to his own death.

19. Zunz and Kahan, *Tocqueville Reader*, 3.

20. I.Introduction, 33.

21. Pascal wrote concerning the choice between belief and unbelief in God: "Let us weigh the gain and the loss in wagering that God is. Let us estimate these two chances. If you gain, you gain all; if you lose, you lose nothing. Wager, then, without hesitation that He is [that is, He exists]." Pascal, *Pensees*, trans. W. F. Trotter, The Great Books of the Western World 33 (Chicago: Encyclopedia Britannica, 1952), III.§233.

hierarchies but also of the historic teachings of the Roman Catholic faith. Tocqueville ultimately could not resist the *philosophes'* rationalist assaults on Catholic dogma, but he continued to believe in the existence of God and in an afterlife with rewards and punishments. Zunz and Kahan asserted that Tocqueville was a deist who continued to look back longingly on the faith he had abandoned as a young man. They write, "He deeply regretted [abandoning his faith], for he had a profound desire for religious certainty ... but was never able to recapture his boyhood faith as a Catholic."[22] Still, his turning away from Roman Catholicism did not compel him to reject the necessity of the public role of religion. Quite the contrary—Tocqueville credited the influence of religion on democracy in America as the most reliable guarantor of liberty.

Tocqueville entered law school in 1824, and by 1827 he had received an appointment as *juge auditeur*, an apprentice judge, at Versailles. Here is where he met Gustave de Beaumont, his travel companion to America, and his future wife, Marie Mottley. As a lawyer, Tocqueville was competent but not impressive enough to attract the attention of influential people who could help him advance his career. By 1830, after Charles X was overthrown by Louis-Philippe, he had determined to get a commission for a trip to America, which he secured early the next year.

Tocqueville and Beaumont hoped for a successful and eventful tour of the United States. They were not to be disappointed. Zunz and Kahan divide the trip into six phases corresponding to Tocqueville and Beaumont's travel itinerary:

a) New York to Albany, Utica, Syracuse, and Buffalo;
b) up the Great Lakes to Michigan, and then to Lower Canada (present-day Quebec);
c) New England;
d) Philadelphia and Baltimore;
e) down the Ohio River from Pittsburgh to Cincinnati and Kentucky, then south along the Mississippi River to New Orleans; and
f) New Orleans to Charleston, South Carolina, north to Washington, D.C., and finally back to New York.[23]

---

22. Zunz and Kahan, *Tocqueville Reader*, 5.
23. Ibid., 11–15.

Tocqueville found an America that was experiencing far-reaching changes, but one that still continued to exhibit some pre-revolutionary features. For example, the United States reached all the way to the Pacific by 1831, thanks to the Louisiana Purchase and the joint occupation with Britain of the Oregon Country, but Texas was still part of Mexico (it would secede in 1836 and become a US state in 1845). Many people were feeling the effects of the Industrial Revolution, perhaps most notably with the widespread use of steamships plying major waterways like the Ohio and Mississippi rivers, but the use of rail power was not yet the common mode of transportation that it would become in subsequent decades.

Most of the American population still lived within a few hundred miles of the Atlantic Ocean.[24] The frontier, while expanding westward at a rapid rate, remained sparsely populated. Slavery was becoming a major divisive issue in the early to mid 19th century when Tocqueville made his visit. In 1831, two key events occurred that served as major forces advancing the cause of abolition: William Lloyd Garrison published the first issue of *The Liberator*, and Nat Turner launched his slave rebellion in Virginia. While slavery had not existed in the North for some decades, it was well ensconced in the South and was expanding into the territories according to the pattern laid down in the 1820 Missouri Compromise. Slavery became the primary 'state's right' that sparked the Civil War in the 1860s, but in 1831 it was not yet the threat to the existence of the Union that it would become. The Nullification Crisis (1828-1833) was the most serious threat to the Union at that time, and while slavery was a major issue in that crisis, it was limited to a dispute between South Carolina and the federal government. In 1835, Tocqueville confessed that he had no idea how slavery would develop as an issue in America, but he was sure that the outcome would not be good.

So Tocqueville saw America in this unique state of transition as it was evolving into an industrial economy and society, while just beginning to seriously grapple with the institution of slavery. One of the

---

24. According to the US Census Bureau, the mean center of population moved from just east of Baltimore, MD to Grant County, VA (now WV) between 1790 and 1830. See this helpful interactive map on the shifting mean center of population, which demonstrates the westward movement of the US population since the first census in 1790, https://www.census.gov/geo/reference/centersofpop/animated-mean2010.html.

most striking examples of this shift comes when Tocqueville, having crossed the Ohio River from Ohio into Kentucky, notes the differences between a slave and free economy. Another is Tocqueville's account of venturing into the wilderness of Michigan to see for himself what the frontier was like. While in New England, Tocqueville received an education on America that was second to none, discussing politics and society with figures such as Alexander Everett (brother of Edward Everett, who shared the dais with Lincoln at the 1863 dedication of Gettysburg National Cemetery), John Quincy Adams (with whom he discussed slavery, in French), Charles Carroll of Maryland (a signer of the Declaration of Independence), Sam Houston (an authority on the Native American tribes of the South, but not yet the heroic president of the Republic of Texas), President Andrew Jackson, and many others. And at the same time Tocqueville and Beaumont were studying American institutions, they were preparing their findings for *Système pénitentiaire*, the book on prison reform that was the fruit of their official visit to the United States. That book won the Montyon Prize in 1833, two years before Tocqueville completed volume 1 of *Democracy*. While the award served to help cover the expenses of the American trip, it was *Democracy* that made Tocqueville's career both as a writer and as a public figure.

What are some of the salient ideas that Tocqueville developed in *Democracy*? For our purposes here, we will consider three: first, Tocqueville's views on the relationship between democracy, equality, and liberty; second, the principle of interest rightly understood; and third, race.

I. Democracy, liberty, equality.

In any discussion of ideas, precision in language is crucial. How did Tocqueville understand terms like "democracy," "equality," "despotism," "liberty," and "manners"? We know that Tocqueville was most profoundly struck by what he called "equality of condition" in America, and that he considered this equality to be the central truth of American civilization. As early as the first page of his introduction, he calls equality of condition "the fundamental fact from which all others seem to be derived, and the central point at which all my observations constantly terminated."[25] Contemporary Americans often use words like "democracy," "equality," and "liberty" as if everyone agrees on what they mean, but such terms can be ambiguous. Tocqueville had specific definitions in mind when he used them, and they are often different than the ways we understand and use them in contemporary discourse. If we are going to grasp the significance of Tocqueville's work, it is important at the outset to understand what he means, so we may think historically and philosophically about *Democracy*.

First, what does Tocqueville mean by "equality of condition"? Importantly, he does not have economic or social leveling in mind. When Tocqueville refers to equality of condition, he means that America had no feudal hierarchies with which to contend, like those that had existed in France for over a thousand years and of which he was a part. No American inherited an aristocratic title. Since America had no feudal past and no formal aristocratic privileges, citizens could enjoy liberty to an extent unlike anything that existed in France. It was not the case in America that only the aristocracy could be considered free by virtue of a noble birth. The basis of rights in America was the individual birthright of freedom. The Declaration of Independence expresses this, and the Constitution forbids aristocracy in the Title of Nobility Clause;[26] therefore, contrary to the European mindset, the concept of "one's betters" did not exist in the minds of Americans like it had existed in feudal Europe since the fall of Rome.

This notion of equality of condition presented itself to Tocqueville most plainly in New England[27] as he observed the centrality of the township and the power of local associations. But we should hasten to add that it was also in New England that Tocqueville first considered the great exception of the Southern states to the notion of equality of condition. In a discussion with John Quincy Adams about the contrast

---

25. I.Introduction, 30.

26. "No title of nobility shall be granted by the United States: and no person holding any office of profit or trust under them, shall, without the consent of the Congress, accept of any present, emolument, office, or title, of any kind whatever, from any king, prince, or foreign state." U. S. Constitution, art. 1, sec. 9, cl. 8. At this point, it is essential to bear in mind that individual rights did not apply to African Americans or Native Americans in 1831.

27. Even more particularly, in Connecticut.

between the North and the South, Tocqueville came to understand that a form of aristocracy did indeed exist in the slave economy of the South. In fact, Tocqueville acknowledged that the Southern states could not be considered truly democratic because of slavery. In volume 2, in his chapter on honor, Tocqueville clarifies, "I speak here of the Americans inhabiting those states where slavery does not exist; they alone can be said to present a complete picture of democratic society."[28] In fact, while Tocqueville did not believe that another revolution was likely in America because of the strength of social equality, he did think it possible for revolution to break out in the South. Race war, Tocqueville says, would be the cause of revolution in the South because of "inequality of condition" there.[29]

But despite slavery and its debilitating effects on both white and black Southern society, Tocqueville believed that equality of condition as it was manifested in New England was the norm in America. In New England, equality tended toward liberty as it did nowhere else. Local institutions helped secure liberty, in large part because they were informed by religion. Tocqueville wrote, "Townships and town arrangements exist in every State; but in no other part of the Union is a township to be met with precisely similar to those of New England. The farther we go towards the South, the less active does the business of the township or parish become; it has fewer magistrates, duties, and rights; the population exercises a less immediate influence on affairs; town-meetings are less frequent, and the subjects of debate less numerous. The power of the elected magistrate is augmented, and that of the voter diminished, whilst the public spirit of the local communities is less excited and less influential."[30] So while equality of condition was the most noteworthy characteristic of American life, it demonstrated itself most purely in New England, and less so in the states of the South. (We will consider Tocqueville's thoughts on racial prejudice and its future impact on the Union later in this introduction.)

How did Tocqueville understand the meaning of democracy, and what was the relationship between democracy and equality as Tocqueville articulated it? Tocqueville thought of "democracy" more

---

28. Alexis de Tocqueville, *Democracy in America* (New York: Knopf, 1994), II, iii, 18, 235n.
29. II.iii.21., 424.
30. I.v., 81.

broadly than we, who in contemporary times often mean government by consent of the people and not much more. For Tocqueville, democracy entailed equality of condition to the extent that "democracy" and "equality" were nearly synonymous. A democracy, for Tocqueville, described a polity, society, and economy that were defined by the absence of hereditary hierarchies. Pierson writes that "democracy" and "equality" were so synonymous in Tocqueville's mind as to be difficult for later translators to discern between the two terms. According to Pierson, Henry Reeve, whose English translation of *Democracy* has been the mainstay since shortly after it was published, suffered from "one capital error"[31] in the transliteration of Tocqueville's title. In French, the work is called *De la Démocratie en Amérique* (*Democracy in America*), but Pierson thought Reeve should have rendered the title "Concerning *Equality* in America."[32] Throughout his work, Tocqueville uses the term *démocratie* polysemantically—that is, he sometimes means "equality," while at other times he refers to the progress of equality, and at still other times he uses *démocratie* to refer to rule by the people. Pierson concludes that "this unconscious lack of precision was unfortunate, for it came to cloud much of Tocqueville's thinking about America and to vitiate for American readers certain parts of his great commentary."[33] Regardless of whether we agree with Pierson about this reality, it is important for modern readers to understand this important feature of Tocqueville's use of language throughout the work.

A common misconception about Tocqueville's *Democracy* is that the work was a celebratory account of American republican institutions—that Tocqueville accepted democracy or equality of condition as an absolute good for society. It is true that Tocqueville accepted the idea that democracy (equality) was an irresistible force, carried along by the will of Providence. But it is not true that Tocqueville believed that this was necessarily a good thing. Americans today conflate democracy and freedom, but Tocqueville was too much of a realist to do so. Tocqueville thought that democracy tends to favor the majority, and majorities tend to concentrate their power in order to preserve and

---

31. Pierson, *Tocqueville in America*, 6n.
32. Ibid. Emphasis mine.
33. Ibid., 158–59n.

extend it. Thus, the "despotism of the majority" can prevail easily in a democracy, much more so than in an aristocracy. An aristocracy has a built-in hierarchical structure to ensure against mob rule. Tocqueville writes, "To concentrate the whole social force in the hands of the legislative body is the natural tendency of democracies; for as this is the power which emanates the most directly from the people, it has the greater share of the people's overwhelming power, and it is naturally led to monopolize every species of influence."[34] Thus, Tocqueville rejected the notion of *vox populi, vox Dei*, that popular majorities always protect the liberty of the people.

This notion leads us to ask, what did Tocqueville mean by liberty, and how is liberty best served in a democracy if democracy naturally tends toward the despotism of the majority? For Tocqueville, "liberty" had both a philosophical and a practical meaning. Philosophically, he borrowed from John Winthrop, first governor of the Massachusetts Bay Colony, in thinking of liberty in two ways, natural and civil. Natural liberty referred to license, the doing of whatever one pleases. According to Winthrop, "man, as he stands in relation to man simply, hath liberty to do what he lists; it is a liberty to evil as well as to good."[35] Furthermore, it rails against God's authority, and in Winthrop's words, "*omnes sumus licentiâ deteriores,*" or, "too much freedom makes us all worse."[36] But there is another form of liberty, which is civil, or moral, liberty. According to Winthrop, this is "a liberty to that only which is good, just, and honest,"[37] and it is apprehended through submission to the divine law. Tocqueville describes Winthrop's formula as a "fine definition of liberty."[38] And for Tocqueville, the key feature that distinguishes civil (moral) from natural liberty is religion, particularly religion that is not coerced by the state. Tocqueville believed that religion that is "unsupported by aught beside its native strength"[39] is

---

34. I.viii., 99.
35. I.ii., 63. In citing Winthrop, Tocqueville relied on an 1820 edition of Cotton Mather's *Magnalia Christi Americana, or the Ecclesiastical History of New England, 1620–1698*, the first history of the Puritan colonies in New England that was originally published in 1702.
36. Ibid.
37. Ibid.
38. I.ii., 63.
39. I.ii., 65.

the steadiest protector of liberty and, furthermore, "the safeguard of morality, and morality as the best security of law, and the surest pledge of the duration of freedom."[40] Tocqueville was astounded not only at the reality of religious liberty in the United States, but also at the fact that Americans from every walk of life agreed that religion was indispensable to the sustenance of liberty. He writes, "I do not know whether all the Americans have a sincere faith in their religion—for who can search the human heart?—but I am certain that they hold it to be indispensable to the maintenance of republican institutions. This opinion is not peculiar to a class of citizens, or to a party, but it belongs to the whole nation, and to every rank of society."[41]

Tocqueville also thought of liberty in practical terms. That is, he thought that individual *liberties* were the manifestation of a prevailing *spirit* of liberty in the land. Again, New England was Tocqueville's paradigm. He described the individual New Englander as taking an active role in governing the township's affairs because there the individual possessed a personal stake in its success. The Connecticut townsman, for example, was not merely a serf working the land on his lord's manor. He was a member of the town, and membership in the town afforded him duties, rights, and privileges. If the government rose or fell, it did so on the merits or demerits of the individuals making up the township. The notion of the "public good" was no abstraction to the townsman in New England, but the individuals in community actively and commonly sought out the specific public goods that benefit everyone. Tocqueville describes it in this way:

> The native of New England is attached to his township because it is independent and free: his co-operation in its affairs insures his attachment to its interest; the well-being it affords him secures his affection; and its welfare is the aim of his ambition and of his future exertions. He takes a part in every occurrence in the place; he practices the art of government in the small sphere within his reach; he accustoms himself to those forms without which liberty can only advance by revolutions; he imbibes their spirit; he acquires a taste for

---

40. Ibid.
41. I.xvii., 153.

order, comprehends the balance of powers, and collects clear practical notions on the nature of his duties and the extent of his rights.[42]

Throughout the book, Tocqueville describes particular liberties, laws, federal relationships, mechanisms, associations, and manners that existed in America that made it a much more legitimate example of a free society than France. Liberty was not understood only in abstract terms. Tocqueville believed that liberty is seen in active terms. The aim of his study was to identify how Americans specifically applied liberty, and how to preserve it under the pressures wrought by the natural tendencies of equality toward despotism.

In order for liberty to survive and thrive then, a local spirit of community was necessary. Tocqueville calls this a "public spirit"[43] when describing the New England township. To nurture this public spirit, members of a local community needed to nurture certain habits, or manners. James T. Schleifer calls these habits "positive liberty." Positive liberty supports negative liberty, which Schleifer describes in formal, explicit terms. "Negative liberty provides specific rights or freedoms—for example, the right to vote, the liberty to associate, or freedom of the press." So every member of a community may possess the legal right to vote, for example, but without the habit of association, or the habit of education, it would not matter whether the right to vote existed or not. Schleifer writes, "Just as the *habits* of liberty give life to the *art* of liberty, positive liberty assures that rights granted are not empty of substance."[44] Thus, Schleifer touches on one of the most important and unique American characteristics that Tocqueville describes—manners, and their profound influence on political and social culture.

Tocqueville defines manners as "the whole moral and intellectual condition of a people."[45] American manners, rooted as they were in religion, were the source of American greatness. Furthermore, manners made democracy in America possible and were key to preserving

---

42. I.v., 79.
43. I.v., 77.
44. James T. Schleifer, *The Chicago Companion to Tocqueville's* Democracy in America (Chicago: University of Chicago Press, 2012), 68. Emphasis original.
45. I.xvii., 148.

liberty. Tocqueville asserts that "the gradual growth of democratic manners and institutions should be regarded, not as the best, but as the only means of preserving freedom."[46] Manners—the moral habits of the citizenry—were more important than laws in society. Indeed, the American laws were based on manners. The laws were meaningless apart from manners, and the centrality and superiority of manners related to the laws is what Schleifer illustrates in his description of the contrast between positive and negative liberty.

Since, as Tocqueville notes, religion informed manners in America, what role did religion play in society as Tocqueville observed it? As we have already seen, for Tocqueville, religion and morality together were indispensable supports of liberty. The great paradox in America was that, while religion had no direct power over the citizenry via establishment, nothing influenced American manners more than the Christian religion. In Tocqueville's assessment, "there is no country in the world where the Christian religion retains a greater influence over the souls of men than in America."[47] Elsewhere, he writes, "The Americans combine the notions of Christianity and of liberty so intimately in their minds, that it is impossible to make them conceive the one without the other."[48] Devotion to God and to his laws were so central to the American mind that love of country was considered an expression of devotion to God, as Tocqueville observed. Russell Kirk writes that, "in the middle of the nineteenth century, American society might have sunk into an irresponsible disintegrating individualism, had it not still been held together by the cement of Christian teaching."[49]

So, for Tocqueville, liberty is distinct from democracy, or equality. While democracy is inexorably supplanting aristocracy by the apparent working of an all-powerful Providence, this is not to suggest that liberty is also inevitable. Rather, in Tocqueville's view, the natural tendency of democracy is toward despotism. But despotism is not inevitable either. Tocqueville insisted that liberty was fundamental to human nature, and while some form of determinism may apply in

---

46. I.xvii., 172.
47. I.xvii., 151.
48. I.xvii., 154.
49. Russell Kirk, *The Roots of American Order* (1974; repr., Wilmington, DE: ISI, 2014), 448–49.

history, human beings were not subject to such a force. People could, by the exercise of their will, defy the natural tendency toward despotism in a democracy, and protect and extend liberty and the public good.

How can despotism prevail in a democracy, and how can the citizenry combat despotism? Kirk says that Tocqueville's "analysis of democratic despotism is his supreme achievement as a political theorist, a sociologist, a liberal, and a conservative."[50] For Tocqueville, democratic despotism was not like an absolute monarchy or what we might recognize as a dictatorship, in which one person or group locates supreme political power in themselves. Democratic despotism, as Kirk understood Tocqueville, was one that no longer pursued any larger purpose but instead satisfied itself with the ordinary. Kirk writes, "Society ought to be designed to encourage the highest moral and intellectual qualities in man; the worst threat of the new democratic system is that mediocrity will not only be encouraged, but may be enforced. Tocqueville dreads the reduction of human society to an insect-like arrangement. ... Variety, individuality, progress: these Tocqueville struggled to conserve."[51] In volume 2, in a chapter titled "What Sort Of Despotism Democratic Nations Have To Fear," Tocqueville describes democratic despotism as a hyper-individualism, in which people are concerned only about themselves and no longer consider the public good or their responsibility to contribute to it. "An immense and tutelary power,"[52] as Tocqueville describes it, would take responsibility for the community, and those members no longer would have a personal stake, or ownership of it. The ever-extending tide of equality of condition has the effect of leveling individuals to this even plane, resulting in self-centeredness and a pursuit of personal desires above all other concerns. Liberty, which is the fount of political responsibility, creativity, expression, innovation, order, and morality, can be devoured by equality, so that little of human dignity remains.

---

50. Russell Kirk, *The Conservative Mind: From Burke to Eliot* (1953; repr., Washington: Regnery, 2001), 206.
51. Ibid., 208–10.
52. II.iv.6., 461.

The tool for preventing this sad state of affairs is the local voluntary association. Churches, townships, reform societies, civic organizations—these and other kinds of local associations that are dedicated to promoting the public good, Tocqueville insisted, are the keys to preserving liberty in the face of a threatening democratic despotism. An aristocracy has an ingrained mechanism to ensure against despotism; in the European feudal system, the aristocrats themselves served as a check against executive overreach. Without aristocratic structure, the people can degenerate from a state of liberty to license (natural liberty), but local associations serve to check this descent. And it is local associations, rather than national ones, that make the difference. Tocqueville saw that it was harder for individuals to concern themselves with national affairs because the more distant the issues, the more abstract they become. Because local affairs are of immediate interest, people are more inclined to take responsibility for them. Tocqueville writes, "Local freedom, then, which leads a great number of citizens to value the affection of their neighbors and of their kindred, perpetually brings men together, and forces them to help one another, in spite of the propensities which sever them."[53] Thus, the concerns of a locality naturally serve to foster community in the form of associations, and this is the best way to check the advance of despotism.

So Tocqueville devoted a great deal of energy to writing about democracy, equality, liberty, and despotism, and the role played by manners, religion, and associations in the American democratic society.

II. Interest rightly understood.

The notion Tocqueville called "interest rightly understood" (*l'intérêt bien entendu*) also played an essential and unique role in American democracy, as yet another guarantor of civil liberty. Tocqueville recognized that Americans were governed not so much by a love of virtue in itself, but more by the practical benefits of virtue, especially when virtue and self-interest were the same. He writes, "In the United States, hardly anybody talks of the beauty of virtue; but they maintain that virtue is useful, and prove it every day. The American moralists do not

---

53. II.ii.4., 311.

profess that men ought to sacrifice themselves for their fellow-creatures *because* it is noble to make such sacrifices; but they boldly aver that such sacrifices are as necessary to him who imposes them upon himself, as to him for whose sake they are made."[54] When individual self-interest could contribute to the public good, civil liberty was preserved and extended. Thus, at the intersection of public good and private interest, Tocqueville located "interest rightly understood." Wilfred M. McClay calls this converging of public and private interest as a "halfway covenant, one that conceded the primacy of unregenerate individualistic vice, being satisfied, to paraphrase Oscar Wilde's witticism, to coax that vice into paying willing tribute to virtue."[55]

In an important respect, liberty itself is entailed in the notion of interest rightly understood, as Tocqueville observed it in Jacksonian America. The old Federalist Party's dream of a classical republic led by wise and virtuous democratic aristocracy had been replaced, especially by the late 1820s and early 1830s, by the era of the common man. The disinterestedness that George Washington so scrupulously observed in order to set the example for his successors also was gone—replaced by, in the words of Gordon Wood, "a democratic marketplace of equally competing individuals with interests to promote."[56] How indeed, Tocqueville asks, is it possible for citizens who have been in America only for a generation or two to conjure up sincere patriotism and profound concern for the issues of their nation, beginning with local concerns and expanding outward to national ones? "It is because every one in his sphere, takes an active part in the government of society."[57] Thus, in the practice of interest rightly understood, we can see manners, religion, freedom of association, and civil liberty working together in American society against concentration of power in the hands of majorities and the "Byzantine dreariness"[58] (in Kirk's words) of democratic despotism.

---

54. II.ii.8., 321.
55. Wilfred M. McClay, *The Masterless: Self and Society in Modern America* (Chapel Hill: University of North Carolina Press, 1994), 45.
56. Gordon S. Wood, *The Idea of America: Reflections on the Birth of the United States* (New York: Penguin, 2011), 162.
57. I.xiv., 126.
58. Kirk, Conservative Mind, 212.

III. Race.

Within his treatment of American equality of condition (the final chapter of volume 1), Tocqueville provides a lengthy discussion on "The Present And Probable Future Condition Of The Three Races Which Inhabit The Territory Of The United States." Tocqueville was clearly disturbed and flummoxed by racial prejudice in America, perpetrated by the white race against the indigenous Native Americans and African Americans. Andrew Jackson signed the Indian Removal Act into law in May 1830, mandating the transfer of native tribes from the South to unsettled lands west of the Mississippi. The state governments of the South, along with the federal government, set themselves against Native Americans such that the tribes' ultimate destruction was assured. Tocqueville writes, "[T]he tyranny of the States obliges the savages to retire; the Union, by its promises and resources, facilitates their retreat; and these measures tend to precisely the same end."[59] Because the Native Americans refused to be amalgamated into Anglo-American society, Tocqueville believed they faced a grim choice from their first encounters with European colonists—"war or civilization."[60] Ultimately, Tocqueville could not foresee any other future for indigenous peoples outside of total destruction: "I believe that the Indian nations of North America are doomed to perish; and that whenever the Europeans shall be established on the shores of the Pacific Ocean, that race of men will have ceased to exist."[61]

The white oppression of the African slaves and their American-born children was not identical to that perpetrated by whites on the Native Americans, but it was just as morally reprehensible to Tocqueville. Racial prejudice against African Americans was so insidious, so potentially devastating to the Union, that Tocqueville confessed ignorance as to how it would ever be resolved. The African American intellectual and activist W. E. B. Du Bois (1868–1963) famously began his classic work, *The Souls of Black Folk*, with the statement: "[T]he problem of the Twentieth Century is the problem of the color-line."[62] Tocqueville could have made the same statement describing the

---

59. I.xviii., 187.

60. I.xviii., 180.

61. Ibid.

62. W. E. B. Du Bois, *The Souls of Black Folk* in *W. E. B. Du Bois: Writings*, ed. Nathan Huggins (New York: Library of America, 1986), 359.

nineteenth century. He writes, "The most formidable of all the ills which threaten the future of the Union arises from the presence of a black population upon its territory."[63] Slavery was an obvious blight on the manners of the South, and Tocqueville observed the contrast between the manners of the North and those of the South simply by considering the two sides of the Ohio River as it separated the free state of Ohio and the slave state of Kentucky. In Ohio, Tocqueville observed movement, industry, and abundance; in Kentucky, he saw an indolence, stagnation, and greed among the whites because of slavery. Slavery dehumanized both the slave and the master. Tocqueville said of the white Kentuckian, he "scorns not only labor, but all the undertakings which labor promotes; as he lives in an idle independence, his tastes are those of an idle man."[64] Thus, Tocqueville observed that the institution of slavery had the effect of altering the manners of the inhabitants of the South. Given what we have considered about the importance Tocqueville assigned to manners in a democratic society, the negative effects of slavery on the people of the South cannot be overstated.

Still, for Tocqueville, slavery was not the real evil that beset African Americans. Racial prejudice was far more problematic because it struck against the fabric of American democracy and liberty. Furthermore, racial prejudice was not as overt as slavery, not as visible to the onlooker as field hands toiling in the sun. Racial prejudice was the basis of American slavery, and even if slavery was abolished at some point in the future, whites would still consider African Americans to be inferior. As an outsider, Tocqueville could easily recognize that the slavery existing in America was nothing like that of the ancient West. In America, "Oppression has, at one stroke, deprived the descendants of the Africans of almost all the privileges of humanity."[65] Because slavery had been legally contained in the Southern states by 1831, because it was so clearly in opposition to liberty and justice, and because its immorality was becoming obvious to more people, Tocqueville believed that slavery could not continue to exist in America indefinitely. Ultimately, it would come to an end either by

---

63. I.xviii., 189.
64. I.xviii., 196.
65. I.xviii., 174.

abolition or by more violent means, such as a race war. Beyond the cessation of slavery in America, Tocqueville could not foresee how the effects of racial prejudice would develop, but of one thing he was certain: no matter how slavery was abolished, either by peaceful means or violence, the future of the relationship between white and black was grim. "By the act of the master, or by the will of the slave, [slavery] will cease," Tocqueville writes, "and, in either case, great calamities may be expected to ensue."[66]

In a very real sense, when it came to slavery in particular, and racial prejudice in general, Americans were untrue to their stated ideals of democracy, liberty, the public good, and ultimately, progress. The enslavement of African Americans and the forced removal and subsequent extermination of Native Americans cried out against American democracy, as to render the concept absurd in the nineteenth century. Worse still, Americans inflicted *upon themselves* a mortal wound that has festered in every period of the country's history. Tocqueville saw that the greatest social ills of 1831 America were rooted in racial prejudice, but at that time he could not see a satisfactory solution. Neither could anyone else, for that matter. There were political settlements, like the Missouri Compromise of 1820 and the Compromise of 1850. There were voluntary societies that sought to colonize free blacks in Africa, like the American Colonization Society. There were those who called for immediate abolition, such as William Lloyd Garrison and Frederick Douglass. There were those who wanted to extend slavery west and south, like James K. Polk, and those who wanted to contain it where it existed, like Abraham Lincoln. And by 1857, the Supreme Court under Roger Taney sought to resolve the slavery question once and for all by essentially legalizing it everywhere in the Union—even in free states—in the infamous Dred Scott decision. The Civil War (1861–65) ultimately brought about slavery's abolition, but racial prejudice remained, just as Tocqueville said it would. Concluding his book *The Suppression of the African Slave Trade to the United States of America*, Du Bois wrote at the end of the nineteenth century:

> [W]e have the somewhat inchoate idea that we are not
> destined to be harassed with great social questions, and

---

66. I.xviii., 212.

that even if we are, and fail to answer them, the fault is with the question and not with us. ... Such an attitude is dangerous; we have and shall have, as other peoples have had, critical, momentous, and pressing questions to answer. The riddle of the Sphinx may be postponed, it may be evasively answered now; sometime it must be fully answered.[67]

Tocqueville was unable to apply the valuable wisdom he gained in America about the power of religion, manners, and liberty to the great evils of his day. Americans have since had to figure out how to answer Du Bois's "riddle of the Sphinx"—a riddle that has always had much more destructive potential to American society than the threat of democratic despotism—largely without Tocqueville's help.

The broad issues of democracy, liberty, and racial prejudice lead us to consider one final idea: American exceptionalism. The political sociologist Seymour Martin Lipset credited Tocqueville with being the first to apply the term "exceptional" to the United States.[68] In the first part of volume 2, Tocqueville writes:

> The position of the Americans is therefore quite exceptional, and it may be believed that no democratic people will ever be placed in a similar one. Their strictly Puritanical origin—their exclusively commercial habits—even the country they inhabit, which seems to divert their minds from the pursuit of science, literature, and the arts—the proximity of Europe, which allows them to neglect these pursuits without relapsing into barbarism,—a thousand special causes, of which I have only

---

67. W. E. B. Du Bois, *The Suppression of the African Slave Trade to the United States of America: 1638 –1870* in *W. E. B. Du Bois: Writings*, ed. Nathan Huggins (New York: Library of America, 1986), 197.

68. "In his great book, Tocqueville is the first to refer to the United States as exceptional. ... He is, therefore, the initiator of the writings on American exceptionalism." Seymour Martin Lipset, *American Exceptionalism: A Double-Edged Sword* (New York: Norton, 1996), 18.

been able to point out the most important—have singularly concurred to fix the mind of the American upon purely practical objects. His passions, his wants, his education, and everything about him, seem to unite in drawing the native of the United States earthward: his religion alone bids him turn, from time to time, a transient and distracted glance to heaven. Let us cease, then, to view all democratic nations under the example of the American people, and attempt to survey them at length with their own features.[69]

Tocqueville uses the term "exceptional" with reference to America only this once, but the notion that America is exceptional is implicit throughout *Democracy*. Lipset describes Tocqueville's meaning as "qualitatively different from all other countries."[70] Thus, for Tocqueville, America was not superior to other countries, but was, as Lipset described, "an outlier"[71] given its origins, its geography, its culture, its federalism, and its experience of being without feudal hierarchies. But Tocqueville recognized that exceptionalism cuts both ways; for example, he lamented the dearth of aesthetic culture in America as a negative feature of American exceptionalism. Still, many who have not carefully read Tocqueville have misunderstood his assessment of American exceptionalism, and have sought to use him to offer credibility to their own notions of American exceptionalism.[72]

Racial prejudice is perhaps the most obvious argument against normative American exceptionalism. Those who would seek to use Tocqueville to advance their own religious or political agenda defined by a normative exceptionalism are forced to reckon with Tocqueville's honest and thorough treatment of racism and its effects on all the inhabitants of America. But this is one important reason why it is still important for Americans to read Tocqueville, not merely as a historical

---

69. II.i.9., 260.

70. Lipset, *American Exceptionalism*, 18.

71. Ibid.

72. Ronald Reagan is an example of someone who frequently cited Tocqueville to argue for normative American exceptionalism. See my book on the history and theology of American exceptionalism as civil religion, John D. Wilsey, *American Exceptionalism and Civil Religion: Reassessing the History of an Idea* (Downers Grove: IVP Academic, 2015).

artifact, but as a sourcebook for the present day. While the America of 1831 is gone forever, American ideals have been passed down to our own generation. Lipset calls these ideals "the American creed," consisting of "liberty, egalitarianism, individualism, populism, and laissez-faire." These are major themes of Tocqueville's book, and while much has changed since *Democracy* was published, the conclusions he reached about human nature and the meaning of democracy are still pertinent and valuable. If the present and future generations enjoy liberty for themselves and desire to safeguard it for their children, they will do so in large measure by heeding Tocqueville's scrupulous examination and timeless sagacity.

—John D. Wilsey
Southwestern Baptist Theological Seminary
Houston, Texas

VOLUME I

★

Author's Introduction

Amongst the novel objects that attracted my attention during my stay in the United States, nothing struck me more forcibly than the general equality of condition among the people. I readily discovered the prodigious influence which this primary fact exercises on the whole course of society; it gives a peculiar direction to public opinion, and a peculiar tenor to the laws; it imparts new maxims to the governing authorities, and peculiar habits to the governed.

I soon perceived that the influence of this fact extends far beyond the political character and the laws of the country, and that it has no less empire over civil society than over the government; it creates opinions, gives birth to new sentiments, founds novel customs, and modifies whatever it does not produce. The more I advanced in the study of American society, the more I perceived that this equality of condition is the fundamental fact from which all others seem to be derived, and the central point at which all my observations constantly terminated.

I then turned my thoughts to our own hemisphere, and thought that I discerned there something analogous to the spectacle which the New World presented to me. I observed that equality of condition, though it has not there reached the extreme limit which it seems to have attained in the United States, is constantly approaching it; and that the democracy which governs the American communities appears to be rapidly rising into power in Europe.

Hence I conceived the idea of the book which is now before the reader.

It is evident to all alike that a great democratic revolution is going on amongst us; but all do not look at it in the same light. To some it appears to be novel but accidental, and, as such, they hope it may still be checked; to others it seems irresistible, because it is the most uniform, the most ancient, and the most permanent tendency which is to be found in history.

I look back for a moment on the situation of France seven hundred years ago, when the territory was divided amongst a small number of families, who were the owners of the soil and the rulers of the inhabitants; the right of governing descended with the family inheritance from generation to generation; force was the only means by which man could act on man; and landed property was the sole source of power.

Soon, however, the political power of the clergy was founded, and began to increase: the clergy opened their ranks to all classes, to the poor and the rich, the vassal and the lord; through the Church, equality penetrated into the Government, and he who as a serf must have vegetated in perpetual bondage took his place as a priest in the midst of nobles, and not infrequently above the heads of kings.

The different relations of men with each other became more complicated and numerous as society gradually became more stable and civilized. Hence the want of civil laws was felt; and the ministers of law soon rose from the obscurity of the tribunals and their dusty chambers, to appear at the court of the monarch, by the side of the feudal barons clothed in their ermine and their mail.

Whilst the kings were ruining themselves by their great enterprises, and the nobles exhausting their resources by private wars, the lower orders were enriching themselves by commerce. The influence of money began to be perceptible in state affairs. The transactions of business opened a new road to power, and the financier rose to a station of political influence in which he was at once flattered and despised.

Gradually the diffusion of intelligence, and the increasing taste for literature and art, caused learning and talent to become a means of government; mental ability led to social power, and the man of letters took a part in the affairs of the state.

The value attached to high birth declined just as fast as new avenues to power were discovered. In the eleventh century, nobility was beyond all price; in the thirteenth, it might be purchased. Nobility was first conferred by gift in 1270; and equality was thus introduced into the government by the aristocracy itself.

In the course of these seven hundred years, it sometimes happened that the nobles, in order to resist the authority of the crown, or to diminish the power of their rivals, granted some political influence to the common people. Or, more frequently, the king permitted the lower orders to have a share in the government, with the intention of depressing the aristocracy.

In France, the kings have always been the most active and the most constant of levelers. When they were strong and ambitious, they spared no pains to raise the people to the level of the nobles; when they were temperate and feeble, they allowed the people to rise above themselves. Some assisted the democracy by their talents, others by their vices. Louis XI. and Louis XIV. reduced all ranks beneath the throne to the same degree of subjection; and, finally, Louis XV. descended, himself and all his court, into the dust.

As soon as land began to be held on any other than a feudal tenure, and personal property in its turn became able to confer influence and power, every discovery in the arts, every improvement in commerce or manufactures, created so many new elements of equality among men. Henceforward every new invention, every new want which it occasioned, and every new desire which craved satisfaction, was a step towards a general leveling. The taste for luxury, the love of war, the empire of fashion, and the most superficial as well as the deepest passions of the human heart, seemed to co-operate to enrich the poor and to impoverish the rich.

From the time when the exercise of the intellect became a source of strength and of wealth, we see that every addition to science, every fresh truth, and every new idea became a germ of power placed within the reach of the people. Poetry, eloquence, and memory, the graces of the mind, the glow of imagination, depth of thought, and all the gifts which Heaven scatters at a venture, turned to the advantage of the democracy; and even when they were in the possession of its adversaries, they still served its cause by throwing into bold relief the natural greatness of man. Its conquests spread, therefore, with those of civilization and knowledge; and literature became an arsenal open to all, where the poor and the weak daily resorted for arms.

In running over the pages of our history for seven hundred years, we shall scarcely find a single great event which has not promoted equality of condition.

The Crusades and the English wars decimated the nobles and divided their possessions: the municipal corporations introduced democratic liberty into the bosom of feudal monarchy; the invention of fire-arms equalized the vassal and the noble on the field of battle; the art of printing opened the same resources to the minds of all classes; the post-office brought knowledge alike to the door of the cottage and to the gate of the palace; and Protestantism proclaimed that all men are alike able to find the road to heaven. The discovery of America opened a thousand new paths to fortune, and led obscure adventurers to wealth and power.

If, beginning with the eleventh century, we examine what has happened in France from one half-century to another, we shall not fail to perceive, at the end of each of these periods, that a twofold revolution has taken place in the state of society. The noble has gone down on the social ladder, and the commoner has gone up; the one descends as the other rises. Every half-century brings them nearer to each other, and they will soon meet.

Nor is this peculiar to France. Whithersoever we turn our eyes, we perceive the same revolution going on throughout the Christian world. The various occurrences of national existence have everywhere turned to the advantage of democracy: all men have aided it by their exertions, both those who have intentionally labored in its cause, and those who have served it unwittingly; those who have fought for it, and those who have declared themselves its opponents, have all been driven along in the same track, have all labored to one end; some ignorantly and some unwillingly, all have been blind instruments in the hands of God.

The gradual development of the principle of equality is, therefore, a Providential fact. It has all the chief characteristics of such a fact: it is universal, it is durable, it constantly eludes all human interference, and all events as well as all men contribute to its progress.

Would it, then, be wise to imagine that a social movement, the causes of which lie so far back, can be checked by the efforts of one generation? Can it be believed that the democracy which has overthrown the feudal system, and vanquished kings, will retreat before tradesmen and capitalists? Will it stop now that it has grown so strong, and its adversaries so weak?

Whither, then, are we tending? No one can say, for terms of comparison already fail us. The conditions of men are more equal in Christian countries at the present day than they have been at any previous time, or in any part of the world; so that the magnitude of what already has been done prevents us from foreseeing what is yet to be accomplished.

The whole book which is here offered to the public has been written under the impression of a kind of religious terror produced in the author's mind by the view of that irresistible revolution which has advanced for centuries in spite of every obstacle, and which is still advancing in the midst of the ruins it has caused.

It is not necessary that God himself should speak in order that we may discover the unquestionable signs of his will. It is enough to ascertain what is the habitual course of nature and the constant tendency of events. I know, without a special revelation, that the planets move in the orbits traced by the Creator's hand.

If the men of our time should be convinced, by attentive observation and sincere reflection, that the gradual and progressive development of social equality is at once the past and the future of their history, this discovery alone would confer the sacred character of a Divine decree upon the change. To attempt to check democracy would be in that case to resist the will of God; and the nations would then be constrained to make the best of the social lot awarded to them by Providence.

The Christian nations of our day seem to me to present a most alarming spectacle; the movement which impels them is already so strong that it cannot be stopped, but it is not yet so rapid that it cannot be guided. Their fate is still in their own hands; yet a little while, and it may be so no longer.

The first of the duties which are at this time imposed upon those who direct our affairs, is to educate the democracy; to renovate, if possible, its religious belief; to purify its morals; to regulate its movements; to substitute by degrees a knowledge of business for its inexperience, and an acquaintance with its true interests for its blind instincts; to adapt its government to time and place, and to make it conform to the occurrences and the men of the times. A new science of politics is needed for a new world.

This, however, is what we think of least; placed in the middle of a rapid stream, we obstinately fix our eyes on the ruins which may still be descried upon the shore we have left, whilst the current hurries us away, and drags us backward toward the gulf.

In no country in Europe has the great social revolution which I have just described made such rapid progress as in France; but it has always advanced without guidance. The heads of the state have made no preparation for it, and it has advanced without their consent or without their knowledge. The most powerful, the most intelligent, and the most moral classes of the nation have never attempted to take hold of it in order to guide it. The democracy has consequently been abandoned to its wild instincts, and it has grown up like those children who have no parental guidance, who receive their education in the public streets, and who are acquainted only with the vices and wretchedness of society. Its existence was seemingly unknown, when suddenly it acquired supreme power. Every one then submitted to its caprices; it was worshipped as the idol of strength; and when afterwards it was enfeebled by its own excesses, the legislator conceived the rash project of destroying it, instead of instructing it and correcting its vices. No attempt was made to fit it to govern, but all were bent on excluding it from the government.

The consequence has been, that the democratic revolution has taken place in the body of society, without that concomitant change in the laws, ideas, customs, and manners, which was necessary to render such a revolution beneficial. Thus we have a democracy, without anything to lessen its vices and bring out its natural advantages; and although we already perceive the evils it brings, we are ignorant of the benefits it may confer.

While the power of the crown, supported by the aristocracy, peaceably governed the nations of Europe, society, in the midst of its wretchedness, had several sources of happiness which can now scarcely be conceived or appreciated. The power of a part of his subjects was an insurmountable barrier to the tyranny of the prince; and the monarch, who felt the almost divine character which he enjoyed in the eyes of the multitude, derived a motive for the just use of his power from the respect which he inspired. The nobles, high as they were placed above the people, could not but take that calm and benevolent interest in their fate which the shepherd feels towards his flock; and without acknowledging the poor as their equals, they watched over the destiny of those whose welfare Providence had entrusted to their care. The people, never having conceived the idea of a social condition different from their own, and never expecting to become equal to their leaders, received benefits from them without discussing their rights. They became attached to them when they were clement and just, and submitted to their exactions without resistance or servility, as to the inevitable visitations of the Deity. Custom and the manners of the time, moreover, had established certain limits to oppression, and put a sort of legal restraint upon violence.

As the noble never suspected that any one would attempt to deprive him of the privileges which he believed to be legitimate, and as the serf looked upon his own inferiority as a consequence of the immutable order of nature, it is easy to imagine that some mutual exchange of good-will took place between two classes so differently gifted by fate. Inequality and wretchedness were then to be found in society; but the souls of neither rank of men were degraded.

Men are not corrupted by the exercise of power, or debased by the habit of obedience; but by the exercise of a power which they believe to be illegitimate, and by obedience to a rule which they consider to be usurped and oppressive.

On the one side were wealth, strength, and leisure, accompanied by the refinements of luxury, the elegance of taste, the pleasures of wit, and the cultivation of the arts; on the other, were labor, clownishness, and ignorance. But in the midst of this coarse and ignorant multitude it was not uncommon to meet with energetic passions, generous sentiments, profound religious convictions, and wild virtues.

The social state thus organized might boast of its stability, its power, and, above all, its glory.

But the scene is now changed. Gradually the distinctions of rank are done away; the barriers which once severed mankind are falling down; property is divided, power is shared by many, the light of intelligence spreads, and the capacities of all classes are equally cultivated. The State becomes democratic, and the empire of democracy is slowly and peaceably introduced into the institutions and the manners of the nation.

I can conceive of a society in which all men would feel an equal love and respect for the laws of which they consider themselves as the authors; in which the authority of the government would be respected as necessary, though not as divine; and in which the loyalty of the subject to the chief magistrate would not be a passion, but a quiet and rational persuasion. Every individual being in the possession of rights which he is sure to retain, a kind of manly confidence and reciprocal courtesy would arise between all classes, alike removed from pride and servility. The people, well acquainted with their own true interests, would understand that, in order to profit by the advantages of society, it is necessary to satisfy its requisitions. The voluntary association of the citizens might then take the place of the individual exertions of the nobles, and the community would be alike protected from anarchy and from oppression.

I admit that, in a democratic state thus constituted, society would not be stationary. But the impulses of the social body might there be regulated and made progressive. If there were less splendor than in the midst of an aristocracy, the contrast of misery would also be less frequent; the pleasures of enjoyment might be less excessive, but those of comfort would be more general; the sciences might be less perfectly cultivated, but ignorance would be less common; the impetuosity of the feelings would be repressed, and the habits of the nation softened; there would be more vices and fewer great crimes.

In the absence of enthusiasm and an ardent faith, great sacrifices may be obtained from the members of a commonwealth by an appeal to their understandings and their experience; each individual will feel the same necessity of union with his fellows to protect his own weakness; and as he knows that he can obtain their help only on condition of helping them, he will readily perceive that his personal interest is identified with the interests of the whole community. The nation, taken as a whole, will be less brilliant, less glorious, and perhaps less strong; but the majority of the citizens will enjoy a greater degree of prosperity, and the people will remain quiet, not because they despair of a change for the better, but because they are conscious that they are well off already.

If all the consequences of this state of things were not good or useful, society would at least have appropriated all such as were useful and good; and having once and for ever renounced the social advantages of aristocracy, mankind would enter into possession of all the benefits which democracy can afford.

But here it may be asked what we have adopted in the place of those institutions, those ideas, and those customs of our forefathers which we have abandoned.

The spell of royalty is broken, but it has not been succeeded by the majesty of the laws. The people have learned to despise all authority, but they still fear it; and fear now extorts more than was formerly paid from reverence and love.

I perceive that we have destroyed those individual powers which were able, single-handed, to cope with tyranny; but it is the government that has inherited the privileges of which families, corporations, and individuals have been deprived; to the power of a small number of persons—which, if it was sometimes oppressive, was often conservative—has succeeded the weakness of the whole community.

The division of property has lessened the distance which separated the rich from the poor; but it would seem that, the nearer they draw to each other, the greater is their mutual hatred, and the more vehement the envy and the dread with which they resist each other's claims to power; the idea of Right does not exist for either party, and Force affords to both the only argument for the present, and the only guaranty for the future.

The poor man retains the prejudices of his forefathers without their faith, and their ignorance without their virtues; he has adopted the doctrine of self-interest as the rule of his actions, without understanding the science which puts it to use; and his selfishness is no less blind than was formerly his devotedness to others.

If society is tranquil, it is not because it is conscious of its strength and its well-being, but because it fears its weakness and its infirmities; a single effort may cost it its life. Everybody feels the evil, but no one has courage or energy enough to seek the cure. The desires, the repinings, the sorrows, and the joys of the present time lead to no visible or permanent result, like the passions of old men, which terminate in impotence.

We have, then, abandoned whatever advantages the old state of things afforded, without receiving any compensation from our present condition; we have destroyed an aristocracy, and we seem inclined to survey its ruins with complacency, and to fix our abode in the midst of them.

The phenomena which the intellectual world presents are not less deplorable. The democracy of France, hampered in its course or abandoned to its lawless passions, has overthrown whatever crossed its path, and has shaken all that it has not destroyed. Its empire has not been gradually introduced, or peaceably established, but it has constantly advanced in the midst of the disorders and the agitations of a conflict. In the heat of the struggle, each partisan is hurried beyond the natural limits of his opinions by the doctrines and the excesses of his opponents, until he loses sight of the end of his exertions, and holds a language which does not express his real sentiments or secret instincts. Hence arises the strange confusion which we are compelled to witness.

I can recall nothing in history more worthy of sorrow and pity, than the scenes which are passing under our eyes. It is as if the natural bond which unites the opinions of man to his tastes, and his actions to his principles, was now broken; the sympathy which has always been observed between the feelings and the ideas of mankind appears to be dissolved, and all the laws of moral analogy to be abolished.

Zealous Christians are still found amongst us, whose minds are nurtured on the thoughts which pertain to a future life, and who readily espouse the cause of human liberty as the source of all moral greatness. Christianity, which has declared that all men are equal in the sight of God, will not refuse to acknowledge that all citizens are equal in the eye of the law. But, by a singular concourse of events, religion has been for a time entangled with those institutions which democracy assails; and it is not infrequently brought to reject the equality which it loves, and to curse that cause of liberty as a foe, whose efforts it might hallow by its alliance.

By the side of these religious men, I discern others whose looks are turned to earth rather than to heaven. These are the partisans of liberty, not only as the source of the noblest virtues, but more especially as the root of all solid advantages; and they sincerely desire to secure its authority, and to impart its blessings to mankind. It is natural that they should hasten to invoke the assistance of religion, for they must know that liberty cannot be established without morality, nor morality without faith. But they have seen religion in the ranks of their adversaries, and they inquire no further; some of them attack it openly, and the remainder are afraid to defend it.

In former ages, slavery was advocated by the venal and slav-ish-minded, whilst the independent and the warmhearted were struggling without hope to save the liberties of mankind. But men of high and generous characters are now to be met with, whose opinions are at variance with their inclinations, and who praise that servility which they have themselves never known. Others, on the contrary, speak of liberty as if they were able to feel its sanctity and its majesty, and loudly claim for humanity those rights which they have always refused to acknowledge.

There are virtuous and peaceful individuals whose pure morality, quiet habits, opulence, and talents fit them to be the leaders of the surrounding population. Their love of country is sincere, and they are ready to make the greatest sacrifices for its welfare. But civilization often finds them among its opponents; they confound its abuses with its benefits, and the idea of evil is inseparable in their minds from that of novelty.

Near these I find others, whose object is to materialize mankind, to hit upon what is expedient without heeding what is just, to acquire knowledge without faith, and prosperity apart from virtue; claiming to be the champions of modern civilization, they place themselves arrogantly at its head, usurping a place which is abandoned to them, and of which they are wholly unworthy.

Where are we, then?

The religionists are the enemies of liberty, and the friends of liberty attack religion; the high-minded and the noble advocate bondage, and the meanest and most servile preach independence; honest and enlightened citizens are opposed to all progress, whilst men without patriotism and without principle put themselves forward as the apostles of civilization and intelligence.

Has such been the fate of the centuries which have preceded our own? and has man always inhabited a world like the present, where all things are out of their natural connections, where virtue is without genius, and genius without honor; where the love of order is confounded with a taste for oppression, and the holy rites of freedom with a contempt of law; where the light thrown by conscience on human actions is dim, and where nothing seems to be any longer forbidden or allowed, honorable or shameful, false or true?

I cannot believe that the Creator made man to leave him in an endless struggle with the intellectual miseries which surround us. God destines a calmer and a more certain future to the communities of Europe. I am ignorant of his designs, but I shall not cease to believe in them because I cannot fathom them, and I had rather mistrust my own capacity than his justice.

There is a country in the world where the great social revolution which I am speaking of seems to have nearly reached its natural limits. It has been effected with ease and quietness; say rather that this country is reaping the fruits of the democratic revolution which we are undergoing, without having had the revolution itself.

The emigrants who colonized the shores of America in the beginning of the seventeenth century somehow separated the democratic principle from all the principles which it had to contend with in the old communities of Europe, and transplanted it alone to the New World. It has there been able to spread in perfect freedom, and peaceably to determine the character of the laws by influencing the manners of the country.

It appears to me beyond a doubt that, sooner or later, we shall arrive, like the Americans, at an almost complete equality of condition. But I do not conclude from this, that we shall ever be necessarily led to draw the same political consequences which the Americans have derived from a similar social organization. I am far from supposing that they have chosen the only form of government which a democracy may adopt; but as the generative cause of laws and manners in the two countries is the same, it is of immense interest for us to know what it has produced in each of them.

It is not, then, merely to satisfy a legitimate curiosity that I have examined America; my wish has been to find there instruction by which we may ourselves profit. Whoever should imagine that I have intended to write a panegyric would be strangely mistaken, and on reading this book, he will perceive that such was not my design: nor has it been my object to advocate any form of government in particular, for I am of opinion that absolute excellence is rarely to be found in any system of laws. I have not even pretended to judge whether the social revolution, which I believe to be irresistible, is advantageous or prejudicial to mankind. I have acknowledged this revolution as a fact already accomplished, or on the eve of its accomplishment; and I have selected the nation, from amongst those which have undergone it, in which its development has been the most peaceful and the most complete, in order to discern its natural consequences, and to find out, if possible, the means of rendering it profitable to mankind. I confess that, in America, I saw more than America; I sought there the image of democracy itself, with its inclinations, its character, its prejudices, and its passions, in order to learn what we have to fear or to hope from its progress.

In the first part of this work, I have attempted to show the direction given to the laws by the democracy of America, which is abandoned almost without restraint to its instinctive propensities; and to exhibit the course it prescribes to the government and the influence it exercises on affairs. I have sought to discover the evils and the advantages which it brings. I have examined the precautions used by the Americans to direct it, as well as those which they have not adopted, and I have undertaken to point out the causes which enable it to govern society. I do not know whether I have succeeded in making known what I saw in America, but I am certain that such has been my sincere desire, and that I have never, knowingly, moulded facts to ideas, instead of ideas to facts.

Whenever a point could be established by the aid of written documents, I have had recourse to the original text, and to the most authentic and approved works. I have cited my authorities in the notes, and any one may refer to them. Whenever opinions, political customs, or remarks on the manners of the country were concerned, I have endeavored to consult the most enlightened men I met with. If the point in question was important or doubtful, I was not satisfied with one testimony, but I formed my opinion on the evidence of several witnesses. Here the reader must necessarily rely upon my word. I could frequently have quoted names which are either known to him, or which deserve to be so, in proof of what I advance; but I have carefully abstained from this practice. A stranger frequently hears important truths at the fireside of his host, which the latter would perhaps conceal from the ear of friendship; he consoles himself with his guest for the silence to which he is restricted, and the shortness of the traveller's stay takes away all fear of his indiscretion. I carefully noted every conversation of this nature as soon as it occurred, but these notes will never leave my writing-case. I had rather injure the success of my statements than add my name to the list of those strangers who repay the generous hospitality they have received by subsequent chagrin and annoyance.

I am aware that, notwithstanding my care, nothing will be easier than to criticize this book, if any one ever chooses to criticize it.

Those readers who may examine it closely will discover, I think, in the whole work, a dominant thought which binds, so to speak, its several parts together. But the diversity of the subjects I have had to treat is exceedingly great, and it will not be difficult to oppose an isolated fact to the body of facts which I cite, or an isolated idea to the body of ideas I put forth. I hope to be read in the spirit which has guided my labors, and that my book may be judged by the general impression it leaves, as I have formed my own judgment not on any single reason, but upon the mass of evidence.

It must not be forgotten that the author who wishes to be understood is obliged to push all his ideas to their utmost theoretical consequences, and often to the verge of what is false or impracticable; for if it be necessary sometimes to depart from the rules of logic in action, such is not the case in discourse, and a man finds it almost as difficult to be inconsistent in his language, as to be consistent in his conduct.

I conclude by myself pointing out what many readers will consider the principal defect of the work. This book is written to favor no particular views, and in composing it, I have entertained no design of serving or attacking any party. I have undertaken, not to see differently from others, but to look further than others, and whilst they are busied for the morrow only, I have turned my thoughts to the whole future.

CHAPTER I

---★---

Exterior Form of North America

N orth America presents in its external form certain general features which it is easy to discriminate at the first glance.

A sort of methodical order seems to have regulated the separation of land and water, mountains and valleys. A simple but grand arrangement is discoverable amidst the confusion of objects and the prodigious variety of scenes.

This continent is divided almost equally into two vast regions, one of which is bounded on the north by the Arctic Pole, and by the two great oceans on the east and west. It stretches toward the south, forming a triangle, whose irregular sides meet at length above the great lakes of Canada. The second region begins where the other terminates, and includes all the remainder of the continent. The one slopes gently toward the Pole, the other toward the Equator.

The territory comprehended in the first region descends toward the north with so imperceptible a slope, that it may almost be said to form a plain. Within the bounds of this immense level tract there are neither high mountains nor deep valleys. Streams meander through it irregularly; great rivers intertwine, separate, and meet again, spread into vast marshes, losing all trace of their channels in the labyrinth of waters they have themselves created, and thus at length, after innumerable windings, fall into the Polar seas. The great lakes which bound this first region are not walled in, like most of those in the Old World, between hills and rocks. Their banks are flat, and rise but a few feet above the level of their waters,—each of them thus forming a vast bowl filled to the brim. The slightest change in the structure of the globe would cause their waters to rush either towards the Pole or to the tropical seas.

The second region has a more broken surface, and is better suited for the habitation of man. Two long chains of mountains divide it, from one extreme to the other: the one, named the Alleghany, follows the direction of the shore of the Atlantic Ocean; the other is parallel with the Pacific.

The space which lies between these two chains of mountains contains 1,341,649 square miles. Its surface is therefore about six times as great as that of France.

This vast territory, however, forms a single valley, one side of which descends from the rounded summits of the Alleghenies, while the other rises in an uninterrupted course to the tops of the Rocky Mountains. At the bottom of the valley flows an immense river, into which the various streams issuing from the mountains fall from all parts. In memory of their native land, the French formerly called this river the St. Louis. The Indians, in their pompous language, have named it the Father of Waters, or the Mississippi.

The Mississippi takes its source at the boundary of the two great regions of which I have spoken, not far from the highest point of the table-land where they unite. Near the same spot rises another river [the Red River of the North], which empties itself into the Polar seas. The course of the Mississippi is at first dubious: it winds several times towards the north, whence it rose; and only at length, after having been delayed in lakes and marshes, does it assume its definite direction, and flow slowly onward to the south.

Sometimes quietly gliding along the argillaceous bed which nature has assigned to it, sometimes swollen by freshets, the Mississippi waters over 2,500 miles in its course. At the distance of 1,364 miles from its mouth, this river attains an average depth of fifteen feet; and it is navigated by vessels of 300 tons burden for a course of nearly 500 miles. Fifty-seven large navigable rivers contribute to swell the waters of the Mississippi; amongst others, the Missouri, which traverses a space of 2,500 miles, the Arkansas, 1,300 miles, the Red River, 1,000 miles, the Ohio, 959 miles; four whose course is from 800 to 1,000 miles in length, viz. the Illinois, the St. Peter's, the St. Francis, and the Des Moines; besides a countless multitude of rivulets which unite from all parts their tributary streams.

The valley which is watered by the Mississippi seems to have been created for it alone, and there, like a god of antiquity, the river dispenses both good and evil. Near the stream, nature displays an inexhaustible fertility; in proportion as you recede from its banks, the powers of vegetation languish, the soil becomes poor, and the plants that survive have a sickly growth. Nowhere have the great convulsions of the globe left more evident traces than in the valley of the Mississippi. The whole aspect of the country shows the powerful effects of water, both by its fertility and its barrenness. The waters of the primeval ocean accumulated enormous beds of vegetable mould in the valley, which they leveled as they retired. Upon the right bank of the river are found immense plains, as smooth as if the husbandman had passed over them with his roller. As you approach the mountains, the soil becomes more and more unequal and sterile; the ground is, as it were, pierced in a thousand places by primitive rocks, which appear like the bones of a skeleton whose flesh has been consumed by time. The surface of the earth is covered with a granitic sand, and huge, irregular masses of stone, among which a few plants force their growth, and give the appearance of a green field covered with the ruins of a vast edifice. These stones and this sand discover, on examination, a perfect analogy with those which compose the arid and broken summits of the Rocky Mountains. The flood of waters which washed the soil to the bottom of the valley, afterwards carried away portions of the rocks themselves; and these, dashed and bruised against the neighboring cliffs, were left scattered like wrecks at their feet.

The valley of the Mississippi is, upon the whole, the most magnificent dwelling-place prepared by God for man's abode; and yet it may be said that at present it is but a mighty desert.

On the eastern side of the Alleghenies, between the base of these mountains and the Atlantic Ocean, there lies a long ridge of rocks and sand, which the sea appears to have left behind as it retired. The mean breadth of this territory does not exceed one hundred miles; but it is about nine hundred miles in length. This part of the American continent has a soil which offers every obstacle to the husbandman, and its vegetation is scanty and unvaried.

Upon this inhospitable coast the first united efforts of human industry were made. This tongue of arid land was the cradle of those English colonies which were destined one day to become the United States of America. The center of power still remains here; whilst in the rear of it the true elements of the great people to whom the future control of the continent belongs are gathering almost in secrecy together.

When the Europeans first landed on the shores of the West Indies, and afterwards on the coast of South America, they thought themselves transported into those fabulous regions of which poets had sung. The sea sparkled with phosphoric light, and the extraordinary transparency of its waters discovered to the view of the navigator all the depths of the abyss. Here and there appeared little islands perfumed with odoriferous plants, and resembling baskets of flowers floating on the tranquil surface of the ocean. Every object which met the sight, in this enchanting region, seemed prepared to satisfy the wants or contribute to the pleasures of man. Almost all the trees were loaded with nourishing fruits, and those which were useless as food delighted the eye by the brilliancy and variety of their colors. In groves of fragrant lemon-trees, wild figs, flowering myrtles, acacias, and oleanders, which were hung with festoons of various climbing-plants, covered with flowers, a multitude of birds unknown in Europe displayed their bright plumage, glittering with purple and azure, and mingled their warbling with the harmony of a world teeming with life and motion.

Underneath this brilliant exterior, death was concealed. But this fact was not then known, and the air of these climates had so enervating an influence, that man, absorbed by present enjoyment, was rendered regardless of the future.

North America appeared under a very different aspect: there, everything was grave, serious, and solemn; it seemed created to be the domain of intelligence, as the South was that of sensual delight. A turbulent and foggy ocean washed its shores. It was girt round by a belt of granitic rocks, or by wide tracts of sand. The foliage of its woods was dark and gloomy; for they were composed of firs, larches, evergreen oaks, wild olive-trees, and laurels.

Beyond this outer belt lay the thick shades of the central forests, where the largest trees which are produced in the two hemispheres grow side by side. The plane, the catalpa, the sugar-maple, and the Virginian poplar mingled their branches with those of the oak, the beech, and the lime.

In these, as in the forests of the Old World, destruction was perpetually going on. The ruins of vegetation were heaped upon each other; but there was no laboring hand to remove them, and their decay was not rapid enough to make room for the continual work of reproduction. Climbing plants, grasses, and other herbs forced their way through the mass of dying trees; they crept along their bending trunks, found nourishment in their dusty cavities, and a passage beneath the lifeless bark. Thus decay gave its assistance to life, and their respective productions were mingled together. The depths of these forests were gloomy and obscure, and a thousand rivulets, undirected in their course by human industry, preserved in them a constant moisture. It was rare to meet with flowers, wild fruits, or birds, beneath their shades. The fall of a tree overthrown by age, the rushing torrent of a cataract, the lowing of the buffalo, and the howling of the wind, were the only sounds which broke the silence of nature.

To the east of the great river, the woods almost disappeared; in their stead were seen prairies of immense extent. Whether Nature in her infinite variety had denied the germs of trees to these fertile plains, or whether they had once been covered with forests, subsequently destroyed by the hand of man, is a question which neither tradition nor scientific research has been able to answer.

These immense deserts were not, however, wholly untenanted by men. Some wandering tribes had been for ages scattered among the forest shades or the green pastures of the prairie. From the mouth of the St. Lawrence to the Delta of the Mississippi, and from the Atlantic to the Pacific Ocean, these savages possessed certain points of resemblance which bore witness of their common origin: but at the same time, they differed from all other known races of men; they were neither white like the Europeans, nor yellow like most of the Asiatics, nor black like the negroes. Their skin was reddish brown, their hair long and shining, their lips thin, and their cheekbones very prominent. The languages spoken by the North American tribes were various as far as regarded their words, but they were subject to the same grammatical rules. These rules differed in several points from such as had been observed to govern the origin of language. The idiom of the Americans seemed to be the product of new combinations; and bespoke an effort of the understanding, of which the Indians of our days would be incapable.

In that land the great experiment was to be made, by civilized man, of the attempt to construct society upon a new basis; and it was there, for the first time, that theories hitherto unknown, or deemed impracticable, were to exhibit a spectacle for which the world had not been prepared by the history of the past.

CHAPTER II

───────★───────

Origin of the Anglo-Americans, and Importance of This Origin in Relation to Their Future Condition

After the birth of a human being, his early years are obscurely spent in the toils or pleasures of childhood. As he grows up, the world receives him, when his manhood begins, and he enters into contact with his fellows. He is then studied for the first time, and it is imagined that the germ of the vices and the virtues of his maturer years is then formed.

This, if I am not mistaken, is a great error. We must begin higher up; we must watch the infant in his mother's arms; we must see the first images which the external world casts upon the dark mirror of his mind, the first occurrences which he witnesses; we must hear the first words which awaken the sleeping powers of thought, and stand by his earliest efforts,—if we would understand the prejudices, the habits, and the passions which will rule his life. The entire man is, so to speak, to be seen in the cradle of the child.

The growth of nations presents something analogous to this; they all bear some marks of their origin. The circumstances which accompanied their birth and contributed to their development affect the whole term of their being.

If we were able to go back to the elements of states, and to examine the oldest monuments of their history, I doubt not that we should discover in them the primal cause of the prejudices, the habits, the ruling passions, and, in short, of all that constitutes what is called the national character. We should there find the explanation of certain customs which now seem at variance with the prevailing manners; of such laws as conflict with established principles; and of such incoherent opinions as are here and there to be met with in society, like those fragments of broken chains which we sometimes see hanging from the vaults of an old edifice, and supporting nothing. This might explain the destinies of certain nations which seem borne on by an unknown force to ends of which they themselves are ignorant. But hitherto facts have been wanting to researches of this kind: the spirit of inquiry has only come upon communities in their latter days; and when they at length contemplated their origin, time had already obscured it, or ignorance and pride adorned it with truth-concealing fables.

America is the only country in which it has been possible to witness the natural and tranquil growth of society, and where the influence exercised on the future condition of states by their origin is clearly distinguishable.

If we carefully examine the social and political state of America, after having studied its history, we shall remain perfectly convinced that not an opinion, not a custom, not a law, I may even say not an event, is upon record which the origin of that people will not explain. The readers of this book will find in the present chapter the germ of all that is to follow, and the key to almost the whole work.

The emigrants who came at different periods to occupy the territory now covered by the American Union differed from each other in many respects; their aim was not the same, and they governed themselves on different principles.

These men had, however, certain features in common, and they were all placed in an analogous situation. The tie of language is, perhaps, the strongest and the most durable that can unite mankind. All the emigrants spoke the same tongue; they were all offsets from the same people. Born in a country which had been agitated for centuries by the struggles of faction, and in which all parties had been obliged in their turn to place themselves under the protection of the laws, their political education had been perfected in this rude school; and they were more conversant with the notions of right, and the principles of true freedom, than the greater part of their European contemporaries. At the period of the first emigrations, the township system, that fruitful germ of free institutions, was deeply rooted in the habits of the English; and with it the doctrine of the sovereignty of the people had been introduced into the bosom of the monarchy of the house of Tudor.

The religious quarrels which have agitated the Christian world were then rife. England had plunged into the new order of things with headlong vehemence. The character of its inhabitants, which had always been sedate and reflective, became argumentative and austere. General information had been increased by intellectual contests, and the mind had received in them a deeper cultivation. Whilst religion was the topic of discussion, the morals of the people became more pure. All these national features are more or less discoverable in the physiognomy of those Englishmen who came to seek a new home on the opposite shores of the Atlantic.

All the British colonies had then a great degree of family likeness at the epoch of their settlement. All of them, from their beginning, seemed destined to witness the growth, not of the aristocratic liberty of their mother country, but of that freedom of the middle and lower orders of which the history of the world had as yet furnished no complete example.

In this general uniformity, however, several striking differences were discernible, which it is necessary to point out. Two branches may be distinguished in the great Anglo-American family, which have hitherto grown up without entirely commingling; the one in the South, the other in the North.

Virginia received the first English colony; the emigrants took possession of it in 1607. The idea that mines of gold and silver are the sources of national wealth was at that time singularly prevalent in Europe; a fatal delusion, which has done more to impoverish the European nations who adopted it, and has cost more lives in America, than the united influence of war and bad laws. The men sent to Virginia were seekers of gold, adventurers without resources and without character, whose turbulent and restless spirit endangered the infant colony, and rendered its progress uncertain. Artisans and agriculturists arrived afterwards; and, although they were a more moral and orderly race of men, they were hardly in any respect above the level of the inferior classes in England. No lofty views, no spiritual conception, presided over the foundation of these new settlements. The colony was scarcely established when slavery was introduced; this was the capital fact which was to exercise an immense influence on the character, the laws, and the whole future of the South. Slavery, as we shall afterwards show, dishonors labor; it introduces idleness into society, and with idleness, ignorance and pride, luxury and distress. It enervates the powers of the mind, and benumbs the activity of man. The influence of slavery, united to the English character, explains the manners and the social condition of the Southern States.

In the North, the same English character as the ground received totally different colors. Here I may be allowed to enter into some details.

In the English colonies of the North, more generally known as the States of New England, the two or three main ideas which now constitute the basis of the social theory of the United States were first combined. The principles of New England spread at first to the neighboring States; they then passed successively to the more distant ones; and at last, if I may so speak, they *interpenetrated* the whole confederation. They now extend their influence beyond its limits, over the whole American world. The civilization of New England has been like a beacon lit upon a hill, which, after it has diffused its warmth immediately around it, also tinges the distant horizon with its glow.

The foundation of New England was a novel spectacle, and all the circumstances attending it were singular and original. Nearly all colonies have been first inhabited, either by men without education and without resources, driven by their poverty and their misconduct from the land which gave them birth, or by speculators and adventurers greedy of gain. Some settlements cannot even boast so honorable an origin; St. Domingo was founded by buccaneers; and, at the present day, the criminal courts of England supply the population of Australia.

The settlers who established themselves on the shores of New England all belonged to the more independent classes of their native country. Their union on the soil of America at once presented the singular phenomenon of a society containing neither lords nor common people, and we may almost say, neither rich nor poor. These men possessed, in proportion to their number, a greater mass of intelligence than is to be found in any European nation of our own time.

All, perhaps without a single exception, had received a good education, and many of them were known in Europe for their talents and their acquirements. The other colonies had been founded by adventurers without families; the emigrants of New England brought with them the best elements of order and morality; they landed on the desert coast accompanied by their wives and children. But what especially distinguished them from all others was the aim of their undertaking. They had not been obliged by necessity to leave their country; the social position they abandoned was one to be regretted, and their means of subsistence were certain. Nor did they cross the Atlantic to improve their situation or to increase their wealth; it was a purely intellectual craving, which called them from the comforts of their former homes; and in facing the inevitable sufferings of exile, their object was the triumph of an idea.

The emigrants, or, as they deservedly styled themselves, the Pilgrims, belonged to that English sect the austerity of whose principles had acquired for them the name of Puritans. Puritanism was not merely a religious doctrine, but it corresponded in many points with the most absolute democratic and republican theories. It was this tendency which had aroused its most dangerous adversaries. Persecuted by the government of the mother country, and disgusted by the habits of a society which the rigor of their own principles condemned, the Puritans went forth to seek some rude and infrequented part of the world, where they could live according to their own opinions, and worship God in freedom.

A few quotations will throw more light upon the spirit of these pious adventurers than all that we can say of them. Nathaniel Morton, the historian of the first years of the settlement, thus opens his subject:—

> Gentle Reader,—I have for some length of time looked upon it as a duty incumbent especially on the immediate successors of those that have had so large experience of those many memorable and signal demonstrations of God's goodness, viz. the first beginners of this Plantation in New England, to commit to writing his gracious dispensations on that behalf; having so many inducements thereunto, not only otherwise, but so plentifully in the Sacred Scriptures: that so, what we have seen, and what our fathers have told us (Psalm 78:3, 4), we

may not hide from our children, showing to the generations to come the praises of the Lord; that especially the seed of Abraham his servant, and the children of Jacob his chosen (Psalm 105:5, 6), may remember his marvelous works in the beginning and progress of the planting of New England, his wonders and the judgments of his mouth; how that God brought a vine into this wilderness; that he cast out the heathen, and planted it; that he made room for it and caused it to take deep root; and it filled the land (Psalm 80:8, 9). And not only so, but also that he hath guided his people by his strength to his holy habitation, and planted them in the mountain of his inheritance in respect of precious Gospel enjoyments: and that as especially God may have the glory of all unto whom it is most due; so also some rays of glory may reach the names of those blessed Saints, that were the main instruments and the beginning of this happy enterprise.

It is impossible to read this opening paragraph without an involuntary feeling of religious awe; it breathes the very savor of Gospel antiquity. The sincerity of the author heightens his power of language. In our eyes, as well as in his own, it was not a mere party of adventurers gone forth to seek their fortune beyond seas, but the germ of a great nation wafted by Providence to a predestined shore.

The author continues, and thus describes the departure of the first pilgrims:—

So they left that goodly and pleasant city of Leyden, which had been their resting-place for above eleven years; but they knew that they were pilgrims and strangers here below, and looked not much on these things, but lifted up their eyes to heaven, their dearest country, where God hath prepared for them a city (Heb. 11:16), and therein quieted their spirits. When they came to Delfs-Haven they found the ship and all things ready; and such of their friends as could not come with them followed after them, and sundry came from Amsterdam to see them shipt, and to take their leaves of them. One night was spent with little sleep with the most, but with friendly entertainment and Christian discourse, and other real expressions of true Christian love. The next day they went on board, and their friends with them, where truly doleful was the sight of that sad and mournful parting, to hear what sighs and sobs and prayers did sound amongst them; what tears did gush from every eye, and pithy speeches pierced each other's heart, that sundry of the Dutch strangers that stood on the Key as spectators could not refrain from tears. But the tide (which stays for no man) calling them away, that were thus loth to depart, their Reverend Pastor, falling down on his knees, and they all with him, with watery cheeks commended them with most fervent prayers unto the Lord and his blessing; and then with mutual embraces and many tears they took their leaves one of another, which proved to be the last leave to many of them.

The emigrants were about 150 in number, including the women and the children. Their object was to plant a colony on the shores of the Hudson; but after having been driven about for some time in the Atlantic Ocean, they were forced to land on the arid coast of New England, at the spot which is now the town of Plymouth. The rock is still shown on which the pilgrims disembarked.

"But before we pass on," continues our historian,

let the reader with me make a pause, and seriously consider this poor people's present condition, the more to be raised up to admiration of God's goodness towards them in their preservation: for being now passed the vast ocean, and a sea of troubles before them in expectation, they had now no friends to welcome them, no inns to entertain or refresh them, no houses, or much less towns, to repair unto to seek for succour: and for the season it was winter, and they that know the winters of the country know them to be sharp and violent, subject to cruel and fierce storms, dangerous to travel to known places, much more to search unknown coasts. Besides, what could they see but a hideous and desolate wilderness, full of wilde beasts, and wilde men? and what multitudes of them there were, they then knew not: for which way soever they turned their eyes (save upward to Heaven) they could have but little solace or content in respect of any outward object; for summer being ended, all things stand in appearance with a weather-beaten face, and the whole country, full of woods and thickets, represented a wild and savage hew; if they looked behind them, there was the mighty ocean which they had passed, and was now as a main bar or gulph to separate them from all the civil parts of the world.

It must not be imagined that the piety of the Puritans was merely speculative, or that it took no cognizance of the course of worldly affairs. Puritanism, as I have already remarked, was scarcely less a political than a religious doctrine. No sooner had the emigrants landed on the barren coast described by Nathaniel Morton, than it was their first care to constitute a society, by subscribing the following Act:—

In the name of God. Amen. We, whose names are under-written, the loyal subjects of our dread Sovereign Lord King James, &c. &c., Having undertaken for the glory of God, and advancement of the Christian Faith, and the honour of our King and country, a voyage to plant the first colony in the northern parts of Virginia; Do by these presents solemnly and mutually, in the presence of God and one another, covenant and combine ourselves together into a civil body politick, for our better ordering and preservation, and furtherance of the ends aforesaid: and by virtue hereof do enact, constitute, and frame such just and equal laws, ordinances, acts, constitutions, and offices, from time to time, as shall be thought most meet and convenient for the general good of the Colony: unto which we promise all due submission and obedience," etc.

This happened in 1620, and from that time forwards the emigration went on. The religious and political passions which ravaged the British empire during the whole reign of Charles I. drove fresh crowds of sectarians every year to the shores of America. In England, the stronghold of Puritanism continued to be in the middle classes; and it was from the middle classes that most of the emigrants came.

The population of New England increased rapidly; and whilst the hierarchy of rank despotically classed the inhabitants of the mother country, the colony approximated more and more the novel spectacle of a community homogeneous in all its parts. A democracy, more perfect than antiquity had dared to dream of, started in full size and panoply from the midst of an ancient feudal society.

The English government was not dissatisfied with a large emigration which removed the elements of fresh discord and further revolutions. On the contrary, it did everything to encourage it, and seemed to have no anxiety about the destiny of those who sought a shelter on the soil of America from the rigor of their laws. It appeared as if New England was a region given up to the dreams of fancy, and the unrestrained experiments of innovators.

The English colonies (and this is one of the main causes of their prosperity) have always enjoyed more internal freedom and more political independence than the colonies of other nations; and this principle of liberty was nowhere more extensively applied than in the States of New England.

It was generally allowed at that period, that the territories of the New World belonged to that European nation which had been the first to discover them. Nearly the whole coast of North America thus became a British possession towards the end of the sixteenth century. The means used by the English government to people these new domains were of several kinds: the king sometimes appointed a governor of his own choice, who ruled a portion of the New World in the name and under the immediate orders of the crown; this is the colonial system adopted by the other countries of Europe. Sometimes, grants of certain tracts were made by the crown to an individual or to a company, in which case all the civil and political power fell into the hands of one or more persons, who, under the inspection and control of the crown, sold the lands and governed the inhabitants. Lastly, a third system consisted in allowing a certain number of emigrants to form themselves into a political society under the protection of the mother country, and to govern themselves in whatever was not contrary to her laws. This mode of colonization, so favorable to liberty, was adopted only in New England.

In 1628, a charter of this kind was granted by Charles I. to the emigrants who went to form the colony of Massachusetts. But, in general, charters were not given to the colonies of New England till their existence had become an established fact. Plymouth, Providence, New Haven, Connecticut, and Rhode Island were founded without the help, and almost without the knowledge, of the mother country. The new settlers did not derive their powers from the head of the empire, although they did not deny its supremacy; they constituted themselves into a society, and it was not till thirty or forty years afterwards, under Charles II., that their existence was legally recognized by a royal charter.

This frequently renders it difficult, in studying the earliest historical and legislative records of New England, to detect the link which connected the emigrants with the land of their forefathers. They continually exercised the rights of sovereignty; they named their magistrates, concluded peace or declared war, made police regulations, and enacted laws, as if their allegiance was due only to God. Nothing can be more curious, and at the same time more instructive, than the legislation of that period; it is there that the solution of the great social problem which the United States now present to the world is to be found.

Amongst these documents we shall notice, as especially characteristic, the code of laws promulgated by the little state of Connecticut in 1650.

The legislators of Connecticut begin with the penal laws, and, strange to say, they borrow their provisions from the text of Holy Writ.

"Whosoever shall worship any other God than the Lord," says the preamble of the Code, "shall surely be put to death." This is followed by ten or twelve enactments of the same kind, copied verbatim from the books of Exodus, Leviticus, and Deuteronomy. Blasphemy, sorcery, adultery, and rape were punished with death; an outrage offered by a son to his parents was to be expiated by the same penalty. The legislation of a rude and half-civilized people was thus applied to an enlightened and moral community. The consequence was, that the punishment of death was never more frequently prescribed by statute, and never more rarely enforced.

The chief care of the legislators, in this body of penal laws, was the maintenance of orderly conduct and good morals in the community: thus they constantly invaded the domain of conscience, and there was scarcely a sin which was not subject to magisterial censure. The reader is aware of the rigor with which these laws punished rape and adultery; intercourse between unmarried persons was likewise severely repressed. The judge was empowered to inflict either a pecuniary penalty, a whipping, or marriage, on the misdemeanants; and if the records of the old courts of New Haven may be believed, prosecutions of this kind were not infrequent. We find a sentence, bearing date the 1st of May, 1660, inflicting a fine and reprimand on a young woman who was accused of using improper language, and of allowing herself to be kissed. The Code of 1650 abounds in preventive measures. It punishes idleness and drunkenness with severity. Innkeepers were forbidden to furnish more than a certain quantity of liquor to each consumer; and simple lying, whenever it may be injurious, is checked by a fine or a flogging. In other places, the legislator, entirely forgetting the great principles of religious toleration which he had himself demanded in Europe, makes attendance on divine service compulsory, and goes so far as to visit with severe punishment, and even with death, Christians who chose to worship God according to a ritual differing from his own. Sometimes, indeed, the zeal for regulation induces him to descend to the most frivolous particulars: thus a law is to be found in the same code which prohibits the use of tobacco. It must not be forgotten that these fantastical and vexatious laws were not imposed by authority, but that they were freely voted by all the persons interested in them, and that the manners of the community were even more austere and puritanical than the laws. In 1649, a solemn association was formed in Boston to check the worldly luxury of long hair.

These errors are no doubt discreditable to human reason; they attest the inferiority of our nature, which is incapable of laying firm hold upon what is true and just, and is often reduced to the alternative of two excesses. In strict connection with this penal legislation, which bears such striking marks of a narrow, sectarian spirit, and of those religious passions which had been warmed by persecution and were still fermenting among the people, a body of political laws is to be found, which, though written two hundred years ago, is still in advance of the liberties of our age.

The general principles which are the groundwork of modern constitutions—principles which, in the seventeenth century, were imperfectly known in Europe, and not completely triumphant even in Great Britain—were all recognized and established by the laws of New

England: the intervention of the people in public affairs, the free voting of taxes, the responsibility of the agents of power, personal liberty, and trial by jury, were all positively established without discussion.

These fruitful principles were there applied and developed to an extent such as no nation in Europe has yet ventured to attempt.

In Connecticut the electoral body consisted, from its origin, of the whole number of citizens; and this is readily to be understood, when we recollect that in this young community there was an almost perfect equality of fortune, and a still greater uniformity of opinions. In Connecticut, at this period, all the executive functionaries were elected, including the Governor of the State. The citizens above the age of sixteen were obliged to bear arms; they formed a national militia, which appointed its own officers, and was to hold itself at all times in readiness to march for the defense of the country.

In the laws of Connecticut, as well as in all those of New England, we find the germ and gradual development of that township independence, which is the life and mainspring of American liberty at the present day. The political existence of the majority of the nations of Europe commenced in the superior ranks of society, and was gradually and imperfectly communicated to the different members of the social body. In America, on the contrary, it may be said that the township was organized before the county, the county before the State, the State before the Union.

In New England, townships were completely and definitively constituted as early as 1650. The independence of the township was the nucleus round which the local interests, passions, rights, and duties collected and clung. It gave scope to the activity of a real political life, thoroughly democratic and republican. The colonies still recognized the supremacy of the mother country; monarchy was still the law of the State; but the republic was already established in every township.

The towns named their own magistrates of every kind, rated themselves, and levied their own taxes. In the New England town, the law of representation was not adopted; but the affairs of the community were discussed, as at Athens, in the market-place, by a general assembly of the citizens.

In studying the laws which were promulgated at this early era of the American republics, it is impossible not to be struck by the remarkable acquaintance with the science of government, and the advanced theory of legislation, which they display. The ideas there formed of the duties of society towards its members are evidently much loftier and more comprehensive than those of European legislators at that time: obligations were there imposed upon it which it elsewhere slighted. In the States of New England, from the first, the condition of the poor was provided for; strict measures were taken for the maintenance of roads, and surveyors were appointed to attend to them; records were established in every town, in which the results of public deliberations, and the births, deaths, and marriages of the citizens, were entered; clerks were directed to keep these records; officers were charged with the administration of vacant inheritances, and with the arbitration of litigated landmarks; and many others were created, whose chief functions were the maintenance of public order in the community. The law enters into a thousand various details to anticipate and satisfy a crowd of social wants which are even now very inadequately felt in France.

But it is by the mandates relating to Public Education that the original character of American civilization is at once placed in the clearest light. "It being," says the law, "one chief project of that old deluder, Satan, to keep men from the knowledge of the Scripture by persuading them from the use of tongues, to the end that learning may not be buried in the graves of our forefathers, in church and commonwealth, the Lord assisting our endeavors." Here follow clauses establishing schools in every township, and obliging the inhabitants, under pain of heavy fines, to support them. Schools of a superior kind were founded in the same manner in the more populous districts. The municipal authorities were bound to enforce the sending of children to school by their parents; they were empowered to inflict fines upon all who refused compliance; and in cases of continued resistance, society assumed the place of the parent, took possession of the child, and deprived the father of those natural rights which he used to so bad a purpose. The reader will undoubtedly have remarked the preamble of these enactments: in America, religion is the road to knowledge, and the observance of the divine laws leads man to civil freedom.

If, after having cast a rapid glance over the state of American society in 1650, we turn to the condition of Europe, and more especially to that of the Continent, at the same period, we cannot fail to be struck with astonishment. On the continent of Europe, at the beginning of the seventeenth century, absolute monarchy had everywhere triumphed over the ruins of the oligarchical and feudal liberties of the Middle Ages. Never perhaps were the ideas of right more completely overlooked, than in the midst of the splendor and literature of Europe; never was there less political activity among the people; never were the principles of true freedom less widely circulated; and at that very time, those principles, which were scorned or unknown by the nations of Europe, were proclaimed in the deserts of the New World, and were accepted as the future creed of a great people. The boldest theories of the human mind were reduced to practice by a community so humble, that not a statesman condescended to attend to it; and a system of legislation without a precedent was produced offhand by the natural originality of men's imaginations. In the bosom of this obscure democracy, which had as yet brought forth neither generals, nor philosophers, nor authors, a man might stand up in the face of a free people, and pronounce with general applause the following fine definition of liberty.

> Concerning liberty, I observe a great mistake in the country about that. There is a twofold liberty, natural (I mean as our nature is now corrupt) and civil or federal. The first is common to man with beasts and other creatures. By this, man, as he stands in relation to man simply, hath liberty to do what he lists; it is a liberty to evil as well as to good. This liberty is incompatible and inconsistent with authority, and cannot endure the least restraint of the most just authority. The exercise and maintaining of this liberty makes men grow more evil, and in time to be worse than brute beasts: *omnes sumus licentiâ deteriores*. This is that great enemy of truth and peace, that wild beast, which all the ordinances of God are bent against, to restrain and subdue it. The other kind of liberty I call civil or federal; it may also be termed moral, in reference to the covenant between God and man, in the moral law, and the politic covenants and constitutions, amongst men themselves. This liberty is the proper end and object of authority, and cannot subsist without it; and it is a liberty to that only which is good, just, and honest. This liberty you are to stand for, with the hazard not only of your

goods, but of your lives, if need be. Whatsoever crosseth this, is not authority, but a distemper thereof. This liberty is maintained and exercised in a way of subjection to authority; it is of the same kind of liberty wherewith Christ hath made us free.

I have said enough to put the character of Anglo-American civilization in its true light. It is the result (and this should be constantly present to the mind) of two distinct elements, which in other places have been in frequent hostility, but which in America have been admirably incorporated and combined with one another. I allude to the spirit of Religion and the spirit of Liberty.

The settlers of New England were at the same time ardent sectarians and daring innovators. Narrow as the limits of some of their religious opinions were, they were free from all political prejudices.

Hence arose two tendencies, distinct but not opposite, which are everywhere discernible in the manners as well as the laws of the country.

One would think that men who had sacrificed their friends, their family, and their native land to a religious conviction would be wholly absorbed in the pursuit of the treasure which they had just purchased at so high a price. And yet we find them seeking with nearly equal zeal for material wealth and moral good,—for well-being and freedom on earth, and salvation in heaven. They moulded and altered at pleasure all political principles, and all human laws and institutions; they broke down the barriers of the society in which they were born; they disregarded the old principles which had governed the world for ages; a career without bounds, a field without a horizon, was opened before them: they precipitate themselves into it, and traverse it in every direction. But, having reached the limits of the political world, they stop of their own accord, and lay aside with awe the use of their most formidable faculties; they no longer doubt or innovate; they abstain from raising even the veil of the sanctuary, and bow with submissive respect before truths which they admit without discussion.

Thus, in the moral world, everything is classified, systematized, foreseen, and decided beforehand; in the political world, everything is agitated, disputed, and uncertain. In the one is a passive though a voluntary obedience; in the other, an independence scornful of experience, and jealous of all authority. These two tendencies, apparently so discrepant, are far from conflicting; they advance together, and mutually support each other.

Religion perceives that civil liberty affords a noble exercise to the faculties of man, and that the political world is a field prepared by the Creator for the efforts of mind. Free and powerful in its own sphere, satisfied with the place reserved for it, religion never more surely establishes its empire than when it reigns in the hearts of men unsupported by aught beside its native strength.

Liberty regards religion as its companion in all its battles and its triumphs,—as the cradle of its infancy, and the divine source of its claims. It considers religion as the safeguard of morality, and morality as the best security of law, and the surest pledge of the duration of freedom.

CHAPTER III

———— ★ ————

Social Condition of the Anglo-Americans

S ocial condition is commonly the result of circumstances, sometimes of laws, oftener still of these two causes united; but when
once established, it may justly be considered as itself the source of
almost all the laws, the usages, and the ideas which regulate the conduct of nations: whatever it does not produce, it modifies.

If we would become acquainted with the legislation and the
manners of a nation, therefore, we must begin by the study of its
social condition.

The striking characteristic of the social condition of
the Anglo-Americans is its essential democracy

Many important observations suggest themselves upon the social
condition of the Anglo-Americans; but there is one which takes pre-
cedence of all the rest. The social condition of the Americans is eminently democratic; this was its character at the foundation of the colonies, and it is still more strongly marked at the present day.

I have stated in the preceding chapter that great equality existed
among the emigrants who settled on the shores of New England. Even
the germs of aristocracy were never planted in that part of the Union.
The only influence which obtained there was that of intellect; the people were used to reverence certain names as the emblems of knowledge and virtue. Some of their fellow-citizens acquired a power over
the others which might truly have been called aristocratic, if it had
been capable of transmission from father to son.

This was the state of things to the east of the Hudson: to the southwest of that river, and as far as the Floridas, the case was different.
In most of the States situated to the southwest of the Hudson some
great English proprietors had settled, who had imported with them

aristocratic principles and the English law of inheritance. I have explained the reasons why it was impossible ever to establish a powerful aristocracy in America; these reasons existed with less force to the southwest of the Hudson.[1] In the South, one man, aided by slaves, could cultivate a great extent of country; it was therefore common to see rich landed proprietors. But their influence was not altogether aristocratic, as that term is understood in Europe, since they possessed no privileges; and the cultivation of their estates being carried on by slaves, they had no tenants depending on them, and consequently no patronage. Still, the great proprietors south of the Hudson constituted a superior class, having ideas and tastes of its own, and forming the center of political action. This kind of aristocracy sympathized with the body of the people, whose passions and interests it easily embraced; but it was too weak and too short-lived to excite either love or hatred. This was the class which headed the insurrection in the South, and furnished the best leaders of the American Revolution.[2]

At this period, society was shaken to its center. The people, in whose name the struggle had taken place, conceived the desire of exercising the authority which it had acquired; its democratic tendencies were

---

1. Earlier in Chapter II, Tocqueville explained that aristocracy did not take hold in America because, since the basis of wealth in an aristocracy is land, class structures that had existed in Europe could not be imported to America. Land parcels were too small in America to support a powerful aristocracy, and furthermore, the produce of the land was not sufficient to provide vast amounts of wealth. Tocqueville's frame of reference for this was, of course, New England. "Laws were made to establish a gradation of ranks; but it was soon found that the soil of America was opposed to a territorial aristocracy. To bring that refractory land into cultivation, the constant and interested exertions of the owner himself were necessary; and when the ground was prepared, its produce was found to be insufficient to enrich a proprietor and a farmer at the same time. The land was then naturally broken up into small portions, which the proprietor cultivated for himself. Land is the basis of an aristocracy, which clings to the soil that supports it; for it is not by privileges alone, nor by birth, but by landed property handed down from generation to generation, that an aristocracy is constituted. A nation may present immense fortunes and extreme wretchedness; but unless those fortunes are territorial, there is no true aristocracy, but simply the class of the rich and that of the poor." -Editor
2. The "insurrection in the South" to which Tocqueville refers is the American Revolution in the Southern colonies. -Editor

awakened; and having thrown off the yoke of the mother country, it aspired to independence of every kind. The influence of individuals gradually ceased to be felt, and custom and law united to produce the same result.

But the law of inheritance was the last step to equality. I am surprised that ancient and modern jurists have not attributed to this law a greater influence on human affairs. It is true that these laws belong to civil affairs; but they ought, nevertheless, to be placed at the head of all political institutions; for they exercise an incredible influence upon the social state of a people, whilst political laws only show what this state already is. They have, moreover, a sure and uniform manner of operating upon society, affecting, as it were, generations yet unborn. Through their means, man acquires a kind of preternatural power over the future lot of his fellow-creatures. When the legislator has once regulated the law of inheritance, he may rest from his labor. The machine once put in motion will go on for ages, and advance, as if self-guided, towards a point indicated beforehand. When framed in a particular manner, this law unites, draws together, and vests property and power in a few hands; it causes an aristocracy, so to speak, to spring out of the ground. If formed on opposite principles, its action is still more rapid; it divides, distributes, and disperses both property and power. Alarmed by the rapidity of its progress, those who despair of arresting its motion endeavor, at least, to obstruct it by difficulties and impediments. They vainly seek to counteract its effect by contrary efforts; but it shatters and reduces to powder every obstacle, until we can no longer see anything but a moving and impalpable cloud of dust, which signals the coming of the Democracy. When the law of inheritance permits, still more when it decrees, the equal division of a father's property amongst all his children, its effects are of two kinds: it is important to distinguish them from each other, although they tend to the same end.

In virtue of the law of partible inheritance, the death of every proprietor brings about a kind of revolution in the property; not only do his possessions change hands, but their very nature is altered, since they are parceled into shares, which become smaller and smaller at each division. This is the direct, and as it were the physical, effect of the law. It follows, then, that, in countries where equality of inheritance is established by law, property, and especially landed property, must constantly tend to division into smaller and smaller parts. The effects, however, of such legislation would only be perceptible after a lapse of time, if the law were abandoned to its own working; for, supposing the family to consist of only two children, (and, in a country peopled as France is, the average number is not above three,) these children, sharing amongst them the fortune of both parents, would not be poorer than their father or mother.

But the law of equal division exercises its influence not merely upon the property itself, but it affects the minds of the heirs, and brings their passions into play. These indirect consequences tend powerfully to the destruction of large fortunes, and especially of large domains.

Among nations whose law of descent is founded upon the right of primogeniture, landed estates often pass from generation to generation without undergoing division,—the consequence of which is, that family feeling is to a certain degree incorporated with the estate. The family represents the estate, the estate the family,—whose name, together with its origin, its glory, its power, and its virtues, is thus perpetuated in an imperishable memorial of the past and a sure pledge of the future.

When the equal partition of property is established by law, the intimate connection is destroyed between family feeling and the preservation of the paternal estate; the property ceases to represent the family; for, as it must inevitably be divided after one or two generations, it has evidently a constant tendency to diminish, and must in the end be completely dispersed. The sons of the great landed proprietor, if they are few in number, or if fortune befriends them, may indeed entertain the hope of being as wealthy as their father, but not of possessing the same property that he did; their riches must be composed of other elements than his. Now, as soon as you divest the land-owner of that interest in the preservation of his estate which he derives from association, from tradition, and from family pride, you may be certain that, sooner or later, he will dispose of it; for there is a strong pecuniary interest in favor of selling, as floating capital produces higher interest than real property, and is more readily available to gratify the passions of the moment.

In America, there are but few wealthy persons; nearly all Americans have to take a profession. Now, every profession requires an apprenticeship. The Americans can devote to general education only the early years of life. At fifteen, they enter upon their calling, and thus their education generally ends at the age when ours begins. Whatever is done afterwards is with a view to some special and lucrative object; a science is taken up as a matter of business, and the only branch of it which is attended to is such as admits of an immediate practical application.

In America, most of the rich men were formerly poor; most of those who now enjoy leisure were absorbed in business during their youth; the consequence of which is, that, when they might have had a taste for study, they had no time for it, and when the time is at their disposal, they have no longer the inclination.

There is no class, then, in America, in which the taste for intellectual pleasures is transmitted with hereditary fortune and leisure, and by which the labors of the intellect are held in honor. Accordingly, there is an equal want of the desire and the power of application to these objects.

A middling standard is fixed in America for human knowledge. All approach as near to it as they can; some as they rise, others as they descend. Of course, a multitude of persons are to be found who entertain the same number of ideas on religion, history, science, political economy, legislation, and government. The gifts of intellect proceed directly from God, and man cannot prevent their unequal distribution. But it is at least a consequence of what we have just said, that although the capacities of men are different, as the Creator intended they should be, Americans find the means of putting them to use are equal.

In America, the aristocratic element has always been feeble from its birth; and if at the present day it is not actually destroyed, it is at any rate so completely disabled, that we can scarcely assign to it any degree of influence on the course of affairs.

The democratic principle, on the contrary, has gained so much strength by time, by events, and by legislation, as to have become not only predominant, but all-powerful. There is no family or corporate authority, and it is rare to find even the influence of individual character enjoy any durability.

America, then, exhibits in her social state an extraordinary phenomenon. Men are there seen on a greater equality in point of fortune
and intellect, or, in other words, more equal in their strength, than in
any other country of the world, or in any age of which history has preserved the remembrance.

———————————

--- ★ ---

The Principle of the Sovereignty of the People in America

W henever the political laws of the United States are to be discussed, it is with the doctrine of the sovereignty of the people that we must begin.

The principle of the sovereignty of the people, which is always to be found, more or less, at the bottom of almost all human institutions, generally remains there concealed from view. It is obeyed without being recognized, or if for a moment it be brought to light, it is hastily cast back into the gloom of the sanctuary.

"The will of the nation" is one of those phrases which have been most largely abused by the wily and the despotic of every age. Some have seen the expression of it in the purchased suffrages of a few of the satellites of power; others, in the votes of a timid or an interested minority; and some have even discovered it in the silence of a people, on the supposition that the fact of submission established the right to command.

In America, the principle of the sovereignty of the people is not either barren or concealed, as it is with some other nations; it is recognized by the customs and proclaimed by the laws; it spreads freely, and arrives without impediment at its most remote consequences. If there be a country in the world where the doctrine of the sovereignty of the people can be fairly appreciated, where it can be studied in its application to the affairs of society, and where its dangers and its advantages may be judged, that country is assuredly America.

At the present day the principle of the sovereignty of the people has acquired, in the United States, all the practical development which the imagination can conceive. It is unencumbered by those fictions which are thrown over it in other countries, and it appears in every possible form, according to the exigency of the occasion. Sometimes the laws are made by the people in a body, as at Athens; and sometimes its representatives, chosen by universal suffrage, transact business in its name, and under its immediate supervision.

In some countries, a power exists which, though it is in a degree foreign to the social body, directs it, and forces it to pursue a certain track. In others, the ruling force is divided, being partly within and partly without the ranks of the people. But nothing of the kind is to be seen in the United States; there society governs itself for itself. All power centers in its bosom; and scarcely an individual is to be met with who would venture to conceive, or, still less, to express, the idea of seeking it elsewhere. The nation participates in the making of its laws by the choice of its legislators, and in the execution of them by the choice of the agents of the executive government; it may almost be said to govern itself, so feeble and so restricted is the share left to the administration, so little do the authorities forget their popular origin and the power from which they emanate. The people reign in the American political world as the Deity does in the universe. They are the cause and the aim of all things; everything comes from them, and everything is absorbed in them.

CHAPTER V

---★---

Necessity of Examining the Condition of the States Before That of the Union at Large

It is proposed to examine, in the following chapter, what is the form of government established in America on the principle of the sovereignty of the people; what are its means of action, its hindrances, its advantages, and its dangers. The first difficulty which presents itself arises from the complex nature of the Constitution of the United States, which consists of two distinct social structures, connected, and, as it were, encased one within the other; two governments, completely separate and almost independent, the one fulfilling the ordinary duties, and responding to the daily and indefinite calls, of a community, the other circumscribed within certain limits, and only exercising an exceptional authority over the general interests of the country. In short, there are twenty-four small sovereign nations, whose agglomeration constitutes the body of the Union. To examine the Union before we have studied the States, would be to adopt a method filled with obstacles. The form of the Federal Government of the United States was the last to be adopted; and it is in fact nothing more than a summary of those republican principles which were current in the whole community before it existed, and independently of its existence. Moreover, the Federal Government is, as I have just observed, the exception; the government of the States is the rule. The author who should attempt to exhibit the picture as a whole, before he had explained its details, would necessarily fall into obscurity and repetition.

The great political principles which now govern American society undoubtedly took their origin and their growth in the State. We must know the State, then, in order to gain a clue to the rest. The States which now compose the American Union all present the same features, as far as regards the external aspect of their institutions. Their political or administrative life is centered in three focuses of action, which may be compared to the different nervous centers which give motion to the human body. The township is the first in order, then the county, and lastly the State.[1]

The American System of Townships

IT is not unintentionally that I begin this subject with the Township. The village or township is the only association which is so perfectly natural, that, wherever a number of men are collected, it seems to constitute itself.

The town or tithing, then, exists in all nations, whatever their laws and customs may be: it is man who makes monarchies and establishes republics, but the township seems to come directly from the hand of God. But although the existence of the township is coeval with that of man, its freedom is an infrequent and fragile thing. A nation can always establish great political assemblies, because it habitually contains a certain number of individuals fitted by their talents, if not by their habits, for the direction of affairs. The township, on the contrary, is composed of coarser materials, which are less easily fashioned by the legislator. The difficulty of establishing its independence rather augments than diminishes with the increasing intelligence of the people. A highly civilized community can hardly tolerate a local independence, is disgusted at its numerous blunders, and is apt to despair of success before the experiment is completed. Again, the immunities of townships, which have been obtained with so much difficulty, are least of all protected against the encroachments of the supreme power. They are unable to struggle, single-handed, against a strong and enterprising government, and they cannot defend themselves with success unless they are identified with the customs of the nation and supported by public opinion. Thus, until the independence of townships is amalgamated with the manners of a people, it is easily destroyed; and it is only after a long existence in the

---

1. Here, we will limit our attention to Tocqueville's discussion of the township. -Editor

laws that it can be thus amalgamated. Municipal freedom is not the fruit of human efforts; it is rarely created by others; but is, as it were, secretly self-produced in the midst of a semi-barbarous state of society. The constant action of the laws and the national habits, peculiar circumstances, and, above all, time, may consolidate it; but there is certainly no nation on the continent of Europe which has experienced its advantages. Yet municipal institutions constitute the strength of free nations. Town-meetings are to liberty what primary schools are to science; they bring it within the people's reach, they teach men how to use and how to enjoy it. A nation may establish a free government, but without municipal institutions, it cannot have the spirit of liberty. Transient passions, the interests of an hour, or the chance of circumstances, may create the external forms of independence; but the despotic tendency which has been driven into the interior of the social system, will, sooner or later, reappear on the surface.

To make the reader understand the general principles on which the political organization of the counties and townships in the United States rests, I have thought it expedient to choose one of the States of New England as an example, to examine in detail the mechanism of its constitution, and then to cast a general glance over the rest of the country.

The township and the county are not organized in the same manner in every part of the Union; it is easy to perceive, however, that nearly the same principles have guided the formation of both of them throughout the Union. I am inclined to believe that these principles have been carried further, and have produced greater results, in New England than elsewhere. Consequently, they stand out there in higher relief, and offer greater facilities to the observations of a stranger.

The township institutions of New England form a complete and regular whole; they are old; they have the support of the laws, and the still stronger support of the manners of the community, over which they exercise a prodigious influence. For all these reasons, they deserve our special attention.

Limits of the Township
The township of New England holds a middle place between the commune and the canton of France. Its average population is from two to three thousand; so that it is not so large, on the one hand, that the

interests of its inhabitants would be likely to conflict, and not so small, on the other, but that men capable of conducting its affairs may always be found among its citizens.

Powers of the Township in New England

In the township, as well as everywhere else, the people are the source of power; but nowhere do they exercise their power more immediately. In America, the people form a master who must be obeyed to the utmost limits of possibility.

In New England, the majority act by representatives in conducting the general business of the State. It is necessary that it should be so. But in the townships, where the legislative and administrative action of the government is nearer to the governed, the system of representation is not adopted. There is no municipal council; but the body of voters, after having chosen its magistrates, directs them in everything that exceeds the simple and ordinary execution of the laws of the State.

Spirit of the Townships of New England

In America, not only do municipal bodies exist, but they are kept alive and supported, by town spirit. The township of New England possesses two advantages, which strongly excite the interest of mankind,—namely, independence and authority. Its sphere is limited, indeed; but within that sphere, its action is unrestrained. This independence alone gives it a real importance, which its extent and population would not insure.

It is to be remembered, too, that the affections of men generally turn towards power. Patriotism is not durable in a conquered nation. The New-Englander is attached to his township, not so much because he was born in it, but because it is a free and strong community, of which he is a member, and which deserves the care spent in managing it. In Europe, the absence of local public spirit is a frequent subject of regret to those who are in power; every one agrees that there is no surer guaranty of order and tranquility, and yet nothing is more difficult to create. If the municipal bodies were made powerful and independent, it is feared that they would become too strong, and expose the state to anarchy. Yet, without power and independence, a town may contain good subjects, but it can have no active citizens. Another important fact is, that the township of New England is so constituted as to excite the warmest of human affections, without arousing the ambitious passions of the heart of man. The officers of the county are not elected, and their authority is very limited. Even the State is only a second-rate community whose tranquil and obscure administration offers no inducement sufficient to draw men away from the home of their interests into the turmoil of public affairs. The Federal Government confers power and honor on the men who conduct it; but these individuals can never be very numerous. The high station of the Presidency can only be reached at an advanced period of life; and the other Federal functionaries of a high class are generally men who have been favored by good luck, or have been distinguished in some other career. Such cannot be the permanent aim of the ambitious. But the township, at the center of the ordinary relations of life, serves as a field for the desire of public esteem, the want of exciting interest, and the taste for authority and popularity; and the passions which commonly embroil society change their character, when they find a vent so near the domestic hearth and the family circle.

In the American townships, power has been disseminated with admirable skill, for the purpose of interesting the greatest possible number of persons in the common weal. Independently of the voters, who are from time to time called into action, the power is divided among innumerable functionaries and officers, who all, in their several spheres, represent the powerful community in whose name they act. The local administration thus affords an unfailing source of profit and interest to a vast number of individuals.

The American system, which divides the local authority among so many citizens, does not scruple to multiply the functions of the town officers. For in the United States, it is believed, and with truth, that patriotism is a kind of devotion which is strengthened by ritual observance. In this manner, the activity of the township is continually perceptible; it is daily manifested in the fulfillment of a duty, or the exercise of a right; and a constant though gentle motion is thus kept up in society, which animates without disturbing it. The American attaches himself to his little community for the same reason that the mountaineer clings to his hills, because the characteristic features

of his country are there more distinctly marked; it has a more striking physiognomy.

The existence of the townships of New England is, in general, a
happy one. Their government is suited to their tastes, and chosen by
themselves. In the midst of the profound peace and general comfort
which reign in America, the commotions of municipal life are infrequent. The conduct of local business is easy. The political education
of the people has long been complete; say rather that it was complete,
when the people first set foot upon the soil. In New England, no tradition exists of a distinction of ranks; no portion of the community is
tempted to oppress the remainder; and the wrongs which may injure
isolated individuals are forgotten in the general contentment which
prevails. If the government has faults, (and it would no doubt be easy
to point out some,) they do not attract notice, for the government really emanates from those it governs, and whether it acts ill or well,
this fact casts the protecting spell of a parental pride over its demerits. Besides, they have nothing wherewith to compare it. England formerly governed the mass of the colonies; but the people was always
sovereign in the township, where its rule is not only an ancient, but a
primitive state.

The native of New England is attached to his township because it is
independent and free: his co-operation in its affairs insures his attachment to its interest; the well-being it affords him secures his affection;
and its welfare is the aim of his ambition and of his future exertions.
He takes a part in every occurrence in the place; he practices the art of
government in the small sphere within his reach; he accustoms himself to those forms without which liberty can only advance by revolutions; he imbibes their spirit; he acquires a taste for order, comprehends the balance of powers, and collects clear practical notions on
the nature of his duties and the extent of his rights.

The Administration of Government in New England
NOTHING is more striking to a European traveller in the United
States, than the absence of what we term the Government, or the
Administration. Written laws exist in America, and one sees the daily

execution of them; but although everything moves regularly, the mover can nowhere be discovered. The hand which directs the social machine is invisible. Nevertheless, as all persons must have recourse to certain grammatical forms, which are the foundation of human language, in order to express their thoughts; so all communities are obliged to secure their existence by submitting to a certain amount of authority, without which they fall into anarchy. This authority may be distributed in several ways, but it must always exist somewhere.

There are two methods of diminishing the force of authority in a nation. The first is to weaken the supreme power in its very principle, by forbidding or preventing society from acting in its own defense under certain circumstances. To weaken authority in this manner is the European way of establishing freedom.

The second manner of diminishing the influence of authority does not consist in stripping society of some of its rights, nor in paralyzing its efforts, but in distributing the exercise of its powers among various hands, and in multiplying functionaries, to each of whom is given the degree of power necessary for him to perform his duty. There may be nations whom this distribution of social powers might lead to anarchy; but in itself, it is not anarchical. The authority thus divided is, indeed, rendered less irresistible and less perilous, but it is not destroyed.

The Revolution of the United States was the result of a mature and reflecting preference of freedom, and not of a vague or ill-defined craving for independence. It contracted no alliance with the turbulent passions of anarchy; but its course was marked, on the contrary, by a love of order and law.

It was never assumed in the United States, that the citizen of a free country has a right to do whatever he pleases; on the contrary, more social obligations were there imposed upon him than anywhere else. No idea was ever entertained of attacking the principle or contesting the rights of society; but the exercise of its authority was divided, in order that the office might be powerful and the officer insignificant, and that the community should be at once regulated and free. In no country in the world does the law hold so absolute a language as in America; and in no country is the right of applying it vested in so many hands. The administrative power in the United States presents nothing either centralized or hierarchical in its constitution; this accounts for its passing unperceived. The power exists, but its representative is nowhere to be seen.

General Remarks on the Administration in the United States

Townships and town arrangements exist in every State; but in no other part of the Union is a township to be met with precisely similar to those of New England. The farther we go towards the South, the less active does the business of the township or parish become; it has fewer magistrates, duties, and rights; the population exercises a less immediate influence on affairs; town-meetings are less frequent, and the subjects of debate less numerous. The power of the elected magistrate is augmented, and that of the voter diminished, whilst the public spirit of the local communities is less excited and less influential. These differences may be perceived to a certain extent in the State of New York; they are very sensible in Pennsylvania; but they become less striking as we advance to the Northwest. The majority of the emigrants who settle in the Northwestern States are natives of New England, and they carry the administrative habits of their mother country with them into the country which they adopt. A township in Ohio is not unlike a township in Massachusetts.

Political Effects of Decentralized Administration in the United States

---

We have shown that, in the United States, there is no centralized administration, and no hierarchy of public functionaries. Local authority has been carried farther than any European nation could endure without great inconvenience, and it has even produced some disadvantageous consequences in America. But in the United States, the centralization of the government is perfect; and it would be easy to prove that the national power is more concentrated there than it has ever been in the old nations of Europe. Not only is there but one legis-lative body in each State,—not only does there exist but one source of political authority,—but numerous assemblies in districts or counties have not, in general, been multiplied, lest they should be tempted to leave their administrative duties and interfere with the government. In America, the legislature of each State is supreme; nothing can impede its authority,—neither privileges, nor local immunities, nor personal influence, nor even the empire of reason, since it represents that majority which claims to be the sole organ of reason. Its own determination is, therefore, the only limit to its action. In juxtaposi-tion with it, and under its immediate control, is the representative of the executive power, whose duty it is to constrain the refractory to submit by superior force. The only symptom of weakness lies in cer-tain details of the action of the government. The American republics have no standing armies to intimidate a discontented minority; but as no minority has as yet been reduced to declare open war, the neces-sity of an army has not been felt. The State usually employs the offi-cers of the township or the county to deal with the citizens. Thus, for instance, in New England, the town assessor fixes the rate of taxes; the town collector receives them; the town treasurer transmits the amount to the public treasury; and the disputes which may arise are brought before the ordinary courts of justice. This method of collect-ing taxes is slow as well as inconvenient, and it would prove a per-petual hindrance to a government whose pecuniary demands were large. It is desirable that, in whatever materially affects its existence, the government should be served by officers of its own, appointed by itself, removable at its pleasure, and accustomed to rapid methods of proceeding. But it will always be easy for the central government, organized as it is in America, to introduce more energetic and effica-cious modes of action according to its wants.

The want of a centralized government will not, then, as has often been asserted, prove the destruction of the republics of the New World; far from the American governments being not sufficiently cen-tralized, I shall prove hereafter that they are too much so. The legisla-tive bodies daily encroach upon the authority of the government, and their tendency, like that of the French Convention, is to appropriate it entirely to themselves. The social power thus centralized is constantly changing hands, because it is subordinate to the power of the people.

It often forgets the maxims of wisdom and foresight in the conscious-ness of its strength. Hence arises its danger. Its vigor, and not its impo-tence, will probably be the cause of its ultimate destruction.

The system of decentralized administration produces several dif-ferent effects in America. The Americans seem to me to have out-stepped the limits of sound policy, in isolating the administration of the government: for order, even in secondary affairs, is a matter of national importance. As the State has no administrative functionaries of its own, stationed on different points of its territory, to whom it can give a common impulse, the consequence is, that it rarely attempts to issue any general police regulations. The want of these regulations is severely felt, and is frequently observed by Europeans. The appear-ance of disorder which prevails on the surface leads him at first to imagine that society is in a state of anarchy: nor does he perceive his mistake till he has gone deeper into the subject. Certain under-takings are of importance to the whole State; but they cannot be put in execution, because there is no State administration to direct them. Abandoned to the exertions of the towns or counties, under the care of elected and temporary agents, they lead to no result, or at least to no durable benefit.

Centralization easily succeeds, indeed, in subjecting the external actions of men to a certain uniformity, which we come at last to love for its own sake, independently of the objects to which it is applied, like those devotees who worship the statue, and forget the deity it rep-resents. Centralization imparts without difficulty an admirable regu-larity to the routine of business; provides skillfully for the details of the social police; represses small disorders and petty misdemeanors; maintains society in a *statu quo* alike secure from improvement and decline; and perpetuates a drowsy regularity in the conduct of affairs, which the heads of the administration are wont to call good order and public tranquility; in short, it excels in prevention, but not in action. Its force deserts it, when society is to be profoundly moved, or accel-erated in its course; and if once the co-operation of private citizens is necessary to the furtherance of its measures, the secret of its impo-tence is disclosed. Even whilst the centralized power, in its despair, invokes the assistance of the citizens, it says to them: "You shall act just as I please, as much as I please, and in the direction which I please. You are to take charge of the details, without aspiring to guide the system; you are to work in darkness; and afterwards you may judge my work by its results." These are not the conditions on which the alliance of the human will is to be obtained; it must be free in its gait, and responsible for its acts, or (such is the constitution of man) the citizen had rather remain a passive spectator, than a dependent actor, in schemes with which he is unacquainted.

Granting, for an instant, that the villages and counties of the United States would be more usefully governed by a central authority, which they had never seen, than by functionaries taken from among them,—admitting, for the sake of argument, that there would be more security in America, and the resources of society would be better employed there, if the whole administration centered in a single arm,—still the *political* advantages which the Americans derive from their decentralized system would induce me to prefer it to the contrary plan. It profits me but little, after all, that a vigilant authority always protects the tranquility of my pleasures, and constantly averts all dangers from my path, without my care or concern, if this same authority is the absolute master of my liberty and my life, and if it so monopolizes movement and life, that when it languishes everything languishes around it, that when it sleeps everything must sleep, and that when it dies the state itself must perish.

There are countries in Europe, where the natives consider themselves as a kind of settlers, indifferent to the fate of the spot which they inhabit. The greatest changes are effected there without their concurrence, and (unless chance may have apprised them of the event) without their knowledge; nay, more, the condition of his village, the police of his street, the repairs of the church or the parsonage, do not concern him; for he looks upon all these things as unconnected with himself, and as the property of a powerful stranger whom he calls the government. He has only a life-interest in these possessions, without the spirit of ownership or any ideas of improvement. This want of interest in his own affairs goes so far, that if his own safety or that of his children is at last endangered, instead of trying to avert the peril, he will fold his arms, and wait till the whole nation comes to his aid. This man, who has so completely sacrificed his own free will, does not, more than any other person, love obedience; he cowers, it is true, before the pettiest officer; but he braves the law with the spirit of a conquered foe, as soon as its superior force is withdrawn: he perpetually oscillates between servitude and license.

When a nation has arrived at this state, it must either change its customs and its laws, or perish; for the source of public virtues is dried up; and though it may contain subjects, it has no citizens. Such communities are a natural prey to foreign conquests; and if they do not wholly disappear from the scene, it is only because they are surrounded by other nations similar or inferior to themselves; it is because they still have an indefinable instinct of patriotism; and an involuntary pride in the name of their country, or a vague reminiscence of its bygone fame, suffices to give them an impulse of self-preservation.

Nor can the prodigious exertions made by certain nations to defend a country in which they had lived, so to speak, as strangers, be adduced in favor of such a system; for it will be found that, in these cases, their main incitement was religion. The permanence, the glory, or the prosperity of the nation were become parts of their faith; and in defending their country, they defended also that Holy City of which they were all citizens. The Turkish tribes have never taken an active share in the conduct of their affairs; but they accomplished stupendous enterprises, as long as the victories of the Sultan were triumphs of the Mohammedan faith. In the present age, they are in rapid decay, because their religion is departing, and despotism only remains. Montesquieu, who attributed to absolute power an authority peculiar to itself, did it, as I conceive, an undeserved honor; for despotism, taken by itself, can maintain nothing durable. On close inspection, we shall find that religion, and not fear, has ever been the cause of the long-lived prosperity of an absolute government. Do what you may, there is no true power among men except in the free union of their will; and patriotism or religion are the only two motives in the world which can long urge all the people towards the same end.

Laws cannot rekindle an extinguished faith; but men may be interested by the laws in the fate of their country. It depends upon the laws to awaken and direct the vague impulse of patriotism, which never abandons the human heart; and if it be connected with the thoughts, the passions, and the daily habits of life, it may be consolidated into a durable and rational sentiment. Let it not be said that it is too late to make the experiment; for nations do not grow old as men do, and every fresh generation is a new people ready for the care of the legislator.

It is not the *administrative,* but the *political* effects of decentralization, that I most admire in America. In the United States, the interests of the country are everywhere kept in view; they are an object of solicitude to the people of the whole Union, and every citizen is as warmly attached to them as if they were his own. He takes pride in the glory of his nation; he boasts of its success, to which he conceives himself to have contributed; and he rejoices in the general prosperity by which he profits. The feeling he entertains toward the state is analogous to that which unites him to his family, and it is by a kind of selfishness that he interests himself in the welfare of his country.

To the European, a public officer represents a superior force; to an American, he represents a right. In America, then, it may be said that no one renders obedience to man, but to justice and to law. If the opinion which the citizen entertains of himself is exaggerated, it is at least salutary; he unhesitatingly confides in his own powers, which appear to him to be all-sufficient. When a private individual meditates an undertaking, however directly connected it may be with the welfare of society, he never thinks of soliciting the co-operation of the government; but he publishes his plan, offers to execute it, courts the assistance of other individuals, and struggles manfully against all obstacles. Undoubtedly he is often less successful than the state might have been in his position; but in the end, the sum of these private undertakings far exceeds all that the government could have done.

It would be easy to adduce several facts in proof of what I advance, but I had rather give only one, with which I am best acquainted. In America, the means which the authorities have at their disposal for the discovery of crimes and the arrest of criminals are few. A state police does not exist, and passports are unknown. The criminal police of the United States cannot be compared to that of France; the magistrates and public agents are not numerous; they do not always initiate the measures for arresting the guilty; and the examinations of prisoners are rapid and oral. Yet I believe that in no country does crime more rarely elude punishment. The reason is, that every one conceives himself to be interested in furnishing evidence of the crime, and in seizing the delinquent. During my stay in the United States, I witnessed the spontaneous formation of committees in a county for the pursuit and prosecution of a man who had committed a great crime. In Europe, a criminal is an unhappy man who is struggling for his life against the agents of power, whilst the people are merely a spectator of the conflict: in America, he is looked upon as an enemy of the human race, and the whole of mankind is against him.

I believe that provincial institutions are useful to all nations, but nowhere do they appear to me to be more necessary than amongst a democratic people. In an aristocracy, order can always be maintained in the midst of liberty; and as the rulers have a great deal to lose, order is to them a matter of great interest. In like manner, an aristocracy protects the people from the excesses of despotism, because it always possesses an organized power ready to resist a despot. But a democracy without provincial institutions has no security against these evils. How can a populace, unaccustomed to freedom in small concerns, learn to use it temperately in great affairs? What resistance can be offered to tyranny in a country where each individual is weak, and where the citizens are not united by any common interest? Those who dread the license of the mob, and those who fear absolute power, ought alike to desire the gradual development of provincial liberties.

I am also convinced, that democratic nations are most likely to fall beneath the yoke of a centralized administration, for several reasons, amongst which is the following.

The constant tendency of these nations is to concentrate all the strength of the government in the hands of the only power which directly represents the people; because, beyond the people, nothing is to be perceived but a mass of equal individuals. But when the same power already has all the attributes of government, it can scarcely refrain from penetrating into the details of the administration, and an opportunity of doing so is sure to present itself in the long run, as was the case in France. In the French Revolution, there were two impulses in opposite directions, which must never be confounded;

the one was favorable to liberty, the other to despotism. Under the ancient monarchy, the king was the sole author of the laws; and below the power of the sovereign, certain vestiges of provincial institutions, half destroyed, were still distinguishable. These provincial institutions were incoherent, ill arranged, and frequently absurd; in the hands of the aristocracy, they had sometimes been converted into instruments of oppression. The Revolution declared itself the enemy at once of royalty and of provincial institutions; it confounded in indiscriminate hatred all that had preceded it,—despotic power and the checks to its abuses; and its tendency was at once to republicanize and to centralize. This double character of the French Revolution is a fact which has been adroitly handled by the friends of absolute power. Can they be accused of laboring in the cause of despotism, when they are defending that centralized administration which was one of the great innovations of the Revolution? In this manner, popularity may be united with hostility to the rights of the people, and the secret slave of tyranny may be the professed lover of freedom.

CHAPTER VI

———————— ★ ————————

Judicial Power in the United States, and Its Influence on Political Society

I have thought it right to devote a separate chapter to the judicial authorities of the United States, lest their great political importance should be lessened in the reader's eyes by a merely incidental mention of them. Confederations have existed in other countries beside America; I have seen republics elsewhere than upon the shores of the New World alone: the representative system of government has been adopted in several states of Europe; but I am not aware that any nation of the globe has hitherto organized a judicial power in the same manner as the Americans. The judicial organization of the United States is the institution which a stranger has the greatest difficulty in understanding. He hears the authority of a judge invoked in the political occurrences of every day, and he naturally concludes that, in the United States, the judges are important political functionaries: nevertheless, when he examines the nature of the tribunals, they offer at the first glance nothing which is contrary to the usual habits and privileges of those bodies; and the magistrates seem to him to interfere in public affairs only by chance, but by a chance which recurs every day.

When the Parliament of Paris remonstrated, or refused to register an edict, or when it summoned a functionary accused of malversation to its bar, its political influence as a judicial body was clearly visible; but nothing of the kind is to be seen in the United States. The Americans have retained all the ordinary characteristics of judicial authority, and have carefully restricted its action to the ordinary circle of its functions.

The first characteristic of judicial power in all nations is the duty of arbitration. But rights must be contested in order to warrant the interference of a tribunal; and an action must be brought before the decision of a judge can be had. As long, therefore, as a law is uncontested, the judicial authority is not called upon to discuss it, and it may exist without being perceived. When a judge in a given case attacks a law relating to that case, he extends the circle of his customary duties, without, however, stepping beyond it, since he is in some measure obliged to decide upon the law in order to decide the case. But if he pronounces upon a law without proceeding from a case, he clearly steps beyond his sphere, and invades that of the legislative authority.

The second characteristic of judicial power is, that it pronounces on special cases, and not upon general principles. If a judge, in deciding a particular point, destroys a general principle by passing a judgment which tends to reject all the inferences from that principle, and consequently to annul it, he remains within the ordinary limits of his functions. But if he directly attacks a general principle without having a particular case in view, he leaves the circle in which all nations have agreed to confine his authority; he assumes a more important, and perhaps a more useful influence, than that of the magistrate; but he ceases to represent the judicial power.

The third characteristic of the judicial power is, that it can only act when it is called upon, or when, in legal phrase, it has taken cognizance of an affair. This characteristic is less general than the other two; but, notwithstanding the exceptions, I think it may be regarded as essential. The judicial power is, by its nature, devoid of action; it must be put in motion in order to produce a result. When it is called upon to repress a crime, it punishes the criminal; when a wrong is to be redressed, it is ready to redress it; when an act requires interpretation, it is prepared to interpret it; but it does not pursue criminals, hunt out wrongs, or examine evidence of its own accord. A judicial functionary who should take the initiative, and usurp the censureship of the laws, would in some measure do violence to the passive nature of his authority.

Whenever a law which the judge holds to be unconstitutional is invoked in a tribunal of the United States, he may refuse to admit it as a rule; this power is the only one which is peculiar to the American magistrate, but it gives rise to immense political influence. In truth, few laws can escape the searching analysis of the judicial power for any length of time, for there are few which are not prejudicial to some private interest or other, and none which may not be brought before a court of justice by the choice of parties, or by the necessity of the case. But as soon as a judge has refused to apply any given law in a case, that law immediately loses a portion of its moral force. Those to whom it is prejudicial learn that means exist of overcoming its authority; and similar suits are multiplied, until it becomes powerless. The alternative, then, is, that the people must alter the constitution, or the legislature must repeal the law. The political power which the Americans have entrusted to their courts of justice is therefore immense; but the evils of this power are considerably diminished by the impossibility of attacking the laws except through the courts of justice. If the judge had been empowered to contest the law on the ground of theoretical generalities,—if he were able to take the initiative, and to censure the legislator,—he would play a prominent political part; and as the champion or the antagonist of a party, he would have brought the hostile passions of the nation into the conflict. But when a judge contests a law in an obscure debate on some particular case, the importance of his attack is concealed from public notice; his decision bears upon the interest of an individual, and the law is slighted only incidentally. Moreover, although it is censured, it is not abolished; its moral force may be diminished, but its authority is not taken away; and its final destruction can be accomplished only by the reiterated attacks of judicial functionaries. It will be seen, also, that by leaving it to private interest to censure the law, and by intimately uniting the trial of the law with the trial of an individual, legislation is protected from wanton assaults, and from the daily aggressions of party spirit. The errors of the legislator are exposed only to meet a real want; and it is always a positive and appreciable fact which must serve as the basis of a prosecution.

I am inclined to believe this practice of the American courts to be at once most favorable to liberty and to public order. If the judge could only attack the legislator openly and directly, he would sometimes be afraid to oppose him; and at other times, party spirit might encourage him to brave it at every turn. The laws would consequently be attacked when the power from which they emanated was weak, and obeyed when it was strong;—that is to say, when it would be useful to respect them, they would often be contested; and when it would be easy to convert them into an instrument of oppression, they would be respected. But the American judge is brought into the political arena independently of his own will. He only judges the law because he is obliged to judge a case. The political question which he is called upon to resolve is connected with the interests of the parties, and he cannot refuse to decide it without a denial of justice. He performs his functions as a citizen, by fulfilling the precise duties which belong to his profession as a magistrate. It is true that, upon this system, the judicial censorship of the courts of justice over the legislature cannot extend to all laws indiscriminately, inasmuch as some of them can never give rise to that precise species of contest which is termed a lawsuit; and even when such a contest is possible, it may happen that no one cares to bring it before a court of justice. The Americans have often felt this inconvenience; but they have left the remedy incomplete, lest they should give it an efficacy which might in some cases prove dangerous. Within these limits, the power vested in the American courts of justice, of pronouncing a statute to be unconstitutional, forms one of the most powerful barriers which has ever been devised against the tyranny of political assemblies.

Other Powers Granted to American Judges

It is hardly necessary to say that, in a free country like America, all the citizens have the right of indicting public functionaries before the ordinary tribunals, and that all the judges have the power of convicting public officers. The right granted to the courts of justice of punishing the agents of the executive government, when they violate the laws, is so natural a one, that it cannot be looked upon as an extraordinary privilege. Nor do the springs of government appear to me to be weakened in the United States, by rendering all public officers responsible to the tribunals. The Americans seem, on the contrary, to have increased by this means that respect which is due to the authorities, and at the same time, to have made these authorities more careful not to offend. I was struck by the small number of political trials which occur in the United States; but I had no difficulty in accounting for this circumstance. A prosecution, of whatever nature it may be, is always a difficult and expensive undertaking. It is easy to attack a public man in the journals, but the motives for bringing him before the tribunals must be serious. A solid ground of complaint must exist, before any one thinks of prosecuting a public officer, and these officers are careful not to furnish such grounds of complaint, when they are afraid of being prosecuted.

This does not depend upon the republican form of American institutions, for the same thing happens in England. These two nations do not regard the impeachment of the principal officers of state as the guaranty of their independence. But they hold that it is rather by minor prosecutions, which the humblest citizen can institute at any time, that liberty is protected, and not by those great judicial procedures, which are rarely employed until it is too late.

In the Middle Ages, when it was very difficult to reach offenders, the judges inflicted frightful punishments on the few who were arrested; but this did not diminish the number of crimes. It has since been discovered that, when justice is more certain and more mild, it is more efficacious. The English and the Americans hold that tyranny and oppression are to be treated like any other crime, by lessening the penalty and facilitating conviction.

In the year VIII. of the French Republic, a constitution was drawn up in which the following clause was introduced: "Art. 75. All the agents of the government below the rank of ministers can be prosecuted for offences relating to their several functions only by virtue of a decree of the Council of State; in which case, the prosecution takes place before the ordinary tribunals." This clause survived the "Constitution of the year VIII.," and is still maintained, in spite of the just complaints of the nation. I have always found a difficulty in explaining its meaning to Englishmen or Americans, and have hardly understood it myself. They at once perceived that, the Council of State in France being a great tribunal established in the center of the kingdom, it was a sort of tyranny to send all complainants before it as a preliminary step. But when I told them that the Council of State was not a judicial body, in the common sense of the term, but an administrative council composed of men dependent on the Crown,—so that the king, after having ordered one of his servants, called a Prefect, to commit an injustice, has the power of commanding another of his servants, called a Councilor of State, to prevent the former from being punished,—when I showed them, that the citizen who has been injured by an order of the sovereign is obliged to ask the sovereign's permission to obtain redress, they refused to credit so flagrant an abuse, and were tempted to accuse me of falsehood or ignorance. It frequently happened, before the Revolution, that a Parliament issued a warrant against a public officer who had committed an offence. Sometimes the royal authority intervened, and quashed the proceedings. Despotism then showed itself openly, and men obeyed it only by submitting to superior force. It is painful to perceive how much lower we are sunk than our forefathers; since we allow things to pass, under the color of justice and the sanction of law, which violence alone imposed upon them.

CHAPTER VII

Political Jurisdiction in the United States

In the United States, as well as in Europe, one branch of the legislature is authorized to impeach, and the other to judge: the House of Representatives arraigns the offender, and the Senate punishes him. But the Senate can only try such persons as are brought before it by the House of Representatives, and those persons must belong to the class of public functionaries. Thus the jurisdiction of the Senate is less extensive than that of the Peers of France, whilst the right of impeachment by the Representatives is more general than that of the Deputies. But the great difference which exists between Europe and America is, that, in Europe, the political tribunals can apply all the enactments of the penal code, whilst in America, when they have deprived the offender of his official rank, and have declared him incapable of filling any political office for the future, their jurisdiction terminates, and that of the ordinary tribunals begins.

The main object of the political jurisdiction which obtains in the United States is, therefore, to take away the power from him who would make a bad use of it, and prevent him from ever acquiring it again. This is evidently an administrative measure, sanctioned by the formalities of a judicial decision. In this matter, the Americans have created a mixed system; they have surrounded the act which removes a public functionary with all the securities of a political trial, and they have deprived political condemnations of their severest penalties.

Every link of the system may easily be traced from this point; we at once perceive why the American constitutions subject all the civil functionaries to the jurisdiction of the Senate, whilst the military, whose crimes are nevertheless more formidable, are exempted from that tribunal. In the civil service, none of the American functionaries can be said to be removable; the places which some of them occupy are inalienable, and the others are chosen for a term which cannot be shortened. It is, therefore, necessary to try them all in order to deprive them of their authority. But military officers are dependent on the chief magistrate of the State, who is himself a civil functionary; and the decision which condemns him is a blow upon them all.

CHAPTER VIII

———— ★ ————

The Federal Constitution

I have hitherto considered each State as a separate whole, and have explained the different springs which the people there put in motion, and the different means of action which it employs. But all the States which I have considered as independent are yet forced to submit, in certain cases, to the supreme authority of the Union. The time is now come to examine the portion of sovereignty which has been granted to the Union, and to cast a rapid glance over the Federal Constitution.

———————

Summary of the Federal Constitution

The first question which awaited the Americans was, so to divide the sovereignty that each of the different States which composed the Union should continue to govern itself in all that concerned its internal prosperity, whilst the entire nation, represented by the Union, should continue to form a compact body, and to provide for all general exigencies. The problem was a complex and difficult one. It was as impossible to determine beforehand, with any degree of accuracy, the share of authority which each of the two governments was to enjoy, as to foresee all the incidents in the life of a nation.

The obligations and the claims of the Federal government were simple and easily definable, because the Union had been formed with the express purpose of meeting certain great general wants; but the claims and obligations of the individual States, on the other hand, were complicated and various, because their government had penetrated into all the details of social life. The attributes of the Federal government were therefore carefully defined, and all that was not included among them was declared to remain to the governments of the several States. Thus the government of the States remained the rule, and that of the Confederation was the exception.

But as it was foreseen that, in practice, questions might arise as to the exact limits of this exceptional authority, and it would be dangerous to submit these questions to the decision of the ordinary courts of justice, established in the different States by the States themselves, a high Federal court was created, one of whose duties was to maintain the balance of power between the two rival governments, as it had been established by the Constitution.

Powers of the Federal Government

The people in themselves are only individuals; and the special reason why they need to be united under one government is, that they may appear to advantage before foreigners. The exclusive right of making peace and war, of concluding treaties of commerce, raising armies, and equipping fleets, was therefore granted to the Union. The necessity of a national government was less imperiously felt in the conduct of the internal affairs of society; but there are certain general interests which can only be attended to with advantage by a general authority. The Union was invested with the power of controlling the monetary system, carrying the mails, and opening the great roads which were to unite the different parts of the country. The independence of the government of each State in its sphere was recognized; yet the Federal government was authorized to interfere in the internal affairs of the States in a few predetermined cases, in which an indiscreet use of their independence might compromise the safety of the whole Union. Thus, whilst the power of modifying and changing their legislation at pleasure was preserved to each of the confederate republics, they are forbidden to enact *ex-post-facto* laws, or to grant any titles of nobility. Lastly, as it was necessary that the Federal government should be able to fulfill its engagements, it has an unlimited power of levying taxes.

In examining the division of powers, as established by the Federal Constitution, remarking on the one hand the portion of sovereignty which has been reserved to the several States, and on the other, the share of power which has been given to the Union, it is evident that the Federal legislators entertained very clear and accurate notions respecting the centralization of government. The United States form not only a republic, but a confederation; yet the national authority is more centralized there than it was in several of the absolute monarchies of Europe. I will cite only two examples.

Thirteen supreme courts of justice existed in France, which, generally speaking, had the right of interpreting the law without appeal; and those provinces which were styled *pays d'État* were authorized to refuse their assent to an impost which had been levied by the sovereign, who represented the nation.

In the Union, there is but one tribunal to interpret, as there is one legislature to make, the laws; and an impost voted by the representatives of the nation is binding upon all the citizens. In these two essential points, therefore, the Union is more centralized than the French monarchy, although the Union is only an assemblage of confederate republics.

In What Respects the Federal Constitution Is Superior to That of the States

The Federal Constitution, as well as the State constitutions, divided the legislative body into two branches. But in the States, these two branches were composed of the same elements, and elected in the same manner. The consequence was, that the passions and inclinations of the populace were as rapidly and easily represented in one chamber as in the other, and that laws were made with violence and precipitation. By the Federal Constitution, the two houses originate in like manner in the choice of the people; but the conditions of eligibility and the mode of election were changed, in order that, if, as is the case in certain nations, one branch of the legislature should not represent the same interests as the other, it might at least represent more wisdom. A mature age was necessary to become a Senator, and the Senate was chosen by an elected assembly of a limited number of members.

To concentrate the whole social force in the hands of the legislative body is the natural tendency of democracies; for as this is the power which emanates the most directly from the people, it has the greater share of the people's overwhelming power, and it is naturally led to monopolize every species of influence. This concentration of power is at once very prejudicial to a well-conducted administration, and favorable to the despotism of the majority. The legislators of the States frequently yielded to these democratic propensities, which were invariably and courageously resisted by the founders of the Union.

Advantages of the Federal System in General, and Its Special Utility in America

In small states, the watchfulness of society penetrates into every part, and the spirit of improvement enters into the smallest details; the ambition of the people being necessarily checked by its weakness, all the efforts and resources of the citizens are turned to the internal well-being of the community, and are not likely to evaporate in the fleeting breath of glory. The powers of every individual being generally limited, his desires are proportionally small. Mediocrity of fortune makes the various conditions of life nearly equal, and the manners of the inhabitants are orderly and simple. Thus, all things considered, and allowance being made for the various degrees of morality and enlightenment, we shall generally find in small nations more persons in easy circumstances, more contentment and tranquility, than in large ones.

When tyranny is established in the bosom of a small state, it is more galling than elsewhere, because, acting in a narrower circle, everything in that circle is affected by it. It supplies the place of those great designs which it cannot entertain, by a violent or exasperating interference in a multitude of minute details; and it leaves the political world, to which it properly belongs, to meddle with the arrangements of private life. Tastes as well as actions are to be regulated; and the families of the citizens, as well as the state, are to be governed. This invasion of rights occurs, however, but seldom, freedom being in truth the natural state of small communities. The temptations which the government offers to ambition are too weak, and the resources of private individuals are too slender, for the sovereign power easily to fall into the grasp of a single man; and should such an event occur, the subjects of the state can easily unite and overthrow the tyrant and the tyranny at once by a common effort.

Small nations have therefore ever been the cradle of political liberty; and the fact that many of them have lost their liberty by becoming larger, shows that their freedom was more a consequence of their small size than of the character of the people.

The history of the world affords no instance of a great nation retaining the form of republican government for a long series of years; and this has led to the conclusion that such a thing is impracticable. For my own part, I think it imprudent to attempt to limit what is possible, and to judge the future, for men who are every day deceived in relation to the actual and the present, and often taken by surprise in the circumstances with which they are most familiar. But it may be said with confidence, that a great republic will always be exposed to more perils than a small one.

It may, therefore, be asserted as a general proposition, that nothing is more opposed to the well-being and the freedom of men than vast empires. Nevertheless, it is important to acknowledge the peculiar advantages of great states. For the very reason that the desire of power is more intense in these communities than amongst ordinary men, the love of glory is also more developed in the hearts of certain citizens, who regard the applause of a great people as a reward worthy of their exertions, and an elevating encouragement to man. If we would learn why great nations contribute more powerfully to the increase of knowledge and the advance of civilization than small states, we shall discover an adequate cause in the more rapid and energetic circulation of ideas, and in those great cities which are the intellectual centers where all the rays of human genius are reflected and combined. To this it may be added, that most important discoveries demand a use of national power which the government of a small state is unable to make: in great nations, the government has more enlarged ideas, and is more completely disengaged from the routine of precedent and the selfishness of local feeling; its designs are conceived with more talent, and executed with more boldness.

In time of peace, the well-being of small nations is undoubtedly more general and complete; but they are apt to suffer more acutely from the calamities of war than those great empires whose distant frontiers may long avert the presence of the danger from the mass of the people, who are therefore more frequently afflicted than ruined by the contest.

But in this matter, as in many others, the decisive argument is the necessity of the case. If none but small nations existed, I do not doubt that mankind would be more happy and more free; but the existence of great nations is unavoidable.

Political strength thus becomes a condition of national prosperity. It profits a state but little to be affluent and free, if it is perpetually exposed to be pillaged or subjugated; its manufactures and commerce are of small advantage, if another nation has the empire of the seas and gives the law in all the markets of the globe. Small nations are often miserable, not because they are small, but because they are weak; and great empires prosper, less because they are great, than because they are strong. Physical strength is therefore one of the first conditions of the happiness, and even of the existence, of nations. Hence it occurs, that, unless very peculiar circumstances intervene, small nations are always united to large empires in the end, either by force or by their own consent. I know not a more deplorable condition than that of a people unable to defend itself or to provide for its own wants.

The Federal system was created with the intention of combining the different advantages which result from the magnitude and the littleness of nations; and a glance at the United States of America discovers the advantages which they have derived from its adoption.

In great centralized nations, the legislator is obliged to give a character of uniformity to the laws, which does not always suit the diversity of customs and of districts; as he takes no cognizance of special cases, he can only proceed upon general principles; and the population are obliged to conform to the exigencies of the legislation, since the legislation cannot adapt itself to the exigencies and the customs of the population; which is a great cause of trouble and misery. This disadvantage does not exist in confederations; Congress regulates the principal measures of the national government; and all the details of the administration are reserved to the provincial legislatures. One can hardly imagine how much this division of sovereignty contributes to the well-being of each of the States which compose the Union. In these small communities, which are never agitated by the desire of aggrandizement or the care of self-defense, all public authority and private energy are turned towards internal improvements. The central government of each State, which is in immediate juxtaposition to the citizens, is daily apprised of the wants which arise in society; and new projects are proposed every year, which are discussed at town-meetings or by the legislature, and which are transmitted by the press to stimulate the zeal and to excite the interest of the citizens. This spirit of improvement is constantly alive in the American republics, without compromising their tranquility; the ambition of power yields to the less refined and less dangerous desire for well-being. It is generally believed in America, that the existence and the permanence of the republican form of government in the New World depend upon the existence and the duration of the Federal system; and it is not unusual to attribute a large share of the misfortunes which have befallen the new States of South America to the injudicious erection of great republics, instead of a divided and confederate sovereignty.

It is incontestably true, that the tastes and the habits of republican government in the United States were first created in the townships and the provincial assemblies. In a small State, like that of Connecticut, for instance, where cutting a canal or laying down a road is a great political question, where the State has no army to pay and no wars to carry on, and where much wealth or much honor cannot be given to the rulers, no form of government can be more natural or more appropriate than a republic. But it is this same republican spirit, it is these manners and customs of a free people, which have been created and nurtured in the different States, which must be afterwards applied to the country at large. The public spirit of the Union is, so to speak, nothing more than an aggregate or summary of the patriotic zeal of the separate provinces. Every citizen of the United States transports, so to speak, his attachment to his little republic into the common store of American patriotism. In defending the Union, he defends the increasing prosperity of his own State or county, the right of conducting its affairs, and the hope of causing measures of improvement to be adopted in it which may be favorable to his own interests; and these are motives which are wont to stir men more than the general interests of the country and the glory of the nation.

On the other hand, if the temper and the manners of the inhabitants especially fitted them to promote the welfare of a great republic, the federal system renders their task less difficult. The confederation of all the American States presents none of the ordinary inconveniences resulting from great agglomerations of men. The Union is a great republic in extent, but the paucity of objects for which its government acts assimilates it to a small State. Its acts are important, but they are rare. As the sovereignty of the Union is limited and incomplete, its exercise is not dangerous to liberty; for it does not excite those insatiable desires of fame and power which have proved so fatal to great republics. As there is no common center to the country, great capital cities, colossal wealth, abject poverty, and sudden revolutions are alike unknown; and political passion, instead of spreading over the land like a fire on the prairies, spends its strength against the interests and the individual passions of every State.

Nevertheless, tangible objects and ideas circulate throughout the Union as freely as in a country inhabited by one people. Nothing checks the spirit of enterprise. The government invites the aid of all who have talents or knowledge to serve it. Inside of the frontiers of the Union, profound peace prevails, as within the heart of some great empire; abroad, it ranks with the most powerful nations of the earth: two thousand miles of coast are open to the commerce of the world; and as it holds the keys of a New World, its flag is respected in the most remote seas. The Union is happy and free as a small people, and glorious and strong as a great nation.

CHAPTER IX

---★---

How it Can Be Strictly Said that the People Govern in the United States

Thus far, I have examined the institutions of the United States; I have passed their legislation in review, and have described the present forms of political society in that country. But above these institutions, and beyond all these characteristic forms, there is a sovereign power—that of the people—which may destroy or modify them at its pleasure. It remains to be shown in what manner this power, superior to the laws, acts; what are its instincts and its passions, what the secret springs which retard, accelerate, or direct its irresistible course, what the effects of its unbounded authority, and what the destiny which is reserved for it.

In America, the people appoint the legislative and the executive power, and furnish the jurors who punish all infractions of the laws. The institutions are democratic, not only in their principle, but in all their consequences; and the people elect their representatives *directly*, and for the most part *annually*, in order to insure their dependence. The people are, therefore, the real directing power; and although the form of government is representative, it is evident that the opinions, the prejudices, the interests, and even the passions of the people are hindered by no permanent obstacles from exercising a perpetual influence on the daily conduct of affairs. In the United States, the majority governs in the name of the people, as is the case in all countries in which the people are supreme. This majority is principally composed of peaceable citizens, who, either by inclination or by interest, sincerely wish the welfare of their country. But they are surrounded by the incessant agitation of parties, who attempt to gain their co-operation and support.

CHAPTER X

---★---

Parties in the United States

A great distinction must be made between parties. Some countries are so large that the different populations which inhabit them, although united under the same government, have contradictory interests; and they may consequently be in a perpetual state of opposition. In this case, the different fractions of the people may more properly be considered as distinct nations than as mere parties; and if a civil war breaks out, the struggle is carried on by rival states rather than by factions in the same state.

But when the citizens entertain different opinions upon subjects which affect the whole country alike,—such, for instance, as the principles upon which the government is to be conducted,—then distinctions arise which may correctly be styled parties. Parties are a necessary evil in free governments; but they have not at all times the same character and the same propensities.

The political parties which I style great are those which cling to principles rather than to their consequences; to general, and not to special cases; to ideas, and not to men. These parties are usually distinguished by nobler features, more generous passions, more genuine convictions, and a more bold and open conduct, than the others. In them, private interest, which always plays the chief part in political passions, is more studiously veiled under the pretext of the public good; and it may even be sometimes concealed from the eyes of the very persons whom it excites and impels.

Minor parties, on the other hand, are generally deficient in political good faith. As they are not sustained or dignified by lofty purposes, they ostensibly display the selfishness of their character in their actions. They glow with a factitious zeal; their language is vehement; but their conduct is timid and irresolute. The means which they employ are as wretched as the end at which they aim. Hence it happens, that, when a calm state succeeds a violent revolution, great men seem suddenly to disappear, and the powers of the human mind to lie concealed. Society is convulsed by great parties, it is only agitated by minor ones; it is torn by the former, by the latter it is degraded; and if the first sometimes save it by a salutary perturbation, the last invariably disturb it to no good end.

CHAPTER XI

★

Liberty of the Press in the United States

The influence of the liberty of the press does not affect political opinions alone, but extends to all the opinions of men, and modifies customs as well as laws. In another part of this work, I shall attempt to determine the degree of influence which the liberty of the press has exercised upon civil society in the United States, and to point out the direction which it has given to the ideas, as well as the tone which it has imparted to the character and the feelings, of the Anglo-Americans. At present, I purpose only to examine the effects produced by the liberty of the press in the political world.

I confess that I do not entertain that firm and complete attachment to the liberty of the press which is wont to be excited by things that are supremely good in their very nature. I approve of it from a consideration more of the evils it prevents, than of the advantages it insures.

If any one could point out an intermediate and yet a tenable position between the complete independence and the entire servitude of opinion, I should, perhaps, be inclined to adopt it; but the difficulty is, to discover this intermediate position. Intending to correct the licentiousness of the press, and to restore the use of orderly language, you first try the offender by a jury; but if the jury acquits him, the opinion which was that of a single individual becomes the opinion of the whole country. Too much and too little has therefore been done; go farther, then. You bring the delinquent before permanent magistrates; but even here, the cause must be heard before it can be decided; and the very principles which no book would have ventured to avow are blazoned forth in the pleadings, and what was obscurely hinted at in a single composition is thus repeated in a multitude of other publications. The language is only the expression, and (if I may so speak) the body, of the thought, but it is not the thought itself. Tribunals may condemn the body, but the sense, the spirit, of the work is too subtle for their authority. Too much has still been done to recede, too little to attain your end; you must go still farther. Establish a censorship of the press. But the tongue of the public speaker will still make itself heard, and your purpose is not yet accomplished; you have only increased the mischief. Thought is not, like physical strength, dependent upon the number of its agents; nor can authors be counted like the troops which compose an army. On the contrary, the authority of a principle is often increased by the small number of men by whom it is expressed. The words of one strong-minded man, addressed to the passions of a listening assembly, have more power than the vociferations of a thousand orators; and if it be allowed to speak freely in any one public place, the consequence is the same as if free speaking was allowed in every village. The liberty of speech must therefore be destroyed, as well as the liberty of the press. And now you have succeeded, everybody is reduced to silence. But your object was to repress the abuses of liberty, and you are brought to the feet of a despot. You have been led from the extreme of independence to the extreme of servitude, without finding a single tenable position on the way at which you could stop.

There are certain nations which have peculiar reasons for cherishing the liberty of the press, independently of the general motives which I have just pointed out. For in certain countries which profess to be free, every individual agent of the government may violate the laws with impunity, since the constitution does not give to those who are injured a right of complaint before the courts of justice. In this case, the liberty of the press is not merely one of the guaranties, but it is the only guaranty, of their liberty and security which the citizens possess. If the rulers of these nations proposed to abolish the independence of the press, the whole people might answer, Give us the right of prosecuting your offences before the ordinary tribunals, and perhaps we may then waive our right of appeal to the tribunal of public opinion.

In countries where the doctrine of the sovereignty of the people ostensibly prevails, the censorship of the press is not only dangerous, but absurd. When the right of every citizen to a share in the government of society is acknowledged, every one must be presumed to be able to choose between the various opinions of his contemporaries, and to appreciate the different facts from which inferences may be drawn. The sovereignty of the people and the liberty of the press may therefore be regarded as correlative; just as the censorship of the press and universal suffrage are two things which are irreconcilably opposed, and which cannot long be retained among the institutions of the same people. Not a single individual of the [thirty] millions who inhabit the United States has, as yet, dared to propose any restrictions on the liberty of the press.

America is perhaps, at this moment, the country of the whole world which contains the fewest germs of revolution; but the press is not less destructive in its principles there than in France, and it displays the same violence without the same reasons for indignation. In America, as in France, it constitutes a singular power, so strangely composed of mingled good and evil, that liberty could not live without it, and public order can hardly be maintained against it. Its power is certainly much greater in France than in the United States; though nothing is more rare in the latter country than to hear of a prosecution being instituted against it. The reason of this is perfectly simple: the Americans, having once admitted the doctrine of the sovereignty of the people, apply it with perfect sincerity. It was never their intention out of elements which are changing every day to create institutions which should last forever; and there is consequently nothing criminal in an attack upon the existing laws, provided a violent infraction of them is not intended. They are also of opinion that courts of justice are powerless to check the abuses of the press; and that, as the subtlety of human language perpetually eludes judicial analysis, offences of this nature somehow escape the hand which attempts to seize them. They hold that, to act with efficacy upon the press, it would be necessary to find a tribunal, not only devoted to the existing order of things, but capable of surmounting the influence of public opinion; a tribunal which should conduct its proceedings without publicity, which should pronounce its decrees without assigning its motives, and punish the intentions, even more than the language, of a writer. Whoever should be able to create and maintain a tribunal of this kind, would waste his time in prosecuting the liberty of the press; for he would be the absolute master of the whole community, and would be as free to rid himself of the authors as of their writings. In this question, therefore, there is no medium between servitude and license; in order to enjoy the inestimable benefits which the liberty of the press insures, it is necessary to submit to the inevitable evils which it creates. To expect to acquire the former, and to escape the latter, is to cherish one of those illusions which commonly mislead nations in their times of sickness, when, tired with faction and exhausted by effort, they attempt to make hostile opinions and contrary principles coexist upon the same soil.

In the United States, the democracy perpetually brings new men to the conduct of public affairs; and the administration consequently seldom preserves consistency or order in its measures. But the general principles of the government are more stable, and the chief opinions which regulate society are more durable, there than in many other countries. When once the Americans have taken up an idea, whether it be well or ill founded, nothing is more difficult than to eradicate it from their minds. The same tenacity of opinion has been observed in England, where, for the last century, greater freedom of thought and more invincible prejudices have existed than in any other country of Europe. I attribute this to a cause which may, at first sight, appear to have an opposite tendency, namely, to the liberty of the press. The nations amongst whom this liberty exists cling to their opinions as much from pride as from conviction. They cherish them because they hold them to be just, and because they chose them of their own free will; and they adhere to them, not only because they are true, but because they are their own. Several other reasons conduce to the same end.

It was remarked by a man of genius, that "ignorance lies at the two ends of knowledge." Perhaps it would have been more correct to say, that strong convictions are found only at the two ends, and that doubt lies in the middle. The human intellect, in truth, may be considered in three distinct states, which frequently succeed one another.

A man believes firmly, because he adopts a proposition without inquiry. He doubts as soon as objections present themselves. But he frequently succeeds in satisfying these doubts, and then he begins again to believe. This time, he has not a dim and casual glimpse of the truth, but sees it clearly before him, and advances by the light it gives.

When the liberty of the press acts upon men who are in the first of these three states, it does not immediately disturb their habit of believing implicitly without investigation, but it changes every day the objects of their unreflecting convictions. The human mind continues to discern but one point at a time upon the whole intellectual horizon, and that point is constantly changing. This is the period of sudden revolutions. Woe to the generations which first abruptly adopt the freedom of the press.

The circle of novel ideas, however, is soon travelled over. Experience comes to undeceive men, and plunges them into doubt and general mistrust. We may rest assured that the majority of mankind will always stop in one of these two states, will either believe they know not wherefore, or will not know what to believe. Few are those who can ever attain to that other state of rational and independent conviction, which true knowledge can produce out of the midst of doubt.

It has been remarked that, in times of great religious fervor, men sometimes change their religious opinions; whereas, in times of general skepticism, every one clings to his old persuasion. The same thing takes place in politics under the liberty of the press. In countries where all the theories of social science have been contested in their turn, men who have adopted one of them stick to it, not so much because they are sure of its truth, as because they are not sure that there is any better to be had. In the present age, men are not very ready to die for their opinions, but they are rarely inclined to change them; there are few martyrs, as well as few apostates.

Another still more valid reason may be adduced: when no opinions are looked upon as certain, men cling to the mere instincts and material interests of their position, which are naturally more tangible, definite, and permanent than any opinions in the world.

It is a very difficult question to decide, whether an aristocracy or a democracy governs the best. But it is certain that democracy annoys one part of the community, and that aristocracy oppresses another. It is a truth which is self-established, and one which it is needless to discuss, that "you are rich and I am poor."

CHAPTER XII

---★---

Political Associations in the United States

In no country in the world has the principle of association been more successfully used, or applied to a greater multitude of objects, than in America. Besides the permanent associations, which are established by law, under the names of townships, cities, and counties, a vast number of others are formed and maintained by the agency of private individuals.

The citizen of the United States is taught from infancy to rely upon his own exertions, in order to resist the evils and the difficulties of life; he looks upon the social authority with an eye of mistrust and anxiety, and he claims its assistance only when he is unable to do without it. This habit may be traced even in the schools, where the children in their games are wont to submit to rules which they have themselves established, and to punish misdemeanors which they have themselves defined. The same spirit pervades every act of social life. If a stoppage occurs in a thoroughfare, and the circulation of vehicles is hindered, the neighbors immediately form themselves into a deliberative body; and this extemporaneous assembly gives rise to an executive power, which remedies the inconvenience before anybody has thought of recurring to a pre-existing authority superior to that of the persons immediately concerned. If some public pleasure is concerned, an association is formed to give more splendor and regularity to the entertainment. Societies are formed to resist evils which are exclusively of a moral nature, as to diminish the vice of intemperance. In the United States, associations are established to promote the public safety, commerce, industry, morality, and religion. There is no end which the human will despairs of attaining through the combined power of individuals united into a society.

I shall have occasion hereafter to show the effects of association in civil life; I confine myself for the present to the political world. When once the right of association is recognized, the citizens may use it in different ways.

An association consists simply in the public assent which a number of individuals give to certain doctrines; and in the engagement which they contract to promote in a certain manner the spread of those doctrines. The right of associating with such views is very analogous to the liberty of unlicensed printing; but societies thus formed possess more authority than the press. When an opinion is represented by a society, it necessarily assumes a more exact and explicit form. It numbers its partisans, and compromises them in its cause: they, on the other hand, become acquainted with each other, and their zeal is increased by their number. An association unites into one channel the efforts of diverging minds, and urges them vigorously towards the one end which it clearly points out.

The second degree in the exercise of the right of association is the power of meeting. When an association is allowed to establish centers of action at certain important points in the country, its activity is increased, and its influence extended. Men have the opportunity of seeing each other; means of execution are combined; and opinions are maintained with a warmth and energy which written language can never attain.

Lastly, in the exercise of the right of political association, there is a third degree: the partisans of an opinion may unite in electoral bodies, and choose delegates to represent them in a central assembly. This is, properly speaking, the application of the representative system to a party.

Thus, in the first instance, a society is formed between individuals professing the same opinion, and the tie which keeps it together is of a purely intellectual nature. In the second case, small assemblies are formed, which represent only a fraction of the party. Lastly, in the third case, they constitute, as it were, a separate nation in the midst of the nation, a government within the government. Their delegates, like the real delegates of the majority, represent the whole collective force of their party; and, like them, also, have an appearance of nationality and all the moral power which results from it. It is true that they have not the right, like the others, of making the laws; but they have the power of attacking those which are in force, and of drawing up beforehand those which ought to be enacted.

If, among a people who are imperfectly accustomed to the exercise of freedom, or are exposed to violent political passions, by the side of the majority who make the laws be placed a minority who only deliberate and get laws ready for adoption, I cannot but believe that public tranquility would there incur very great risks. There is doubtless a wide difference between proving that one law is in itself better than another, and proving that the former ought to be substituted for the latter. But the imagination of the multitude is very apt to overlook this difference, which is so apparent to the minds of thinking men. It sometimes happens that a nation is divided into two nearly equal parties, each of which affects to represent the majority. If, near the directing power, another power be established, which exercises almost as much moral authority as the former, we are not to believe that it will long be content to speak without acting; or that it will always be restrained by the abstract consideration that associations are meant to direct opinions, but not to enforce them,—to suggest, but not to make, the laws.

The more I consider the independence of the press in its principal consequences, the more am I convinced that, in the modern world, it is the chief, and, so to speak, the constitutive element of liberty. A nation which is determined to remain free is therefore right in demanding, at any price, the exercise of this independence. But the *unlimited* liberty of political association cannot be entirely assimilated to the liberty of the press. The one is at the same time less necessary, and more dangerous, than the other. A nation may confine it within certain limits without forfeiting any part of its self-directing power; and it may sometimes be obliged to do so, in order to maintain its own authority.

The omnipotence of the majority appears to me to be so full of peril to the American republics, that the dangerous means used to bridle it seem to be more advantageous than prejudicial. And here I will express an opinion which may remind the reader of what I said when speaking of the freedom of townships. There are no countries in which associations are more needed, to prevent the despotism of faction or the arbitrary power of a prince, than those which are democratically constituted. In aristocratic nations, the body of the nobles and the wealthy are in themselves natural associations, which check the abuses of power. In countries where such associations do not exist, if private individuals cannot create an artificial and temporary substitute for them, I can see no permanent protection against the most galling tyranny; and a great people may be oppressed with impunity by a small faction, or by a single individual.

The meeting of a great political convention, (for there are conventions of all kinds,) which may frequently become a necessary measure, is always a serious occurrence, even in America, and one which judicious patriots cannot regard without alarm. This was very perceptible in the Convention of 1831, at which all the most distinguished members strove to moderate its language, and to restrain its objects within certain limits. It is probable that this Convention exercised a great influence on the minds of the malcontents, and prepared them for the open revolt against the commercial laws of the Union which took place in 1832.

It cannot be denied that the unrestrained liberty of association for political purposes is the privilege which a people is longest in learning how to exercise. If it does not throw the nation into anarchy, it perpetually augments the chances of that calamity. On one point, however, this perilous liberty offers a security against dangers of another kind; in countries where associations are free, secret societies are unknown. In America, there are factions, but no conspiracies.

CHAPTER XIII

—————— ★ ——————

Government of the Democracy in America

I am well aware of the difficulties which attend this part of my subject; but although every expression which I am about to use may clash, upon some points, with the feelings of the different parties which divide my country, I shall still speak my whole thought.

In Europe, we are at a loss how to judge the true character and the permanent instincts of democracy, because in Europe two conflicting principles exist, and we do not know what to attribute to the principles themselves, and what to the passions which the contest produces. Such, however, is not the case in America; there the people reign without impediment, and they have no perils to dread, and no injuries to avenge. In America, democracy is given up to its own propensities; its course is natural, and its activity is unrestrained; there, consequently, its real character must be judged. And to no people can this inquiry be more vitally interesting than to the French nation, who are blindly driven onwards, by a daily and irresistible impulse, towards a state of things which may prove either despotic or republican, but which will assuredly be democratic.

Universal Suffrage

I have already observed that universal suffrage has been adopted in all the States of the Union: it consequently exists in communities which occupy very different positions in the social scale. I have had opportunities of observing its effects in different localities, and amongst races of men who are nearly strangers to each other in their language, their religion, and their modes of life; in Louisiana as well as in New England, in Georgia as in Canada. I have remarked that universal suffrage is far from producing in America either all the good or all the evil consequences which may be expected from it in Europe, and that its effects generally differ very much from those which are attributed to it.

The Choice of the People, and the Instinctive Preferences of the American Democracy

Many people in Europe are apt to believe without saying it, or to say without believing it, that one of the great advantages of universal suffrage is, that it entrusts the direction of affairs to men who are worthy of the public confidence. They admit that the people are unable to govern of themselves, but they aver that the people always wish the welfare of the state, and instinctively designate those who are animated by the same good wishes, and who are the most fit to wield the supreme authority. I confess that the observations I made in America by no means coincide with these opinions. On my arrival in the United States, I was surprised to find so much distinguished talent among the subjects, and so little among the heads of the government. It is a constant fact, that, at the present day, the ablest men in the United States are rarely placed at the head of affairs; and it must be acknowledged that such has been the result, in proportion as democracy has outstepped all its former limits. The race of American statesmen has evidently dwindled most remarkably in the course of the last fifty years.

Several causes may be assigned for this phenomenon. It is impossible, after the most strenuous exertions, to raise the intelligence of the people above a certain level. Whatever may be the facilities of acquiring information, whatever may be the profusion of easy methods and cheap science, the human mind can never be instructed and developed without devoting considerable time to these objects.

The greater or the less possibility of subsisting without labor is therefore the necessary boundary of intellectual improvement. This boundary is more remote in some countries, and more restricted in others; but it must exist somewhere, as long as the people are constrained to work in order to procure the means of subsistence, that is to say, as long as they continue to be the people. It is therefore quite as difficult to imagine a state in which all the citizens should be very well informed, as a state in which they should all be wealthy; these two difficulties are correlative. I readily admit that the mass of the citizens sincerely wish to promote the welfare of the country; nay, more, I even allow that the lower classes mix fewer considerations of personal interest with their patriotism than the higher orders; but it is always more or less difficult for them to discern the best means of attaining the end which they sincerely desire. Long and patient observation and much acquired knowledge are requisite to form a just estimate of the character of a single individual. Men of the greatest genius often fail to do it, and can it be supposed that the vulgar will always succeed? The people have neither the time nor the means for an investigation of this kind. Their conclusions are hastily formed from a superficial inspection of the more prominent features of a question. Hence it often happens that mountebanks of all sorts are able to please the people, whilst their truest friends frequently fail to gain their confidence.

Moreover, the democracy not only lack that soundness of judgment which is necessary to select men really deserving of their confidence, but often have not the desire or the inclination to find them out. It cannot be denied that democratic institutions strongly tend to promote the feeling of envy in the human heart; not so much because they afford to every one the means of rising to the same level with others, as because those means perpetually disappoint the persons who employ them. Democratic institutions awaken and foster a passion for equality which they can never entirely satisfy. This complete equality eludes the grasp of the people at the very moment when they think they have grasped it, and "flies," as Pascal says, "with an eternal flight"; the people are excited in the pursuit of an advantage, which is more precious because it is not sufficiently remote to be unknown, or sufficiently near to be enjoyed. The lower orders are agitated by the chance of success, they are irritated by its uncertainty; and they pass from the enthusiasm of pursuit to the exhaustion of ill-success, and lastly to the acrimony of disappointment. Whatever transcends their own limits appears to be an obstacle to their desires, and there is no superiority, however legitimate it may be, which is not irksome in their sight.

It has been supposed that the secret instinct, which leads the lower orders to remove their superiors as much as possible from the direction of public affairs, is peculiar to France. This, however, is an error; the instinct to which I allude is not French, it is democratic; it may have been heightened by peculiar political circumstances, but it owes its origin to a higher cause.

In the United States, the people do not hate the higher classes of society, but are not favorably inclined towards them, and carefully exclude them from the exercise of authority. They do not dread distinguished talents, but are rarely fond of them. In general, every one who rises without their aid seldom obtains their favor.

Whilst the natural instincts of democracy induce the people to reject distinguished citizens as their rulers, an instinct not less strong induces able men to retire from the political arena, in which it is so difficult to retain their independence, or to advance without becoming servile. This opinion has been candidly expressed by Chancellor Kent, who says, in speaking with high praise of that part of the Constitution which empowers the executive to nominate the judges: "It is indeed probable that the men who are best fitted to discharge the duties of this high office would have too much reserve in their manners, and too much austerity in their principles, for them to be returned by the majority at an election where universal suffrage is adopted." Such were the opinions which were printed without contradiction in America in the year 1830!

I hold it to be sufficiently demonstrated, that universal suffrage is by no means a guaranty of the wisdom of the popular choice. Whatever its advantages may be, this is not one of them.

CHAPTER XIV

———— ★ ————

What Are the Real Advantages
Which American Society Derives
from a Democratic Government

B efore entering upon the present chapter, I must remind the reader of what I have more than once observed in this book. The political constitution of the United States appears to me to be one of the forms of government which a democracy may adopt; but I do not regard the American Constitution as the best, or as the only one, which a democratic people may establish. In showing the advantages which the Americans derive from the government of democracy, I am therefore very far from affirming, or believing, that similar advantages can be obtained only from the same laws.

General Tendency of the Laws Under the American Democracy, and Instincts of Those Who Apply Them

The defects and weaknesses of a democratic government may readily be discovered; they are demonstrated by flagrant instances, whilst its salutary influence is insensible, and, so to speak, occult. A glance suffices to detect its faults, but its good qualities can be discerned only by long observation. The laws of the American democracy are frequently defective or incomplete; they sometimes attack vested rights, or sanction others which are dangerous to the community; and even if they were good, their frequency would still be a great evil. How comes it, then, that the American republics prosper and continue?

In the consideration of laws, a distinction must be carefully observed between the end at which they aim, and the means by which they pursue that end; between their absolute and their relative excellence. If it be the intention of the legislator to favor the interests of the minority at the expense of the majority, and if the measures he takes are so combined as to accomplish the object he has in view with the least possible expense of time and exertion, the law may be well drawn up, although its purpose is bad; and the more efficacious it is, the more dangerous it will be.

Democratic laws generally tend to promote the welfare of the greatest possible number; for they emanate from the majority of the citizens, who are subject to error, but who cannot have an interest opposed, to their own advantage. The laws of an aristocracy tend, on the contrary, to concentrate wealth and power in the hands of the minority; because an aristocracy, by its very nature, constitutes a minority. It may therefore be asserted, as a general proposition, that the purpose of a democracy in its legislation is more useful to humanity than that of an aristocracy. This is, however, the sum total of its advantages.

Aristocracies are infinitely more expert in the science of legislation than democracies ever can be. They are possessed of a self-control which protects them from the errors of temporary excitement; and they form far-reaching designs, which they know how to mature till a favorable opportunity arrives. Aristocratic government proceeds with the dexterity of art; it understands how to make the collective force of all its laws converge at the same time to a given point. Such is not the case with democracies, whose laws are almost always ineffective or inopportune. The means of democracy are therefore more imperfect than those of aristocracy, and the measures which it unwittingly adopts are frequently opposed to its own cause; but the object it has in view is more useful.

Let us now imagine a community so organized by nature, or by its constitution, that it can support the transitory action of bad laws, and that it can await, without destruction, the *general tendency* of its legislation: we shall then conceive how a democratic government, notwithstanding its faults, may be best fitted to produce the prosperity of this community. This is precisely what has occurred in the United States; and I repeat, what I have before remarked, that the great advantage of the Americans consists in their being able to commit faults which they may afterwards repair.

An analogous observation may be made respecting public officers. It is easy to perceive that the American democracy frequently errs in the choice of the individuals to whom it entrusts the power of the administration; but it is more difficult to say why the state prospers under their rule. In the first place, it is to be remarked, that if, in a democratic state, the governors have less honesty and less capacity than elsewhere, the governed are more enlightened and more attentive to their interests. As the people in democracies are more constantly vigilant in their affairs, and more jealous of their rights, they prevent their representatives from abandoning that general line of conduct which their own interest prescribes. In the second place, it must be remembered, that, if the democratic magistrate is more apt to misuse his power, he possesses it for a shorter time. But there is yet another reason which is still more general and conclusive. It is no doubt of importance to the welfare of nations that they should be governed by men of talents and virtue; but it is perhaps still more important for them that the interests of those men should not differ from the interests of the community at large; for if such were the case, their virtues might become almost useless, and their talents might be turned to a bad account. I have said that it is important that the interests of the persons in authority should not differ from or oppose the interests of the community at large; but I do not insist upon their having the same interests as the *whole* population, because I am not aware that such a state of things ever existed in any country.

No political form has hitherto been discovered which is equally favorable to the prosperity and the development of all the classes into which society is divided. These classes continue to form, as it were, so many distinct communities in the same nation; and experience has shown that it is no less dangerous to place the fate of these classes exclusively in the hands of any one of them, than it is to make one people the arbiter of the destiny of another. When the rich alone govern, the interest of the poor is always endangered; and when the poor make the laws, that of the rich incurs very serious risks. The advantage of democracy does not consist, therefore, as has sometimes been asserted, in favoring the prosperity of all, but simply in contributing to the well-being of the greatest number.

The men who are entrusted with the direction of public affairs in the United States are frequently inferior, both in capacity and morality, to those whom an aristocracy would raise to power. But their interest is identified and confounded with that of the majority of their fellow-citizens. They may frequently be faithless, and frequently mistaken; bat they will never systematically adopt a line of conduct hostile to the majority; and they cannot give a dangerous or exclusive tendency to the government.

The maladministration of a democratic magistrate, moreover, is an isolated fact, which has influence only during the short period for which he is elected. Corruption and incapacity do not act as common interests, which may connect men permanently with one another. A corrupt or incapable magistrate will not concert his measures with another magistrate, simply because the latter is as corrupt and incapable as himself; and these two men will never unite their endeavors to promote the corruption and inaptitude of their remote posterity. The ambition and the maneuvers of the one will serve, on the contrary, to unmask the other. The vices of a magistrate, in democratic states, are usually wholly personal.

But under aristocratic governments, public men are swayed by the interest of their order, which, if it is sometimes confounded with the interests of the majority, is very frequently distinct from them. This interest is the common and lasting bond which unites them together; it induces them to coalesce and combine their efforts to attain an end which is not always the happiness of the greatest number: and it serves not only to connect the persons in authority with each other, but to unite them with a considerable portion of the community, since a numerous body of citizens belong to the aristocracy, without being invested with official functions. The aristocratic magistrate is therefore constantly supported by a portion of the community, as well as by the government of which he is a member.

The common purpose which, in aristocracies, connects the interest of the magistrates with that of a portion of their contemporaries, identifies it also with that of future generations; they labor for the future as well as for the present. The aristocratic magistrate is urged at the same time, towards the same point, by the passions of the community, by his own, and, I may almost add, by those of his posterity. Is it, then, wonderful that he does not resist such repeated impulses? And, indeed, aristocracies are often carried away by their class-spirit, without being corrupted by it; and they unconsciously fashion society to their own ends, and prepare it for their own descendants.

The English aristocracy is perhaps the most liberal which has ever existed, and no body of men has ever, uninterruptedly, furnished so many honorable and enlightened individuals to the government of a country. It cannot, however, escape observation, that, in the legislation of England, the interests of the poor have been often sacrificed to the advantage of the rich, and the rights of the majority to the privileges of a few. The consequence is, that England, at the present day, combines the extremes of good and evil fortune in the bosom of her society; and the miseries and privations of her poor almost equal her power and renown.

In the United States, where the public officers have no class-interests to promote, the general and constant influence of the government is beneficial, although the individuals who conduct it are frequently unskillful, and sometimes contemptible. There is, indeed, a secret tendency in democratic institutions, which makes the exertions of the citizens subservient to the prosperity of the community, in spite of their vices and mistakes; whilst in aristocratic institutions, there is a secret bias, which, notwithstanding the talents and virtues of those who conduct the government, leads them to contribute to the evils which oppress their fellow-creatures. In aristocratic governments, public men may frequently do harm without intending it; and in democratic states, they bring about good results which they never thought of.

Public Spirit in the United States
There is one sort of patriotic attachment, which principally arises from that instinctive, disinterested, and indefinable feeling which connects the affections of man with his birthplace. This natural fondness is united with a taste for ancient customs, and a reverence for traditions of the past; those who cherish it love their country as they love the mansion of their fathers. They love the tranquility which it affords them; they cling to the peaceful habits which they have contracted within its bosom; they are attached to the reminiscences which it awakens; and they are even pleased by living there in a state of obedience. This patriotism is sometimes stimulated by religious enthusiasm, and then it is capable of making prodigious efforts. It is in itself a kind of religion: it does not reason, but it acts from the impulse of faith and sentiment. In some nations, the monarch is regarded as a

personification of the country; and, the fervor of patriotism being converted into the fervor of loyalty, they take a sympathetic pride in his conquests, and glory in his power. There was a time, under the ancient monarchy, when the French felt a sort of satisfaction in the sense of their dependence upon the arbitrary will of their king; and they were wont to say with pride, "We live under the most powerful king in the world."

How happens it that in the United States, where the inhabitants arrived but as yesterday upon the soil which they now occupy, and brought neither customs nor traditions with them there; where they met each other for the first time with no previous acquaintance; where, in short, the instinctive love of country can scarcely exist;—how happens it that every one takes as zealous an interest in the affairs of his township, his county, and the whole State, as if they were his own? It is because every one, in his sphere, takes an active part in the government of society.

———★———

Unlimited Power of the Majority in the United States, and its Consequences

The very essence of democratic government consists in the absolute sovereignty of the majority; for there is nothing in democratic states which is capable of resisting it. Most of the American constitutions have sought to increase this natural strength of the majority by artificial means.

In the United States, political questions cannot be taken up in so general and absolute a manner; and all parties are willing to recognize the rights of the majority, because they all hope at some time to be able to exercise them to their own advantage. The majority, therefore, in that country, exercise a prodigious actual authority, and a power of opinion which is nearly as great; no obstacles exist which can impede or even retard its progress, so as to make it heed the complaints of those whom it crushes upon its path. This state of things is harmful in itself, and dangerous for the future.

———

Tyranny of the Majority

I hold it to be an impious and detestable maxim, that, politically speaking, the people have a right to do anything; and yet I have asserted that all authority originates in the will of the majority. Am I, then, in contradiction with myself?

A general law, which bears the name of justice, has been made and sanctioned, not only by a majority of this or that people, but by a majority of mankind. The rights of every people are therefore confined within the limits of what is just. A nation may be considered as a jury which is empowered to represent society at large, and to apply justice, which is its law. Ought such a jury, which represents society, to have more power than the society itself, whose laws it executes?

When I refuse to obey an unjust law, I do not contest the right of the majority to command, but I simply appeal from the sovereignty of the people to the sovereignty of mankind. Some have not feared to assert that a people can never outstep the boundaries of justice and reason in those affairs which are peculiarly its own; and that consequently full power may be given to the majority by which they are represented. But this is the language of a slave.

A majority taken collectively is only an individual, whose opinions, and frequently whose interests, are opposed to those of another individual, who is styled a minority. If it be admitted that a man possessing absolute power may misuse that power by wronging his adversaries, why should not a majority be liable to the same reproach? Men do not change their characters by uniting with each other; nor does their patience in the presence of obstacles increase with their strength. For my own part, I cannot believe it; the power to do everything, which I should refuse to one of my equals, I will never grant to any number of them.

I do not think that, for the sake of preserving liberty, it is possible to combine several principles in the same government so as really to oppose them to one another. The form of government which is usually termed *mixed* has always appeared to me a mere chimera. Accurately speaking, there is no such thing as a *mixed government*, in the sense usually given to that word, because, in all communities, some one principle of action may be discovered which preponderates over the others. England, in the last century,—which has been especially cited as an example of this sort of government,—was essentially an aristocratic state, although it comprised some great elements of democracy; for the laws and customs of the country were such that the aristocracy could not but preponderate in the long run, and direct public affairs according to its own will. The error arose from seeing the interests of the nobles perpetually contending with those of the people, without considering the issue of the contest, which was really the important point. When a community actually has a mixed government,—that is to say, when it is equally divided between adverse principles,—it must either experience a revolution, or fall into anarchy.

I am therefore of opinion, that social power superior to all others must always be placed somewhere; but I think that liberty is endangered when this power finds no obstacle which can retard its course, and give it time to moderate its own vehemence.

Unlimited power is in itself a bad and dangerous thing. Human beings are not competent to exercise it with discretion. God alone can be omnipotent, because his wisdom and his justice are always equal to his power. There is no power on earth so worthy of honor in itself, or clothed with rights so sacred, that I would admit its uncontrolled and all-predominant authority. When I see that the right and the means of absolute command are conferred on any power whatever, be it called a people or a king, an aristocracy or a democracy, a monarchy or a republic, I say there is the germ of tyranny, and I seek to live elsewhere, under other laws.

In my opinion, the main evil of the present democratic institutions of the United States does not arise, as is often asserted in Europe, from their weakness, but from their irresistible strength. I am not so much alarmed at the excessive liberty which reigns in that country, as at the inadequate securities which one finds there against tyranny.

When an individual or a party is wronged in the United States, to whom can he apply for redress? If to public opinion, public opinion constitutes the majority; if to the legislature, it represents the majority, and implicitly obeys it; if to the executive power, it is appointed by the majority, and serves as a passive tool in its hands. The public force consists of the majority under arms; the jury is the majority invested with the right of hearing judicial cases; and in certain States, even the judges are elected by the majority. However iniquitous or absurd the measure of which you complain, you must submit to it as well as you can.

If, on the other hand, a legislative power could be so constituted as to represent the majority without necessarily being the slave of its passions, an executive so as to retain a proper share of authority, and a judiciary so as to remain independent of the other two powers, a government would be formed which would still be democratic, without incurring hardly any risk of tyranny.

I do not say that there is a frequent use of tyranny in America at the present day; but I maintain that there is no sure barrier against it, and that the causes which mitigate the government there are to be found in the circumstances and the manners of the country, more than in its laws.

Effects of the Omnipotence of the Majority upon the Arbitrary Authority of American Public Officers

A distinction must be drawn between tyranny and arbitrary power. Tyranny may be exercised by means of the law itself, and in that case it is not arbitrary; arbitrary power may be exercised for the public good, in which case it is not tyrannical. Tyranny usually employs arbitrary means, but, if necessary, it can do without them.

In the United States, the omnipotence of the majority, which is favorable to the legal despotism of the legislature, likewise favors the arbitrary authority of the magistrate. The majority has absolute power both to make the law and to watch over its execution; and as it has equal authority over those who are in power, and the community at large, it considers public officers as its passive agents, and readily confides to them the task of carrying out its designs. The details of their office, and the privileges which they are to enjoy, are rarely defined beforehand. It treats them as a master does his servants, since they are always at work in his sight, and he can direct or reprimand them at any instant.

In general, the American functionaries are far more independent within the sphere which is prescribed to them than the French civil officers. Sometimes, even, they are allowed by the popular authority to exceed those bounds; and as they are protected by the opinion, and backed by the power, of the majority, they dare do things which even a European, accustomed as he is to arbitrary power, is astonished at. By this means, habits are formed in the heart of a free country which may some day prove fatal to its liberties.

Effects of the Tyranny of the Majority upon the National Character of the Americans.— The Courtier-Spirit In The United States

The tendencies which I have just mentioned are as yet but slightly perceptible in political society; but they already exercise an unfavorable influence upon the national character of the Americans.

I attribute the small number of distinguished men in political life to the ever-increasing despotism of the majority in the United States.

When the American Revolution broke out, they arose in great numbers; for public opinion then served, not to tyrannize over, but to direct the exertions of individuals. Those celebrated men, sharing the agitation of mind common at that period, had a grandeur peculiar to themselves, which was reflected back upon the nation, but was by no means borrowed from it.

In absolute governments, the great nobles who are nearest to the throne flatter the passions of the sovereign, and voluntarily truckle to his caprices. But the mass of the nation does not degrade itself by servitude; it often submits from weakness, from habit, or from ignorance, and sometimes from loyalty. Some nations have been known to sacrifice their own desires to those of the sovereign with pleasure and pride, thus exhibiting a sort of independence of mind in the very act of submission. These nations are miserable, but they are not degraded. There is a great difference between doing what one does not approve, and feigning to approve what one does; the one is the weakness of a feeble person, the other befits the temper of a lackey.

In free countries, where every one is more or less called upon to give his opinion on affairs of state,—in democratic republics, where public life is incessantly mingled with domestic affairs, where the sovereign authority is accessible on every side, and where its attention can always be attracted by vociferation,—more persons are to be met with who speculate upon its weaknesses, and live upon ministering to its passions, than in absolute monarchies. Not because men are naturally worse in these states than elsewhere, but the temptation is stronger and of easier access at the same time. The result is a more extensive debasement of character.

Democratic republics extend the practice of currying favor with the many, and introduce it into all classes at once: this is the most serious reproach that can be addressed to them. This is especially true in democratic states organized like the American republics, where the power of the majority is so absolute and irresistible that one must give up his rights as a citizen, and almost abjure his qualities as a man, if he intends to stray from the track which it prescribes.

In that immense crowd which throngs the avenues to power in the United States, I found very few men who displayed that manly candor and masculine independence of opinion which frequently distinguished the Americans in former times, and which constitutes the leading feature in distinguished characters wherever they may be found. It seems, at first sight, as if all the minds of the Americans were formed upon one model, so accurately do they follow the same route. A stranger does, indeed, sometimes meet with Americans who dissent from the rigor of these formularies,—with men who deplore the defects of the laws, the mutability and the ignorance of democracy,— who even go so far as to observe the evil tendencies which impair the national character, and to point out such remedies as it might be possible to apply; but no one is there to hear them except yourself, and you, to whom these secret reflections are confided, are a stranger and a bird of passage. They are very ready to communicate truths which are useless to you, but they hold a different language in public.

If ever these lines are read in America, I am well assured of two things;—in the first place, that all who peruse them will raise their voices to condemn me; and, in the second place, that many of them will acquit me at the bottom of their conscience.

I have heard of patriotism in the United States, and I have found true patriotism among the people, but never among the leaders of the people. This may be explained by analogy: despotism debases the oppressed much more than the oppressor: in absolute monarchies, the king often has great virtues, but the courtiers are invariably servile. It is true that American courtiers do not say "Sire," or "Your Majesty,"—a distinction without a difference They are forever talking of the natural intelligence of the people whom they serve: they do not debate the question which of the virtues of their master is pre-eminently worthy of admiration, for they assure him that he possesses all the virtues without having acquired them, or without caring to acquire them; they do not give him their daughters and their wives to be raised at his pleasure to the rank of his concubines; but, by sacrificing their opinions, they prostitute themselves. Moralists and philosophers in America are not obliged to conceal their opinions under the veil of allegory; but before they venture upon a harsh truth, they say, "We are aware that the people whom we are addressing are too superior to the weaknesses of human nature to lose the command of their temper for an instant. We should not hold this language if we were not speaking to men whom their virtues and their intelligence render more worthy of freedom than all the rest of the world." The sycophants of Louis XIV. could not flatter more dexterously.

For my part, I am persuaded that, in all governments, whatever their nature may be, servility will cower to force, and adulation will follow power. The only means of preventing men from degrading themselves is to invest no one with that unlimited authority which is the sure method of debasing them.

The Greatest Dangers of the American Republics
Proceed from the Omnipotence of the Majority

Governments usually perish from impotence or from tyranny. In the former case, their power escapes from them; it is wrested from their grasp in the latter. Many observers who have witnessed the anarchy of democratic states, have imagined that the government of those states was naturally weak and impotent. The truth is, that, when war is once begun between parties, the government loses its control over society. But I do not think that a democratic power is naturally without force or resources; say, rather, that it is almost always by the abuse of its force, and the misemployment of its resources, that it becomes a failure. Anarchy is almost always produced by its tyranny or its mistakes, but not by its want of strength.

It is important not to confound stability with force, or the greatness of a thing with its duration. In democratic republics, the power which directs society is not stable; for it often changes hands, and assumes a new direction. But, whichever way it turns, its force is almost irresistible. The governments of the American republics appear to me to be as much centralized as those of the absolute monarchies of Europe, and more energetic than they are. I do not, therefore, imagine that they will perish from weakness.

If ever the free institutions of America are destroyed, that event may be attributed to the omnipotence of the majority, which may at some future time urge the minorities to desperation, and oblige them to have recourse to physical force. Anarchy will then be the result, but it will have been brought about by despotism.

Mr. Madison expresses the same opinion in the Federalist, No. 51.

> It is of great importance in a republic, not only to guard the society against the oppression of its rulers, but to guard one part of the society against the injustice of the

other part. Justice is the end of government. It is the end of civil society. It ever has been, and ever will be, pursued until it be obtained, or until liberty be lost in the pursuit. In a society, under the forms of which the stronger faction can readily unite and oppress the weaker, anarchy may as truly be said to reign as in a state of nature, where the weaker individual is not secured against the violence of the stronger: and as, in the latter state, even the stronger individuals are prompted by the uncertainty of their condition to submit to a government which may protect the weak as well as themselves, so, in the former state, will the more powerful factions be gradually induced by a like motive to wish for a government which will protect all parties, the weaker as well as the more powerful. It can be little doubted, that, if the State of Rhode Island was separated from the Confederacy and left to itself, the insecurity of right under the popular form of government within such narrow limits would be displayed by such reiterated oppressions of the factious majorities, that some power altogether independent of the people would soon be called for by the voice of the very factions whose misrule had proved the necessity of it.

Jefferson also said: "The executive power in our government is not the only, perhaps not even the principal, object of my solicitude. The tyranny of the legislature is really the danger most to be feared, and will continue to be so for many years to come. The tyranny of the executive power will come in its turn, but at a more distant period."

I am glad to cite the opinion of Jefferson upon this subject rather than that of any other, because I consider him the most powerful advocate democracy has ever had.

CHAPTER XVI

───────────★───────────

Causes Which Mitigate the Tyranny of the Majority in the United States

Absence of Centralized Administration

I have already pointed out the distinction between a centralized government and a centralized administration. The former exists in America, but the latter is nearly unknown there. If the directing power of the American communities had both these instruments of government at its disposal, and united the habit of executing its commands to the right of commanding; if, after having established the general principles of government, it descended to the details of their application; and if, having regulated the great interests of the country, it could descend to the circle of individual interests, freedom would soon be banished from the New World.

But in the United States, the majority, which so frequently displays the tastes and the propensities of a despot, is still destitute of the most perfect instruments of tyranny.

In the American republics, the central government has never as yet busied itself but with a small number of objects, sufficiently prominent to attract its attention. The secondary affairs of society have never been regulated by its authority; and nothing has hitherto betrayed its desire of even interfering in them. The majority is become more and more absolute, but has not increased the prerogatives of the central government; those great prerogatives have been confined to a certain sphere; and, although the despotism of the majority may be galling upon one point, it cannot be said to extend to all. However the predominant party in the nation may be carried away by its passions, however ardent it may be in the pursuit of its projects, it cannot oblige all the citizens to comply with its desires in the same manner, and at the same time, throughout the country. When the central government which represents that majority has issued a decree, it must entrust the execution of its will to agents, over whom it frequently has no control, and whom it cannot perpetually direct. The townships, municipal bodies, and counties form so many concealed breakwaters, which check or part the tide of popular determination. If an oppressive law were passed, liberty would still be protected by the mode of executing that law; the majority cannot descend to the details and what may be called the puerilities of administrative tyranny. It does not even imagine that it can do so, for it has not a full consciousness of its authority. It knows only the extent of its natural powers, but is unacquainted with the art of increasing them.

This point deserves attention; for if a democratic republic, similar to that of the United States, were ever founded in a country where the power of one man had previously established a centralized administration, and had sunk it deep into the habits and the laws of the people, I do not hesitate to assert, that, in such a republic, a more insufferable despotism would prevail than in any of the absolute monarchies of Europe; or, indeed, than any which could be found on this side of Asia.

The Profession of the Law in the United States Serves to Counterpoise the Democracy

In visiting the Americans and studying their laws, we perceive that the authority they have entrusted to members of the legal profession, and the influence which these individuals exercise in the government, is the most powerful existing security against the excesses of democracy. This effect seems to me to result from a general cause, which it is useful to investigate, as it may be reproduced elsewhere.

The members of the legal profession have taken a part in all the movements of political society in Europe for the last five hundred years. At one time, they have been the instruments of the political authorities, and at another, they have succeeded in converting the political authorities into their instruments. In the Middle Ages, they afforded a powerful support to the Crown; and since that period, they have exerted themselves effectively to limit the royal prerogative. In England, they have contracted a close alliance with the aristocracy: in France, they have shown themselves its most dangerous enemies. Under all these circumstances, have the members of the legal profession been swayed by sudden and fleeting impulses, or have they been more or less impelled by instincts which are natural to them, and which will always recur in history? I am incited to this investigation, for perhaps this particular class of men will play a prominent part in the political society which is soon to be created.

Men who have made a special study of the laws derive from this occupation certain habits of order, a taste for formalities, and a kind of instinctive regard for the regular connection of ideas, which naturally render them very hostile to the revolutionary spirit and the unreflecting passions of the multitude.

The special information which lawyers derive from their studies insures them a separate rank in society, and they constitute a sort of privileged body in the scale of intellect. This notion of their superiority perpetually recurs to them in the practice of their profession: they are the masters of a science which is necessary, but which is not very generally known: they serve as arbiters between the citizens; and the habit of directing to their purpose the blind passions of parties in litigation, inspires them with a certain contempt for the judgment of the multitude. Add to this, that they naturally constitute *a body*; not by any previous understanding, or by an agreement which directs them to a common end; but the analogy of their studies and the uniformity of their methods connect their minds together, as a common interest might unite their endeavors.

Some of the tastes and the habits of the aristocracy may consequently be discovered in the characters of lawyers. They participate in the same instinctive love of order and formalities; and they entertain the same repugnance to the actions of the multitude, and the same secret contempt of the government of the people. I do not mean to say that the natural propensities of lawyers are sufficiently strong to sway them irresistibly; for they, like most other men, are governed by their private interests, and especially by the interests of the moment.

In a state of society in which the members of the legal profession cannot hold that rank in the political world which they enjoy in private life, we may rest assured that they will be the foremost agents of revolution. But it must then be inquired, whether the cause which then induces them to innovate and destroy results from a permanent disposition or from an accident. It is true that lawyers mainly contributed to the overthrow of the French monarchy in 1789; but it remains to be seen whether they acted thus because they had studied the laws, or because they were prohibited from making them.

Five hundred years ago, the English nobles headed the people, and spoke in their name; at the present time, the aristocracy support the throne, and defend the royal prerogative. But aristocracy has, notwithstanding this, its peculiar instincts and propensities. We must be careful not to confound isolated members of a body with the body itself. In all free governments, of whatsoever form they may be, members of the legal profession will be found in the front ranks of all parties. The same remark is also applicable to the aristocracy; almost all the democratic movements which have agitated the world have been directed by nobles. A privileged body can never satisfy the ambition of all its members: it has always more talents and more passions than it can find places to content and employ; so that a considerable number of individuals are usually to be met with, who are inclined to attack those very privileges which they cannot soon enough turn to their own account.

I do not, then, assert that *all* the members of the legal profession are, at *all* times, the friends of order and the opponents of innovation, but merely that most of them are usually so. In a community in which lawyers are allowed to occupy without opposition that high station which naturally belongs to them, their general spirit will be eminently conservative and anti-democratic. When an aristocracy excludes the leaders of that profession from its ranks, it excites enemies who are the more formidable as they are independent of the nobility by their labors, and feel themselves to be their equals in intelligence, though inferior in opulence and power. But whenever an aristocracy consents to impart some of its privileges to these same individuals, the two classes coalesce very readily, and assume, as it were, family interests.

I am, in like manner, inclined to believe that a monarch will always be able to convert legal practitioners into the most serviceable instruments of his authority. There is a far greater affinity between this class of persons and the executive power, than there is between them and the people, though they have often aided to overturn the former; just as there is a greater natural affinity between the nobles and the monarch, than between the nobles and the people, although the higher orders of society have often, in concert with the lower classes, resisted the prerogative of the crown.

Lawyers are attached to public order beyond every other consideration, and the best security of public order is authority. It must not be forgotten, also, that, if they prize freedom much, they generally value legality still more: they are less afraid of tyranny than of arbitrary power; and, provided the legislature undertakes of itself to deprive men of their independence, they are not dissatisfied.

I am therefore convinced that the prince who, in presence of an encroaching democracy, should endeavor to impair the judicial authority in his dominions, and to diminish the political influence of lawyers, would commit a great mistake: he would let slip the substance of authority to grasp the shadow. He would act more wisely in introducing lawyers into the government; and if he entrusted despotism to them under the form of violence, perhaps he would find it again in their hands under the external features of justice and law.

The government of democracy is favorable to the political power of lawyers; for when the wealthy, the noble, and the prince are excluded from the government, the lawyers take possession of it, in their own right, as it were, since they are the only men of information and sagacity, beyond the sphere of the people, who can be the object of the popular choice. If, then, they are led by their tastes towards the aristocracy and the prince, they are brought in contact with the people by their interests. They like the government of democracy, without participating in its propensities and without imitating its weaknesses; whence they derive a twofold authority from it and over it. The people in democratic states do not mistrust the members of the legal profession, because it is known that they are interested to serve the popular cause; and the people listen to them without irritation, because they do not attribute to them any sinister designs. The lawyers do not, indeed, wish to overthrow the institutions of democracy, but they constantly endeavor to turn it away from its real direction by means which are foreign to its nature. Lawyers belong to the people by birth and interest, and to the aristocracy by habit and taste; they may be looked upon as the connecting link of the two great classes of society.

The profession of the law is the only aristocratic element which can be amalgamated without violence with the natural elements of democracy, and be advantageously and permanently combined with them. I am not ignorant of the defects inherent in the character of this body of men; but without this admixture of lawyer-like sobriety with the democratic principle, I question whether democratic institutions could long be maintained; and I cannot believe that a republic could hope to exist at the present time, if the influence of lawyers in public business did not increase in proportion to the power of the people.

This aristocratic character, which I hold to be common to the legal profession, is much more distinctly marked in the United States and in England than in any other country. This proceeds not only from the legal studies of the English and American lawyers, but from the nature of the law, and the position which these interpreters of it occupy, in the two countries. The English and the Americans have retained the law of precedents; that is to say, they continue to found their legal opinions and the decisions of their courts upon the opinions and decisions of their predecessors. In the mind of an English or American lawyer, a taste and a reverence for what is old is almost always united with a love of regular and lawful proceedings.

This predisposition has another effect upon the character of the legal profession and upon the general course of society. The English and American lawyers investigate what has been done; the French advocate inquires what should have been done: the former produce precedents; the latter, reasons. A French observer is surprised to hear how often an English or an American lawyer quotes the opinions of others, and how little he alludes to his own; whilst the reverse occurs in France. There the most trifling litigation is never conducted without the introduction of an entire system of ideas peculiar to the counsel employed; and the fundamental principles of law are discussed in order to obtain a perch of land by the decision of the court. This abnegation of his own opinion, and this implicit deference to the opinion of his forefathers, which are common to the English and American lawyer, this servitude of thought which he is obliged to profess, necessarily give him more timid habits and more conservative inclinations in England and America than in France.

The French codes are often difficult of comprehension, but they can be read by every one; nothing, on the other hand, can be more obscure and strange to the uninitiated, than a legislation founded upon precedents. The absolute need of legal aid which is felt in England and the United States, and the high opinion which is entertained of the ability of the legal profession, tend to separate it more and more from the people, and to erect it into a distinct class. The French lawyer is simply a man extensively acquainted with the statutes of his country; but the English or American lawyer resembles the hierophants of Egypt, for, like them, he is the sole interpreter of an occult science.

The position which lawyers occupy in England and America exercises no less influence upon their habits and opinions. The English aristocracy, which has taken care to attract to its sphere whatever is at all analogous to itself, has conferred a high degree of importance and authority upon the members of the legal profession. In English society, lawyers do not occupy the first rank, but they are contented with the station assigned to them: they constitute, as it were, the younger branch of the English aristocracy; and they are attached to their elder brothers, although they do not enjoy all their privileges. The English lawyers consequently mingle the aristocratic tastes and ideas of the circles in which they move, with the aristocratic interests of their profession.

And, indeed, the lawyer-like character which I am endeavoring to depict is most distinctly to be met with in England: there, laws are esteemed not so much because they are good as because they are old; and if it be necessary to modify them in any respect, to adapt them to the changes which time operates in society, recourse is had to the most inconceivable subtleties in order to uphold the traditional fabric, and to maintain that nothing has been done which does not square with the intentions, and complete the labors, of former generations. The very individuals who conduct these changes disclaim any desire of innovation, and had rather resort to absurd expedients than plead guilty to so great a crime. This spirit appertains more especially to the English lawyers; they appear indifferent to the real meaning of what they treat, and they direct all their attention to the letter,—seeming inclined to abandon reason and humanity, rather than to swerve one tittle from the law. English legislation may be compared to the stock of an old tree, upon which lawyers have engrafted the most dissimilar shoots, in the hope that, although their fruits may differ, their foliage at least will be confounded with the venerable trunk which supports them all.

In America, there are no nobles or literary men, and the people are apt to mistrust the wealthy; lawyers consequently form the highest political class, and the most cultivated portion of society. They have therefore nothing to gain by innovation, which adds a conservative interest to their natural taste for public order. If I were asked where I place the American aristocracy, I should reply, without hesitation, that it is not among the rich, who are united by no common tie, but that it occupies the judicial bench and the bar.

The more we reflect upon all that occurs in the United States, the more shall we be persuaded that the lawyers, as a body, form the most powerful, if not the only, counterpoise to the democratic element. In that country, we easily perceive how the legal profession is qualified by its attributes, and even by its faults, to neutralize the vices inherent in popular government. When the American people are intoxicated by passion, or carried away by the impetuosity of their ideas, they are checked and stopped by the almost invisible influence of their legal counselors. These secretly oppose their aristocratic propensities to the nation's democratic instincts, their superstitious attachment to what is old to its love of novelty, their narrow views to its immense designs, and their habitual procrastination to its ardent impatience.

The courts of justice are the visible organs by which the legal profession is enabled to control the democracy. The judge is a lawyer, who, independently of the taste for regularity and order which he has contracted in the study of law, derives an additional love of stability from the inalienability of his own functions. His legal attainments have already raised him to a distinguished rank amongst his fellows; his political power completes the distinction of his station, and gives him the instincts of the privileged classes.

Armed with the power of declaring the laws to be unconstitutional, the American magistrate perpetually interferes in political affairs. He cannot force the people to make laws, but at least he can oblige them not to disobey their own enactments, and not to be inconsistent with themselves. I am aware that a secret tendency to diminish the judicial power exists in the United States; and by most of the Constitutions of the several States, the government can, upon the demand of the two houses of the legislature, remove the judges from their station. Some other State Constitutions make the members of the judiciary elective, and they are even subjected to frequent re-elections. I venture to predict that these innovations will sooner or later be attended with fatal consequences; and that it will be found out at some future period, that, by thus lessening the independence of the judiciary, they have attacked not only the judicial power, but the democratic republic itself.

It must not, moreover, be supposed that the legal spirit is confined, in the United States, to the courts of justice; it extends far beyond them. As the lawyers form the only enlightened class whom the people do not mistrust, they are naturally called upon to occupy most of the public stations. They fill the legislative assemblies, and are at the head of the administration; they consequently exercise a powerful influence upon the formation of the law, and upon its execution. The lawyers are, however, obliged to yield to the current of public opinion, which is too strong for them to resist; but it is easy to find indications of what they would do, if they were free to act. The Americans, who have made so many innovations in their political laws, have introduced very sparing alterations in their civil laws, and that with great difficulty, although many of these laws are repugnant to their social condition. The reason of this is, that, in matters of civil law, the majority are obliged to defer to the authority of the legal profession, and the American lawyers are disinclined to innovate when they are left to their own choice.

It is curious for a Frenchman to hear the complaints which are made in the United States, against the stationary spirit of legal men, and their prejudices in favor of existing institutions.

The influence of legal habits extends beyond the precise limits I have pointed out. Scarcely any political question arises in the United States which is not resolved, sooner or later, into a judicial question. Hence all parties are obliged to borrow, in their daily controversies, the ideas, and even the language, peculiar to judicial proceedings. As most public men are, or have been, legal practitioners, they introduce the customs and technicalities of their profession into the management of public affairs. The jury extends this habitude to all classes. The language of the law thus becomes, in some measure, a vulgar tongue; the spirit of the law, which is produced in the schools and courts of justice, gradually penetrates beyond their walls into the bosom of society, where it descends to the lowest classes, so that at last the whole people contract the habits and the tastes of the judicial magistrate. The lawyers of the United States form a party which is but little feared and scarcely perceived, which has no badge peculiar to itself, which adapts itself with great flexibility to the exigencies of the time, and accommodates itself without resistance to all the movements of the social body. But this party extends over the whole community, and penetrates into all the classes which compose it; it acts upon the country imperceptibly, but finally fashions it to suit its own purposes.

★

Principal Causes Which Tend to Maintain the Democratic Republic in the United States

A Democratic republic exists in the United States; and the principal object of this book has been to explain the causes of its existence. Several of these causes have been involuntarily passed by, or only hinted at, as I was borne along by my subject. Others I have been unable to discuss at all; and those on which I have dwelt most are, as it were, buried in the details of this work.

I think, therefore, that, before I proceed to speak of the future, I ought to collect within a small compass the reasons which explain the present. In this retrospective chapter I shall be brief; for I shall take care to remind the reader only very summarily of what he already knows, and shall select only the most prominent of those facts which I have not yet pointed out.

All the causes which contribute to the maintenance of the democratic republic in the United States are reducible to three heads:—

    a) The peculiar and accidental situation in which Providence has placed the Americans.

    b) The laws.

    c) The manners and customs of the people.

Accidental or Providential Causes Which Contribute to Maintain the Democratic Republic in the United States

A thousand circumstances, independent of the will of man, facilitate the maintenance of a democratic republic in the United States. Some of these are known, the others may easily be pointed out; but I shall confine myself to the principal ones.

The Americans have no neighbors, and consequently they have no great wars, or financial crises, or inroads, or conquest, to dread; they require neither great taxes, nor large armies, nor great generals; and they have nothing to fear from a scourge which is more formidable to republics than all these evils combined, namely, military glory. It is impossible to deny the inconceivable influence which military glory exercises upon the spirit of a nation. General Jackson, whom the Americans have twice elected to be the head of their government, is a man of violent temper and very moderate talents; nothing in his whole career ever proved him qualified to govern a free people; and indeed, the majority of the enlightened classes of the Union has always opposed him. But he was raised to the Presidency, and has been maintained there, solely by the recollection of a victory which he gained, twenty years ago, under the walls of New Orleans; a victory which was, however, a very ordinary achievement, and which could only be remembered in a country where battles are rare. Now the people who are thus carried away by the illusions of glory are unquestionably the most cold and calculating, the most unmilitary, if I may so speak, and the most prosaic, of all the nations of the earth.

America has no great capital city, whose direct or indirect influence is felt over the whole extent of the country; this I hold to be one of the first causes of the maintenance of republican institutions in the United States. In cities, men cannot be prevented from concerting together, and awakening a mutual excitement which prompts sudden and passionate resolutions. Cities may be looked upon as large assemblies, of which all the inhabitants are members; their populace exercise a prodigious influence upon the magistrates, and frequently execute their own wishes without the intervention of public officers.

To subject the provinces to the metropolis is, therefore, to place the destiny of the empire in the hands, not only of a portion of the community, which is unjust, but in the hands of a populace carrying out its own impulses, which is very dangerous. The preponderance of capital cities is therefore a serious injury to the representative system; and it exposes modern republics to the same defect as the republics of antiquity, which all perished from not having known this system.

It would be easy for me to enumerate many secondary causes which have contributed to establish, and now concur to maintain, the democratic republic of the United States. But among these favorable circumstances I discern two principal ones, which I hasten to point out. I have already observed that the origin of the Americans, or what I have called their point of departure, may be looked upon as the first and most efficacious cause to which the present prosperity of the United States may be attributed. The Americans had the chances of birth in their favor; and their forefathers imported that equality of condition and of intellect into the country whence the democratic republic has very naturally taken its rise. Nor was this all; for besides this republican condition of society, the early settlers bequeathed to their descendants the customs, manners, and opinions which contribute most to the success of a republic. When I reflect upon the consequences of this primary fact, methinks I see the destiny of America embodied in the first Puritan who landed on those shores, just as the whole human race was represented by the first man.

The chief circumstance which has favored the establishment and the maintenance of a democratic republic in the United States, is the nature of the territory which the Americans inhabit. Their ancestors gave them the love of equality and of freedom; but God himself gave them the means of remaining equal and free, by placing them upon a boundless continent. General prosperity is favorable to the stability of all governments, but more particularly of a democratic one, which depends upon the will of the majority, and especially upon the will of that portion of the community which is most exposed to want. When the people rule, they must be rendered happy, or they will overturn the state: and misery stimulates them to those excesses to which ambition rouses kings. The physical causes, independent of the laws, which promote general prosperity, are more numerous in America than they ever have been in any other country in the world, at any other period of history. In the United States, not only is legislation democratic, but Nature herself favors the cause of the people.

Influence of the Laws Upon the Maintenance of the Democratic Republic in the United States

The principal aim of this book has been to make known the laws of the United States; if this purpose has been accomplished, the reader is already enabled to judge for himself which are the laws that really tend to maintain the democratic republic, and which endanger its existence. If I have not succeeded in explaining this in the whole course of my work, I cannot hope to do so in a single chapter. It is not my intention to retrace the path I have already pursued; and a few lines will suffice to recapitulate what I have said.

Three circumstances seem to me to contribute more than all others to the maintenance of the democratic republic in the United States.

The first is that federal form of government which the Americans have adopted, and which enables the Union to combine the power of a great republic with the security of a small one;

The second consists in those township institutions which limit the despotism of the majority, and at the same time impart to the people a taste for freedom, and the art of being free;

The third is to be found in the constitution of the judicial power. I have shown how the courts of justice serve to repress the excesses of democracy, and how they check and direct the impulses of the majority without stopping its activity.

Influence of Manners upon the Maintenance of the Democratic Republic in the United States

I have previously remarked that the manners of the people may be considered as one of the great general causes to which the maintenance of a democratic republic in the United States is attributable. I here use the word *manners* with the meaning which the ancients attached to the word *mores*; for I apply it not only to manners properly so called,—that is, to what might be termed *the habits of the heart*,—but to the various notions and opinions current among men, and to the mass of those ideas which constitute their character of mind. I comprise under this term, therefore, the whole moral and intellectual condition of a people. My intention is not to draw a picture of American manners, but simply to point out such features of them as are favorable to the maintenance of their political institutions.

Religion Considered as a Political Institution, Which Powerfully Contributes to the Maintenance of the Democratic Republic amongst the Americans

By the side of every religion is to be found a political opinion, which is connected with it by affinity. If the human mind be left to follow its own bent, it will regulate the temporal and spiritual institutions of society in a uniform manner; and man will endeavor, if I may so speak, to *harmonize* earth with heaven.

The greatest part of British America was peopled by men who, after having shaken off the authority of the Pope, acknowledged no other religious supremacy: they brought with them into the New World a form of Christianity, which I cannot better describe than by styling it a democratic and republican religion. This contributed powerfully to the establishment of a republic and a democracy in public affairs; and from the beginning, politics and religion contracted an alliance which has never been dissolved.

About fifty years ago, Ireland began to pour a Catholic population into the United States; and on their part, the Catholics of America made proselytes, so that, at the present moment, more than a million of Christians, professing the truths of the Church of Rome, are to be found in the Union. These Catholics are faithful to the observances of their religion; they are fervent and zealous in the belief of their doctrines. Yet they constitute the most republican and the most democratic class in the United States. This fact may surprise the observer at first, but the causes of it may easily be discovered upon reflection.

I think that the Catholic religion has erroneously been regarded as the natural enemy of democracy. Amongst the various sects of Christians, Catholicism seems to me, on the contrary, to be one of the most favorable to equality of condition among men. In the Catholic Church, the religious community is composed of only two elements; the priest and the people. The priest alone rises above the rank of his flock, and all below him are equal.

On doctrinal points, the Catholic faith places all human capacities upon the same level; it subjects the wise and ignorant, the man of genius and the vulgar crowd, to the details of the same creed; it imposes the same observances upon the rich and needy, it inflicts the same austerities upon the strong and the weak; it listens to no compromise with mortal man, but, reducing all the human race to the same standard, it confounds all the distinctions of society at the foot of the same altar, even as they are confounded in the sight of God. If Catholicism predisposes the faithful to obedience, it certainly does not prepare them for inequality: but the contrary may be said of Protestantism, which generally tends to make men independent, more than to render them equal. Catholicism is like an absolute monarchy; if the sovereign be removed, all the other classes of society are more equal than in republics.

It has not infrequently occurred that the Catholic priest has left the service of the altar to mix with the governing powers of society, and to take his place amongst the civil ranks of men. This religious influence has sometimes been used to secure the duration of that political state of things to which he belonged. Thus we have seen Catholics taking the side of aristocracy from a religious motive. But no sooner is the priesthood entirely separated from the government, as is the case in the United States, than it is found that no class of men are more naturally disposed than the Catholics to transfer the doctrine of the equality of condition into the political world.

If, then, the Catholic citizens of the United States are not forcibly led by the nature of their tenets to adopt democratic and republican principles, at least they are not necessarily opposed to them; and their social position, as well as their limited number, obliges them to adopt these opinions. Most of the Catholics are poor, and they have no chance of taking a part in the government unless it be open to all the citizens. They constitute a minority, and all rights must be respected in order to insure to them the free exercise of their own privileges. These two causes induce them, even unconsciously, to adopt political doctrines which they would perhaps support with less zeal if they were rich and preponderant.

The Catholic clergy of the United States have never attempted to oppose this political tendency; but they seek rather to justify it. The Catholic priests in America have divided the intellectual world into two parts: in the one, they place the doctrines of revealed religion, which they assent to without discussion; in the other, they leave those political truths, which they believe the Deity has left open to free inquiry. Thus the Catholics of the United States are at the same time the most submissive believers and the most independent citizens.

It may be asserted, then, that in the United States no religious doctrine displays the slightest hostility to democratic and republican institutions. The clergy of all the different sects there hold the same language; their opinions are in agreement with the laws, and the human mind flows onwards, so to speak, in one undivided current.

Indirect Influence of Religious Opinions Upon Political Society In The United States

I have just shown what the direct influence of religion upon politics is in the United States; but its indirect influence appears to me to be still more considerable, and it never instructs the Americans more fully in the art of being free than when it says nothing of freedom.

The sects which exist in the United States are innumerable. They all differ in respect to the worship which is due to the Creator; but they all agree in respect to the duties which are due from man to man. Each sect adores the Deity in its own peculiar manner; but all sects preach the same moral law in the name of God. If it be of the highest importance to man, as an individual, that his religion should be true, it is not so to society. Society has no future life to hope for or to fear; and provided the citizens profess a religion, the peculiar tenets of that religion are of little importance to its interests. Moreover, all the sects of the United States are comprised within the great unity of Christianity, and Christian morality is everywhere the same.

It may fairly be believed, that a certain number of Americans pursue a peculiar form of worship from habit more than from conviction. In the United States, the sovereign authority is religious, and consequently hypocrisy must be common; but there is no country in the world where the Christian religion retains a greater influence over the souls of men than in America; and there can be no greater proof of its utility, and of its conformity to human nature, than that its influence is powerfully felt over the most enlightened and free nation of the earth.

I have remarked that the American clergy in general, without even excepting those who do not admit religious liberty, are all in favor of civil freedom; but they do not support any particular political system.

They keep aloof from parties, and from public affairs. In the United States, religion exercises but little influence upon the laws, and upon the details of public opinion; but it directs the manners of the community, and, by regulating domestic life, it regulates the state.

I do not question that the great austerity of manners which is observable in the United States arises, in the first instance, from religious faith. Religion is often unable to restrain man from the numberless temptations which chance offers; nor can it check that passion for gain which everything contributes to arouse: but its influence over the mind of woman is supreme, and women are the protectors of morals. There is certainly no country in the world where the tie of marriage is more respected than in America, or where conjugal happiness is more highly or worthily appreciated. In Europe, almost all the disturbances of society arise from the irregularities of domestic life. To despise the natural bonds and legitimate pleasures of home, is to contract a taste for excesses, a restlessness of heart, and fluctuating desires. Agitated by the tumultuous passions which frequently disturb his dwelling, the European is galled by the obedience which the legislative powers of the state exact. But when the American retires from the turmoil of public life to the bosom of his family, he finds in it the image of order and of peace. There his pleasures are simple and natural, his joys are innocent and calm; and as he finds that an orderly life is the surest path to happiness, he accustoms himself easily to moderate his opinions as well as his tastes. Whilst the European endeavors to forget his domestic troubles by agitating society, the American derives from his own home that love of order which he afterwards carries with him into public affairs.

In the United States, the influence of religion is not confined to the manners, but it extends to the intelligence, of the people. Amongst the Anglo-Americans, some profess the doctrines of Christianity from a sincere belief in them, and others do the same because they fear to be suspected of unbelief. Christianity, therefore, reigns without obstacle, by universal consent; the consequence is, as I have before observed, that every principle of the moral world is fixed and determinate, although the political world is abandoned to the debates and the experiments of men. Thus the human mind is never left to wander over a boundless field; and, whatever may be its pretensions, it is checked from time to time by barriers which it cannot surmount.

Before it can innovate, certain primary principles are laid down, and the boldest conceptions are subjected to certain forms which retard and stop their completion.

The imagination of the Americans, even in its greatest flights, is circumspect and undecided; its impulses are checked, and its works unfinished. These habits of restraint recur in political society, and are singularly favorable both to the tranquility of the people and the durability of the institutions they have established. Nature and circumstances have made the inhabitants of the United States bold, as is sufficiently attested by the enterprising spirit with which they seek for fortune. If the mind of the Americans were free from all trammels, they would shortly become the most daring innovators and the most persistent disputants in the world. But the revolutionists of America are obliged to profess an ostensible respect for Christian morality and equity, which does not permit them to violate wantonly the laws that oppose their designs; nor would they find it easy to surmount the scruples of their partisans, even if they were able to get over their own. Hitherto, no one in the United States has dared to advance the maxim that everything is permissible for the interests of society,—an impious adage, which seems to have been invented in an age of freedom to shelter all future tyrants. Thus, whilst the law permits the Americans to do what they please, religion prevents them from conceiving, and forbids them to commit, what is rash or unjust.

Religion in America takes no direct part in the government of society, but it must be regarded as the first of their political institutions; for if it does not impart a taste for freedom, it facilitates the use of it. Indeed, it is in this same point of view that the inhabitants of the United States themselves look upon religious belief. I do not know whether all the Americans have a sincere faith in their religion,—for who can search the human heart?—but I am certain that they hold it to be indispensable to the maintenance of republican institutions. This opinion is not peculiar to a class of citizens, or to a party, but it belongs to the whole nation, and to every rank of society.

In the United States, if a politician attacks a sect, this may not prevent the partisans of that very sect from supporting him; but if he attacks all the sects together, every one abandons him, and he remains alone.

Whilst I was in America, a witness, who happened to be called at the Sessions of the county of Chester (State of New York), declared that he did not believe in the existence of God, or in the immortality of the soul. The judge refused to admit his evidence, on the ground that the witness had destroyed beforehand all the confidence of the court in what he was about to say. The newspapers related the fact without any further comment.

The Americans combine the notions of Christianity and of liberty so intimately in their minds, that it is impossible to make them conceive the one without the other; and with them, this conviction does not spring from that barren, traditional faith which seems to vegetate rather than to live in the soul.

I have known of societies formed by the Americans to send out ministers of the Gospel into the new Western States, to found schools and churches there, lest religion should be suffered to die away in those remote settlements, and the rising States be less fitted to enjoy free institutions than the people from whom they came. I met with wealthy New-Englanders who abandoned the country in which they were born, in order to lay the foundations of Christianity and of freedom on the banks of the Missouri, or in the prairies of Illinois. Thus religious zeal is perpetually warmed in the United States by the fires of patriotism. These men do not act exclusively from a consideration of a future life; eternity is only one motive of their devotion to the cause. If you converse with these missionaries of Christian civilization, you will be surprised to hear them speak so often of the goods of this world, and to meet a politician where you expected to find a priest. They will tell you, that "all the American republics are collectively involved with each other; if the republics of the West were to fall into anarchy, or to be mastered by a despot, the republican institutions which now flourish upon the shores of the Atlantic Ocean would be in great peril. It is therefore our interest that the new States should be religious, in order that they may permit us to remain free."

Such are the opinions of the Americans: and if any hold that the religious spirit which I admire is the very thing most amiss in America, and that the only element wanting to the freedom and happiness of the human race on the other side of the ocean is to believe with Spinoza in the eternity of the world, or with Cabanis that thought is secreted by the brain, I can only reply, that those who hold this language have never been in America, and that they have never seen a religious or a free nation. When they return from a visit to that country, we shall hear what they have to say.

There are persons in France who look upon republican institutions only as a means of obtaining grandeur; they measure the immense space which separates their vices and misery from power and riches, and they aim to fill up this gulf with ruins, that they may pass over it. These men are the *condottieri* of liberty, and fight for their own advantage, whatever be the colors they wear. The republic will stand long enough, they think, to draw them up out of their present degradation. It is not to these that I address myself. But there are others who look forward to a republican form of government as a tranquil and lasting state, towards which modern society is daily impelled by the ideas and manners of the time, and who sincerely desire to prepare men to be free. When these men attack religious opinions, they obey the dictates of their passions, and not of their interests. Despotism may govern without faith, but liberty cannot. Religion is much more necessary in the republic which they set forth in glowing colors, than in the monarchy which they attack; it is more needed in democratic republics than in any others. How is it possible that society should escape destruction, if the moral tie be not strengthened in proportion as the political tie is relaxed? and what can be done with a people who are their own masters, if they be not submissive to the Deity?

Principal Causes Which Render Religion Powerful in America

The philosophers of the eighteenth century explained in a very simple manner the gradual decay of religious faith. Religious zeal, said they, must necessarily fail the more generally liberty is established and knowledge diffused. Unfortunately, the facts by no means accord with their theory. There are certain populations in Europe whose unbelief is only equaled by their ignorance and debasement; whilst in America, one of the freest and most enlightened nations in the world fulfill with fervor all the outward duties of religion.

On my arrival in the United States, the religious aspect of the country was the first thing that struck my attention; and the longer I stayed there, the more I perceived the great political consequences resulting from this new state of things. In France, I had almost always seen the spirit of religion and the spirit of freedom marching in opposite directions. But in America, I found they were intimately united, and that they reigned in common over the same country. My desire to discover the causes of this phenomenon increased from day to day. In order to satisfy it, I questioned the members of all the different sects; I sought especially the society of the clergy, who are the depositaries of the different creeds, and are especially interested in their duration. As a member of the Roman Catholic Church, I was more particularly brought into contact with several of its priests, with whom I became intimately acquainted. To each of these men I expressed my astonishment and explained my doubts: I found that they differed upon matters of detail alone, and that they all attributed the peaceful dominion of religion in their country mainly to the separation of church and state. I do not hesitate to affirm, that, during my stay in America, I did not meet a single individual, of the clergy or the laity, who was not of the same opinion upon this point.

This led me to examine more attentively than I had hitherto done the station which the American clergy occupy in political society. I learned with surprise that they filled no public appointments; I did not see one of them in the administration, and they are not even represented in the legislative assemblies. In several States, the law excludes them from political life, public opinion in all. And when I came to inquire into the prevailing spirit of the clergy, I found that most of its members seemed to retire of their own accord from the exercise of power, and that they made it the pride of their profession to abstain from politics.

I heard them inveigh against ambition and deceit, under whatever political opinions these vices might chance to lurk; but I learned from their discourses that men are not guilty in the eye of God for any opinions concerning political government which they may profess with sincerity, any more than they are for their mistakes in building a house, or in driving a furrow. I perceived that these ministers of the Gospel eschewed all parties, with the anxiety attendant upon personal interest. These facts convinced me that what I had been told was true; and it then became my object to investigate their causes, and to inquire how it happened that the real authority of religion was increased by a state of things which diminished its apparent force: these causes did not long escape my researches.

The short space of threescore years can never content the imagination of man; nor can the imperfect joys of this world satisfy his heart. Man alone, of all created beings, displays a natural contempt of existence, and yet a boundless desire to exist; he scorns life, but he dreads annihilation. These different feelings incessantly urge his soul to the contemplation of a future state, and religion directs his musings thither. Religion, then, is simply another form of hope; and it is no less natural to the human heart than hope itself. Men cannot abandon their religious faith without a kind of aberration of intellect, and a sort of violent distortion of their true nature; they are invincibly brought back to more pious sentiments. Unbelief is an accident, and faith is the only permanent state of mankind. If we consider religious institutions merely in a human point of view, they may be said to derive an inexhaustible element of strength from man himself, since they belong to one of the constituent principles of human nature.

I am aware that, at certain times, religion may strengthen this influence, which originates in itself, by the artificial power of the laws, and by the support of those temporal institutions which direct society. Religions intimately united with the governments of the earth have been known to exercise sovereign power founded on terror and faith; but when a religion contracts an alliance of this nature, I do not hesitate to affirm that it commits the same error as a man who should sacrifice his future to his present welfare; and in obtaining a power to which it has no claim, it risks that authority which is rightfully its own. When a religion founds its empire only upon the desire of immortality which lives in every human heart, it may aspire to universal dominion; but when it connects itself with a government, it must adopt maxims which are applicable only to certain nations. Thus, in forming an alliance with a political power, religion augments its authority over a few, and forfeits the hope of reigning over all.

As long as a religion rests only upon those sentiments which are the consolation of all affliction, it may attract the affections of all mankind. But if it be mixed up with the bitter passions of the world, it may be constrained to defend allies whom its interests, and not the principle of love, have given to it; or to repel as antagonists men who are still attached to it, however opposed they may be to the powers with which it is allied. The church cannot share the temporal power of the state, without being the object of a portion of that animosity which the latter excites.

The political powers which seem to be most firmly established have frequently no better guaranty for their duration than the opinions of a generation, the interests of the time, or the life of an individual. A law may modify the social condition which seems to be most fixed and determinate; and with the social condition, everything else must change. The powers of society are more or less fugitive, like the years which we spend upon earth; they succeed each other with rapidity, like the fleeting cares of life; and no government has ever yet been founded upon an invariable disposition of the human heart, or upon an imperishable interest.

As long as a religion is sustained by those feelings, propensities, and passions which are found to occur under the same forms at all periods of history, it may defy the efforts of time; or, at least, it can be destroyed only by another religion. But when religion clings to the interests of the world, it becomes almost as fragile a thing as the powers of earth. It is the only one of them all which can hope for immortality; but if it be connected with their ephemeral power, it shares their fortunes, and may fall with those transient passions which alone supported them. The alliance which religion contracts with political powers must needs be onerous to itself, since it does not require their assistance to live, and by giving them its assistance it may be exposed to decay.

The danger which I have just pointed out always exists, but it is not always equally visible. In some ages, governments seem to be imperishable; in others, the existence of society appears to be more precarious than the life of man. Some constitutions plunge the citizens into a lethargic somnolence, and others rouse them to feverish excitement. When governments seem so strong, and laws so stable, men do not perceive the dangers which may accrue from a union of church and state. When governments appear weak, and laws inconstant, the danger is self-evident, but it is no longer possible to avoid it. We must therefore learn how to perceive it from afar.

In proportion as a nation assumes a democratic condition of society, and as communities display democratic propensities, it becomes more and more dangerous to connect religion with political institutions; for the time is coming when authority will be bandied from hand to hand, when political theories will succeed each other, and when men, laws, and constitutions will disappear or be modified from day to day, and this not for a season only, but unceasingly. Agitation and mutability are inherent in the nature of democratic republics, just as stagnation and sleepiness are the law of absolute monarchies.

If the Americans, who change the head of the government once in four years, who elect new legislators every two years, and renew the State officers every twelvemonth,—if the Americans, who have given up the political world to the attempts of innovators, had not placed religion beyond their reach, where could it take firm hold in the ebb and flow of human opinions? where would be that respect which belongs to it, amidst the struggles of faction? and what would become of its immortality, in the midst of universal decay? The American clergy were the first to perceive this truth, and to act in conformity with it. They saw that they must renounce their religious influence, if they were to strive for political power; and they chose to give up the support of the state, rather than to share its vicissitudes.

In America, religion is perhaps less powerful than it has been at certain periods and among certain nations; but its influence is more lasting. It restricts itself to its own resources, but of these none can deprive it: its circle is limited, but it pervades it and holds it under undisputed control.

On every side in Europe, we hear voices complaining of the absence of religious faith, and inquiring the means of restoring to religion some remnant of its former authority. It seems to me that we must first attentively consider what ought to be *the natural state* of men, with regard to religion, at the present time; and when we know what we have to hope and to fear, we may discern the end to which our efforts ought to be directed.

The two great dangers which threaten the existence of religion are schism and indifference. In ages of fervent devotion, men sometimes abandon their religion, but they only shake one off in order to adopt another. Their faith changes its objects, but suffers no decline. The old religion then excites enthusiastic attachment or bitter enmity in either party; some leave it with anger, others cling to it with increased devotedness, and although persuasions differ, irreligion is unknown. Such, however, is not the case when a religious belief is secretly undermined by doctrines which may be termed negative, since they deny the truth of one religion without affirming that of any other. Prodigious revolutions then take place in the human mind, without the apparent co-operation of the passions of man, and almost without his knowledge. Men lose the objects of their fondest hopes, as if through forgetfulness. They are carried away by an imperceptible current, which they have not the courage to stem, but which they follow with regret, since it bears them away from a faith they love, to a skepticism that plunges them into despair.

In ages which answer to this description, men desert their religious opinions from lukewarmness rather than from dislike; they are not rejected, but they fall away. But if the unbeliever does not admit religion to be true, he still considers it useful. Regarding religious institutions in a human point of view, he acknowledges their influence upon manners and legislation. He admits that they may serve to make men live in peace, and prepare them gently for the hour of death. He regrets the faith which he has lost; and as he is deprived of a treasure of which he knows the value, he fears to take it away from those who still possess it.

On the other hand, those who continue to believe are not afraid openly to avow their faith. They look upon those who do not share their persuasion as more worthy of pity than of opposition; and they are aware, that, to acquire the esteem of the unbelieving, they are not obliged to follow their example. They are not hostile, then, to any one in the world; and as they do not consider the society in which they live as an arena in which religion is bound to face its thousand deadly foes, they love their contemporaries, whilst they condemn their weaknesses and lament their errors.

As those who do not believe conceal their incredulity, and as those who believe display their faith, public opinion pronounces itself in favor of religion: love, support, and honor are bestowed upon it, and it is only by searching the human soul that we can detect the wounds which it has received. The mass of mankind, who are never without the feeling of religion, do not perceive anything at variance with the established faith. The instinctive desire of a future life brings the crowd about the altar, and opens the hearts of men to the precepts and consolations of religion.

But this picture is not applicable to us; for there are men amongst us who have ceased to believe in Christianity, without adopting any other religion; others are in the perplexities of doubt, and already affect not to believe; and others, again, are afraid to avow that Christian faith which they still cherish in secret.

Amidst these lukewarm partisans and ardent antagonists, a small number of believers exists, who are ready to brave all obstacles, and to scorn all dangers, in defense of their faith. They have done violence to human weakness, in order to rise superior to public opinion. Excited by the effort they have made, they scarcely know where to stop; and as they know that the first use which the French made of independence was to attack religion, they look upon their contemporaries with dread, and recoil in alarm from the liberty which their fellow-citizens are seeking to obtain. As unbelief appears to them to be a novelty, they comprise all that is new in one indiscriminate animosity. They are at war with their age and country, and they look upon every opinion which is put forth there as the necessary enemy of faith.

Such is not the natural state of men with regard to religion at the present day; and some extraordinary or incidental cause must be at work in France, to prevent the human mind from following its natural inclination, and drive it beyond the limits at which it ought naturally to stop.

I am fully convinced that this extraordinary and incidental cause is the close connection of politics and religion. The unbelievers of Europe attack the Christians as their political opponents, rather than as their religious adversaries; they hate the Christian religion as the opinion of a party, much more than as an error of belief; and they reject the clergy less because they are the representatives of the Deity, than because they are the allies of government.

In Europe, Christianity has been intimately united to the powers of the earth. Those powers are now in decay, and it is, as it were, buried under their ruins. The living body of religion has been bound down to the dead corpse of superannuated polity; cut but the bonds which restrain it, and it will rise once more. I know not what could restore the Christian Church of Europe to the energy of its earlier days; that power belongs to God alone; but it may be for human policy to leave to faith the full exercise of the strength which it still retains.

How the Education, the Habits, and the Practical Experience of the Americans Promote the Success of Their Democratic Institutions

I have but little to add to what I have already said, concerning the influence which the instruction and the habits of the Americans exercise upon the maintenance of their political institutions.

America has hitherto produced very few writers of distinction; it possesses no great historians, and not a single eminent poet. The inhabitants of that country look upon literature properly so called with a kind of disapprobation; and there are towns of second-rate importance in Europe, in which more literary works are annually published than in the twenty-four States of the Union put together. The spirit of the Americans is averse to general ideas; it does not seek theoretical discoveries. Neither politics nor manufactures direct them to such speculations; and although new laws are perpetually enacted in the United States, no great writers there have hitherto inquired into the general principles of legislation. The Americans have lawyers and commentators, but no jurists; and they furnish examples rather than lessons to the world. The same observation applies to the mechanical arts. In America, the inventions of Europe are adopted with sagacity; they are perfected, and adapted with admirable skill to the wants of the country. Manufactures exist, but the science of manufacture is not cultivated; and they have good workmen, but very few inventors. Fulton was obliged to proffer his services to foreign nations for a long time, before he was able to devote them to his own country.

The observer who is desirous of forming an opinion on the state of instruction amongst the Anglo-Americans must consider the same object from two different points of view. If he singles out only the learned, he will be astonished to find how few they are; but if he counts the ignorant, the American people will appear to be the most enlightened in the world. The whole population, as I observed in another place, is situated between these two extremes.

In New England, every citizen receives the elementary notions of human knowledge; he is taught, moreover, the doctrines and the evidences of his religion, the history of his country, and the leading features of its Constitution. In the States of Connecticut and Massachusetts, it is extremely rare to find a man imperfectly acquainted with all these things, and a person wholly ignorant of them is a sort of phenomenon.

When I compare the Greek and Roman republics with these American States; the manuscript libraries of the former, and their rude population, with the innumerable journals and the enlightened people of the latter; when I remember all the attempts which are made to judge the modern republics by the aid of those of antiquity, and to infer what will happen in our time from what took place two thousand years ago,—I am tempted to burn my books, in order to apply none but novel ideas to so novel a condition of society.

What I have said of New England must not, however, be applied indistinctly to the whole Union: as we advance towards the West or the South, the instruction of the people diminishes. In the States which border on the Gulf of Mexico, a certain number of individuals may be found, as in France, who are devoid even of the rudiments of instruction. But there is not a single district in the United States sunk in complete ignorance, and for a very simple reason. The nations of Europe started from the darkness of a barbarous condition, to advance towards the light of civilization: their progress has been unequal; some of them have improved apace, whilst others have loitered in their course, and some have stopped, and are still sleeping upon the way.

Such has not been the case in the United States. The Anglo-Americans, already civilized, settled upon that territory which their descendants occupy; they had not to begin to learn, and it was sufficient for them not to forget. Now the children of these same Americans are the persons who, year by year, transport their dwellings into the wilds, and, with their dwellings, their acquired information and their esteem for knowledge. Education has taught them the utility of instruction, and has enabled them to transmit that instruction to their posterity. In the United States, society has no infancy, but it is born in man's estate.

The Americans never use the word "peasant," because they have no idea of the class which that term denotes; the ignorance of more remote ages, the simplicity of rural life, and the rusticity of the villager, have not been preserved amongst them; and they are alike unacquainted with the virtues, the vices, the coarse habits, and the simple graces of an early stage of civilization. At the extreme borders of the Confederate States, upon the confines of society and the wilderness, a population of bold adventurers have taken up their abode, who pierce the solitudes of the American woods, and seek a country there, in order to escape the poverty which awaited them in their native home. As soon as the pioneer reaches the place which is to serve him for a retreat, he fells a few trees and builds a log-house. Nothing can offer a more miserable aspect than these isolated dwellings. The traveller who approaches one of them towards nightfall sees the flicker of the hearth-flame through the chinks in the walls; and at night, if the wind rises, he hears the roof of boughs shake to and fro in the midst of the great forest-trees. Who would not suppose that this poor hut is the asylum of rudeness and ignorance? Yet no sort of comparison can be drawn between the pioneer and the dwelling which shelters him. Everything about him is primitive and wild, but he is himself the result of the labor and experience of eighteen centuries. He wears the dress and speaks the language of cities; he is acquainted with the past, curious about the future, and ready for argument upon the present; he is, in short, a highly civilized being, who consents for a time to inhabit the backwoods, and who penetrates into the wilds of the New World with the Bible, an axe, and some newspapers. It is difficult to imagine the incredible rapidity with which thought circulates in the midst of these deserts. I do not think that so much intellectual activity exists in the most enlightened and populous districts of France.

It cannot be doubted that, in the United States, the instruction of the people powerfully contributes to the support of the democratic republic; and such must always be the case, I believe, where the instruction which enlightens the understanding is not separated from the moral education which amends the heart. But I would not exaggerate this advantage, and I am still further from thinking, as so many people do think in Europe, that men can be instantaneously made citizens by teaching them to read and write. True information is mainly derived from experience; and if the Americans had not been gradually accustomed to govern themselves, their book-learning would not help them much at the present day.

I have lived much with the people in the United States, and I cannot express how much I admire their experience and their good sense. An American should never be led to speak of Europe; for he will then probably display much presumption and very foolish pride. He will take up with those crude and vague notions which are so useful to the ignorant all over the world. But if you question him respecting his own country, the cloud which dimmed his intelligence will immediately disperse; his language will become as clear and precise as his thoughts. He will inform you what his rights are, and by what means he exercises them; he will be able to point out the customs which obtain in the political world. You will find that he is well acquainted with the rules of the administration, and that he is familiar with the mechanism of the laws. The citizen of the United States does not acquire his practical science and his positive notions from books; the instruction he has acquired may have prepared him for receiving those ideas, but it did not furnish them. The American learns to know the laws by participating in the act of legislation; and he takes a lesson in the forms of government from governing. The great work of society is ever going on before his eyes, and, as it were, under his hands.

In the United States, politics are the end and aim of education; in Europe, its principal object is to fit men for private life. The interference of the citizens in public affairs is too rare an occurrence to be provided for beforehand. Upon casting a glance over society in the two hemispheres, these differences are indicated even by their external aspect.

In Europe, we frequently introduce the ideas and habits of private life into public affairs; and as we pass at once from the domestic circle to the government of the state, we may frequently be heard to discuss the great interests of society in the same manner in which we converse with our friends. The Americans, on the other hand, transport the habits of public life into their manners in private; in their country, the jury is introduced into the games of schoolboys, and parliamentary forms are observed in the order of a feast.

The Laws Contribute More to the Maintenance of the Democratic Republic in the United States than the Physical Circumstances of the Country, and the Manners More than the Laws

I have remarked that the maintenance of democratic institutions in the United States is attributable to the circumstances, the laws, and the manners of that country. Most Europeans are acquainted with only the first of these three causes, and they are apt to give it a preponderant importance which it does not really possess.

It is true that the Anglo-Americans settled in the New World in a state of social equality; the low-born and the noble were not to be found amongst them; and professional prejudices were always as unknown as the prejudices of birth. Thus, as the condition of society was democratic, the rule of democracy was established without difficulty. But this circumstance is not peculiar to the United States; almost all the American colonies were founded by men equal amongst themselves, or who became so by inhabiting them. In no one part of the New World have Europeans been able to create an aristocracy. Nevertheless, democratic institutions prosper nowhere but in the United States.

The American Union has no enemies to contend with; it stands in the wilds like an island in the ocean. But the Spaniards of South America were no less isolated by nature; yet their position has not relieved them from the charge of standing armies. They make war upon each other when they have no foreign enemies to oppose; and the Anglo-American democracy is the only one which has hitherto been able to maintain itself in peace.

The territory of the Union presents a boundless field to human activity, and inexhaustible materials for labor. The passion for wealth takes the place of ambition, and the heat of faction is mitigated by a consciousness of prosperity. But in what portion of the globe shall we find more fertile plains, mightier rivers, or more unexplored and inexhaustible riches, than in South America? Yet South America has been unable to maintain democratic institutions. If the welfare of nations depended on their being placed in a remote position, with an unbounded space of habitable territory before them, the Spaniards of South America would have no reason to complain of their fate. And although they might enjoy less prosperity than the inhabitants of the United States, their lot might still be such as to excite the envy of some nations in Europe. There are, however, no nations upon the face of the earth more miserable than those of South America.

Thus, not only are physical causes inadequate to produce results analogous to those which occur in North America, but they cannot raise the population of South America above the level of European states, where they act in a contrary direction. Physical causes do not therefore affect the destiny of nations so much as has been supposed.

I have met with men in New England who were on the point of leaving a country where they might have remained in easy circumstances, to seek their fortune in the wilds. Not far from that region, I found a French population in Canada, closely crowded on a narrow territory, although the same wilds were at hand; and whilst the emigrant from the United States purchased an extensive estate with the earnings of a short term of labor, the Canadian paid as much for land as he would have done in France. Thus Nature offers the solitudes of the New World to Europeans also; but they do not always know how to make use of her gifts. Other inhabitants of America have the same physical conditions of prosperity as the Anglo-Americans, but without their laws and their manners; and these people are miserable. The laws and manners of the Anglo-Americans are therefore that special and predominant cause of their greatness which is the object of my inquiry.

I am far from supposing that the American laws are preeminently good in themselves: I do not hold them to be applicable to all democratic nations; and several of them seem to me to be dangerous, even in the United States. But it cannot be denied that American legislation, taken as a whole, is extremely well adapted to the genius of the people and the nature of the country which it is intended to govern. The American laws are therefore good, and to them must be attributed a large portion of the success which attends the government of democracy in America: but I do not believe them to be the principal cause of that success; and if they seem to me to have more influence than the nature of the country upon the social happiness of the Americans, there is still reason to believe that their effect is inferior to that produced by the manners of the people.

The manners of the Americans of the United States are, then, the peculiar cause which renders that people the only one of the American nations that is able to support a democratic government; and it is the influence of manners which produces the different degrees of order and prosperity that may be distinguished in the several Anglo-American democracies. Thus the effect which the geographical position of a country may have upon the duration of democratic institutions is exaggerated in Europe. Too much importance is attributed to legislation, too little to manners. These three great causes serve, no doubt, to regulate and direct the American democracy; but if they were to be classed in their proper order, I should say that physical circumstances are less efficient than the laws, and the laws infinitely less so than the manners of the people. I am convinced that the most advantageous situation and the best possible laws cannot maintain a constitution in spite of the manners of a country; whilst the latter may turn to some advantage the most unfavorable positions and the worst laws. The importance of manners is a common truth to which study and experience incessantly direct our attention. It may be regarded as a central point in the range of observation, and the common termination of all my inquiries. So seriously do I insist upon this head, that, if I have hitherto failed in making the reader feel the important influence of the practical experience, the habits, the opinions, in short, of the manners of the Americans, upon the maintenance of their institutions, I have failed in the principal object of my work.

Whether Laws and Manners Are Sufficient to Maintain Democratic Institutions in Other Countries Besides America

I have asserted that the success of democratic institutions in the United States is more attributable to the laws themselves, and the manners of the people, than to the nature of the country. But does it follow that the same causes would of themselves produce the same results, if they were put in operation elsewhere; and if the country is no adequate substitute for laws and manners, can laws and manners in their turn take the place of a country? It will readily be understood that the elements of a reply to this question are wanting: other inhabitants are to be found in the New World besides the Anglo-Americans, and, as these are affected by the same physical circumstances as the latter, they may fairly be compared with them. But there are no nations out of America which have adopted the same laws and manners, though destitute of the physical advantages peculiar to the Anglo-Americans. No standard of comparison therefore exists, and we can only hazard an opinion.

It appears to me, in the first place, that a careful distinction must be made between the institutions of the United States and democratic institutions in general. When I reflect upon the state of Europe, its mighty nations, its populous cities, its formidable armies, and the complex nature of its politics, I cannot suppose that even the Anglo-Americans, if they were transported to our hemisphere, with their ideas, their religion, and their manners, could exist without considerably altering their laws. But a democratic nation may be imagined, organized differently from the American people. Is it then impossible to conceive a government really established upon the will of the majority, but in which the majority, repressing its natural instinct of equality, should consent, with a view to the order and the stability of the state, to invest a family or an individual with all the attributes of executive power? Might not a democratic society be imagined, in which the forces of the nation would be more centralized than they are in the United States; where the people would exercise a less direct and less irresistible influence upon public affairs, and yet every citizen, invested with certain rights, would participate, within his sphere, in the conduct of the government? What I have seen amongst the Anglo-Americans induces me to believe that democratic institutions of this kind, prudently introduced into society, so as gradually to mix with the habits, and to be interfused with the opinions of the people, might exist in other countries besides America. If the laws of the United States were the only imaginable democratic laws, or the most perfect which it is possible to conceive, I should admit that their success in America affords no proof of the success of democratic institutions in general, in a country less favored by nature. But as the laws of America appear to me to be defective in several respects, and as I can readily imagine others, the peculiar advantages of that country do not prove to me that democratic institutions cannot succeed in a nation less favored by circumstances, if ruled by better laws.

If human nature were different in America from what it is elsewhere, or if the social condition of the Americans created habits and opinions amongst them different from those which originate in the same social condition in the Old World, the American democracies would afford no means of predicting what may occur in other democracies. If the Americans displayed the same propensities as all other democratic nations, and if their legislators had relied upon the nature

of the country and the favor of circumstances to restrain those propensities within due limits, the prosperity of the United States, being
attributable to purely physical causes, would afford no encouragement to a people inclined to imitate their example, without sharing
their natural advantages. But neither of these suppositions is borne
out by facts.

In America, the same passions are to be met with as in Europe,—
some originating in human nature, others in the democratic condition of society. Thus, in the United States, I found that restlessness
of heart which is natural to men when all ranks are nearly equal, and
the chances of elevation are the same to all. I found there the democratic feeling of envy expressed under a thousand different forms.
I remarked that the people there frequently displayed, in the conduct
of affairs, a mixture of ignorance and presumption; and I inferred
that, in America, men are liable to the same failings and exposed to
the same evils as amongst ourselves. But, upon examining the state of
society more attentively, I speedily discovered that the Americans had
made great and successful efforts to counteract these imperfections of
human nature, and to correct the natural defects of democracy. Their
divers municipal laws appeared to me so many means of restraining
the restless ambition of the citizens within a narrow sphere, and of
turning those same passions which might have worked havoc in the
state, to the good of the township or the parish. The American legislators seem to have succeeded to some extent in opposing the idea of
right to the feelings of envy; the permanence of religious morality to
the continual shifting of politics; the experience of the people to their
theoretical ignorance; and their practical knowledge of business to
the impatience of their desires.

The Americans, then, have not relied upon the nature of their
country to counterpoise those dangers which originate in their
Constitution and their political laws. To evils which are common to
all democratic nations, they have applied remedies which none but
themselves had ever thought of; and, although they were the first
to make the experiment, they have succeeded in it. The manners
and laws of the Americans are not the only ones which may suit a
democratic people; but the Americans have shown that it would be
wrong to despair of regulating democracy by the aid of manners and
laws. If other nations should borrow this general and pregnant idea

from the Americans, without, however, intending to imitate them in the peculiar application which they have made of it; if they should attempt to fit themselves for that social condition which it seems to be the will of Providence to impose upon the generations of this age, and so to escape from the despotism or the anarchy which threatens them,—what reason is there to suppose that their efforts would not be crowned with success? The organization and the establishment of democracy in Christendom is the great political problem of our times. The Americans, unquestionably, have not resolved this problem, but they furnish useful data to those who undertake to resolve it.

Importance of What Precedes with Respect to the State Of Europe

It may readily be discovered with what intention I undertook the foregoing inquiries. The question here discussed is interesting not only to the United States, but to the whole world; it concerns, not a nation only, but all mankind. If those nations whose social condition is democratic could remain free only while they inhabit uncultivated regions, we must despair of the future destiny of the human race; for democracy is rapidly acquiring a more extended sway, and the wilds are gradually peopled with men. If it were true that laws and manners are insufficient to maintain democratic institutions, what refuge would remain open to the nations, except the despotism of one man? I am aware that there are many worthy persons at the present time who are not alarmed at this alternative, and who are so tired of liberty as to be glad of repose far from its storms. But these persons are ill acquainted with the haven towards which they are bound. Preoccupied by their remembrances, they judge of absolute power by what it has been, and not by what it might become in our times.

Is not this deserving of consideration? If men must really come to this point, that they are to be entirely emancipated or entirely enslaved,— all their rights to be made equal, or all to be taken away from them;

if the rulers of society were compelled either gradually to raise the crowd to their own level, or to allow all the citizens to fall below that of humanity,—would not the doubts of many be resolved, the consciences of many be confirmed, and the community prepared to make great sacrifices with little difficulty? In that case, the gradual growth of democratic manners and institutions should be regarded, not as the best, but as the only means of preserving freedom; and, without liking the government of democracy, it might be adopted as the most applicable, and the fairest remedy for the present ills of society.

---★---

CHAPTER XVIII

The Present and Probable Future Condition of the Three Races Which Inhabit the Territory of the United States

The principal task which I had imposed upon myself is now performed: I have shown, as far as I was able, the laws and the manners of the American democracy. Here I might stop; but the reader would perhaps feel that I had not satisfied his expectations.

An absolute and immense democracy is not all that we find in America; the inhabitants of the New World may be considered from more than one point of view. In the course of this work, my subject has often led me to speak of the Indians and the Negroes; but I have never had time to stop in order to show what place these two races occupy in the midst of the democratic people whom I was engaged in describing. I have shown in what spirit and according to what laws the Anglo-American Union was formed; but I could give only a hurried and imperfect glance at the dangers which menace that confederation, and could not furnish a detailed account of its chances of duration independently of its laws and manners. When speaking of the united republics, I hazarded no conjectures upon the permanence of republican forms in the New World; and when making frequent allusion to the commercial activity which reigns in the Union, I was unable to inquire into the future of the Americans as a commercial people.

These topics are collaterally connected with my subject without forming a part of it; they are American, without being democratic; and to portray democracy has been my principal aim. It was therefore necessary to postpone these questions, which I now take up as the proper termination of my work.

The territory now occupied or claimed by the American Union spreads from the shores of the Atlantic to those of the Pacific Ocean. On the east and west, its limits are those of the continent itself. On the south, it advances nearly to the Tropics, and it extends upward to the icy regions of the North.

The human beings who are scattered over this space do not form, as in Europe, so many branches of the same stock. Three races, naturally distinct, and, I might almost say, hostile to each other, are discoverable amongst them at the first glance. Almost insurmountable barriers had been raised between them by education and law, as well as by their origin and outward characteristics; but fortune has brought them together on the same soil, where, although they are mixed, they do not amalgamate, and each race fulfills its destiny apart.

Amongst these widely differing families of men, the first which attracts attention—the superior in intelligence, in power, and in enjoyment—is the White, or European, the MAN pre-eminently so called; below him appear the Negro and the Indian. These two unhappy races have nothing in common, neither birth, nor features, nor language, nor habits. Their only resemblance lies in their misfortunes. Both of them occupy an equally inferior position in the country they inhabit; both suffer from tyranny; and if their wrongs are not the same, they originate from the same authors.

If we reasoned from what passes in the world, we should almost say that the European is to the other races of man kind what man himself is to the lower animals: he makes them subservient to his use, and when he cannot subdue, he destroys them. Oppression has, at one stroke, deprived the descendants of the Africans of almost all the privileges of humanity. The Negro of the United States has lost even the remembrance of his country; the language which his forefathers spoke is never heard around him; he abjured their religion and forgot their customs when he ceased to belong to Africa, without acquiring any claim to European privileges. But he remains half-way between the two communities, isolated between two races; sold by the one, repulsed by the other; finding not a spot in the universe to call by the name of country, except the faint image of a home which the shelter of his master's roof affords.

The Negro has no family: woman is merely the temporary companion of his pleasures, and his children are on an equality with himself from the moment of their birth. Am I to call it a proof of God's mercy, or a visitation of his wrath, that man, in certain states, appears to be insensible to his extreme wretchedness, and almost obtains a depraved taste for the cause of his misfortunes? The Negro, plunged in this abyss of evils, scarcely feels his own calamitous situation. Violence made him a slave, and the habit of servitude gives him the thoughts and desires of a slave; he admires his tyrants more than he hates them, and finds his joy and his pride in the servile imitation of those who oppress him. His understanding is degraded to the level of his soul.

The Negro enters upon slavery as soon as he is born; nay, he may have been purchased in the womb, and have begun his slavery before he began his existence. Equally devoid of wants and of enjoyment, and useless to himself, he learns, with his first notions of existence, that he is the property of another, who has an interest in preserving his life, and that the care of it does not devolve upon himself; even the power of thought appears to him a useless gift of Providence, and he quietly enjoys all the privileges of his debasement.

If he becomes free, independence is often felt by him to be a heavier burden than slavery; for, having learned, in the course of his life, to submit to everything except reason, he is too unacquainted with her dictates to obey them. A thousand new desires beset him, and he has not the knowledge and energy necessary to resist them: these are masters which it is necessary to contend with, and he has learnt only to submit and obey. In short, he is sunk to such a depth of wretchedness, that, while servitude brutalizes, liberty destroys him.

Oppression has been no less fatal to the Indian than to the Negro race, but its effects are different. Before the arrival of white men in the New World, the inhabitants of North America lived quietly in their woods, enduring the vicissitudes and practicing the virtues and vices common to savage nations. The Europeans, having dispersed the Indian tribes and driven them into the deserts, condemned them to a wandering life, full of inexpressible sufferings.

Savage nations are only controlled by opinion and custom. When the North American Indians had lost the sentiment of attachment to their country; when their families were dispersed, their traditions obscured, and the chain of their recollections broken; when all their habits were changed, and their wants increased beyond measure,—European tyranny rendered them more disorderly and less civilized than they were before. The moral and physical condition of these tribes continually grew worse, and they became more barbarous as they became more wretched. Nevertheless, the Europeans have not been able to change the character of the Indians; and, though they have had power to destroy, they have never been able to subdue and civilize them.

The lot of the Negro is placed on the extreme limit of servitude, while that of the Indian lies on the uttermost verge of liberty; and slavery does not produce more fatal effects upon the first, than independence upon the second. The Negro has lost all property in his own person, and he cannot dispose of his existence without committing a sort of fraud. But the savage is his own master as soon as he is able to act; parental authority is scarcely known to him; he has never bent his will to that of any of his kind, nor learned the difference between voluntary obedience and a shameful subjection; and the very name of law is unknown to him. To be free, with him, signifies to escape from all the shackles of society. As he delights in this barbarous independence, and would rather perish than sacrifice the least part of it, civilization has little hold over him.

The Negro makes a thousand fruitless efforts to insinuate himself amongst men who repulse him; he conforms to the tastes of his oppressors, adopts their opinions, and hopes by imitating them to form a part of their community. Having been told from infancy that his race is naturally inferior to that of the whites, he assents to the proposition, and is ashamed of his own nature. In each of his features he discovers a trace of slavery, and, if it were in his power, he would willingly rid himself of everything that makes him what he is.

The Indian, on the contrary, has his imagination inflated with the pretended nobility of his origin, and lives and dies in the midst of these dreams of pride. Far from desiring to conform his habits to ours, he loves his savage life as the distinguishing mark of his race, and repels every advance to civilization, less, perhaps, from hatred of it, than from a dread of resembling the Europeans. While he has nothing to oppose to our perfection in the arts but the resources of the desert, to our tactics nothing but undisciplined courage,—whilst our well-digested plans are met only by the spontaneous instincts of savage life,— who can wonder if he fails in this unequal contest?

The Negro, who earnestly desires to mingle his race with that of the European, cannot do so; while the Indian, who might succeed to a certain extent, disdains to make the attempt. The servility of the one dooms him to slavery, the pride of the other to death.

The Present and Probable Future Condition of the Indian Tribes Which Inhabit the Territory Possessed by the Union

None of the Indian tribes which formerly inhabited the territory of New England—the Narragansetts, the Mohicans, the Pequots—have any existence but in the recollection of man. The Lenapes, who received William Penn, a hundred and fifty years ago, upon the banks of the Delaware, have disappeared; and I myself met with the last of the Iroquois, who were begging alms. The nations I have mentioned formerly covered the country to the sea-coast; but a traveller at the present day must penetrate more than a hundred leagues into the interior of the continent to find an Indian. Not only have these wild tribes receded, but they are destroyed; and as they give way or perish, an immense and increasing people fill their place. There is no instance upon record of so prodigious a growth or so rapid a destruction: the manner in which the latter change takes place is not difficult to describe.

When the Indians were the sole inhabitants of the wilds whence they have since been expelled, their wants were few. Their arms were of their own manufacture, their only drink was the water of the brook, and their clothes consisted of the skins of animals, whose flesh furnished them with food.

The Europeans introduced amongst the savages of North America fire-arms, ardent spirits, and iron: they taught them to exchange for manufactured stuffs the rough garments which had previously satisfied their untutored simplicity. Having acquired new tastes, without the arts by which they could be gratified, the Indians were obliged to have recourse to the workmanship of the whites; but in return for their productions, the savage had nothing to offer except the rich furs which still abounded in his woods. Hence the chase became necessary, not merely to provide for his subsistence, but to satisfy the frivolous desires of Europeans. He no longer hunted merely to obtain food, but to procure the only objects of barter which he could offer. Whilst the wants of the natives were thus increasing, their resources continued to diminish.

From the moment when a European settlement is formed in the neighborhood of the territory occupied by the Indians, the beasts of chase take the alarm. Thousands of savages, wandering in the forests, and destitute of any fixed dwelling, did not disturb them; but as soon as the continuous sounds of European labor are heard in their neighborhood, they begin to flee away, and retire to the West, where their instinct teaches them that they will still find deserts of immeasurable extent. "The buffalo is constantly receding," say Messrs. Clarke and Cass in their Report of the year 1829; "a few years since they approached the base of the Alleghany; and a few years hence they may even be rare upon the immense plains which extend to the base of the Rocky Mountains." I have been assured that this effect of the approach of the whites is often felt at two hundred leagues' distance from their frontier. Their influence is thus exerted over tribes whose name is unknown to them; and who suffer the evils of usurpation long before they are acquainted with the authors of their distress.

Bold adventurers soon penetrate into the country the Indians have deserted, and when they have advanced about fifteen or twenty leagues from the extreme frontiers of the whites, they begin to build habitations for civilized beings in the midst of the wilderness. This is done without difficulty, as the territory of a hunting nation is ill defined; it is the common property of the tribe, and belongs to no one in particular, so that individual interests are not concerned in protecting any part of it.

A few European families, occupying points very remote from each other, soon drive away the wild animals which remain between their places of abode. The Indians, who had previously lived in a sort of abundance, then find it difficult to subsist, and still more difficult to procure the articles of barter which they stand in need of. To drive away their game has the same effect as to render sterile the fields of our agriculturists; deprived of the means of subsistence, they are reduced, like famished wolves, to prowl through the forsaken woods in quest of prey. Their instinctive love of country attaches them to the soil which gave them birth, even after it has ceased to yield anything but misery and death. At length, they are compelled to acquiesce and depart: they follow the traces of the elk, the buffalo, and the beaver, and are guided by these wild animals in the choice of their future country. Properly speaking, therefore, it is not the Europeans who drive away the natives of America; it is famine;—a happy distinction, which had escaped the casuists of former times, and for which we are indebted to modern discovery!

It is impossible to conceive the frightful sufferings which attend these forced migrations. They are undertaken by a people already exhausted and reduced; and the countries to which the new-comers betake themselves are inhabited by other tribes, which receive them with jealous hostility. Hunger is in the rear, war awaits them, and misery besets them on all sides. To escape from so many enemies, they separate, and each individual endeavors to procure secretly the means of supporting his existence by isolating himself, living in the immensity of the desert like an outcast in civilized society. The social tie, which distress had long since weakened, is then dissolved; they have no longer a country, and soon they will not be a people; their very families are obliterated; their common name is forgotten; their language perishes; and all traces of their origin disappear. Their nation has ceased to exist, except in the recollection of the antiquaries of America, and a few of the learned of Europe.

I should be sorry to have my reader suppose that I am coloring the picture too highly: I saw with my own eyes many of the miseries which I have just described, and was the witness of sufferings which I have not the power to portray.

At the end of the year 1831, whilst I was on the left bank of the Mississippi, at a place named by Europeans Memphis, there arrived a numerous band of Choctaws (or Chactas, as they are called by the French in Louisiana). These savages had left their country, and were endeavoring to gain the right bank of the Mississippi, where they hoped to find an asylum which had been promised them by the American government. It was then the middle of winter, and the cold was unusually severe; the snow had frozen hard upon the ground, and the river was drifting huge masses of ice. The Indians had their families with them; and they brought in their train the wounded and the sick, with children newly born, and old men upon the verge of death. They possessed neither tents nor wagons, but only their arms and some provisions. I saw them embark to pass the mighty river, and never will that solemn spectacle fade from my remembrance. No cry, no sob, was heard amongst the assembled crowd; all were silent. Their calamities were of ancient date, and they knew them to be irremediable. The Indians had all stepped into the bark which was to carry them across, but their dogs remained upon the bank. As soon as these animals perceived that their masters were finally leaving the shore, they set up a dismal howl, and, plunging all together into the icy waters of the Mississippi, swam after the boat.

The ejectment of the Indians often takes place at the present day in a regular, and, as it were, a legal manner. When the European population begins to approach the limit of the desert inhabited by a savage tribe, the government of the United States usually sends forward envoys, who assemble the Indians in a large plain, and, having first eaten and drunk with them, address them thus: "What have you to do in the land of your fathers? Before long, you must dig up their bones in order to live. In what respect is the country you inhabit better than another? Are there no woods, marshes, or prairies, except where you dwell? And can you live nowhere but under your own sun? Beyond those mountains which you see at the horizon, beyond the lake which bounds your territory on the west, there lie vast countries where beasts of chase are yet found in great abundance; sell us your lands, then, and go to live happily in those solitudes." After holding this language, they spread before the eyes of the Indians fire-arms, woolen garments, kegs of brandy, glass necklaces, bracelets of tinsel, ear-rings, and looking-glasses. If, when they have beheld all these riches, they still hesitate, it is insinuated that they cannot refuse the required consent, and that the government itself will not long have the power of protecting them in their rights. What are they to do? Half convinced and half compelled, they go to inhabit new deserts, where the importunate whites will not let them remain ten years in peace. In this manner do the Americans obtain, at a very low price, whole provinces, which the richest sovereigns of Europe could not purchase.

These are great evils; and it must be added that they appear to me to be irremediable. I believe that the Indian nations of North America are doomed to perish; and that whenever the Europeans shall be established on the shores of the Pacific Ocean, that race of men will have ceased to exist. The Indians had only the alternative of war or civilization; in other words, they must either destroy the Europeans or become their equals.

At the first settlement of the colonies, they might have found it possible, by uniting their forces, to deliver themselves from the small bodies of strangers who landed on their continent. They several times attempted to do it, and were on the point of succeeding; but the disproportion of their resources at the present day, when compared with those of the whites, is too great to allow such an enterprise to be thought of. But from time to time among the Indians, men of sagacity and energy foresee the final destiny which awaits the native population, and exert themselves to unite all the tribes in common hostility to the Europeans; but their efforts are unavailing. The tribes which are in the neighborhood of the whites are too much weakened to offer an effectual resistance; whilst the others, giving way to that childish carelessness of the morrow which characterizes savage life, wait for the near approach of danger before they prepare to meet it: some are unable, others are unwilling, to act.

It is easy to foresee that the Indians will never civilize themselves, or that it will be too late when they may be inclined to make the experiment.

Civilization is the result of a long social process, which takes place in the same spot, and is handed down from one generation to another, each one profiting by the experience of the last. Of all nations, those submit to civilization with the most difficulty who habitually live by the chase. Pastoral tribes, indeed, often change their place of abode; but they follow a regular order in their migrations, and often return to their old stations, whilst the dwelling of the hunter varies with that of the animals he pursues.

Several attempts have been made to diffuse knowledge amongst the Indians, leaving unchecked their wandering propensities, by the Jesuits in Canada, and by the Puritans in New England; but none of these endeavors have been crowned by any lasting success. Civilization began in the cabin, but soon retired to expire in the woods. The great error of these legislators of the Indians was their not understanding that, in order to succeed in civilizing a people, it is first necessary to fix them, which cannot be done without inducing them to cultivate the soil; the Indians ought in the first place to have been accustomed to agriculture. But not only are they destitute of this indispensable preliminary to civilization,—they would even have great difficulty in acquiring it. Men who have once abandoned themselves to the restless and adventurous life of the hunter feel an insurmountable disgust for the constant and regular labor which tillage requires. We see this proved even in our own societies; but it is far more visible among races whose partiality for the chase is a part of their national character.

Independently of this general difficulty, there is another, which applies peculiarly to the Indians. They consider labor not merely as an evil, but as a disgrace; so that their pride contends against civilization as obstinately as their indolence.

There is no Indian so wretched as not to retain under his hut of bark a lofty idea of his personal worth; he considers the cares of industry as degrading occupations; he compares the husbandman to the ox which traces the furrow; and in each of our handicrafts, he can see only the labor of slaves. Not that he is devoid of admiration for the power and intellectual greatness of the whites; but, although the result of our efforts surprises him, he contemns the means by which we obtain it; and while he acknowledges our ascendency, he still believes in his own superiority. War and hunting are the only pursuits which appear to him worthy of a man. The Indian, in the dreary solitudes of his woods, cherishes the same ideas, the same opinions, as the noble of the Middle Ages in his castle; and he only needs to become a conqueror to complete the resemblance. Thus, however strange it may seem, it is in the forests of the New World, and not amongst the Europeans who people its coasts, that the ancient prejudices of Europe still exist.

More than once, in the course of this work, I have endeavored to explain the prodigious influence which the social condition appears to exercise upon the laws and the manners of men; and I beg to add a few words on the same subject.

When I perceive the resemblance which exists between the political institutions of our ancestors, the Germans, and the wandering tribes of North America,—between the customs described by Tacitus, and those of which I have sometimes been a witness,—I cannot help thinking that the same cause has brought about the same results in both hemispheres; and that, in the midst of the apparent diversity of human affairs, certain primary facts may be discovered, from which all the others are derived. In what we usually call the German institutions, then, I am inclined to perceive only barbarian habits, and the opinions of savages in what we style feudal principles.

However strongly the vices and prejudices of the North American Indians may be opposed to their becoming agricultural and civilized, necessity sometimes drives them to it. Several of the Southern tribes, considerably numerous, and amongst others the Cherokees and the Creeks, found themselves, as it were, surrounded by Europeans, who had landed on the shores of the Atlantic, and, either descending the Ohio, or proceeding up the Mississippi, arrived simultaneously upon their borders. These tribes had not been driven from place to place, like their Northern brethren; but they had been gradually shut up within narrow limits, like game driven into an enclosure before the huntsmen plunge among them. The Indians, who were thus placed between civilization and death, found themselves obliged to live igno-miniously by labor, like the whites. They took to agriculture, and, without entirely forsaking their old habits or manners, sacrificed only as much as was necessary to their existence.

The Cherokees went further; they created a written language, established a permanent form of government, and, as everything proceeds rapidly in the New World, before they all of them had clothes, they set up a newspaper.

The development of European habits has been much accelerated among these Indians by the mixed race which has sprung up. Deriving intelligence from the father's side, without entirely losing the savage customs of the mother, the half-blood forms the natural link between civilization and barbarism. Wherever this race has multiplied, the savage state has become modified, and a great change has taken place in the manners of the people.

The success of the Cherokees proves that the Indians are capable of civilization, but it does not prove that they will succeed in it. This difficulty which the Indians find in submitting to civilization proceeds from a general cause, the influence of which it is almost impossible for them to escape. An attentive survey of history demonstrates that, in general, barbarous nations have raised themselves to civilization by degrees, and by their own efforts. Whenever they derived knowledge from a foreign people, they stood towards them in the relation of conquerors, and not of a conquered nation. When the conquered nation is enlightened, and the conquerors are half savage, as in the invasion of the Roman empire by the Northern nations, or that of China by the Mongols, the power which victory bestows upon the barbarian is sufficient to keep up his importance among civilized men, and permit him to rank as their equal until he becomes their rival. The one has might on his side, the other has intelligence; the former admires the knowledge and the arts of the conquered, the latter envies the power of the conquerors. The barbarians at length admit civilized man into their palaces, and he in turn opens his schools to the barbarians. But when the side on which the physical force lies also possesses an intellectual superiority, the conquered party seldom become civilized; it retreats, or is destroyed. It may therefore be said, in a general way, that savages go forth in arms to seek knowledge, but do not receive it when it comes to them.

If the Indian tribes which now inhabit the heart of the continent could summon up energy enough to attempt to civilize themselves, they might possibly succeed. Superior already to the barbarous nations which surround them, they would gradually gain strength and experience, and when the Europeans should appear upon their borders, they would be in a state, if not to maintain their independence, at least to assert their right to the soil, and to incorporate themselves with the conquerors. But it is the misfortune of Indians to be brought into contact with a civilized people, who are also (it must be owned) the most grasping nation on the globe, whilst they are still semi-barbarian; to find their masters in their instructors, and to receive knowledge and oppression at once. Living in the freedom of the woods, the North American Indian was destitute, but he had no feeling of inferiority towards any one; as soon, however, as he desires to penetrate into the social scale of the whites, he can only take the lowest rank in society, for he enters, ignorant and poor, within the pale of science and wealth. After having led a life of agitation, beset with evils and dangers, but at the same time filled with proud emotions, he is obliged to submit to a wearisome, obscure, and degraded state. To gain the bread which nourishes him by hard and ignoble labor,—this is in his eyes the only result of which civilization can boast; and even this he is not always sure to obtain.

The Indians, in the little which they have done, have unquestionably displayed as much natural genius as the peoples of Europe in their greatest undertakings; but nations as well as men require time to learn, whatever may be their intelligence and their zeal. Whilst the savages were endeavoring to civilize themselves, the Europeans continued to surround them on every side, and to confine them within narrower limits; the two races gradually met, and they are now in immediate contact with each other. The Indian is already superior to his barbarous parent, but he is still far below his white neighbor. With their resources and acquired knowledge, the Europeans soon appropriated to themselves most of the advantages which the natives might have derived from the possession of the soil: they have settled among them, have purchased land at a low rate, or have occupied it by force, and the Indians have been ruined by a competition which they had not the means of sustaining. They were isolated in their own country, and their race only constituted a little colony of troublesome strangers in the midst of a numerous and dominant people.

Washington said, in one of his messages to Congress, "We are more enlightened and more powerful than the Indian nations; we are therefore bound in honor to treat them with kindness, and even with generosity." But this virtuous and high-minded policy has not been followed. The rapacity of the settlers is usually backed by the tyranny of the government. Although the Cherokees and the Creeks are established upon territory which they inhabited before the arrival of the Europeans, and although the Americans have frequently treated with them as with foreign nations, the surrounding States have not been willing to acknowledge them as an independent people, and have undertaken to subject these children of the woods to Anglo-American magistrates, laws, and customs. Destitution had driven these unfortunate Indians to civilization, and oppression now drives them back to barbarism: many of them abandon the soil which they had begun to clear, and return to the habits of savage life.

If we consider the tyrannical measures which have been adopted by the legislatures of the Southern States, the conduct of their Governors, and the decrees of their courts of justice, we shall be convinced that the entire expulsion of the Indians is the final result to which all the efforts of their policy are directed. The Americans of that part of the Union look with jealousy upon the lands which the natives still possess; they are aware that these tribes have not yet lost the traditions of savage life, and before civilization has permanently fixed them to the soil, it is intended to force them to depart by reducing them to despair. The Creeks and Cherokees, oppressed by the several States, have appealed to the central government, which is by no means insensible to their misfortunes, and is sincerely desirous of saving the remnant of the natives, and of maintaining them in the free possession of that territory which the Union has guaranteed to them. But the several States oppose so formidable a resistance to the execution of this design, that the government is obliged to consent to the extirpation of a few barbarous tribes, already half destroyed, in order not to endanger the safety of the American Union.

But the Federal government, which is not able to protect the Indians, would fain mitigate the hardships of their lot; and, with this intention, it has undertaken to transport them into remote regions at the public cost.

Between the 33d and 37th degrees of north latitude, a vast tract of country lies, which has taken the name of Arkansas, from the principal river that waters it. It is bounded on the one side by the confines of Mexico, on the other by the Mississippi. Numberless streams cross it in every direction; the climate is mild, and the soil productive, and it is inhabited only by a few wandering hordes of savages. The government of the Union wishes to transport the broken remnants of the indigenous population of the South to the portion of this country which is nearest to Mexico, and at a great distance from the American settlements.

We were assured, towards the end of the year 1831, that 10,000 Indians had already gone to the shores of the Arkansas, and fresh detachments were constantly following them. But Congress has been unable to create a unanimous determination in those whom it is disposed to protect. Some, indeed, joyfully consent to quit the seat of oppression; but the most enlightened members of the community refuse to abandon their recent dwellings and their springing crops; they are of opinion that the work of civilization, once interrupted, will never be resumed; they fear that those domestic habits which have been so recently contracted may be irrevocably lost in the midst of a country which is still barbarous, and where nothing is prepared for the subsistence of an agricultural people; they know that their entrance into those wilds will be opposed by hostile hordes, and that they have lost the energy of barbarians, without having yet acquired the resources of civilization to resist their attacks. Moreover, the Indians readily discover that the settlement which is proposed to them is merely temporary. Who can assure them that they will at length be allowed to dwell in peace in their new retreat? The United States pledge themselves to maintain them there; but the territory which they now occupy was formerly secured to them by the most solemn oaths. The American government does not indeed now rob them of their lands, but it allows perpetual encroachments on them. In a few years, the same white population which now flocks around them will doubtless track them anew to the solitudes of the Arkansas; they will then be exposed to the same evils, without the same remedies; and as the limits of the earth will at last fail them, their only refuge is the grave.

The Union treats the Indians with less cupidity and violence than the several States, but the two governments are alike deficient in good faith. The States extend what they call the benefits of their laws to the Indians, believing that the tribes will recede rather than submit to them; and the central government, which promises a permanent refuge to these unhappy beings in the West, is well aware of its inability to secure it to them. Thus the tyranny of the States obliges the savages to retire; the Union, by its promises and resources, facilitates their retreat; and these measures tend to precisely the same end.

"By the will of our Father in Heaven, the Governor of the whole world," said the Cherokees, in their petition to Congress, "the red man of America has become small, and the white man great and renowned. When the ancestors of the people of these United States first came to the shores of America, they found the red man strong: though he was ignorant and savage, yet he received them kindly, and gave them dry land to rest their weary feet. They met in peace, and shook hands in token of friendship. Whatever the white man wanted and asked of the Indian, the latter willingly gave. At that time, the Indian was the lord, and the white man the suppliant. But now the scene has changed. The strength of the red man has become weakness. As his neighbors increased in numbers, his power became less and less; and now, of the many and powerful tribes who once covered these United States, only a few are to be seen,—a few whom a sweeping pestilence has left.

The Northern tribes, who were once so numerous and powerful, are now nearly extinct. Thus it has happened to the red man of America. Shall we, who are remnants, share the same fate?

"The land on which we stand we have received as an inheritance from our fathers, who possessed it from time immemorial, as a gift from our common Father in Heaven. They bequeathed it to us as their children, and we have sacredly kept it, as containing the remains of our beloved men. This right of inheritance we have never ceded, nor ever forfeited. Permit us to ask, what better right can the people have to a country than the right of inheritance and immemorial peaceable possession? We know it is said of late by the State of Georgia and by the Executive of the United States, that we have forfeited this right; but we think this is said gratuitously. At what time have we made the forfeit? What great crime have we committed, whereby we must forever be divested of our country and rights? Was it when we were hostile to the United States, and took part with the king of Great Britain, during the struggle for independence? If so, why was not this forfeiture declared in the first treaty of peace between the United States and our beloved men? Why was not such an article as the following inserted in the treaty: 'The United States give peace to the Cherokees, but, for the part they took in the late war, declare them to be but tenants at will, to be removed when the convenience of the States within whose chartered limits they live shall require it'? That was the proper time to assume such a possession. But it was not thought of; nor would our forefathers have agreed to any treaty whose tendency was to deprive them of their rights and their country."

Such is the language of the Indians: what they say is true; what they foresee seems inevitable. From whichever side we consider the destinies of the aborigines of North America, their calamities appear irremediable: if they continue barbarous, they are forced to retire; if they attempt to civilize themselves, the contact of a more civilized community subjects them to oppression and destitution. They perish if they continue to wander from waste to waste, and if they attempt to settle, they still must perish. The assistance of Europeans is necessary to instruct them, but the approach of Europeans corrupts and repels them into savage life. They refuse to change their habits as long as their solitudes are their own, and it is too late to change them when at last they are constrained to submit.

The Spaniards pursued the Indians with blood-hounds, like wild beasts; they sacked the New World like a city taken by storm, with no discernment or compassion; but destruction must cease at last, and frenzy has a limit: the remnant of the Indian population which had escaped the massacre mixed with its conquerors, and adopted in the end their religion and their manners. The conduct of the Americans of the United States towards the aborigines is characterized, on the other hand, by a singular attachment to the formalities of law. Provided that the Indians retain their barbarous condition, the Americans take no part in their affairs; they treat them as independent nations, and do not possess themselves of their hunting-grounds without a treaty of purchase; and if an Indian nation happen to be so encroached upon as to be unable to subsist upon their territory, they kindly take them by the hand and transport them to a grave far from the land of their fathers.

The Spaniards were unable to exterminate the Indian race by those unparalleled atrocities which brand them with indelible shame, nor did they even succeed in wholly depriving it of its rights; but the Americans of the United States have accomplished this twofold purpose with singular felicity, tranquilly, legally, philanthropically, without shedding blood, and without violating a single great principle of morality in the eyes of the world. It is impossible to destroy men with more respect for the laws of humanity.

Situation of the Black Population in the United States, and Dangers with Which its Presence Threatens the Whites

The Indians will perish in the same isolated condition in which they have lived; but the destiny of the Negroes is in some measure interwoven with that of the Europeans. These two races are fastened to each other without intermingling; and they are alike unable to separate entirely or to combine. The most formidable of all the ills which threaten the future of the Union arises from the presence of a black population upon its territory; and in contemplating the cause of the present embarrassments, or the future dangers of the United States, the observer is invariably led to this as a primary fact.

Generally speaking, men must make great and unceasing efforts before permanent evils are created; but there is one calamity which penetrated furtively into the world, and which was at first scarcely distinguishable amidst the ordinary abuses of power: it originated with an individual whose name history has not preserved; it was wafted like some accursed germ upon a portion of the soil; but it afterwards nurtured itself, grew without effort, and spread naturally with the society to which it belonged. This calamity is slavery. Christianity suppressed slavery, but the Christians of the sixteenth century re-established it,—as an exception, indeed, to their social system, and restricted to one of the races of mankind; but the wound thus inflicted upon humanity, though less extensive, was far more difficult of cure.

It is important to make an accurate distinction between slavery itself and its consequences. The immediate evils produced by slavery were very nearly the same in antiquity as they are amongst the moderns; but the consequences of these evils were different. The slave, amongst the ancients, belonged to the same race as his master, and was often the superior of the two in education and intelligence. Freedom was the only distinction between them; and when freedom was conferred, they were easily confounded together. The ancients, then, had a very simple means of ridding themselves of slavery and its consequences,—that of enfranchisement; and they succeeded as soon as they adopted this measure generally. Not but that, in ancient states, the vestiges of servitude subsisted for some time after servitude itself was abolished. There is a natural prejudice which prompts men to despise whomsoever has been their inferior long after he is become their equal; and the real inequality which is produced by fortune or by law is always succeeded by an imaginary inequality which is implanted in the manners of the people. But, among the ancients, this secondary consequence of slavery had a natural limit; for the freedman bore so entire a resemblance to those born free, that it soon became impossible to distinguish him from them.

The greatest difficulty in antiquity was that of altering the law; amongst the moderns, it is that of altering the manners; and, as far as we are concerned, the real obstacles begin where those of the ancients left off. This arises from the circumstance that, amongst the moderns, the abstract and transient fact of slavery is fatally united with the physical and permanent fact of color. The tradition of slavery dishonors the race, and the peculiarity of the race perpetuates the tradition of slavery. No African has ever voluntarily emigrated to the shores of the New World, whence it follows that all the blacks who are now found there are either slaves or freedmen. Thus the Negro transmits the eternal mark of his ignominy to all his descendants; and although the law may abolish slavery, God alone can obliterate the traces of its existence.

The modern slave differs from his master not only in his condition, but in his origin. You may set the Negro free, but you cannot make him otherwise than an alien to the European. Nor is this all; we scarcely acknowledge the common features of humanity in this stranger whom slavery has brought amongst us. His physiognomy is to our eyes hideous, his understanding weak, his tastes low; and we are almost inclined to look upon him as a being intermediate between man and the brutes. The moderns, then, after they have abolished slavery, have three prejudices to contend against, which are less easy to attack, and far less easy to conquer, than the mere fact of servitude,—the prejudice of the master, the prejudice of the race, and the prejudice of color.

It is difficult for us, who have had the good fortune to be born amongst men like ourselves by nature, and our equals by law, to conceive the irreconcilable differences which separate the Negro from the European in America. But we may derive some faint notion of them from analogy. France was formerly a country in which numerous inequalities existed, that had been created by law. Nothing can be more fictitious than a purely legal inferiority,—nothing more contrary to the instinct of mankind than these permanent divisions established between beings evidently similar. Yet these divisions subsisted for ages; they still subsist in many places; and everywhere they have left imaginary vestiges, which time alone can efface. If it be so difficult to root out an inequality which originates solely in the law, how are those distinctions to be destroyed which seem to be based upon the immutable laws of Nature herself? When I remember the extreme difficulty with which aristocratic bodies, of whatever nature they may be, are commingled with the mass of the people, and the exceeding care which they take to preserve for ages the ideal boundaries of their caste inviolate, I despair of seeing an aristocracy disappear which is founded upon visible and indelible signs. Those who hope that the Europeans will ever be amalgamated with the Negroes appear to me to delude themselves: I am not led to any such conclusion by my reason, or by the evidence of facts. Hitherto, wherever the whites have been the most powerful, they have held the blacks in degradation or in slavery; wherever the Negroes have been strongest, they have destroyed the whites: this has been the only balance which has ever taken place between the two races.

I see that, in a certain portion of the territory of the United States, at the present day, the legal barrier which separated the two races is falling away, but not that which exists in the manners of the country; slavery recedes, but the prejudice to which it has given birth is immovable. Whoever has inhabited the United States must have perceived, that, in those parts of the Union in which the Negroes are no longer slaves, they have in no wise drawn nearer to the whites. On the contrary, the prejudice of race appears to be stronger in the States which have abolished slavery, than in those where it still exists; and nowhere is it so intolerant as in those States where servitude has never been known.

It is true, that in the North of the Union marriages may be legally contracted between Negroes and whites; but public opinion would stigmatize as infamous a man who should connect himself with a Negress, and it would be difficult to cite a single instance of such a union. The electoral franchise has been conferred upon the Negroes in almost all the States in which slavery has been abolished; but if they come forward to vote, their lives are in danger. If oppressed, they may bring an action at law, but they will find none but whites amongst their judges; and although they may legally serve as jurors, prejudice repels them from that office. The same schools do not receive the children of the black and of the European. In the theatres, gold cannot procure a seat for the servile race beside their former masters; in the hospitals, they lie apart; and although they are allowed to invoke the same God as the whites, it must be at a different altar, and in their own churches, with their own clergy. The gates of Heaven are not closed against them; but their inferiority is continued to the very confines of the other world. When the Negro dies, his bones are cast aside, and the distinction of condition prevails even in the equality of death. Thus the Negro is free, but he can share neither the rights, nor the pleasures, nor the labor, nor the afflictions, nor the tomb of him whose equal he has been declared to be; and he cannot meet him upon fair terms in life or in death.

In the South, where slavery still exists, the Negroes are less carefully kept apart; they sometimes share the labors and the recreations of the whites; the whites consent to intermix with them to a certain extent, and although legislation treats them more harshly, the habits of the people are more tolerant and compassionate. In the South, the master is not afraid to raise his slave to his own standing, because he knows that he can in a moment reduce him to the dust, at pleasure. In the North, the white no longer distinctly perceives the barrier which separates him from the degraded race, and he shuns the Negro with the more pertinacity, since he fears lest they should some day be confounded together.

Amongst the Americans of the South, Nature sometimes reasserts her rights, and restores a transient equality between the blacks and the whites; but in the North, pride restrains the most imperious of human passions. The American of the Northern States would, perhaps, allow the Negress to share his licentious pleasures, if the laws of his country did not declare that she may aspire to be the legitimate partner of his bed; but he recoils with horror from her who might become his wife.

Thus it is, in the United States, that the prejudice which repels the Negroes seems to increase in proportion as they are emancipated, and inequality is sanctioned by the manners whilst it is effaced from the laws of the country. But if the relative position of the two races which inhabit the United States is such as I have described, why have the Americans abolished slavery in the North of the Union, why do they maintain it in the South, and why do they aggravate its hardships? The answer is easily given. It is not for the good of the Negroes, but for that of the whites, that measures are taken to abolish slavery in the United States.

The first Negroes were imported into Virginia about the year 1621. In America, therefore, as well as in the rest of the globe, slavery originated in the South. Thence it spread from one settlement to another; but the number of slaves diminished towards the Northern States, and the Negro population was always very limited in New England.

A century had scarcely elapsed since the foundation of the Colonies, when the attention of the planters was struck by the extraordinary fact, that the provinces which were comparatively destitute of slaves increased in population, in wealth, and in prosperity more rapidly than those which contained many of them. In the former, however, the inhabitants were obliged to cultivate the soil themselves, or by hired laborers; in the latter, they were furnished with hands for which they paid no wages. Yet, though labor and expense were on the one side, and ease with economy on the other, the former had the more advantageous system. This result seemed the more difficult to explain, since the settlers, who all belonged to the same European race, had the same habits, the same civilization, the same laws, and their shades of difference were extremely slight.

Time, however, continued to advance; and the Anglo-Americans, spreading beyond the coasts of the Atlantic Ocean, penetrated farther and farther into the solitudes of the West; they met there with a new soil and an unwonted climate; they had to overcome obstacles of the most various character; their races intermingled, the inhabitants of the South going up towards the North, those of the North descending to the South. But in the midst of all these causes, the same result occurred at every step; in general, the colonies in which there were no slaves became more populous and more prosperous than those in which slavery flourished. The farther they went, the more was it shown that slavery, which is so cruel to the slave, is prejudicial to the master.

But this truth was most satisfactorily demonstrated when civilization reached the banks of the Ohio. The stream which the Indians had distinguished by the name of Ohio, or the Beautiful River, waters one of the most magnificent valleys which has ever been made the abode of man. Undulating lands extend upon both shores of the Ohio, whose soil affords inexhaustible treasures to the laborer; on either bank, the air is equally wholesome and the climate mild; and each of them forms the extreme frontier of a vast State: that which follows the numerous windings of the Ohio upon the left is called Kentucky; that upon the right bears the name of the river. These two States differ only in a single respect; Kentucky has admitted slavery, but the State of Ohio has prohibited the existence of slaves within its borders. Thus the traveller who floats down the current of the Ohio, to the spot where that river falls into the Mississippi, may be said to sail between liberty and servitude; and a transient inspection of surrounding objects will convince him which of the two is more favorable to humanity.

Upon the left bank of the stream, the population is sparse,—from time to time, one descries a troop of slaves loitering in the half-desert fields; the primeval forest reappears at every turn; society seems to be asleep, man to be idle, and nature alone offers a scene of activity and life.

From the right bank, on the contrary, a confused hum is heard, which proclaims afar the presence of industry; the fields are covered with abundant harvests; the elegance of the dwellings announces the taste and activity of the laborers; and man appears to be in the enjoyment of that wealth and contentment which is the reward of labor.

The State of Kentucky was founded in 1775, the State of Ohio only twelve years later; but twelve years are more in America than half a century in Europe; and, at the present day, the population of Ohio exceeds that of Kentucky by two hundred and fifty thousand souls. These different effects of slavery and freedom may readily be understood; and they suffice to explain many of the differences which we remark between the civilization of antiquity and that of our own time.

Upon the left bank of the Ohio, labor is confounded with the idea of slavery, while upon the right bank, it is identified with that of prosperity and improvement; on the one side, it is degraded, on the other, it is honored; on the former territory, no white laborers can be found, for they would be afraid of assimilating themselves to the Negroes,—all the work is done by slaves; on the latter, no one is idle, for the white population extend their activity and intelligence to every kind of employment. Thus, the men whose task it is to cultivate the rich soil of Kentucky are ignorant and apathetic; whilst those who are active and enlightened either do nothing, or pass over into Ohio, where they may work without shame.

It is true that, in Kentucky, the planters are not obliged to pay the slaves whom they employ; but they derive small profits from their labor, whilst the wages paid to free workmen would be returned with interest in the value of their services. The free workman is paid, but he does his work quicker than the slave; and rapidity of execution is one of the great elements of economy. The white sells his services, but they are only purchased when they may be useful; the black can claim no remuneration for his toil, but the expense of his maintenance is perpetual; he must be supported in his old age as well as in manhood, in his profitless infancy as well as in the productive years of youth, in sickness as well as in health. Payment must equally be made in order to obtain the services of either class of men: the free workman receives his wages in money; the slave in education, in food, in care, and in clothing. The money which a master spends in the maintenance of his slaves goes gradually and in detail, so that it is scarcely perceived; the salary of the free workman is paid in a round sum, and appears to enrich only him who receives it; but in the end, the slave has cost more than the free servant, and his labor is less productive.

The influence of slavery extends still further: it affects the character of the master, and imparts a peculiar tendency to his ideas and tastes. Upon both banks of the Ohio, the character of the inhabitants is enterprising and energetic; but this vigor is very differently exercised in the two States. The white inhabitant of Ohio, obliged to subsist by his own exertions, regards temporal prosperity as the chief aim of his existence; and as the country which he occupies presents inexhaustible resources to his industry, and ever-varying lures to his activity, his acquisitive ardor surpasses the ordinary limits of human cupidity: he is tormented by the desire of wealth, and he boldly enters upon every path which fortune opens to him; he becomes a sailor, a pioneer, an artisan, or a cultivator, with the same indifference, and supports with equal constancy the fatigues and the dangers incidental to these various professions; the resources of his intelligence are astonishing, and his avidity in the pursuit of gain amounts to a species of heroism.

But the Kentuckian scorns not only labor, but all the undertakings which labor promotes; as he lives in an idle independence, his tastes are those of an idle man; money has lost a portion of its value in his eyes; he covets wealth much less than pleasure and excitement; and the energy which his neighbor devotes to gain, turns with him to a passionate love of field sports and military exercises; he delights in violent bodily exertion, he is familiar with the use of arms, and is accustomed from a very early age to expose his life in single combat. Thus slavery not only prevents the whites from becoming opulent, but even from desiring to become so.

As the same causes have been continually producing opposite effects for the last two centuries in the British colonies of North America, they have at last established a striking difference between the commercial capacity of the inhabitants of the South and those of the North. At the present day, it is only the Northern States which are in possession of shipping, manufactures, railroads, and canals. This difference is perceptible, not only in comparing the North with the South, but in comparing the several Southern States. Almost all those who carry on commercial operations, or endeavor to turn slave labor to account, in the most southern districts of the Union, have emigrated from the North. The natives of the Northern States are constantly spreading over that portion of the American territory, where they have less to fear from competition; they discover resources there which escaped the notice of the inhabitants; and, as they comply with a system which they do not approve, they succeed in turning it to better advantage than those who first founded, and who still maintain it.

Were I inclined to continue this parallel, I could easily prove that almost all the differences which may be remarked between the characters of the Americans in the Southern and in the Northern States have originated in slavery; but this would divert me from my subject, and my present intention is not to point out all the consequences of servitude, but those effects which it has produced upon the material prosperity of the countries which have admitted it.

The influence of slavery upon the production of wealth must have been very imperfectly known in antiquity, as slavery then obtained throughout the civilized world; and the nations which were unacquainted with it were barbarians. And, indeed, Christianity only abolished slavery by advocating the claims of the slave; at the present time, it may be attacked in the name of the master; and, upon this point, interest is reconciled with morality.

As these truths became apparent in the United States, slavery receded before the progress of experience. Servitude had begun in the South, and had thence spread toward the North; but it now retires again. Freedom, which started from the North, now descends uninterruptedly toward the South. Amongst the great States, Pennsylvania now constitutes the extreme limit of slavery to the North; but, even within those limits, the slave system is shaken: Maryland, which is immediately below Pennsylvania, is preparing for its abolition; and Virginia, which comes next to Maryland, is already discussing its utility and its dangers.

No great change takes place in human institutions, without involving amongst its causes the law of inheritance. When the law of primogeniture obtained in the South, each family was represented by a wealthy individual, who was neither compelled nor induced to labor; and he was surrounded, as by parasitic plants, by the other members of his family, who were then excluded by law from sharing the common inheritance, and who led the same kind of life as himself. The same thing then occurred in all the families of the South which still happens in the noble families of some countries in Europe, namely, that the younger sons remain in the same state of idleness as their elder brother, without being as rich as he is. This identical result seems to be produced in Europe and in America by wholly analogous causes. In the South of the United States, the whole race of whites formed an aristocratic body, headed by a certain number of privileged individuals, whose wealth was permanent, and whose leisure was hereditary. These leaders of the American nobility kept alive the traditional prejudices of the white race in the body of which they were the representatives, and maintained idleness in honor. This aristocracy contained many who were poor, but none who would work; its members preferred want to labor; consequently, Negro laborers and slaves met with no competition; and, whatever opinion might be entertained as to the utility of their industry, it was necessary to employ them, since there was no one else to work.

No sooner was the law of primogeniture abolished, than fortunes began to diminish, and all the families of the country were simultaneously reduced to a state in which labor became necessary to existence,—several of them have since entirely disappeared,—and all of them learned to look forward to the time when it would be necessary for every one to provide for his own wants. Wealthy individuals are still to be met with, but they no longer constitute a compact and hereditary body, nor have they been able to adopt a line of conduct in which they could persevere, and which they could infuse into all ranks of society. The prejudice which stigmatized labor was, in the first place, abandoned by common consent, the number of needy men was increased, and the needy were allowed to gain a subsistence by labor without blushing for their toil. Thus, one of the most immediate consequences of the equal division of estates has been, to create a class of free laborers. As soon as competition began between the free laborer and the slave, the inferiority of the latter became manifest, and slavery was attacked in its fundamental principle, which is, the interest of the master.

As slavery recedes, the black population follows its retrograde course, and returns with it towards those tropical regions whence it originally came. However singular this fact may at first appear to be, it may readily be explained. Although the Americans abolish the principle of slavery, they do not set their slaves free. To illustrate this remark, I will quote the example of the State of New York. In 1788, this State prohibited the sale of slaves within its limits, which was an indirect method of prohibiting the importation of them. Thenceforward the number of Negroes could only increase according to the ratio of the natural increase of population. But eight years later, a more decisive measure was taken, and it was enacted that all children born of slave parents after the 4th of July, 1799, should be free. No increase could then take place, and, although slaves still existed, slavery might be said to be abolished.

As soon as a Northern State thus prohibited the importation, no slaves were brought from the South to be sold in its markets. On the other hand, as the sale of slaves was forbidden in that State, an owner could no longer get rid of his slave (who thus became a burdensome possession) otherwise than by transporting him to the South. But when a Northern State declared that the son of the slave should be born free, the slave lost a large portion of his market-value, since his posterity was no longer included in the bargain, and the owner had then a strong interest in transporting him to the South. Thus the same law prevents the slaves of the South from coming North, and drives those of the North to the South.

But there is another cause more powerful than any that I have described. The want of free hands is felt in a State in proportion as the number of slaves decreases. But in proportion as labor is performed by free hands, slave-labor becomes less productive; and the slave is then a useless or onerous possession, whom it is important to export to the South, where the same competition is not to be feared. Thus the abolition of slavery does not set the slave free, but merely transfers him to another master, and from the North to the South.

The emancipated Negroes, and those born after the abolition of slavery, do not, indeed, migrate from the North to the South; but their situation with regard to the Europeans is not unlike that of the

Indians; they remain half civilized, and deprived of their rights in the midst of a population which is far superior to them in wealth and knowledge, where they are exposed to the tyranny of the laws and the intolerance of the people. On some accounts they are still more to be pitied than the Indians, since they are haunted by the reminiscence of slavery, and they cannot claim possession of any part of the soil: many of them perish miserably, and the rest congregate in the great towns, where they perform the meanest offices, and lead a wretched and precarious existence.

But even if the number of Negroes continued to increase as rapidly as when they were still in slavery, as the number of whites augments with twofold rapidity after the abolition of slavery, the blacks would soon be, as it were, lost in the midst of a strange population.

A district which is cultivated by slaves is in general less populous than a district cultivated by free labor: moreover, America is still a new country, and a State is therefore not half peopled when it abolishes slavery. No sooner is an end put to slavery, than the want of free labor is felt, and a crowd of enterprising adventurers immediately arrive from all parts of the country, who hasten to profit by the fresh resources which are then opened to industry. The soil is soon divided amongst them, and a family of white settlers takes possession of each portion. Besides, European emigration is exclusively directed to the free States; for what would a poor emigrant do who crosses the Atlantic in search of ease and happiness, if he were to land in a country where labor is stigmatized as degrading?

Thus the white population grows by its natural increase, and, at the same time, by the immense influx of emigrants; whilst the black population receives no emigrants, and is upon its decline. The proportion which existed between the two races is soon inverted. The Negroes constitute a scanty remnant, a poor tribe of vagrants, lost in the midst of an immense people who own the land; and the presence of the blacks is only marked by the injustice and the hardships of which they are the victims.

In several of the Western States, the Negro race never made its appearance; and in all the Northern States, it is rapidly declining. Thus the great question of its future condition is confined within a narrow circle, where it becomes less formidable, though not more easy of solution. The more we descend towards the South, the more difficult does it become to abolish slavery with advantage; and this arises from several physical causes which it is important to point out.

The first of these causes is the climate: it is well known that, in proportion as Europeans approach the tropics, labor becomes more difficult to them. Many of the Americans even assert that, within a certain latitude, it is fatal to them, while the Negroes can work there without danger; but I do not think that this opinion, which is so favorable to the indolence of the inhabitants of the South, is confirmed by experience. The southern parts of the Union are not hotter than the south of Italy and of Spain; and it may be asked why the European cannot work as well there as in the latter two countries. If slavery has been abolished in Italy and in Spain, without causing the destruction of the masters, why should not the same thing take place in the Union? I cannot believe that Nature has prohibited the Europeans in Georgia and the Floridas, under pain of death, from raising the means of subsistence from the soil; but their labor would unquestionably be more irksome and less productive to them than to the inhabitants of New England. As the free workman thus loses a portion of his superiority over the slave in the Southern States, there are fewer inducements to abolish slavery.

All the plants of Europe grow in the northern parts of the Union; the South has special productions of its own. It has been observed that slave labor is a very expensive method of cultivating cereal grain. The farmer of corn land, in a country where slavery is unknown, habitually retains only a small number of laborers in his service, and at seed-time and harvest he hires additional hands, who only live at his cost for a short period. But the agriculturist in a slave state is obliged to keep a large number of slaves the whole year round, in order to sow his fields and to gather in his crops, although their services are required only for a few weeks; for slaves are unable to wait till they are hired, and to subsist by their own labor in the mean time, like free laborers; in order to have their services, they must be bought. Slavery, independently of its general disadvantages, is therefore still more inapplicable to countries in which corn is cultivated, than to those which produce crops of a different kind. The cultivation of tobacco, of cotton, and especially of the sugar-cane, demands, on the other hand, unremitting attention: and women and children are employed in it, whose services are of little use in the cultivation of wheat. Thus slavery is naturally more fitted to the countries from which these productions are derived.

Tobacco, cotton, and the sugar-cane are exclusively grown in the South, and they form the principal sources of the wealth of those States. If slavery were abolished, the inhabitants of the South would be driven to this alternative: they must either change their system of cultivation,—and then they would come into competition with the more active and more experienced inhabitants of the North; or, if they continued to cultivate the same produce without slave labor, they would have to support the competition of the other States of the South, which might still retain their slaves. Thus, peculiar reasons for maintaining slavery exist in the South which do not operate in the North.

But there is yet another motive, which is more cogent than all the others: the South might, indeed, rigorously speaking, abolish slavery; but how should it rid its territory of the black population? Slaves and slavery are driven from the North by the same law; but this twofold result cannot be hoped for in the South.

In proving that slavery is more natural and more advantageous in the South than in the North, I have shown that the number of slaves must be far greater in the former. It was to the southern settlements that the first Africans were brought, and it is there that the greatest number of them have always been imported. As we advance towards the South, the prejudice which sanctions idleness increases in power. In the States nearest to the tropics, there is not a single white laborer; the Negroes are consequently much more numerous in the South than in the North. And, as I have already observed, this disproportion increases daily, since the Negroes are transferred to one part of the Union as soon as slavery is abolished in the other. Thus, the black population augments in the South, not only by its natural fecundity, but by the compulsory emigration of the Negroes from the North; and the African race has causes of increase in the South very analogous to those which accelerate the growth of the European race in the North.

In the State of Maine there is one Negro in three hundred inhabitants; in Massachusetts, one in one hundred; in New York, two in one hundred; in Pennsylvania, three in the same number; in Maryland, thirty-four; in Virginia, forty-two; and lastly, in South Carolina, fifty-five per cent of the inhabitants are black. Such was the proportion of the black population to the whites in the year 1830. But this proportion is perpetually changing, as it constantly decreases in the North, and augments in the South.

It is evident that the most southern States of the Union cannot abolish slavery without incurring great dangers, which the North had no reason to apprehend when it emancipated its black population. We have already shown how the Northern States made the transition from slavery to freedom, by keeping the present generation in chains, and setting their descendants free; by this means, the Negroes are only gradually introduced into the society; and whilst the men who might abuse their freedom are kept in servitude, those who are emancipated may learn the art of being free before they become their own masters. But it would be difficult to apply this method in the South. To declare that all the Negroes born after a certain period shall be free, is to introduce the principle and the notion of liberty into the heart of slavery; the blacks whom the law thus maintains in a state of slavery from which their children are delivered, are astonished at so unequal a fate, and their astonishment is only the prelude to their impatience and irritation. Thenceforward slavery loses, in their eyes, that kind of moral power which it derived from time and habit; it is reduced to a mere palpable abuse of force. The Northern States had nothing to fear from the contrast, because in them the blacks were few in number, and the white population was very considerable. But if this faint dawn of freedom were to show two millions of men their true position, the oppressors would have reason to tremble. After having enfranchised the children of their slaves, the Europeans of the Southern States would very shortly be obliged to extend the same benefit to the whole black population.

In the North, as I have already remarked, a twofold migration ensues upon the abolition of slavery, or even precedes that event when circumstances have rendered it probable; the slaves quit the country to be transported southwards; and the whites of the Northern States, as well as the emigrants from Europe, hasten to fill their place. But these two causes cannot operate in the same manner in the Southern States. On the one hand, the mass of slaves is too great to allow any expectation of their being removed from the country; and on the other hand, the Europeans and Anglo-Americans of the North are afraid to come to inhabit a country in which labor has not yet been reinstated in its rightful honors. Besides, they very justly look upon the States in which the number of the Negroes equals or exceeds that of the whites, as exposed to very great dangers; and they refrain from turning their activity in that direction.

Thus the inhabitants of the South would not be able, while abolishing slavery, like their Northern countrymen, to initiate the slaves gradually into a state of freedom; they have no means of perceptibly diminishing the black population, and they would remain unsupported to repress its excesses. Thus, in the course of a few years, a great people of free Negroes would exist in the heart of a white nation of equal size.

The same abuses of power which now maintain slavery would then become the source of the most alarming perils to the white population of the South. At the present time, the descendants of the Europeans are the sole owners of the land, and the absolute masters of all labor; they alone possess wealth, knowledge, and arms. The black is destitute of all these advantages, but can subsist without them because he is a slave. If he were free, and obliged to provide for his own subsistence, would it be possible for him to remain without these things and to support life? Or would not the very instruments of the present superiority of the white, whilst slavery exists, expose him to a thousand dangers if it were abolished?

As long as the Negro remains a slave, he may be kept in a condition not far removed from that of the brutes; but, with his liberty, he cannot but acquire a degree of instruction which will enable him to appreciate his misfortunes, and to discern a remedy for them. Moreover, there exists a singular principle of relative justice, which is firmly implanted in the human heart. Men are much more forcibly struck by those inequalities which exist within the same class, than with those which may be remarked between different classes. One can understand slavery; but how allow several millions of citizens to exist under a load of eternal infamy and hereditary wretchedness? In the North, the population of freed Negroes feels these hardships and indignities, but its numbers and its powers are small, whilst in the South it would be numerous and strong.

As soon as it is admitted that the whites and the emancipated blacks are placed upon the same territory in the situation of two foreign communities, it will readily be understood that there are but two chances for the future; the Negroes and the whites must either wholly part, or wholly mingle. I have already expressed my conviction as to the latter event. I do not believe that the white and black races will ever live in any country upon an equal footing. But I believe the difficulty to be still greater in the United States than elsewhere. An isolated individual may surmount the prejudices of religion, of his country, or of his race; and if this individual is a king, he may effect surprising changes in society; but a whole people cannot rise, as it were, above itself. A despot who should subject the Americans and their former slaves to the same yoke, might perhaps succeed in commingling their races; but as long as the American democracy remains at the head of affairs, no one will undertake so difficult a task; and it may be foreseen that, the freer the white population of the United States becomes, the more isolated will it remain.

I have previously observed that the mixed race is the true bond of union between the Europeans and the Indians; just so, the Mulattoes are the true means of transition between the white and the Negro; so that, wherever Mulattoes abound, the intermixture of the two races is not impossible. In some parts of America, the European and the Negro races are so crossed by one another, that it is rare to meet with a man who is entirely black, or entirely white: when they are arrived at this point, the two races may really be said to be combined, or, rather, to have been absorbed in a third race, which is connected with both without being identical with either.

Of all Europeans, the English are those who have mixed least with the Negroes. More Mulattoes are to be seen in the South of the Union than in the North, but infinitely fewer than in any other European colony: Mulattoes are by no means numerous in the United States; they have no force peculiar to themselves, and when quarrels originating in differences of color take place, they generally side with the whites,—just as the lackeys of the great in Europe assume the contemptuous airs of nobility toward the lower orders.

The pride of origin, which is natural to the English, is singularly augmented by the personal pride which democratic liberty fosters amongst the Americans: the white citizen of the United States is proud of his race, and proud of himself. But if the whites and the Negroes do not intermingle in the North of the Union, how should they mix in the South? Can it be supposed for an instant, that an American of the Southern States, placed, as he must forever be, between the white man, with all his physical and moral superiority, and the Negro, will ever think of being confounded with the latter? The Americans of the Southern States have two powerful passions, which will always keep them aloof;—the first is the fear of being assimilated to the Negroes, their former slaves; and the second, the dread of sinking below the whites, their neighbors.

If I were called upon to predict the future, I should say that the abolition of slavery in the South will, in the common course of things, increase the repugnance of the white population for the blacks. I found this opinion upon the analogous observation I have already made at the North. I have remarked that the white inhabitants of the North avoid the Negroes with increasing care, in proportion as the legal barriers of separation are removed by the legislature; and why should not the same result take place in the South? In the North, the whites are deterred from intermingling with the blacks by an imaginary danger; in the South, where the danger would be real, I cannot believe that the fear would be less.

If, on the one hand, it be admitted (and the fact is unquestionable) that the colored population perpetually accumulate in the extreme South, and increase more rapidly than the whites; and if, on the other hand, it be allowed that it is impossible to foresee a time at which the whites and the blacks will be so intermingled as to derive the same benefits from society,—must it not be inferred that the blacks and the whites will, sooner or later, come to open strife in the Southern States? But if it be asked what the issue of the struggle is likely to be, it will readily be understood that we are here left to vague conjectures. The human mind may succeed in tracing a wide circle, as it were, which includes the future; but, within that circle, chance rules, and eludes all our foresight. In every picture of the future there is a dim spot which the eye of the understanding cannot penetrate. It appears, however, extremely probable that, in the West India Islands, the white race is destined to be subdued, and, upon the continent, the blacks.

In the West India Islands, the white planters are isolated amidst an immense black population; on the continent, the blacks are placed between the ocean and an innumerable people, who already extend above them, in a compact mass, from the icy confines of Canada to the frontiers of Virginia, and from the banks of the Missouri to the shores of the Atlantic. If the white citizens of North America remain united, it is difficult to believe that the Negroes will escape the destruction which menaces them; they must be subdued by want or by the sword. But the black population accumulated along the coast of the Gulf of Mexico have a chance of success, if the American Union should be dissolved when the struggle between the two races begins. The Federal tie once broken, the people of the South could not rely upon any lasting succor from their Northern countrymen. The latter are well aware that the danger can never reach them; and unless they are constrained to march to the assistance of the South by a positive obligation, it may be foreseen that the sympathy of race will be powerless.

Yet, at whatever period the strife may break out, the whites of the South, even if they are abandoned to their own resources, will enter the lists with an immense superiority of knowledge and the means of warfare: but the blacks will have numerical strength and the energy of despair upon their side; and these are powerful resources to men who have taken up arms. The fate of the white population of the Southern States will, perhaps, be similar to that of the Moors in Spain. After having occupied the land for centuries, it will, perhaps, retire by degrees to the country whence its ancestors came, and abandon to the Negroes the possession of a territory which Providence seems to have destined for them, since they can subsist and labor in it more easily than the whites.

The danger of a conflict between the white and the black inhabitants of the Southern States of the Union—a danger which, however remote it may be, is inevitable—perpetually haunts the imagination of the Americans, like a painful dream. The inhabitants of the North make it a common topic of conversation, although directly they have nothing to fear from it; but they vainly endeavor to devise some means of obviating the misfortunes which they foresee. In the Southern States, the subject is not discussed: the planter does not allude to the future in conversing with strangers; he does not communicate his apprehensions to his friends,—he seeks to conceal them from himself. But there is something more alarming in the tacit forebodings of the South, than in the clamorous fears of the North.

This all-pervading disquietude has given birth to an undertaking as yet but little known, but which may change the fate of a portion of the human race. From apprehension of the dangers which I have just described, some American citizens have formed a society for the purpose of exporting to the coast of Guinea, at their own expense, such free Negroes as may be willing to escape from the oppression to which they are subject.

In 1820, the society to which I allude formed a settlement in Africa, upon the seventh degree of north latitude, which bears the name of Liberia. The most recent intelligence informs us that two thousand five hundred Negroes are collected there. They have introduced the democratic institutions of America into the country of their forefathers. Liberia has a representative system of government, Negro jurymen, Negro magistrates, and Negro priests; churches have been built, newspapers established, and, by a singular turn in the vicissitudes of the world, white men are prohibited from establishing themselves within the settlement.

This is indeed a strange caprice of fortune. Two hundred years have now elapsed since the inhabitants of Europe undertook to tear the Negro from his family and his home, in order to transport him to the shores of North America. Now the European settlers are engaged in sending back the descendants of those very Negroes to the continent whence they were originally taken: the barbarous Africans have learned civilization in the midst of bondage, and have become acquainted with free political institutions in slavery. Up to the present time, Africa has been closed against the arts and sciences of the whites; but the inventions of Europe will perhaps penetrate into those regions, now that they are introduced by Africans themselves. The settlement of Liberia is founded upon a lofty and fruitful idea; but, whatever may be its results with regard to Africa, it can afford no remedy to the New World.

In twelve years, the Colonization Society has transported two thousand five hundred Negroes to Africa; in the same space of time, about seven hundred thousand blacks were born in the United States. If the colony of Liberia were able to receive thousands of new inhabitants every year, and if the Negroes were in a state to be sent thither with advantage; if the Union were to supply the society with annual subsidies, and to transport the Negroes to Africa in the vessels of the state,—it would still be unable to counterpoise the natural increase of population amongst the blacks; and, as it could not remove as many men in a year as are born upon its territory within that time, it could not prevent the growth of the evil which is daily increasing in the

States. The Negro race will never leave those shores of the American continent to which it was brought by the passions and the vices of Europeans; and it will not disappear from the New World as long as it continues to exist. The inhabitants of the United States may retard the calamities which they apprehend, but they cannot now destroy their efficient cause.

I am obliged to confess that I do not regard the abolition of slavery as a means of warding off the struggle of the two races in the Southern States. The Negroes may long remain slaves without complaining; but if they are once raised to the level of freemen, they will soon revolt at being deprived of almost all their civil rights; and, as they cannot become the equals of the whites, they will speedily show themselves as enemies. In the North, everything facilitated the emancipation of the slaves; and slavery was abolished without rendering the free Negroes formidable, since their number was too small for them ever to claim their rights. But such is not the case in the South. The question of slavery was a commercial and manufacturing question for the slave-owners in the North; for those of the South, it is a question of life and death. God forbid that I should seek to justify the principle of Negro slavery, as has been done by some American writers! I say only, that all the countries which formerly adopted that execrable principle are not equally able to abandon it at the present time.

When I contemplate the condition of the South, I can only discover two modes of action for the white inhabitants of those States; viz. either to emancipate the Negroes, and to intermingle with them, or, remaining isolated from them, to keep them in slavery as long as possible. All intermediate measures seem to me likely to terminate, and that shortly, in the most horrible of civil wars, and perhaps in the extirpation of one or the other of the two races. Such is the view which the Americans of the South take of the question, and they act consistently with it. As they are determined not to mingle with the Negroes, they refuse to emancipate them.

Not that the inhabitants of the South regard slavery as necessary to the wealth of the planter; on this point, many of them agree with their Northern countrymen, in freely admitting that slavery is prejudicial to their interests; but they are convinced that the removal of this evil would peril their own existence. The instruction which is now diffused in the South has convinced the inhabitants that slavery is injurious to the slave-owner, but it has also shown them, more clearly than before, that it is almost an impossibility to get rid of it. Hence arises a singular contrast; the more the utility of slavery is contested, the more firmly is it established in the laws; and whilst its principle is gradually abolished in the North, that self-same principle gives rise to more and more rigorous consequences in the South.

The legislation of the Southern States with regard to slaves presents at the present day such unparalleled atrocities as suffice to show that the laws of humanity have been totally perverted, and to betray the desperate position of the community in which that legislation has been promulgated. The Americans of this portion of the Union have not, indeed, augmented the hardships of slavery; they have, on the contrary, bettered the physical condition of the slaves. The only means by which the ancients maintained slavery were fetters and death; the Americans of the South of the Union have discovered more intellectual securities for the duration of their power. They have employed their despotism and their violence against the human mind. In antiquity, precautions were taken to prevent the slave from breaking his chains; at the present day, measures are adopted to deprive him even of the desire of freedom. The ancients kept the bodies of their slaves in bondage, but placed no restraint upon the mind and no check upon education and they acted consistently with their established principle, since a natural termination of slavery then existed, and one day or other the slave might be set free, and become the equal of his master. But the Americans of the South, who do not admit that the Negroes can ever be commingled with themselves, have forbidden them, under severe penalties, to be taught to read or write; and, as they will not raise them to their own level, they sink them as nearly as possible to that of the brutes.

The hope of liberty had always been allowed to the slave, to cheer the hardships of his condition. But the Americans of the South are well aware that emancipation cannot but be dangerous, when the freed man can never be assimilated to his former master. To give a man his freedom, and to leave him in wretchedness and ignominy, is nothing less than to prepare a future chief for a revolt of the slaves. Moreover, it has long been remarked, that the presence of a free Negro vaguely agitates the minds of his less fortunate brethren, and conveys to them a dim notion of their rights. The Americans of the

South have consequently taken away from slave-owners the right of emancipating their slaves in most cases,—not indeed by positive prohibition, but by subjecting that step to various formalities which it is difficult to comply with.

I happened to meet with an old man, in the South of the Union, who had lived in illicit intercourse with one of his Negresses, and had had several children by her, who were born the slaves of their father. He had, indeed, frequently thought of bequeathing to them at least their liberty; but years had elapsed before he could surmount the legal obstacles to their emancipation, and in the mean while his old age was come, and he was about to die. He pictured to himself his sons dragged from market to market, and passing from the authority of a parent to the rod of the stranger, until these horrid anticipations worked his expiring imagination into frenzy. When I saw him, he was a prey to all the anguish of despair; and I then understood how awful is the retribution of Nature upon those who have broken her laws.

These evils are unquestionably great, but they are the necessary and foreseen consequences of the very principle of modern slavery. When the Europeans chose their slaves from a race differing from their own,—which many of them considered as inferior to the other races of mankind, and any notion of intimate union with which they all repelled with horror,—they must have believed that slavery would last forever, since there is no intermediate state which can be durable between the excessive inequality produced by servitude and the complete equality which originates in independence. The Europeans did imperfectly feel this truth, but without acknowledging it even to themselves. Whenever they have had to do with Negroes, their conduct has either been dictated by their interest and their pride, or by their compassion. They first violated every right of humanity by their treatment of the Negro, and they afterwards informed him that those rights were precious and inviolable. They affected to open their ranks to the slaves, but the Negroes who attempted to penetrate into the community were driven back with scorn; and they have incautiously and involuntarily been led to admit freedom instead of slavery, without having the courage to be wholly iniquitous, or wholly just.

If it be impossible to anticipate a period at which the Americans of the South will mingle their blood with that of the Negroes, can they allow their slaves to become free without compromising their own security? And if they are obliged to keep that race in bondage in order to save their own families, may they not be excused for availing themselves of the means best adapted to that end? The events which are taking place in the Southern States appear to me to be at once the most horrible and the most natural results of slavery. When I see the order of nature overthrown, and when I hear the cry of humanity in its vain struggle against the laws, my indignation does not light upon the men of our own time who are the instruments of these outrages; but I reserve my execration for those who, after a thousand years of freedom, brought back slavery into the world once more.

Whatever may be the efforts of the Americans of the South to maintain slavery, they will not always succeed. Slavery, now confined to a single tract of the civilized earth, attacked by Christianity as unjust, and by political economy as prejudicial, and now contrasted with democratic liberty and the intelligence of our age, cannot survive. By the act of the master, or by the will of the slave, it will cease; and, in either case, great calamities may be expected to ensue. If liberty be refused to the Negroes of the South, they will, in the end, forcibly seize it for themselves; if it be given, they will, erelong, abuse it.

What Are the Chances of Duration of the American Union, and What Dangers Threaten It

The maintenance of the existing institutions of the several States depends in part upon the maintenance of the Union itself. We must therefore first inquire into the probable fate of the Union. One point may be assumed at once: if the present confederation were dissolved, it appears to me to be incontestable that the States of which it is now composed would not return to their original isolated condition, but that several Unions would then be formed in the place of one. It is not my intention to inquire into the principles upon which these new Unions would probably be established, but merely to show what the causes are which may effect the dismemberment of the existing confederation.

With this object, I shall be obliged to retrace some of the steps which I have already taken, and to revert to topics which I have before discussed. I am aware that the reader may accuse me of repetition, but the importance of the matter which still remains to be treated is my excuse: I had rather say too much, than not be thoroughly understood; and I prefer injuring the author to slighting the subject.

The legislators who formed the Constitution of 1789 endeavored to confer a separate existence and superior strength upon the federal power. But they were confined by the conditions of the task which they had undertaken to perform. They were not appointed to constitute the government of a single people, but to regulate the association of several States; and, whatever their inclinations might be, they could not but divide the exercise of sovereignty.

In order to understand the consequences of this division, it is necessary to make a short distinction between the functions of government. There are some objects which are national by their very nature,—that is to say, which affect the nation as a whole, and can only be entrusted to the man or the assembly of men who most completely represent the entire nation. Amongst these may be reckoned war and diplomacy. There are other objects which are provincial by their very nature,—that is to say, which only affect certain localities, and which can only be properly treated in that locality. Such, for instance, is the budget of a municipality. Lastly, there are objects of a mixed nature, which are national inasmuch as they affect all the citizens who compose the nation, and which are provincial inasmuch as it is not necessary that the nation itself should provide for them all. Such are the rights which regulate the civil and political condition of the citizens. No society can exist without civil and political rights. These rights, therefore, interest all the citizens alike; but it is not always necessary to the existence and the prosperity of the nation that these rights should be uniform, nor, consequently, that they should be regulated by the central authority.

But sometimes the sovereign authority is composed of pre-organized political bodies, by virtue of circumstances anterior to their union; and, in this case, the provincial governments assume the control, not only of those affairs which more peculiarly belong to them, but of all or a part of the mixed objects in question. For the confederate nations, which were independent sovereignties before their union, and which still represent a considerable share of the sovereign power, have consented to cede to the general government the exercise only of those rights which are indispensable to the Union.

When the national government, independently of the prerogatives inherent in its nature, is invested with the right of regulating the mixed objects of sovereignty, it possesses a preponderant influence. Not only are its own rights extensive, but all the rights which it does not possess exist by its sufferance; and it is to be feared that the provincial governments may be deprived by it of their natural and necessary prerogatives.

When, on the other hand, the provincial governments are invested with the power of regulating those same affairs of mixed interest, an opposite tendency prevails in society. The preponderant force resides in the province, not in the nation; and it may be apprehended that the national government may, in the end, be stripped of the privileges which are necessary to its existence.

Single nations have therefore a natural tendency to centralization, and confederations to dismemberment.

It now remains to apply these general principles to the American Union. The several States necessarily retained the right of regulating all purely provincial affairs. Moreover, these same States kept the rights of determining the civil and political competency of the citizens, of regulating the reciprocal relations of the members of the community, and of dispensing justice,—rights which are general in their nature, but do not necessarily appertain to the national government. We have seen that the government of the Union is invested with the power of acting in the name of the whole nation, in those cases in which the nation has to appear as a single and undivided power; as, for instance, in foreign relations, and in offering a common resistance to a common enemy; in short, in conducting those affairs which I have styled exclusively national.

In this division of the rights of sovereignty, the share of the Union seems at first sight more considerable than that of the States, but a more attentive investigation shows it to be less so. The undertakings of the government of the Union are more vast, but it has less frequent occasion to act at all. Those of the provincial governments are comparatively small, but they are incessant, and they keep alive the authority which they represent. The government of the Union watches over the general interests of the country; but the general interests of a people have but a questionable influence upon individual happiness, whilst provincial interests produce an immediate effect upon the welfare of the inhabitants. The Union secures the independence and the greatness of the nation, which do not immediately affect private citizens; but the several States maintain the liberty, regulate the rights, protect the fortune, and secure the life and the whole future prosperity, of every citizen.

The Federal government is far removed from its subjects, whilst the provincial governments are within the reach of them all, and are ready to attend to the smallest appeal. The central government has upon its side the passions of a few superior men who aspire to conduct it; but upon the side of the provincial governments are the interests of all those second-rate individuals who can only hope to obtain power within their own State, and who nevertheless exercise more authority over the people because they are nearer to them.

The Americans have, therefore, much more to hope and to fear from the States than from the Union; and, according to the natural tendency of the human mind, they are more likely to attach themselves strongly to the former than to the latter. In this respect, their habits and feelings harmonize with their interests.

When a compact nation divides its sovereignty, and adopts a confederate form of government, the traditions, the customs, and the manners of the people for a long time struggle against the laws, and give an influence to the central government which the laws forbid. But when a number of confederate states unite to form a single nation, the same causes operate in an opposite direction. I have no doubt that, if France were to become a confederate republic like that of the United States, the government would at first be more energetic than that of the Union; and if the Union were to alter its constitution to a monarchy like that of France, I think that the American government would long remain weaker than the French. When the national existence of the Anglo-Americans began, their provincial existence was already of long standing; necessary relations were established between the townships and the individual citizens of the same States; and they were accustomed to consider some objects as common to them all, and to conduct other affairs as exclusively relating to their own special interests.

The Union is a vast body, which presents no definite object to patriotic feeling. The forms and limits of the state are distinct and circumscribed, since it represents a certain number of objects which are familiar to the citizens, and dear to them all. It is identified with the soil; with the right of property and the domestic affections; with the recollections of the past, the labors of the present, and the hopes of the future. Patriotism, then, which is frequently a mere extension of individual selfishness, is still directed to the State, and has not passed over to the Union. Thus, the tendency of the interests, the habits, and the feelings of the people is to center political activity in the States in preference to the Union.

It is easy to estimate the different strength of the two governments, by remarking the manner in which they exercise their respective powers. Whenever the government of a State addresses an individual or an assembly of individuals, its language is clear and imperative,—and such is also the tone of the Federal government when it speaks to individuals; but, no sooner has it anything to do with a State, than it begins to parley, to explain its motives and justify its conduct, to argue, to advise, -and, in short, anything but to command. If doubts are raised as to the limits of the constitutional powers of either government, the provincial government prefers its claim with boldness, and takes prompt and energetic steps to support it. Meanwhile the government of the Union reasons; it appeals to the interests, the good sense, the glory of the nation; it temporizes, it negotiates, and does not consent to act until it is reduced to the last extremity. At first sight, it might readily be imagined that it is the provincial government which is armed with the authority of the nation, and that Congress represents a single State.

The Federal government is, therefore, notwithstanding the precautions of those who founded it, naturally so weak, that, more than any other, it requires the free consent of the governed to enable it to subsist. It is easy to perceive that its object is to enable the States to realize with facility their determination of remaining united; and, as long as this preliminary condition exists, it is wise, strong, and active. The Constitution fits the government to control individuals, and easily to surmount such obstacles as they may be inclined to offer, but it was by no means established with a view to the possible voluntary separation of one or more of the States from the Union.

If the sovereignty of the Union were to engage in a struggle with that of the States, at the present day, its defeat may be confidently predicted; and it is not probable that such a struggle would be seriously undertaken. As often as a steady resistance is offered to the Federal government, it will be found to yield. Experience has hitherto shown that, whenever a State has demanded anything with perseverance and resolution, it has invariably succeeded; and that, if it has distinctly refused to act, it was left to do as it thought fit.

But even if the government of the Union had any strength inherent in itself, the physical situation of the country would render the exercise of that strength very difficult. The United States cover an immense territory, they are separated from each other by great distances, and the population is disseminated over the surface of a country which is still half a wilderness. If the Union were to undertake to enforce by arms the allegiance of the confederate States, it would be in a position very analogous to that of England at the time of the war of independence.

However strong a government may be, it cannot easily escape from the consequences of a principle which it has once admitted as the foundation of its constitution. The Union was formed by the voluntary agreement of the States; and these, in uniting together, have not forfeited their nationality, nor have they been reduced to the condition of one and the same people. If one of the States chose to withdraw its name from the contract, it would be difficult to disprove its right of doing so, and the Federal government would have no means of maintaining its claims directly, either by force or by right. In order to enable the Federal government easily to conquer the resistance which may be offered to it by any of its subjects, it would be necessary that one or more of them should be specially interested in the existence of the Union, as has frequently been the case in the history of confederations.

If it be supposed that amongst the States which are united by the Federal tie there are some which exclusively enjoy the principal advantages of union, or whose prosperity entirely depends on the duration of that union, it is unquestionable that they will always be ready to support the central government in enforcing the obedience of the others. But the government would then be exerting a force not derived from itself, but from a principle contrary to its nature. States form confederations in order to derive equal advantages from their union; and in the case just alluded to, the Federal government would derive its power from the unequal distribution of those benefits amongst the States.

In America, the existing Union is advantageous to all the States, but it is not indispensable to any one of them. Several of them might break the Federal tie without compromising the welfare of the others, although the sum of their joint prosperity would be less. As the existence and the happiness of none of the States are wholly dependent on the present Constitution, they would none of them be disposed to make great personal sacrifices to maintain it. On the other hand, there is no State which seems hitherto to have its ambition much interested in the maintenance of the existing Union. They certainly do not all exercise the same influence in the Federal councils; but no one can hope to domineer over the rest, or to treat them as its inferiors or as its subjects.

It appears to me unquestionable, that, if any portion of the Union seriously desired to separate itself from the other States, they would not be able, nor indeed would they attempt, to prevent it; and that the present Union will only last as long as the States which compose it choose to continue members of the confederation. If this point be admitted, the question becomes less difficult; and our object is, not to inquire whether the States of the existing Union are capable of separating, but whether they will choose to remain united.

Amongst the various reasons which tend to render the existing Union useful to the Americans, two principal ones are especially evident to the observer. Although the Americans are, as it were, alone upon their continent, commerce gives them for neighbors all the nations with which they trade. Notwithstanding their apparent isolation, then, the Americans need to be strong, and they can be strong only by remaining united. If the States were to split, they would not only diminish the strength which they now have against foreigners, but they would soon create foreign powers upon their own territory. A system of inland custom-houses would then be established; the valleys would be divided by imaginary boundary lines; the courses of the rivers would be impeded, and a multitude of hindrances would prevent the Americans from using that vast continent which Providence has given them for a dominion. At present, they have no invasion to fear, and consequently no standing armies to maintain, no taxes to levy. If the Union were dissolved, all these burdensome things would erelong be required. The Americans are, then, most deeply interested in the maintenance of their Union. On the other hand, it is almost impossible to discover any private interest which might now tempt a portion of the Union to separate from the other States.

The inhabitants of the United States talk much of their attachment to their country; but I confess that I do not rely upon that calculating patriotism which is founded upon interest, and which a change in the interests may destroy. Nor do I attach much importance to the language of the Americans, when they manifest, in their daily conversation, the intention of maintaining the Federal system adopted by their forefathers. A government retains its sway over a great number of citizens far less by the voluntary and rational consent of the multitude, than by that instinctive, and to a certain extent involuntary, agreement which results from similarity of feelings and resemblances of opinion. I will never admit that men constitute a social body simply because they obey the same head and the same laws. Society can only exist when a great number of men consider a great number of things under the same aspect, when they hold the same opinions upon many subjects, and when the same occurrences suggest the same thoughts and impressions to their minds.

The observer who examines what is passing in the United States upon this principle, will readily discover that their inhabitants, though divided into twenty-four distinct sovereignties, still constitute a single people; and he may perhaps be led to think that the Anglo-American Union is more truly a united society than some nations of Europe which live under the same legislation and the same prince.

Although the Anglo-Americans have several religious sects, they all regard religion in the same manner. They are not always agreed upon the measures which are most conducive to good government, and they vary upon some of the forms of government which it is

expedient to adopt; but they are unanimous upon the general principles which ought to rule human society. From Maine to the Floridas,
and from the Missouri to the Atlantic Ocean, the people are held to
be the source of all legitimate power. The same notions are entertained respecting liberty and equality, the liberty of the press, the
right of association, the jury, and the responsibility of the agents
of government.

If we turn from their political and religious opinions to the
moral and philosophical principles which regulate the daily actions
of life, and govern their conduct, we still find the same uniformity.
The Anglo-Americans acknowledge the moral authority of the reason of the community, as they acknowledge the political authority
of the mass of citizens; and they hold that public opinion is the surest arbiter of what is lawful or forbidden, true or false. The majority of them believe that a man, by following his own interest rightly
understood, will be led to do what is just and good. They hold that
every man is born in possession of the right of self-government, and
that no one has the right of constraining his fellow-creatures to be
happy. They have all a lively faith in the perfectibility of man; they
judge that the diffusion of knowledge must necessarily be advantageous, and the consequences of ignorance fatal; they all consider society as a body in a state of improvement, humanity as a changing scene,
in which nothing is, or ought to be, permanent; and they admit that
what appears to them to-day to be good, may be superseded by something better to-morrow. I do not give all these opinions as true, but as
American opinions.

The Anglo-Americans are not only united by these common
opinions, but they are separated from all other nations by a feeling
of pride. For the last fifty years, no pains have been spared to convince the inhabitants of the United States that they are the only religious, enlightened, and free people. They perceive that, for the present, their own democratic institutions prosper, whilst those of other
countries fail; hence they conceive a high opinion of their superiority, and are not very remote from believing themselves to be a distinct
species of mankind.

Thus, the dangers which threaten the American Union do not originate in diversity of interests or of opinions; but in the various characters and passions of the Americans. The men who inhabit the vast

territory of the United States are almost all the issue of a common stock; but climate, and more especially slavery, have gradually introduced marked differences between the British settler of the Southern States and the British settler of the North. In Europe, it is generally believed that slavery has rendered the interests of one part of the Union contrary to those of the other; but I have not found this to be the case. Slavery has not created interests in the South contrary to those of the North, but it has modified the character and changed the habits of the natives of the South.

I have already explained the influence of slavery upon the commercial ability of the Americans in the South; and this same influence equally extends to their manners. The slave is a servant who never remonstrates, and who submits to everything without complaint. He may sometimes assassinate, but he never withstands, his master. In the South, there are no families so poor as not to have slaves. The citizen of the Southern States becomes a sort of domestic dictator from infancy; the first notion he acquires in life is, that he is born to command, and the first habit which he contracts is that of ruling without resistance. His education tends, then, to give him the character of a haughty and hasty man,—irascible, violent, ardent in his desires, impatient of obstacles, but easily discouraged if he cannot succeed upon his first attempt.

The American of the North sees no slaves around him in his childhood; he is even unattended by free servants, for he is usually obliged to provide for his own wants. As soon as he enters the world, the idea of necessity assails him on every side: he soon learns to know exactly the natural limits of his power; he never expects to subdue by force those who withstand him; and he knows that the surest means of obtaining the support of his fellow-creatures is to win their favor. He therefore becomes patient, reflecting, tolerant, slow to act, and persevering in his designs.

In the Southern States, the more pressing wants of life are always supplied; the inhabitants, therefore, are not occupied with the material cares of life, from which they are relieved by others; and their imagination is diverted to more captivating and less definite objects. The American of the South is fond of grandeur, luxury, and renown, of gayety, pleasure, and, above all, of idleness; nothing obliges him to exert himself in order to subsist; and as he has no necessary occupations, he gives way to indolence, and does not even attempt what would be useful.

But the equality of fortunes and the absence of slavery in the North plunge the inhabitants in those material cares which are disdained by the white population of the South. They are taught from infancy to combat want, and to place wealth above all the pleasures of the intellect or the heart. The imagination is extinguished by the trivial details of life; and the ideas become less numerous and less general, but far more practical, clearer, and more precise. As prosperity is the sole aim of exertion, it is excellently well attained; nature and men are turned to the best pecuniary advantage; and society is dexterously made to contribute to the welfare of each of its members, whilst individual selfishness is the source of general happiness.

The American of the North has not only experience, but knowledge; yet he values science not as an enjoyment, but as a means, and is only anxious to seize its useful applications. The American of the South is more given to act upon impulse; he is more clever, more frank, more generous, more intellectual, and more brilliant. The former, with a greater degree of activity, common sense, information, and general aptitude, has the characteristic good and evil qualities of the middle classes. The latter has the tastes, the prejudices, the weaknesses, and the magnanimity of all aristocracies.

If two men are united in society, who have the same interests, and, to a certain extent, the same opinions, but different characters, different acquirements, and a different style of civilization, it is most probable that these men will not agree. The same remark is applicable to a society of nations.

Slavery, then, does not attack the American Union directly in its interests, but indirectly in its manners.

The States which gave their assent to the Federal contract in 1790 were thirteen in number; the Union now consists of twenty-four members. The population, which amounted to nearly four millions in 1790, had more than tripled in the space of forty years; in 1830, it amounted to nearly thirteen millions. Changes of such magnitude cannot take place without danger.

A society of nations, as well as a society of individuals, has three principal chances of duration,—namely, the wisdom of its members, their individual weakness, and their limited number. The Americans who quit the coasts of the Atlantic Ocean to plunge into the Western wilderness are adventurers, impatient of restraint, greedy of wealth, and frequently men expelled from the States in which they were born. When they arrive in the deserts, they are unknown to each other; they have neither traditions, family feeling, nor the force of example to check their excesses. The authority of the laws is feeble amongst them,—that of morality is still weaker. The settlers who are constantly peopling the valley of the Mississippi are, then, in every respect, inferior to the Americans who inhabit the older parts of the Union. But they already exercise a great influence in its councils; and they arrive at the government of the commonwealth before they have learnt to govern themselves.

The greater the individual weakness of the contracting parties, the greater are the chances of the duration of the contract; for their safety is then dependent upon their union. When, in 1790, the most populous of the American republics did not contain 500,000 inhabitants, each of them felt its own insignificance as an independent people, and this feeling rendered compliance with the Federal authority more easy. But, when one of the confederate States reckons, like the State of New York, two millions [three and a half millions] of inhabitants, and covers an extent of territory equal to a quarter of France, it feels its own strength; and, although it may still support the Union as useful to its prosperity, it no longer regards it as necessary to its existence; and, while consenting to continue in it, it aims at preponderance in the Federal councils. The mere increase in number of the States weakens the tie that holds them together. All men who are placed at the same point of view do not look at the same objects in the same manner. Still less do they do so when the point of view is different. In proportion, then, as the American republics become more numerous, there is less chance of their unanimity in matters of legislation. At present, the interests of the different parts of the Union are not at variance; but who can foresee the various changes of the future in a country in which new towns are founded every day, and new States almost every year?

Since the first settlement of the British Colonies, the number of inhabitants has about doubled every twenty-two years. I perceive no causes which are likely to check this ratio of increase of the Anglo-American population for the next hundred years; and, before that time has elapsed, I believe that the territories and dependencies of the United States will be covered by more than a hundred millions of inhabitants, and divided into forty States. I admit that these hundred millions of men have no different interests. I suppose, on the contrary, that they are all equally interested in the maintenance of the Union; but I still say that, for the very reason that they are a hundred millions, forming forty distinct nations unequally strong, the continuance of the Federal government can only be a fortunate accident.

Whatever faith I may have in the perfectibility of man, until human nature is altered, and men wholly transformed, I shall refuse to believe in the duration of a government which is called upon to hold together forty different nations, spread over a territory equal to one half of Europe, to avoid all rivalry, ambition, and struggles between them, and to direct their independent activity to the accomplishment of the same designs.

But the greatest peril to which the Union is exposed by its increase arises from the continual displacement of its internal forces. The distance from Lake Superior to the Gulf of Mexico is more than twelve hundred miles, as the crow flies. The frontier of the United States winds along the whole of this immense line; sometimes falling within its limits, but more frequently extending far beyond it, into the waste. It has been calculated that the whites advance every year a mean distance of seventeen miles along the whole of this vast boundary. Obstacles, such as an unproductive district, a lake, or an Indian nation, are sometimes encountered. The advancing column then halts for a while; its two extremities curve round upon themselves, and, as soon as they are reunited, they proceed onwards. This gradual and continuous progress of the European race towards the Rocky Mountains has the solemnity of a providential event; it is like a deluge of men rising unabatedly, and daily driven onwards by the hand of God.

Within this front line of conquering settlers, towns are built, and vast States founded. In 1790, there were only a few thousand pioneers sprinkled along the valleys of the Mississippi; at the present day, these valleys contain as many inhabitants as were to be found in the whole Union in 1790. Their population amounts to nearly four millions. The city of Washington was founded in 1800, in the very center of the Union; but such are the changes which have taken place, that it now stands at one of the extremities; and the delegates of the most remote

Western States, in order to take their seats in Congress, are already obliged to perform a journey as long as that from Vienna to Paris.

All the States are borne onwards at the same time in the path of fortune, but they do not all increase and prosper in the same proportion. In the North of the Union, the detached branches of the Alleghany chain, extending as far as the Atlantic Ocean, form spacious roads and ports, constantly accessible to the largest vessels. But from the Potomac, following the shore, to the mouth of the Mississippi, the coast is sandy and flat. In this part of the Union, the mouths of almost all the rivers are obstructed; and the few harbors which exist amongst these lagoons afford shallower water to vessels, and much fewer commercial advantages, than those of the North.

This first and natural cause of inferiority is united to another cause proceeding from the laws. We have seen that slavery, which is abolished in the North, still exists in the South; and I have pointed out its fatal consequences upon the prosperity of the planter himself.

The North is therefore superior to the South both in commerce and manufacture; the natural consequence of which is the more rapid increase of population and wealth within its borders. The States on the shores of the Atlantic Ocean are already half peopled. Most of the land is held by an owner; and they cannot therefore receive so many emigrants as the Western States, where a boundless field is still open to industry. The valley of the Mississippi is far more fertile than the coast of the Atlantic Ocean. This reason, added to all the others, contributes to drive the Europeans westward,—a fact which may be rigorously demonstrated by figures. It is found that the sum total of the population of all the United States has about tripled in the course of forty years. But in the new States adjacent to the Mississippi, the population has increased thirty-one fold within the same time.

The center of the Federal power is continually displaced. Forty years ago, the majority of the citizens of the Union was established upon the coast of the Atlantic, in the environs of the spot where Washington now stands; but the great body of the people are now advancing inland and to the North, so that, in twenty years, the majority will unquestionably be on the western side of the Alleghenies. If the Union continues, the basin of the Mississippi is evidently marked out, by its fertility and its extent, to be the permanent center of the Federal government. In thirty or forty years, that tract of country will have assumed its natural rank. It is easy to calculate that its population, compared with that of the coast of the Atlantic, will then be, in round numbers, as 40 to 11. In a few years, the States which founded the Union will lose the direction of its policy, and the population of the valley of the Mississippi will preponderate in the Federal assemblies.

This constant gravitation of the Federal power and influence towards the Northwest is shown every ten years, when a general census of the population is made, and the number of delegates which each State sends to Congress is settled anew. In 1790, Virginia had nineteen representatives in Congress. This number continued to increase until 1813, when it reached twenty-three; from that time it began to decrease, and, in 1833, Virginia elected only twenty-one. During the same period, the State of New York followed the contrary direction: in 1790, it had ten representatives in Congress; in 1813, twenty-seven; in 1823, thirty-four; and in 1833, forty. The State of Ohio had only one representative in 1803; and in 1833, it had already nineteen. [Virginia now has thirteen, New York thirty-three, and Ohio twenty-one representatives.]

It is difficult to imagine a durable union of a nation which is rich and strong with one which is poor and weak, even if it were proved that the strength and wealth of the one are not the causes of the weakness and poverty of the other. But union is still more difficult to maintain at a time when one party is losing strength, and the other is gaining it. This rapid and disproportionate increase of certain States threatens the independence of the others. New York might perhaps succeed, with its two millions of inhabitants and its forty representatives, in dictating to the other States in Congress. But, even if the more powerful States make no attempt to oppress the smaller ones, the danger still exists; for there is almost as much in the possibility of the act as in the act itself. The weak generally mistrust the justice and the reason of the strong. The States which increase less rapidly than the others look upon those which are more favored by fortune with envy and suspicion. Hence arise the deep-seated uneasiness and ill-defined agitation which are observable in the South, and which form so striking a contrast to the confidence and prosperity which are common to other parts of the Union. I am inclined to think that the hostile attitude taken by the South recently, is attributable to no other cause. The inhabitants of the Southern States are, of all the Americans, those who are most interested in the maintenance of the Union; they would assuredly suffer most from being left to themselves; and yet they are the only ones who threaten to break the tie of confederation. It is easy to perceive that the South, which has given four Presidents— Washington, Jefferson, Madison, and Monroe—to the Union, which perceives that it is losing its Federal influence, and that the number of its representatives in Congress is diminishing from year to year, whilst those of the Northern and Western States are increasing,—the South, which is peopled with ardent and irascible men, is becoming more and more irritated and alarmed. Its inhabitants reflect upon their present position, and remember their past influence, with the melancholy uneasiness of men who suspect oppression. If they discover a law of the Union which is not unequivocally favorable to their interests, they protest against it as an abuse of force; and if their ardent petitions are not listened to, they threaten to quit an association which loads them with burdens whilst it deprives them of the profits. "The Tariff," said the inhabitants of Carolina in 1832, "enriches the North and ruins the South; for, if this were not the case, to what can we attribute the continually increasing power and wealth of the North, with its inclement skies and arid soil; whilst the South, which may be styled the garden of America, is rapidly declining."

If the changes which I have described were gradual, so that each generation at least might have time to disappear with the order of things under which it had lived, the danger would be less; but the progress of society in America is precipitate, and almost revolutionary. The same citizen may have lived to see his State take the lead in the Union, and afterwards become powerless in the Federal assemblies; and an Anglo-American republic has been known to grow as rapidly as a man, passing from birth and infancy to maturity in the course of thirty years. It must not be imagined, however, that the States which lose their preponderance also lose their population or their riches: no stop is put to their prosperity, and they even go on to increase more rapidly than any kingdom in Europe. But they believe themselves to be impoverished because their wealth does not augment as rapidly as that of their neighbors; and they think that their power is lost because they suddenly come in contact with a power greater than their own: thus they are more hurt in their feelings and their passions than in their interests. But this is amply sufficient to endanger the maintenance of the Union. If kings and peoples had only had their true interests in view, ever since the beginning of the world, war would scarcely be known among mankind.

Thus the prosperity of the United States is the source of their most serious dangers, since it tends to create in some of the confederate States that intoxication which accompanies a rapid increase of fortune; and to awaken in others those feelings of envy, mistrust, and regret which usually attend the loss of it. The Americans contemplate this extraordinary progress with exultation; but they would be wiser to consider it with sorrow and alarm. The Americans of the United States must inevitably become one of the greatest nations in the world; their offspring will cover almost the whole of North America; the continent which they inhabit is their dominion, and it cannot escape them. What urges them to take possession of it so soon? Riches, power, and renown cannot fail to be theirs at some future time; but they rush upon this immense fortune as if but a moment remained for them to make it their own.

I think that I have demonstrated, that the existence of the present confederation depends entirely on the continued assent of all the confederates; and, starting from this principle, I have inquired into the causes which may induce some of the States to separate from the others. The Union may, however, perish in two different ways: one of the confederate States may choose to retire from the compact, and so forcibly to sever the Federal tie; and it is to this supposition that most of the remarks that I have made apply: or the authority of the Federal government may be gradually lost by the simultaneous tendency of the united republics to resume their independence. The central power, successively stripped of all its prerogatives, and reduced to impotence by tacit consent, would become incompetent to fulfill its purpose; and the second union would perish, like the first, by a sort of senile imbecility. The gradual weakening of the Federal tie, which may finally lead to the dissolution of the Union, is a distinct circumstance, that may produce a variety of minor consequences before it operates so violent a change. The confederation might still subsist, although its government were reduced to such a degree of inanition as to paralyze the nation, to cause internal anarchy, and to check the general prosperity of the country.

———————

---★---

Conclusion

I am approaching the close of my inquiry: hitherto, in speaking of the future destiny of the United States, I have endeavored to divide my subject into distinct portions, in order to study each of them with more attention. My present object is to embrace the whole from one point of view; the remarks I shall make will be less detailed, but they will be more sure. I shall perceive each object less distinctly, but I shall descry the principal facts with more certainty. A traveller, who has just left a vast city, climbs the neighboring hill; as he goes farther off, he loses sight of the men whom he has just quitted; their dwellings are confused in a dense mass; he can no longer distinguish the public squares, and can scarcely trace out the great thoroughfares; but his eye has less difficulty in following the boundaries of the city, and for the first time he sees the shape of the whole. Such is the future destiny of the British race in North America to my eye; the details of the immense picture are lost in the shade, but I conceive a clear idea of the entire subject.

The territory now occupied or possessed by the United States of America forms about one twentieth part of the habitable earth. But extensive as these bounds are, it must not be supposed that the Anglo-American race will always remain within them; indeed, it has already gone far beyond them.

There was a time when we also might have created a great French nation in the American wilds, to counterbalance the influence of the English upon the destinies of the New World. France formerly possessed a territory in North America scarcely less extensive than the whole of Europe. The three greatest rivers of that continent then flowed within her dominions. The Indian tribes which dwelt between the mouth of the St. Lawrence and the delta of the Mississippi were unaccustomed to any other tongue than ours; and all the European settlements scattered over that immense region recalled the traditions of our country. Louisburg, Montmorency, Duquesne, Saint-Louis, Vincennes, New Orleans, (for such were the names they bore,) are words dear to France and familiar to our ears.

But a course of circumstances, which it would be tedious to enumerate, have deprived us of this magnificent inheritance. Wherever the French settlers were numerically weak and partially established, they have disappeared: those who remain are collected on a small extent of country, and are now subject to other laws. The 400,000 French inhabitants of Lower Canada constitute at the present time the remnant of an old nation lost in the midst of a new people. A foreign population is increasing around them unceasingly and on all sides, who already penetrate amongst the former masters of the country, predominate in their cities, and corrupt their language. This population is identical with that of the United States; it is therefore with truth that I asserted that the British race is not confined within the frontiers of the Union, since it already extends to the northeast.

To the northwest, nothing is to be met with but a few insignificant Russian settlements; but to the southwest, Mexico presents a barrier to the Anglo-Americans. Thus, the Spaniards and the Anglo-Americans are, properly speaking, the two races which divide the possession of the New World. The limits of separation between them have been settled by treaty; but although the conditions of that treaty are favorable to the Anglo-Americans, I do not doubt that they will shortly infringe it. Vast provinces, extending beyond the frontiers of the Union towards Mexico, are still destitute of inhabitants. The natives of the United States will people these solitary regions before their rightful occupants. They will take possession of the soil, and establish social institutions, so that, when the legal owner at length arrives, he will find the wilderness under cultivation, and strangers quietly settled in the midst of his inheritance.

The lands of the New World belong to the first occupant; they are the natural reward of the swiftest pioneer. Even the countries which are already peopled will have some difficulty in securing themselves from this invasion. I have already alluded to what is taking place in the province of Texas. The inhabitants of the United States are perpetually migrating to Texas, where they purchase land; and although they conform to the laws of the country, they are gradually founding the empire of their own language and their own manners. The province of Texas is still part of the Mexican dominions, but it will soon contain no Mexicans; the same thing has occurred wherever the Anglo-Americans have come in contact with a people of a different origin.

It cannot be denied that the British race has acquired an amazing preponderance over all other European races in the New World; and it is very superior to them in civilization, industry, and power. As long as it is surrounded only by desert or thinly-peopled countries, as long as it encounters no dense population upon its route, through which it cannot work its way, it will assuredly continue to spread. The lines marked out by treaties will not stop it; but it will everywhere overleap these imaginary barriers.

The geographical position of the British race in the New World is peculiarly favorable to its rapid increase. Above its northern frontiers the icy regions of the Pole extend; and a few degrees below its southern confines lies the burning climate of the Equator. The Anglo-Americans are therefore placed in the most temperate and habitable zone of the continent.

It is generally supposed that the prodigious increase of population in the United States is posterior to their Declaration of Independence. But this is an error: the population increased as rapidly under the colonial system as at the present day; that is to say, it doubled in about twenty-two years. But this proportion, which is now applied to millions, was then applied to thousands, of inhabitants; and the same fact, which was scarcely noticeable a century ago, is now evident to every observer.

The English in Canada, who are dependent on a king augment and spread almost as rapidly as the British settlers of the United States, who live under a republican government. During the war of Independence, which lasted eight years, the population continued to increase without intermission in the same ratio. Although powerful Indian nations allied with the English existed, at that time, upon the western frontiers, the emigration westward was never checked. Whilst the enemy laid waste the shores of the Atlantic, Kentucky, the western parts of Pennsylvania, and the States of Vermont and of Maine, were filling with inhabitants. Nor did the unsettled state of things which succeeded the war prevent the increase of the population, or stop its progress across the wilds. Thus, the difference of laws, the various conditions of peace and war, of order or anarchy, have exercised no perceptible influence upon the continued development of the Anglo-Americans. This may be readily understood, for no causes are sufficiently general to exercise a simultaneous influence over the whole of so extensive a territory. One portion of the country always offers a sure retreat from the calamities which afflict another part; and however great may be the evil, the remedy which is at hand is greater still.

It must not, then, be imagined that the impulse of the British race in the New World can be arrested. The dismemberment of the Union, and the hostilities which might ensue, the abolition of republican institutions, and the tyrannical government which might succeed, may retard this impulse, but they cannot prevent the people from ultimately fulfilling their destinies. No power upon earth can shut out the emigrants from that fertile wilderness which offers resources to all industry, and a refuge from all want. Future events, whatever they may be, will not deprive the Americans of their climate or their inland seas, their great rivers or their exuberant soil. Nor will bad laws, revolutions, and anarchy be able to obliterate that love of prosperity and spirit of enterprise which seem to be the distinctive characteristics of their race, or extinguish altogether the knowledge which guides them on their way.

Thus, in the midst of the uncertain future, one event at least is sure. At a period which may be said to be near,—for we are speaking of the life of a nation,—the Anglo-Americans alone will cover the immense space contained between the polar regions and the tropics, extending from the coasts of the Atlantic to those of the Pacific Ocean. The territory which will probably be occupied by the Anglo-Americans may perhaps equal three quarters of Europe in extent. The climate of the Union is, upon the whole, preferable to that of Europe, and its natural advantages are as great; it is therefore evident that its population will at some future time be proportionate to our own. Europe, divided as it is between so many nations, and torn as it has been by incessant wars growing out of the barbarous manners of the Middle Ages, has yet attained a population of 410 inhabitants to the square league. What cause can prevent the United States from having as numerous a population in time?

Many ages must elapse before the different offsets of the British race in America will cease to present the same physiognomy; and the time cannot be foreseen at which a permanent inequality of condition can be established in the New World. Whatever differences may arise, from peace or war, freedom or oppression, prosperity or want, between the destinies of the different descendants of the great Anglo-American family, they will all preserve at least a similar social condition, and will hold in common the customs and opinions to which that social condition has given birth.

In the Middle Ages, the tie of religion was sufficiently powerful to unite all the different populations of Europe in the same civilization. The British of the New World have a thousand other reciprocal ties; and they live at a time when the tendency to equality is general amongst mankind. The Middle Ages were a period when everything was broken up,—when each people, each province, each city, and each family tended strongly to maintain its distinct individuality. At the present time, an opposite tendency seems to prevail, and the nations seem to be advancing to unity. Our means of intellectual intercourse unite the remotest parts of the earth; and men cannot remain strangers to each other, or be ignorant of what is taking place in any corner of the globe. The consequence is, that there is less difference at the present day between the Europeans and their descendants in the New World, in spite of the ocean which divides them, than there was between certain towns in the thirteenth century, which were separated only by a river. If this tendency to assimilation brings foreign nations closer to each other, it must a fortiori prevent the descendants of the same people from becoming aliens to each other.

The time will therefore come, when one hundred and fifty millions of men will be living in North America, equal in condition, all belonging to one family, owing their origin to the same cause, and preserving the same civilization, the same language, the same religion, the same habits, the same manners, and imbued with the same opinions, propagated under the same forms. The rest is uncertain, but this is certain; and it is a fact new to the world,—a fact which the imagination strives in vain to grasp.

There are at the present time two great nations in the world, which started from different points, but seem to tend towards the same end. I allude to the Russians and the Americans. Both of them have grown up unnoticed; and whilst the attention of mankind was directed else-where, they have suddenly placed themselves in the front rank among the nations, and the world learned their existence and their greatness at almost the same time.

All other nations seem to have nearly reached their natural limits, and they have only to maintain their power; but these are still in the act of growth. All the others have stopped, or continue to advance with extreme difficulty; these alone are proceeding with ease and celerity along a path to which no limit can be perceived. The American strug-gles against the obstacles which nature opposes to him; the adversar-ies of the Russian are men. The former combats the wilderness and savage life; the latter, civilization with all its arms. The conquests of the American are therefore gained by the ploughshare; those of the Russian by the sword. The Anglo-American relies upon personal interest to accomplish his ends, and gives free scope to the unguided strength and common sense of the people; the Russian centers all the authority of society in a single arm. The principal instrument of the former is freedom; of the latter, servitude. Their starting-point is dif-ferent, and their courses are not the same; yet each of them seems marked out by the will of Heaven to sway the destinies of half the globe.

VOLUME II

──────★──────

FIRST BOOK

Influence of Democracy Upon the Action of Intellect in the United States

CHAPTER I

★

Philosophical Method of the Americans

I think that in no country in the civilized world is less attention paid to philosophy than in the United States. The Americans have no philosophical school of their own; and they care but little for all the schools into which Europe is divided, the very names of which are scarcely known to them.

Yet it is easy to perceive that almost all the inhabitants of the United States conduct their understanding in the same manner, and govern it by the same rules; that is to say, without ever having taken the trouble to define the rules, they have a philosophical method common to the whole people.

To evade the bondage of system and habit, of family-maxims, class-opinions, and, in some degree, of national prejudices; to accept tradition only as a means of information, and existing facts only as a lesson to be used in doing otherwise and doing better; to seek the reason of things for one's self, and in one's self alone; to tend to results without being bound to means, and to aim at the substance through the form;—such are the principal characteristics of what I shall call the philosophical method of the Americans.

CHAPTER II

———★———

Of the Principal Source of Belief
Among Democratic Nations

When the ranks of society are unequal, and men unlike each other in condition, there are some individuals wielding the power of superior intelligence, learning, and enlightenment, whilst the multitude are sunk in ignorance and prejudice. Men living at these aristocratic periods are therefore naturally induced to shape their opinions by the standard of a superior person, or superior class of persons, whilst they are averse to recognize the infallibility of the mass of the people.

The contrary takes place in ages of equality. The nearer the people are drawn to the common level of an equal and similar condition, the less prone does each man become to place implicit faith in a certain man or a certain class of men. But his readiness to believe the multitude increases, and opinion is more than ever mistress of the world. Not only is common opinion the only guide which private judgment retains amongst a democratic people, but amongst such a people it possesses a power infinitely beyond what it has elsewhere. At periods of equality, men have no faith in one another, by reason of their common resemblance; but this very resemblance gives them almost unbounded confidence in the judgment of the public; for it would not seem probable, as they are all endowed with equal means of judging, but that the greater truth should go with the greater number.

When the inhabitant of a democratic country compares himself individually with all those about him, he feels with pride that he is the equal of any one of them; but when he comes to survey the totality of his fellows, and to place himself in contrast with so huge a body, he is instantly overwhelmed by the sense of his own insignificance and weakness. The same equality which renders him independent of each of his fellow-citizens, taken severally, exposes him alone and unprotected to the influence of the greater number. The public has therefore, among a democratic people, a singular power, which aristocratic nations cannot conceive of; for it does not persuade to certain opinions, but it enforces them, and infuses them into the intellect by a sort of enormous pressure of the minds of all upon the reason of each.

In the United States, the majority undertakes to supply a multitude of ready-made opinions for the use of individuals, who are thus relieved from the necessity of forming opinions of their own. Everybody there adopts great numbers of theories, on philosophy, morals, and politics, without inquiry, upon public trust; and if we look to it very narrowly, it will be perceived that religion herself holds sway there much less as a doctrine of revelation than as a commonly received opinion.

Thus intellectual authority will be different, but it will not be diminished; and far from thinking that it will disappear, I augur that it may readily acquire too much preponderance, and confine the action of private judgment within narrower limits than are suited either to the greatness or the happiness of the human race. In the principle of equality I very clearly discern two tendencies; the one leading the mind of every man to untried thoughts, the other which would prohibit him from thinking at all. And I perceive how, under the dominion of certain laws, democracy would extinguish that liberty of the mind to which a democratic social condition is favorable; so that, after having broken all the bondage once imposed on it by ranks or by men, the human mind would be closely fettered to the general will of the greatest number.

If the absolute power of a majority were to be substituted, by democratic nations, for all the different powers which checked or retarded overmuch the energy of individual minds, the evil would only have changed character. Men would not have found the means of independent life; they would simply have discovered (no easy task) a new physiognomy of servitude. There is,—and I cannot repeat it too often,—there is here matter for profound reflection to those who look on freedom of thought as a holy thing, and who hate not only the despot, but despotism. For myself, when I feel the hand of power lie heavy on my brow, I care but little to know who oppresses me; and I am not the more disposed to pass beneath the yoke because it is held out to me by the arms of a million of men.

CHAPTER III

———— ★ ————

Why the Americans Show More Aptitude and Taste for General Ideas Than Their Forefathers, the English

———————

The English have long been a very enlightened and a very aristocratic nation; their enlightened condition urged them constantly to generalize, and their aristocratic habits confined them to the particular. Hence arose that philosophy, at once bold and timid, broad and narrow, which has hitherto prevailed in England, and which still obstructs and stagnates so many minds in that country.

Independently of the causes I have pointed out in what goes before, others may be discerned less apparent, but no less efficacious, which produce amongst almost every democratic people a taste, and frequently a passion, for general ideas. A distinction must be taken between ideas of this kind. Some of them are the result of slow, minute, and conscientious labor of the mind, and these extend the sphere of human knowledge; others spring up at once from the first rapid exercise of the wits, and beget none but very superficial and uncertain notions.

Men who live in ages of equality have a great deal of curiosity and little leisure; their life is so practical, so confused, so excited, so active, that but little time remains to them for thought. Such men are prone to general ideas, because they spare them the trouble of studying particulars; they contain, if I may so speak, a great deal in a little compass, and give, in a little time, a great return. If, then, upon a brief and inattentive investigation, they think they discern a common relation between certain objects, inquiry is not pushed any further; and without examining in detail how far these several objects agree or differ, they are hastily arranged under one formulary, in order to pass to another subject.

One of the distinguishing characteristics of a democratic period is the taste which all men then have for easy success and present enjoyment. This occurs in the pursuits of the intellect as well as in all others. Most of those who live at a time of equality are full of an ambition at once aspiring and relaxed: they would fain succeed brilliantly and at once, but they would be dispensed from great efforts to obtain success. These conflicting tendencies lead straight to the research of general ideas, by aid of which they flatter themselves that they can delineate vast objects with little pains, and draw the attention of the public without much trouble.

And I know not that they are wrong in thinking thus. For their readers are as much averse to investigating anything to the bottom as they are; and what is generally sought in the productions of mind is easy pleasure and information without labor.

If aristocratic nations do not make sufficient use of general ideas, and frequently treat them with inconsiderate disdain, it is true, on the other hand, that a democratic people is ever ready to carry ideas of this kind to excess, and to espouse them with injudicious warmth.

————— ★ —————

Why the Americans Have Never Been So Eager As the French for General Ideas in Political Affairs

I have Observed that the Americans show a less decided taste for general ideas than the French. This is more especially true in politics.

———————————

This difference between the Americans and the French originates in several causes, but principally in the following one. The Americans form a democratic people, who have always directed public affairs themselves. The French are a democratic people, who, for a long time, could only speculate on the best manner of conducting them. The social condition of the French led them to conceive very general ideas on the subject of government, whilst their political constitution prevented them from correcting those ideas by experiment, and from gradually detecting their insufficiency; whereas, in America, the two things constantly balance and correct each other.

———————————

Thus it happens, that the democratic institutions which compel every citizen to take a practical part in the government moderate that excessive taste for general theories in politics which the principle of equality suggests.

CHAPTER V

———————★———————

How Religion in the United States
Avails Itself of Democratic Tendencies

I have shown, in a preceding chapter, that men cannot do without dogmatical belief; and even that it is much to be desired that such belief should exist amongst them. I now add, that, of all the kinds of dogmatical belief, the most desirable appears to me to be dogmatical belief in matters of religion; and this is a clear inference, even from no higher consideration than the interests of this world.

There is hardly any human action, however particular it may be, which does not originate in some very general idea men have conceived of the Deity, of his relation to mankind, of the nature of their own souls, and of their duties to their fellow-creatures. Nor can anything prevent these ideas from being the common spring whence all the rest emanates.

Men are therefore immeasurably interested in acquiring fixed ideas of God, of the soul, and of their general duties to their Creator and their fellow-men; for doubt on these first principles would abandon all their actions to chance, and would condemn them in some way to disorder and impotence.

This is, then, the subject on which it is most important for each of us to have fixed ideas; and unhappily it is also the subject on which it is most difficult for each of us, left to himself, to settle his opinions by the sole force of his reason. None but minds singularly free from the ordinary cares of life—minds at once penetrating, subtile, and trained by thinking—can, even with much time and care, sound the depths of these so necessary truths. And, indeed, we see that philosophers are themselves almost always surrounded with uncertainties; that at every step the natural light which illuminates their path grows dimmer and less secure; and that, in spite of all their efforts, they have as yet only discovered a few conflicting notions, on which the mind of man has been tossed about for thousands of years, without ever firmly grasping the truth, or finding novelty even in its errors. Studies of this nature are far above the average capacity of men; and, even if the majority of mankind were capable of such pursuits, it is evident that leisure to cultivate them would still be wanting.

Fixed ideas about God and human nature are indispensable to the daily practice of men's lives; but the practice of their lives prevents them from acquiring such ideas.

The difficulty appears to be without a parallel. Amongst the sciences, there are some which are useful to the mass of mankind, and are within its reach; others can be approached only by the few, and are not cultivated by the many, who require nothing beyond their more remote applications: but the daily practice of the science I speak of is indispensable to all, although the study of it is inaccessible to the greater number.

General ideas respecting God and human nature are therefore the ideas above all others which it is most suitable to withdraw from the habitual action of private judgment, and in which there is most to gain and least to lose by recognizing a principle of authority.

The first object, and one of the principal advantages, of religion is to furnish to each of these fundamental questions a solution which is at once clear, precise, intelligible to the mass of mankind, and lasting. There are religions which are false and very absurd; but it may be affirmed that any religion which remains within the circle I have just traced, without pretending to go beyond it, (as many religions have attempted to do, for the purpose of restraining on every side the free movement of the human mind,) imposes a salutary restraint on the intellect; and it must be admitted that, if it do not save men in another world, it is at least very conducive to their happiness and their greatness in this.

This is more especially true of men living in free countries. When the religion of a people is destroyed, doubt gets hold of the higher powers of the intellect, and half paralyzes all the others. Every man accustoms himself to have only confused and changing notions on the subjects most interesting to his fellow-creatures and himself. His opinions are ill-defended and easily abandoned; and, in despair of ever resolving by himself the hard problems respecting the destiny of man, he ignobly submits to think no more about them.

Such a condition cannot but enervate the soul, relax the springs of the will, and prepare a people for servitude. Not only does it happen, in such a case, that they allow their freedom to be taken from them; they frequently themselves surrender it. When there is no longer any principle of authority in religion, any more than in politics, men are speedily frightened at the aspect of this unbounded independence. The constant agitation of all surrounding things alarms and exhausts them. As everything is at sea in the sphere of the mind, they determine at least that the mechanism of society shall be firm and fixed; and, as they cannot resume their ancient belief, they assume a master.

For my own part, I doubt whether man can ever support at the same time complete religious independence and entire political freedom. And I am inclined to think that, if faith be wanting in him, he must be subject; and if he be free, he must believe.

Perhaps, however, this great utility of religions is still more obvious amongst nations where equality of conditions prevails, than amongst others. It must be acknowledged that equality, which brings great benefits into the world, nevertheless suggests to men (as will be shown hereafter) some very dangerous propensities. It tends to isolate them from each other, to concentrate every man's attention upon himself; and it lays open the soul to an inordinate love of material gratification.

The greatest advantage of religion is to inspire diametrically contrary principles. There is no religion which does not place the object of man's desires above and beyond the treasures of earth, and which does not naturally raise his soul to regions far above those of the senses. Nor is there any which does not impose on man some duties toward his kind, and thus draw him at times from the contemplation of himself. This occurs in religions the most false and dangerous.

Religious nations are therefore naturally strong on the very point on which democratic nations are weak, which shows of what importance it is for men to preserve their religion as their conditions become more equal.

I have neither the right nor the intention of examining the supernatural means which God employs to infuse religious belief into the heart of man. I am at this moment considering religions in a purely human point of view; my object is to inquire by what means they may most easily retain their sway in the democratic ages upon which we are entering.

It has been shown that, at times of general cultivation and equality, the human mind consents only with reluctance to adopt dogmatical opinions, and feels their necessity acutely only in spiritual matters. This proves, in the first place, that, at such times, religions ought, more cautiously than at any other, to confine themselves within their own precincts; for in seeking to extend their power beyond religious matters, they incur a risk of not being believed at all. The circle within which they seek to restrict the human intellect ought therefore to be carefully traced, and, beyond its verge, the mind should be left entirely free to its own guidance.

Mohammed professed to derive from Heaven, and has inserted in the Koran, not only religious doctrines, but political maxims, civil and criminal laws, and theories of science. The Gospel, on the contrary, only speaks of the general relations of men to God and to each other, beyond which it inculcates and imposes no point of faith. This alone, besides a thousand other reasons, would suffice to prove that the former of these religions will never long predominate in a cultivated and democratic age, whilst the latter is destined to retain its sway at these as at all other periods.

In continuation of this same inquiry, I find that, for religions to maintain their authority, humanly speaking, in democratic ages, not only must they confine themselves strictly within the circle of spiritual matters, but their power also will depend very much on the nature of the belief they inculcate, on the external forms they assume, and on the obligations they impose.

The preceding observation, that equality leads men to very general and very vast ideas, is principally to be understood in respect to religion. Men who are similar and equal in the world readily conceive the idea of the one God, governing every man by the same laws, and granting to every man future happiness on the same conditions. The idea of the unity of mankind constantly leads them back to the idea of the unity of the Creator; whilst, on the contrary, in a state of society where men are broken up into very unequal ranks, they are apt to devise as many deities as there are nations, castes, classes, or families, and to trace a thousand private roads to Heaven.

It cannot be denied that Christianity itself has felt, to some extent, the influence which social and political conditions exercise on religious opinions.

In speaking of philosophical method among the Americans, I have shown that nothing is more repugnant to the human mind, in an age of equality, than the idea of subjection to forms. Men living at such times are impatient of figures; to their eyes, symbols appear to be puerile artifices used to conceal or to set off truths which should more naturally be bared to the light of day: they are unmoved by ceremonial observances, and are disposed to attach only a secondary importance to the details of public worship.

Those who have to regulate the external forms of religion in a democratic age should pay a close attention to these natural propensities of the human mind, in order not to run counter to them unnecessarily.

I firmly believe in the necessity of forms, which fix the human mind in the contemplation of abstract truths, and aid it in embracing them warmly and holding them with firmness. Nor do I suppose that it is possible to maintain a religion without external observances; but, on the other hand, I am persuaded that, in the ages upon which we are entering, it would be peculiarly dangerous to multiply them beyond measure; and that they ought rather to be limited to as much as is absolutely necessary to perpetuate the doctrine itself, which is the substance of religion, of which the ritual is only the form. A religion which should become more minute, more peremptory, and more charged with small observances, at a time when men are becoming more equal, would soon find itself reduced to a band of fanatical zealots in the midst of an infidel people.

I anticipate the objection that, as all religions have general and eternal truths for their object, they cannot thus shape themselves to the shifting inclinations of every age, without forfeiting their claim to certainty in the eyes of mankind. To this I reply again, that the principal opinions which constitute a creed, and which theologians call articles of faith, must be very carefully distinguished from the accessories connected with them. Religions are obliged to hold fast to the former, whatever be the peculiar spirit of the age; but they should take good care not to bind themselves in the same manner to the latter, at a time when everything is in transition, and when the mind, accustomed to the moving pageant of human affairs, reluctantly allows itself to be fixed on any point. The fixity of eternal and secondary things can afford a chance of duration only when civil society is itself fixed; under any other circumstances, I hold it to be perilous.

We shall see that, of all the passions which originate in or are fostered by equality, there is one which it renders peculiarly intense, and which it also infuses into the heart of every man,—I mean the love of well-being. The taste for well-being is the prominent and indelible feature of democratic times.

It may be believed that a religion which should undertake to destroy so deep-seated a passion, would in the end be destroyed by it; and if it attempted to wean men entirely from the contemplation of the good things of this world, in order to devote their faculties exclusively to the thought of another, it may be foreseen that the minds of men would at length escape its grasp, to plunge into the exclusive enjoyment of present and material pleasures.

The chief concern of religion is to purify, to regulate, and to restrain the excessive and exclusive taste for well-being which men feel at periods of equality; but it would be an error to attempt to overcome it completely, or to eradicate it. Men cannot be cured of the love of riches; but they may be persuaded to enrich themselves by none but honest means.

This brings me to a final consideration, which comprises, as it were, all the others. The more the conditions of men are equalized and assimilated to each other, the more important is it for religion; whilst it carefully abstains from the daily turmoil of secular affairs, not needlessly to run counter to the ideas which generally prevail, or to the permanent interests which exist in the mass of the people. For, as public opinion grows to be more and more the first and most irresistible of existing powers, the religious principle has no external support strong enough to enable it long to resist its attacks. This is not less true of a democratic people ruled by a despot, than of a republic. In ages of equality kings may often command obedience, but the majority always commands belief: to the majority, therefore, deference is to be paid in whatsoever is not contrary to the faith.

I showed in my former volume how the American clergy stand aloof from secular affairs. This is the most obvious, but not the only, example of their self-restraint. In America, religion is a distinct sphere, in which the priest is sovereign, but out of which he takes care never to go. Within its limits, he is master of the mind; beyond them, he leaves men to themselves, and surrenders them to the independence and instability which belong to their nature and their age. I have seen no country in which Christianity is clothed with fewer forms, figures, and observances than in the United States; or where it presents more distinct, simple, and general notions to the mind. Although the Christians of America are divided into a multitude of sects, they all look upon their religion in the same light. This applies to Roman Catholicism as well as to the other forms of belief. There are no Romish priests who show less taste for the minute individual observances, for extraordinary or peculiar means of salvation, or who cling more to the spirit, and less to the letter, of the law, than the Roman Catholic priests of the United States. Nowhere is that doctrine of the Church which prohibits the worship reserved to God alone from being offered to the saints, more clearly inculcated or more generally followed. Yet the Roman Catholics of America are very submissive and very sincere.

Another remark is applicable to the clergy of every communion. The American ministers of the Gospel do not attempt to draw or to fix all the thoughts of man upon the life to come; they are willing to surrender a portion of his heart to the cares of the present; seeming to consider the goods of this world as important, though secondary, objects. If they take no part themselves in productive labor, they are at least interested in its progress, and they applaud its results; and whilst they never cease to point to the other world as the great object of the hopes and fears of the believer, they do not forbid him honestly to court prosperity in this. Far from attempting to show that these things are distinct and contrary to one another, they study rather to find out on what point they are most nearly and closely connected.

All the American clergy know and respect the intellectual supremacy exercised by the majority: they never sustain any but necessary conflicts with it. They take no share in the altercations of parties, but they readily adopt the general opinions of their country and their age: and they allow themselves to be borne away without opposition in the current of feeling and opinion by which everything around them is carried along. They endeavor to amend their contemporaries, but they do not quit fellowship with them. Public opinion is therefore never hostile to them: it rather supports and protects them; and their belief owes its authority at the same time to the strength which is its own, and to that which it borrows from the opinions of the majority.

Thus it is, that, by respecting all democratic tendencies not absolutely contrary to herself, and by making use of several of them for her own purposes, Religion sustains a successful struggle with that spirit of individual independence which is her most dangerous opponent.

---★---

CHAPTER VI

The Progress of Roman Catholicism in the United States

A merica is the most democratic country in the world, and it is at the same time (according to reports worthy of belief) the country in which the Roman Catholic religion makes most progress. At first sight, this is surprising.

Two things must here be accurately distinguished: equality inclines men to wish to form their own opinions; but, on the other hand, it imbues them with the taste and the idea of unity, simplicity, and impartiality in the power which governs society. Men living in democratic times are therefore very prone to shake off all religious authority; but if they consent to subject themselves to any authority of this kind, they choose at least that it should be single and uniform. Religious powers not radiating from a common center are naturally repugnant to their minds; and they almost as readily conceive that there should be no religion, as that there should be several.

At the present time, more than in any preceding age, Roman Catholics are seen to lapse into infidelity, and Protestants to be converted to Roman Catholicism. If the Roman Catholic faith be considered within the pale of the Church, it would seem to be losing ground; without that pale, to be gaining it. Nor is this difficult of explanation. The men of our days are naturally little disposed to believe; but, as soon as they have any religion, they immediately find in themselves a latent instinct which urges them unconsciously towards Catholicism. Many of the doctrines and practices of the Romish Church astonish them; but they feel a secret admiration for its discipline, and its great unity attracts them. If Catholicism could at length withdraw itself from the political animosities to which it has given rise, I have hardly any doubt but that the same spirit of the age which appears to be so opposed to it would become so favorable as to admit of its great and sudden advancement.

One of the most ordinary weaknesses of the human intellect is to seek to reconcile contrary principles, and to purchase peace at the expense of logic. Thus there have ever been, and will ever be, men who, after having submitted some portion of their religious belief to the principle of authority, will seek to exempt several other parts of their faith from it, and to keep their minds floating at random between liberty and obedience. But I am inclined to believe that the number of these thinkers will be less in democratic than in other ages; and that our posterity will tend more and more to a division into only two parts,—some relinquishing Christianity entirely, and others returning to the Church of Rome.

CHAPTER VII

———————★———————

What Causes Democratic Nations
to Incline Towards Pantheism

I shall show hereafter how the preponderating taste of a democratic people for very general ideas manifests itself in politics; but I wish to point out, at present, its principal effect on philosophy.

It cannot be denied that pantheism has made great progress in our age. The writings of a part of Europe bear visible marks of it: the Germans introduce it into philosophy, and the French into literature. Most of the works of imagination published in France contain some opinions or some tinge caught from pantheistical doctrines, or they disclose some tendency to such doctrines in their authors. This appears to me not to proceed only from an accidental, but from a permanent cause.

When the conditions of society are becoming more equal, and each individual man becomes more like all the rest, more weak and insignificant, a habit grows up of ceasing to notice the citizens, and considering only the people,—of overlooking individuals, to think only of their kind. At such times, the human mind seeks to embrace a multitude of different objects at once; and it constantly strives to connect a variety of consequences with a single cause. The idea of unity so possesses man, and is sought by him so generally, that, if he thinks he has found it, he readily yields himself to repose in that belief. Not content with the discovery that there is nothing in the world but a creation and a Creator, he is still embarrassed by this primary division of things, and seeks to expand and simplify his conception by including God and the Universe in one great Whole.

If there be a philosophical system which teaches that all things material and immaterial, visible and invisible, which the world contains, are to be considered only as the several parts of an immense

Being, who alone remains eternal amidst the continual change and ceaseless transformation of all that constitutes him, we may readily infer that such a system, although it destroy the individuality of man,—nay, rather because it destroys that individuality,—will have secret charms for men living in democracies. All their habits of thought prepare them to conceive it, and predispose them to adopt it. It naturally attracts and fixes their imagination; it fosters the pride, whilst it soothes the indolence, of their minds.

Amongst the different systems by whose aid Philosophy endeavors to explain the Universe, I believe pantheism to be one of those most fitted to seduce the human mind in democratic times. Against it, all who abide in their attachment to the true greatness of man should combine and struggle.

CHAPTER VIII

———— ★ ————

How Equality Suggests to the Americans the Idea of the Indefinite Perfectibility of Man

E quality suggests to the human mind several ideas which would not have originated from any other source, and it modifies almost all those previously entertained. I take as an example the idea of human perfectibility, because it is one of the principal notions that the intellect can conceive, and because it constitutes of itself a great philosophical theory, which is everywhere to be traced by its consequences in the conduct of human affairs.

Although man has many points of resemblance with the brutes, one trait is peculiar to himself,—he improves: they are incapable of improvement. Mankind could not fail to discover this difference from the beginning. The idea of perfectibility is therefore as old as the world; equality did not give birth to it, but has imparted to it a new character.

When the citizens of a community are classed according to rank, profession, or birth, and when all men are constrained to follow the career which chance has opened before them, every one thinks that the utmost limits of human power are to be discerned in proximity to himself, and no one seeks any longer to resist the inevitable law of his destiny. Not, indeed, that an aristocratic people absolutely deny man's faculty of self-improvement, but they do not hold it to be indefinite; they can conceive amelioration, but not change: they imagine that the future condition of society may be better, but not essentially different; and, whilst they admit that humanity has made progress, and may still have some to make, they assign to it beforehand certain impassable limits.

Thus, they do not presume that they have arrived at the supreme good or at absolute truth, (what people or what man was ever wild enough to imagine it?) but they cherish a persuasion that they have pretty nearly reached that degree of greatness and knowledge which our imperfect nature admits of; and, as nothing moves about them, they are willing to fancy that everything is in its fit place. Then it is that the legislator affects to lay down eternal laws; that kings and nations will raise none but imperishable monuments; and that the present generation undertakes to spare generations to come the care of regulating their destinies.

In proportion as castes disappear and the classes of society approximate,—as manners, customs, and laws vary, from the tumultuous intercourse of men,—as new facts arise,—as new truths are brought to light,—as ancient opinions are dissipated, and others take their place,—the image of an ideal but always fugitive perfection presents itself to the human mind. Continual changes are then every instant occurring under the observation of every man: the position of some is rendered worse; and he learns but too well that no people and no individual, how enlightened soever they may be, can lay claim to infallibility: the condition of others is improved; whence he infers that man is endowed with an indefinite faculty of improvement. His reverses teach him that none have discovered absolute good,—his success stimulates him to the never-ending pursuit of it. Thus, forever seeking, forever falling to rise again,—often disappointed, but not discouraged,—he tends unceasingly towards that unmeasured greatness so indistinctly visible at the end of the long track which humanity has yet to tread.

It can hardly be believed how many facts naturally flow from the philosophical theory of the indefinite perfectibility of man, or how strong an influence it exercises even on those who, living entirely for the purposes of action and not of thought, seem to conform their actions to it, without knowing anything about it.

I accost an American sailor, and inquire why the ships of his country are built so as to last but for a short time; he answers without hesitation, that the art of navigation is every day making such rapid progress, that the finest vessel would become almost useless if it lasted beyond a few years. In these words, which fell accidentally, and on a particular subject, from an uninstructed man, I recognize the general and systematic idea upon which a great people direct all their concerns.

Aristocratic nations are naturally too apt to narrow the scope of human perfectibility; democratic nations, to expand it beyond reason.

———————★———————

The Example of the Americans Does Not Prove That a Democratic People Can Have No Aptitude and No Taste for Science, Literature, or Art.

It must be acknowledged that in few of the civilized nations of our time have the higher sciences made less progress than in the United States; and in few have great artists, distinguished poets, or celebrated writers, been more rare. Many Europeans, struck by this fact, have looked upon it as a natural and inevitable result of equality; and they have thought that, if a democratic state of society and democratic institutions were ever to prevail over the whole earth, the human mind would gradually find its beacon-lights grow dim, and men would relapse into a period of darkness.

To reason thus is, I think, to confound several ideas which it is important to divide and examine separately: it is to mingle, unintentionally, what is democratic with what is only American.

The religion professed by the first emigrants, and bequeathed by them to their descendants,—simple in its forms, austere and almost harsh in its principles, and hostile to external symbols and to ceremonial pomp,—is naturally unfavorable to the fine arts, and only yields reluctantly to the pleasures of literature. The Americans are a very old and a very enlightened people, who have fallen upon a new and unbounded country, where they may extend themselves at pleasure, and which they may fertilize without difficulty. This state of things is without a parallel in the history of the world. In America, every one finds facilities unknown elsewhere for making or increasing his fortune. The spirit of gain is always on the stretch, and the human mind, constantly diverted from the pleasures of imagination and the labors of the intellect, is there swayed by no impulse but the pursuit of wealth. Not only are manufacturing and commercial classes to be found in the United States, as they are in all other countries; but, what never occurred elsewhere, the whole community are simultaneously engaged in productive industry and commerce.

But I am convinced that, if the Americans had been alone in the world, with the freedom and the knowledge acquired by their forefathers, and the passions which are their own, they would not have been slow to discover that progress cannot long be made in the application of the sciences without cultivating the theory of them; that all the arts are perfected by one another: and, however absorbed they might have been by the pursuit of the principal object of their desires, they would speedily have admitted that it is necessary to turn aside from it occasionally, in order the better to attain it in the end.

The taste for the pleasures of mind is moreover so natural to the heart of civilized man, that amongst the polite nations, which are least disposed to give themselves up to these pursuits, a certain number of persons are always to be found who take part in them. This intellectual craving, once felt, would very soon have been satisfied.

But at the very time when the Americans were naturally inclined to require nothing of science but its special applications to the useful arts and the means of rendering life comfortable, learned and literary Europe was engaged in exploring the common sources of truth, and in improving at the same time all that can minister to the pleasures or satisfy the wants of man.

At the head of the enlightened nations of the Old World the inhabitants of the United States more particularly distinguished one, to which they were closely united by a common origin and by kindred habits. Amongst this people they found distinguished men of science, able artists, writers of eminence, and they were enabled to enjoy the treasures of the intellect without laboring to amass them. In spite of the ocean which intervenes, I cannot consent to separate America from Europe. I consider the people of the United States as that portion of the English people who are commissioned to explore the forests of the New World; whilst the rest of the nation, enjoying more leisure and less harassed by the drudgery of life, may devote their energies to thought, and enlarge in all directions the empire of mind.

The position of the Americans is therefore quite exceptional, and it may be believed that no democratic people will ever be placed in a similar one. Their strictly Puritanical origin,—their exclusively commercial habits,—even the country they inhabit, which seems to divert their minds from the pursuit of science, literature, and the arts,—the proximity of Europe, which allows them to neglect these pursuits without relapsing into barbarism,—a thousand special causes, of which I have only been able to point out the most important,—have singularly concurred to fix the mind of the American upon purely practical objects. His passions, his wants, his education, and everything about him, seem to unite in drawing the native of the United States earthward: his religion alone bids him turn, from time to time, a transient and distracted glance to heaven. Let us cease, then, to view all democratic nations under the example of the American people, and attempt to survey them at length with their own features.

It is possible to conceive a people not subdivided into any castes or scale of ranks; among whom the law, recognizing no privileges, should divide inherited property into equal shares; but which, at the same time, should be without knowledge and without freedom. Nor is this an empty hypothesis: a despot may find that it is his interest to render his subjects equal and to leave them ignorant, in order more easily to keep them slaves. Not only would a democratic people of this kind show neither aptitude nor taste for science, literature, or art, but it would probably never arrive at the possession of them. The law of descent would of itself provide for the destruction of large fortunes at each succeeding generation; and no new fortunes would be acquired. The poor man, without either knowledge or freedom, would not so much as conceive the idea of raising himself to wealth; and the rich man would allow himself to be degraded to poverty, without a notion of self-defence. Between these two members of the community complete and invincible equality would soon be established. No one would then have time or taste to devote himself to the pursuits or pleasures of the intellect; but all men would remain paralyzed in a state of common ignorance and equal servitude.

When I conceive a democratic society of this kind, I fancy myself in one of those low, close, and gloomy abodes, where the light which breaks in from without soon faints and fades away. A sudden heaviness overpowers me, and I grope through the surrounding darkness, to find an opening which will restore me to the air and the light of day. But all this is not applicable to men already enlightened who retain their freedom, after having abolished those peculiar and hereditary rights which perpetuated the tenure of property in the hands of certain individuals or certain classes.

When men living in a democratic state of society are enlightened, they readily discover that they are not confined and fixed by any limits which constrain them to take up with their present fortune. They all, therefore, conceive the idea of increasing it,—if they are free, they all attempt it; but all do not succeed in the same manner. The legislature, it is true, no longer grants privileges, but nature grants them. As natural inequality is very great, fortunes become unequal as soon as every man exerts all his faculties to get rich.

The law of descent prevents the establishment of wealthy families, but it does not prevent the existence of wealthy individuals. It constantly brings back the members of the community to a common level, from which they as constantly escape; and the inequality of fortunes augments in proportion as their knowledge is diffused and their liberty increased.

A sect which arose in our time, and was celebrated for its talents and its extravagance, proposed to concentrate all property in the hands of a central power, whose function it should afterwards be to parcel it out to individuals, according to their merits. This would have been a method of escaping from that complete and eternal equality which seems to threaten democratic society. But it would be a simpler and less dangerous remedy to grant no privilege to any, giving to all equal cultivation and equal independence, and leaving every one to determine his own position. Natural inequality will soon make way for itself, and wealth will spontaneously pass into the hands of the most capable.

It is therefore not true to assert, that men living in democratic times are naturally indifferent to science, literature, and the arts: only it must be acknowledged that they cultivate them after their own fashion, and bring to the task their own peculiar qualifications and deficiencies.

CHAPTER X

★

Why the Americans Are More Addicted
To Practical Than To Theoretical Science

If a democratic state of society and democratic institutions do not retard the onward course of the human mind, they incontestably guide it in one direction in preference to another. Their efforts, thus circumscribed, are still exceedingly great; and I may be pardoned if I pause for a moment to contemplate them.

We had occasion, in speaking of the philosophical method of the American people, to make several remarks, which must here be turned to account.

Equality begets in man the desire of judging of everything for himself: it gives him, in all things, a taste for the tangible and the real, a contempt for tradition and for forms. These general tendencies are principally discernible in the peculiar subject of this chapter.

Those who cultivate the sciences amongst a democratic people are always afraid of losing their way in visionary speculation. They mistrust systems; they adhere closely to facts, and study facts with their own senses. As they do not easily defer to the mere name of any fellow-man, they are never inclined to rest upon any man's authority; but, on the contrary, they are unremitting in their efforts to find out the weaker points of their neighbors' doctrine. Scientific precedents have little weight with them; they are never long detained by the subtilty of the schools, nor ready to accept big words for sterling coin; they penetrate, as far as they can, into the principal parts of the subject which occupies them, and they like to expound them in the vulgar tongue. Scientific pursuits then follow a freer and safer course, but a less lofty one.

The mind may, as it appears to me, divide science into three parts.

The first comprises the most theoretical principles, and those more abstract notions, whose application is either unknown or very remote.

The second is composed of those general truths which still belong to pure theory, but lead nevertheless by a straight and short road to practical results.

Methods of application and means of execution make up the third.

Each of these different portions of science may be separately cultivated, although reason and experience prove that neither of them can prosper long, if it be absolutely cut off from the two others.

In America, the purely practical part of science is admirably understood, and careful attention is paid to the theoretical portion, which is immediately requisite to application. On this head, the Americans always display a clear, free, original, and inventive power of mind. But hardly any one in the United States devotes himself to the essentially theoretical and abstract portion of human knowledge. In this respect, the Americans carry to excess a tendency which is, I think, discernible, though in a less degree, amongst all democratic nations.

Nothing is more necessary to the culture of the higher sciences, or of the more elevated departments of science, than meditation; and nothing is less suited to meditation than the structure of democratic society. We do not find there, as amongst an aristocratic people, one class which keeps in repose because it is well off; and another, which does not venture to stir because it despairs of improving its condition. Every one is in motion: some in quest of power, others of gain. In the midst of this universal tumult,—this incessant conflict of jarring interests,—this continual striving of men after fortune,—where is that calm to be found which is necessary for the deeper combinations of the intellect? How can the mind dwell upon any single point, when everything whirls around it, and man himself is swept and beaten onwards by the heady current which rolls all things in its course?

Men who live in democratic communities not only seldom indulge in meditation, but they naturally entertain very little esteem for it. A democratic state of society and democratic institutions keep the greater part of men in constant activity; and the habits of mind which are suited to an active life are not always suited to a contemplative one.

The man of action is frequently obliged to content himself with the best he can get, because he would never accomplish his purpose if he chose to carry every detail to perfection. He has perpetually occasion to rely on ideas which he has not had leisure to search to the bottom; for he is much more frequently aided by the seasonableness of an idea than by its strict accuracy; and, in the long run, he risks less in making use of some false principles, than in spending his time in establishing all his principles, on the basis of truth. The world is not led by long or learned demonstrations: a rapid glance at particular incidents, the daily study of the fleeting passions of the multitude, the accidents of the moment and the art of turning them to account, decide all its affairs.

In the ages in which active life is the condition of almost every one, men are therefore generally led to attach an excessive value to the rapid bursts and superficial conceptions of the intellect; and, on the other hand, to depreciate unduly its slower and deeper labors. This opinion of the public influences the judgment of the men who cultivate the sciences; they are persuaded that they may succeed in those pursuits without meditation, or are deterred from such pursuits as demand it.

There are several methods of studying the sciences. Amongst a multitude of men you will find a selfish, mercantile, and trading taste for the discoveries of the mind, which must not be confounded with that disinterested passion which is kindled in the heart of a few. A desire to utilize knowledge is one thing; the pure desire to know is another. I do not doubt that in a few minds, and at long intervals, an ardent, inexhaustible love of truth springs up, self-supported, and living in ceaseless fruition, without ever attaining full satisfaction. This ardent love it is—this proud, disinterested love of what is true—which raises men to the abstract sources of truth, to draw their mother knowledge thence.

If Pascal had had nothing in view but some large gain, or even if he had been stimulated by the love of fame alone, I cannot conceive that he would ever have been able to rally all the powers of his mind, as he did, for the better discovery of the most hidden things of the Creator. When I see him, as it were, tear his soul from all the cares of life to devote it wholly to these researches, and, prematurely snapping the links which bind the frame to life, die of old age before forty, I stand amazed, and perceive that no ordinary cause is at work to produce efforts so extraordinary.

The future will prove whether these passions, at once so rare and so productive, come into being and into growth as easily in the midst of democratic as in aristocratic communities. For myself, I confess that I am slow to believe it.

In aristocratic societies, the class which gives the tone to opinion, and has the guidance of affairs, being permanently and hereditarily placed above the multitude, naturally conceives a lofty idea of itself and of man. It loves to invent for him noble pleasures, to carve out splendid objects for his ambition. Aristocracies often commit very tyrannical and inhuman actions, but they rarely entertain grovelling thoughts; and they show a kind of haughty contempt of little plea-sures, even whilst they indulge in them. The effect is greatly to raise the general pitch of society. In aristocratic ages, vast ideas are com-monly entertained of the dignity, the power, and the greatness of man. These opinions exert their influence on those who cultivate the sciences, as well as on the rest of the community. They facilitate the natural impulse of the mind to the highest regions of thought; and they naturally prepare it to conceive a sublime, almost a divine, love of truth.

Men of science at such periods are consequently carried away towards theory; and it even happens that they frequently conceive an inconsiderate contempt for practice. "Archimedes," says Plutarch, "was of so lofty a spirit, that he never condescended to write any trea-tise on the manner of constructing all these engines of war. And as he held this science of inventing and putting together engines, and all arts generally speaking which tended to any useful end in practice, to be vile, low, and mercenary, he spent his talents and his studious hours in writing of those things only whose beauty and subtilty had in them no admixture of necessity." Such is the aristocratic aim of sci-ence: it cannot be the same in democratic nations.

The greater part of the men who constitute these nations are extremely eager in the pursuit of actual and physical gratification. As they are always dissatisfied with the position which they occupy, and are always free to leave it, they think of nothing but the means of changing their fortune, or increasing it. To minds thus predisposed, every new method which leads by a shorter road to wealth, every machine which spares labor, every instrument which diminishes the cost of production, every discovery which facilitates pleasures or augments them, seems to be the grandest effort of the human intellect. It is chiefly from these motives that a democratic people addicts itself to scientific pursuits,—that it understands and respects them. In aristocratic ages, science is more particularly called upon to furnish gratification to the mind; in democracies, to the body.

You may be sure that the more a nation is democratic, enlightened, and free, the greater will be the number of these interested promoters of scientific genius, and the more will discoveries immediately applicable to productive industry confer gain, fame, and even power, on their authors. For in democracies, the working class take a part in public affairs; and public honors, as well as pecuniary remuneration, may be awarded to those who deserve them.

In a community thus organized, it may easily be conceived that the human mind may be led insensibly to the neglect of theory; and that it is urged, on the contrary, with unparalleled energy, to the applications of science, or at least to that portion of theoretical science which is necessary to those who make such applications. In vain will some instinctive inclination raise the mind towards the loftier spheres of the intellect; interest draws it down to the middle zone. There it may develop all its energy and restless activity, and bring forth wonders. These very Americans, who have not discovered one of the general laws of mechanics, have introduced into navigation an engine which changes the aspect of the world.

Assuredly I do not contend that the democratic nations of our time are destined to witness the extinction of the great luminaries of man's intelligence, or even that they will never bring new lights into existence. At the age at which the world has now arrived, and amongst so many cultivated nations perpetually excited by the fever of productive industry, the bonds which connect the different parts of science cannot fail to strike the observer; and the taste for practical science itself, if it be enlightened, ought to lead men not to neglect theory. In the midst of so many attempted applications of so many experiments, repeated every day, it is almost impossible that general laws should not frequently be brought to light; so that great discoveries would be frequent, though great inventors may be few.

I believe, moreover, in high scientific vocations. If the democratic principle does not, on the one hand, induce men to cultivate science for its own sake, on the other, it enormously increases the number of those who do cultivate it. Nor is it credible that, amid so great a multitude, a speculative genius should not from time to time arise inflamed by the love of truth alone. Such an one, we may be sure, would dive into the deepest mysteries of nature, whatever be the spirit of his country and his age. He requires no assistance in his course,—it is enough that he is not checked in it. All that I mean to say is this: permanent inequality of conditions leads men to confine themselves to the arrogant and sterile research of abstract truths, whilst the social condition and the institutions of democracy prepare them to seek the immediate and useful practical results of the sciences. This tendency is natural and inevitable: it is curious to be acquainted with it, and it may be necessary to point it out.

——————★——————

CHAPTER XI

In What Spirit the Americans
Cultivate the Arts

It would be to waste the time of my readers and my own, if I strove to demonstrate how the general mediocrity of fortunes, the absence of superfluous wealth, the universal desire of comfort, and the constant efforts by which every one attempts to procure it, make the taste for the useful predominate over the love of the beautiful in the heart of man. Democratic nations, amongst whom all these things exist, will therefore cultivate the arts which serve to render life easy, in preference to those whose object is to adorn it. They will habitually prefer the useful to the beautiful, and they will require that the beautiful should be useful.

But I propose to go further; and, after having pointed out this first feature, to sketch several others.

It commonly happens that, in the ages of privilege, the practice of almost all the arts becomes a privilege; and that every profession is a separate walk, upon which it is not allowable for every one to enter. Even when productive industry is free, the fixed character which belongs to aristocratic nations gradually segregates all the persons who practise the same art, till they form a distinct class, always composed of the same families, whose members are all known to each other, and amongst whom a public opinion of their own, and a species of corporate pride, soon spring up. In a class or guild of this kind, each artisan has not only his fortune to make, but his reputation to preserve. He is not exclusively swayed by his own interest, or even by that of his customer, but by that of the body to which he belongs; and the interest of that body is, that each artisan should produce the best possible workmanship. In aristocratic ages, the object of the arts is therefore to manufacture as well as possible,—not with the greatest despatch, or at the lowest rate.

When, on the contrary, every profession is open to all,—when a multitude of persons are constantly embracing and abandoning it,—and when its several members are strangers, indifferent to, and from their numbers hardly seen by, each other,—the social tie is destroyed, and each workman, standing alone, endeavors simply to gain the most money at the least cost. The will of the customer is then his only limit. But at the same time, a corresponding change takes place in the customer also. In countries in which riches, as well as power, are concentrated and retained in the hands of a few, the use of the greater part of this world's goods belongs to a small number of individuals, who are always the same. Necessity, public opinion, or moderate desires, exclude all others from the enjoyment of them. As this aristocratic class remains fixed at the pinnacle of greatness on which it stands, without diminution or increase, it is always acted upon by the same wants, and affected by them in the same manner. The men of whom it is composed naturally derive from their superior and hereditary position a taste for what is extremely well made and lasting. This affects the general way of thinking of the nation in relation to the arts. It often occurs, among such a people, that even the peasant will rather go without the objects he covets, than procure them in a state of imperfection. In aristocracies, then, the handicraftsmen work for only a limited number of fastidious customers: the profit they hope to make depends principally on the perfection of their workmanship.

Such is no longer the case when, all privileges being abolished, ranks are intermingled, and men are forever rising or sinking upon the social scale. Amongst a democratic people, a number of citizens always exist whose patrimony is divided and decreasing. They have contracted, under more prosperous circumstances, certain wants, which remain after the means of satisfying such wants are gone; and they are anxiously looking out for some surreptitious method of providing for them. On the other hand, there are always in democracies a large number of men whose fortune is upon the increase, but whose desires grow much faster than their fortunes: and who gloat upon the gifts of wealth in anticipation, long before they have means to command them. Such men are eager to find some short cut to these gratifications, already almost within their reach. From the combination of these two causes the result is, that in democracies there is always a multitude of persons whose wants are above their means, and who are very willing to take up with imperfect satisfaction, rather than abandon the object of their desires altogether.

The artisan readily understands these passions, for he himself partakes in them: in an aristocracy, he would seek to sell his workmanship at a high price to the few; he now conceives that the more expeditious way of getting rich is to sell them at a low price to all. But there are only two ways of lowering the price of commodities. The first is to discover some better, shorter, and more ingenious method of producing them: the second is to manufacture a larger quantity of goods, nearly similar, but of less value. Amongst a democratic population, all the intellectual faculties of the workman are directed to these two objects: he strives to invent methods which may enable him not only to work better, but quicker and cheaper; or, if he cannot succeed in that, to diminish the intrinsic quality of the thing he makes, without rendering it wholly unfit for the use for which it is intended. When none but the wealthy had watches, they were almost all very good ones: few are now made which are worth much, but everybody has one in his pocket. Thus the democratic principle not only tends to direct the human mind to the useful arts, but it induces the artisan to produce with great rapidity many imperfect commodities, and the consumer to content himself with these commodities.

Not that, in democracies, the arts are incapable, in case of need, of producing wonders. This may occasionally be the case, if customers appear who are ready to pay for time and trouble. In this rivalry of every kind of industry, in the midst of this immense competition and these countless experiments, some excellent workmen are formed, who reach the utmost limits of their craft. But they have rarely an opportunity of showing what they can do; they are scrupulously sparing of their powers; they remain in a state of accomplished mediocrity, which judges itself, and, though well able to shoot beyond the mark before it, aims only at what it hits. In aristocracies, on the contrary, workmen always do all they can; and when they stop, it is because they have reached the limit of their art.

CHAPTER XII

———————★———————

Why the Americans Raise Some Insignificant Monuments, and Others That Are Very Grand

I have just observed, that, in democratic ages, monuments of the arts tend to become more numerous and less important. I now hasten to point out the exception to this rule.

In a democratic community, individuals are very weak; but the state, which represents them all, and contains them all in its grasp, is very powerful. Nowhere do citizens appear so insignificant as in a democratic nation; nowhere does the nation itself appear greater, or does the mind more easily take in a wide survey of it. In democratic communities, the imagination is compressed when men consider themselves; it expands indefinitely when they think of the state. Hence it is that the same men who live on a small scale in narrow dwellings, frequently aspire to gigantic splendor in the erection of their public monuments.

The Americans have traced out the circuit of an immense city on the site which they intended to make their capital, but which, up to the present time, is hardly more densely peopled than Pontoise, though, according to them, it will one day contain a million of inhabitants. They have already rooted up trees for ten miles round, lest they should interfere with the future citizens of this imaginary metropolis. They have erected a magnificent palace for Congress in the center of the city, and have given it the pompous name of the Capitol.

The several States of the Union are every day planning and erecting for themselves prodigious undertakings, which would astonish the engineers of the great European nations.

Thus democracy not only leads men to a vast number of inconsiderable productions; it also leads them to raise some monuments on the largest scale: but between these two extremes there is a blank. A few scattered specimens of enormous buildings can therefore teach us nothing of the social condition and the institutions of the people by whom they were raised. I may add, though the remark is out of my subject, that they do not make us better acquainted with its greatness, its civilization, and its real prosperity. Whenever a power of any kind shall be able to make a whole people co-operate in a single undertaking, that power, with a little knowledge and a great deal of time, will succeed in obtaining something enormous from efforts so multiplied. But this does not lead to the conclusion that the people are very happy, very enlightened, or even very strong.

CHAPTER XIII

---★---

Literary Characteristics
of Democratic Times

When a traveller goes into a bookseller's shop in the United States, and examines the American books upon the shelves, the number of works appears very great; whilst that of known authors seems, on the contrary, extremely small. He will first find a multitude of elementary treatises, destined to teach the rudiments of human knowledge. Most of these books are written in Europe; the Americans reprint them, adapting them to their own use. Next comes an enormous quantity of religious works, Bibles, sermons, edifying anecdotes, controversial divinity, and reports of charitable societies; lastly appears the long catalogue of political pamphlets. In America, parties do not write books to combat each other's opinions, but pamphlets, which are circulated for a day with incredible rapidity, and then expire.

In the midst of all these obscure productions of the human brain appear the more remarkable works of a small number of authors, whose names are, or ought to be, known to Europeans.

Although America is perhaps in our days the civilized country in which literature is least attended to, still a large number of persons there take an interest in the productions of mind, and make them, if not the study of their lives, at least the charm of their leisure hours. But England supplies these readers with most of the books which they require. Almost all important English books are republished in the United States. The literary genius of Great Britain still darts its rays into the recesses of the forests of the New World. There is hardly a pioneer's hut which does not contain a few odd volumes of Shakespeare. I remember that I read the feudal drama of Henry V. for the first time in a log-house.

Not only do the Americans constantly draw upon the treasures of English literature, but it may be said with truth that they find the literature of England growing on their own soil. The larger part of that small number of men in the United States who are engaged in the composition of literary works are English in substance, and still more so in form. Thus they transport into the midst of democracy the ideas and literary fashions which are current amongst the aristocratic nation they have taken for their model. They paint with colors borrowed from foreign manners; and as they hardly ever represent the country they were born in as it really is, they are seldom popular there.

The citizens of the United States are themselves so convinced that it is not for them that books are published, that, before they can make up their minds upon the merit of one of their authors, they generally wait till his fame has been ratified in England; just as, in pictures, the author of an original is held entitled to judge of the merit of a copy.

The inhabitants of the United States have then, at present, properly speaking, no literature. The only authors whom I acknowledge as American are the journalists. They indeed are not great writers, but they speak the language of their country, and make themselves heard. Other authors are aliens; they are to the Americans what the imitators of the Greeks and Romans were to us at the revival of learning,—an object of curiosity, not of general sympathy. They amuse the mind, but they do not act upon the manners of the people.

I have already said that this state of things is far from originating in democracy alone, and that the causes of it must be sought for in several peculiar circumstances independent of the democratic principle. If the Americans, retaining the same laws and social condition, had had a different origin, and had been transported into another country, I do not question that they would have had a literature. Even as they are, I am convinced that they will ultimately have one; but its character will be different from that which marks the American literary productions of our time, and that character will be peculiarly its own. Nor is it impossible to trace this character beforehand.

CHAPTER XIV

---★---

The Trade of Literature

Democracy not only infuses a taste for letters among the trading classes, but introduces a trading spirit into literature.

In aristocracies, readers are fastidious and few in number; in democracies, they are far more numerous and far less difficult to please. The consequence is, that among aristocratic nations no one can hope to succeed without great exertion, and this exertion may earn great fame, but can never procure much money; whilst among democratic nations a writer may flatter himself that he will obtain at a cheap rate a moderate reputation and a large fortune. For this purpose he need not be admired, it is enough that he is liked.

The ever-increasing crowd of readers, and their continual craving for something new, insures the sale of books which nobody much esteems.

In democratic times, the public frequently treat authors as kings do their courtiers; they enrich and despise them. What more is needed by the venal souls who are born in courts, or are worthy to live there?

Democratic literature is always infested with a tribe of writers who look upon letters as a mere trade; and for some few great authors who adorn it, you may reckon thousands of idea-mongers.

———— ★ ————

The Study of Greek and Latin Literature Is Peculiarly Useful in Democratic Communities

It is evident, that, in democratic communities, the interest of individuals, as well as the security of the commonwealth, demands that the education of the greater number should be scientific, commercial, and industrial, rather than literary. Greek and Latin should not be taught in all the schools; but it is important that those who, by their natural disposition or their fortune, are destined to cultivate letters or prepared to relish them, should find schools where a complete knowledge of ancient literature may be acquired, and where the true scholar may be formed. A few excellent universities would do more towards the attainment of this object than a multitude of bad grammar-schools, where superfluous matters, badly learned, stand in the way of sound instruction in necessary studies.

All who aspire to literary excellence in democratic nations ought frequently to refresh themselves at the springs of ancient literature: there is no more wholesome medicine for the mind. Not that I hold the literary productions of the ancients to be irreproachable; but I think that they have some special merits, admirably calculated to counterbalance our peculiar defects. They are a prop on the side on which we are in most danger of falling.

CHAPTER XVI

---★---

How the American Democracy Has Modified the English Language

I f the reader has rightly understood what I have already said on the subject of literature in general, he will have no difficulty in understanding that species of influence which a democratic social condition and democratic institutions may exercise over language itself, which is the chief instrument of thought.

American authors may truly be said to live rather in England than in their own country; since they constantly study the English writers, and take them every day for their models. But it is not so with the bulk of the population, which is more immediately subjected to the peculiar causes acting upon the United States. It is not then to the written, but to the spoken language, that attention must be paid, if we would detect the changes which the idiom of an aristocratic people may undergo when it becomes the language of a democracy.

Englishmen of education, and more competent judges than I can be of the nicer shades of expression, have frequently assured me that the language of the educated classes in the United States is notably different from that of the educated classes in Great Britain. They complain, not only that the Americans have brought into use a number of new words,—the difference and the distance between the two countries might suffice to explain that much,—but that these new words are more especially taken from the jargon of parties, the mechanical arts, or the language of trade. They assert, in addition to this, that old English words are often used by the Americans in new acceptations; and lastly, that the inhabitants of the United States frequently intermingle phraseology in the strangest manner, and sometimes place words together which are always kept apart in the language of the mother country. These remarks, which were made to me at various times by persons who appeared to be worthy of credit, led me to reflect upon the subject; and my reflections brought me, by theoretical reasoning, to the same point at which my informants had arrived by practical observation.

In aristocracies, language must naturally partake of that state of repose in which everything remains. Few new words are coined, because few new things are made; and, even if new things were made, they would be designated by known words, whose meaning had been determined by tradition. If it happens that the human mind bestirs itself at length, or is roused by light breaking in from without, the novel expressions which are introduced have a learned, intellectual, and philosophical character, which shows that they do not originate in a democracy. After the fall of Constantinople had turned the tide of science and letters towards the west, the French language was almost immediately invaded by a multitude of new words, which all had Greek or Latin roots. An erudite neologism then sprang up in France, which was confined to the educated classes, and which produced no sensible effect, or at least a very gradual one, upon the people.

All the nations of Europe successively exhibited the same change. Milton alone introduced more than six hundred words into the English language, almost all derived from the Latin, the Greek, or the Hebrew. The constant agitation which prevails in a democratic community tends unceasingly, on the contrary, to change the character of the language, as it does the aspect of affairs. In the midst of this general stir and competition of minds, a great number of new ideas are formed, old ideas are lost, or reappear, or are subdivided into an infinite variety of minor shades. The consequence is, that many words must fall into desuetude, and others must be brought into use.

Besides, democratic nations love change for its own sake; and this is seen in their language as much as in their politics. Even when they have no need to change words, they sometimes have the desire.

The genius of a democratic people is not only shown by the great number of words they bring into use, but also by the nature of the ideas these new words represent. Amongst such a people, the majority lays down the law in language, as well as in everything else; its prevailing spirit is as manifest in this as in other respects. But the majority is more engaged in business than in study; in political and commercial interests, than in philosophical speculation or literary pursuits. Most of the words coined or adopted for its use will bear the mark of these habits; they will mainly serve to express the wants of business, the passions of party, or the details of the public administration. In these departments, the language will constantly grow, whilst it will gradually lose ground in metaphysics and theology.

As to the source whence democratic nations are wont to derive their new expressions, and the manner in which they coin them, both may easily be described. Men living in democratic countries know but little of the language which was spoken at Athens or at Rome, and they do not care to dive into the lore of antiquity to find the expression which they want. If they have sometimes recourse to learned etymologies, vanity will induce them to search for roots from the dead languages; but erudition does not naturally furnish them its resources. The most ignorant, it sometimes happens, will use them most. The eminently democratic desire to get above their own sphere will often lead them to seek to dignify a vulgar profession by a Greek or Latin name. The lower the calling is, and the more remote from learning, the more pompous and erudite is its appellation. Thus, the French rope-dancers have transformed themselves into "Acrobates" and "Funambules."

Having little knowledge of the dead languages, democratic nations are apt to borrow words from living tongues; for they have constant mutual intercourse, and the inhabitants of different countries imitate each other the more readily as they grow more like each other every day.

But it is principally upon their own languages that democratic nations attempt to make innovations. From time to time they resume and restore to use forgotten expressions in their vocabulary, or they borrow from some particular class of the community a term peculiar to it, which they introduce with a figurative meaning into the language of daily life. Many expressions which originally belonged to the technical language of a profession or a party, are thus drawn into general circulation.

The most common expedient employed by democratic nations to make an innovation in language consists in giving an unwonted meaning to an expression already in use. This method is very simple, prompt, and convenient; no learning is required to use it aright, and ignorance itself rather facilitates the practice; but that practice is most dangerous to the language. When a democratic people double the meaning of a word in this way, they sometimes render the signification which it retains as ambiguous as that which it acquires. An author begins by a slight deflection of a known expression from its primitive meaning, and, thus modified, he adapts it as well as he can to his subject. A second writer twists the sense of the expression in another way; a third takes possession of it for another purpose; and as there is no common appeal to the sentence of a permanent tribunal which may definitively settle the signification of the word, it remains in an ambulatory condition. The consequence is, that writers hardly ever appear to dwell upon a single thought, but they always seem to aim at a group of ideas, leaving the reader to judge which of them has been hit.

This is a deplorable consequence of democracy. I had rather that the language should be made hideous with words imported from the Chinese, the Tartars, or the Hurons, than that the meaning of a word in our own language should become indeterminate. Harmony and uniformity are only secondary beauties in composition: many of these things are conventional, and, strictly speaking, it is possible to do without them; but without clear phraseology there is no good language.

The principle of equality necessarily introduces several other changes into language.

In aristocratic ages, when each nation tends to stand aloof from all others, and likes to have a physiognomy of its own, it often happens that several communities which have a common origin become nevertheless strangers to each other; so that, without ceasing to understand the same language, they no longer all speak it in the same manner. In these ages, each nation is divided into a certain number of classes, which see but little of each other, and do not intermingle. Each of these classes contracts, and invariably retains, habits of mind peculiar to itself, and adopts by choice certain words and certain terms, which afterwards pass from generation to generation, like their estates. The same idiom then comprises a language of the poor and a language of the rich,—a language of the commoner and a language of the nobility,—a learned language and a vulgar one. The deeper the divisions, and the more impassable the barriers of society become, the more must this be the case. I would lay a wager that amongst the castes of India there are amazing variations of language, and that there is almost as much difference between the language of a Pariah and that of a Brahmin, as there is in their dress.

When, on the contrary, men, being no longer restrained by ranks, meet on terms of constant intercourse,—when castes are destroyed, and the classes of society are recruited from and intermixed with each other, all the words of a language are mingled. Those which are unsuitable to the greater number perish: the remainder form a common store, whence every one chooses pretty nearly at random. Almost all the different dialects which divided the idioms of European nations are manifestly declining: there is no *patois* in the New World, and it is disappearing every day from the old countries.

The influence of this revolution in social condition is as much felt in style as it is in language. Not only does every one use the same words, but a habit springs up of using them without discrimination. The rules which style had set up are almost abolished: the line ceases to be drawn between expressions which seem by their very nature vulgar, and others which appear to be refined. Persons springing from different ranks of society carry the terms and expressions they are accustomed to use with them, into whatever circumstances they may pass; thus the origin of words is lost like the origin of individuals, and there is as much confusion in language as there is in society.

CHAPTER XVII

---★---

Of Some Sources of Poetry
Amongst Democratic Nations

Many different significations have been given to the word Poetry. It would weary my readers if I were to lead them to discuss which of these definitions ought to be selected: I prefer telling them at once that which I have chosen. In my opinion, Poetry is the search after, and the delineation of, the Ideal.

The Poet is he who, by suppressing a part of what exists, by adding some imaginary touches to the picture, and by combining certain real circumstances which do not in fact happen together, completes and extends the work of nature. Thus, the object of poetry is not to represent what is true, but to adorn it, and to present to the mind some loftier image. Verse, regarded as the ideal beauty of language, may be eminently poetical; but verse does not of itself constitute poetry.

I now proceed to inquire whether, amongst the actions, the sentiments, and the opinions of democratic nations, there are any which lead to a conception of the ideal, and which may for this reason be considered as natural sources of poetry.

It must, in the first place, be acknowledged that the taste for ideal beauty, and the pleasure derived from the expression of it, are never so intense or so diffused amongst a democratic as amongst an aristocratic people. In aristocratic nations, it sometimes happens that the body acts as it were spontaneously, whilst the higher faculties are bound and burdened by repose. Amongst these nations, the people will often display poetic tastes, and their fancy sometimes ranges beyond and above what surrounds them.

But in democracies, the love of physical gratification, the notion of bettering one's condition, the excitement of competition, the charm of anticipated success, are so many spurs to urge men onward in the active professions they have embraced, without allowing them to deviate for an instant from the track. The main stress of the faculties is to this point. The imagination is not extinct; but its chief function is to devise what may be useful, and to represent what is real. The principle of equality not only diverts men from the description of ideal beauty; it also diminishes the number of objects to be described.

Aristocracy, by maintaining society in a fixed position, is favorable to the solidity and duration of positive religions, as well as to the stability of political institutions. It not only keeps the human mind within a certain sphere of belief, but it predisposes the mind to adopt one faith rather than another. An aristocratic people will always be prone to place intermediate powers between God and man. In this respect, it may be said that the aristocratic element is favorable to poetry. When the universe is peopled with supernatural beings, not palpable to sense, but discovered by the mind, the imagination ranges freely; and poets, finding a thousand subjects to delineate, also find a countless audience to take an interest in their productions.

In democratic ages, it sometimes happens, on the contrary, that men are as much afloat in matters of faith as they are in their laws. Skepticism then draws the imagination of poets back to earth, and confines them to the real and visible world. Even when the principle of equality does not disturb religious conviction, it tends to simplify it, and to divert attention from secondary agents, to fix it principally on the Supreme Power.

Aristocracy naturally leads the human mind to the contemplation of the past, and fixes it there. Democracy, on the contrary, gives men a sort of instinctive distaste for what is ancient. In this respect, aristocracy is far more favorable to poetry; for things commonly grow larger and more obscure as they are more remote; and, for this twofold reason, they are better suited to the delineation of the ideal.

After having deprived poetry of the past, the principle of equality robs it in part of the present. Amongst aristocratic nations, there are a certain number of privileged personages, whose situation is, as it were, without and above the condition of man: to these, power, wealth, fame, wit, refinement, and distinction in all things appear peculiarly to belong. The crowd never sees them very closely, or does not watch them in minute details; and little is needed to make the description of such men poetical. On the other hand, amongst the same people, you will meet with classes so ignorant, low, and enslaved, that they are no less fit objects for poetry, from the excess of their rudeness and wretchedness, than the former are from their greatness and refinement. Besides, as the different classes of which an aristocratic community is composed are widely separated, and imperfectly acquainted with each other, the imagination may always represent them with some addition to, or some subtraction from, what they really are.

In democratic communities, where men are all insignificant and very much alike, each man instantly sees all his fellows when he surveys himself. The poets of democratic ages can never, therefore, take any man in particular as the subject of a piece; for an object of slender importance, which is distinctly seen on all sides, will never lend itself to an ideal conception.

Thus the principle of equality, in proportion as it has established itself in the world, has dried up most of the old springs of poetry. Let us now attempt to show what new ones it may disclose.

When skepticism had depopulated heaven, and the progress of equality had reduced each individual to smaller and better-known proportions, the poets, not yet aware of what they could substitute for the great themes which were departing together with the aristocracy, turned their eyes to inanimate nature. As they lost sight of gods and heroes, they set themselves to describe streams and mountains. Thence originated, in the last century, that kind of poetry which has been called, by way of distinction, *descriptive*. Some have thought that this embellished delineation of all the physical and inanimate objects which cover the earth was the kind of poetry peculiar to democratic ages; but I believe this to be an error, and that it belongs only to a period of transition.

I am persuaded that, in the end, democracy diverts the imagination from all that is external to man, and fixes it on man alone. Democratic nations may amuse themselves for a while with considering the productions of nature; but they are excited in reality only by a survey of themselves. Here, and here alone, the true sources of poetry amongst such nations are to be found; and it may be believed that the poets who shall neglect to draw their inspirations hence, will lose all sway over the minds which they would enchant, and will be left in the end with none but unimpassioned spectators of their transports.

I have shown how the ideas of progression and of the indefinite perfectibility of the human race belong to democratic ages. Democratic nations care but little for what has been, but they are haunted by visions of what will be; in this direction, their unbounded imagination grows and dilates beyond all measure. Here, then, is the widest range open to the genius of poets, which allows them to remove their performances to a sufficient distance from the eye. Democracy, which shuts the past against the poet, opens the future before him.

As all the citizens who compose a democratic community are nearly equal and alike, the poet cannot dwell upon any one of them; but the nation itself invites the exercise of his powers. The general similitude of individuals, which renders any one of them taken separately an improper subject of poetry, allows poets to include them all in the same imagery, and to take a general survey of the people itself. Democratic nations have a clearer perception than any others of their own aspect; and an aspect so imposing is admirably fitted to the delineation of the ideal.

I readily admit that the Americans have no poets; I cannot allow that they have no poetic ideas. In Europe, people talk a great deal of the wilds of America, but the Americans themselves never think about them: they are insensible to the wonders of inanimate nature, and they may be said not to perceive the mighty forests which surround them till they fall beneath the hatchet. Their eyes are fixed upon another sight: the American people views its own march across these wilds,—drying swamps, turning the course of rivers, peopling solitudes, and subduing nature. This magnificent image of themselves does not meet the gaze of the Americans at intervals only; it may be said to haunt every one of them in his least as well as in his most important actions, and to be always flitting before his mind.

Nothing conceivable is so petty, so insipid, so crowded with paltry interests, in one word, so anti-poetic, as the life of a man in the United States. But amongst the thoughts which it suggests, there is always one which is full of poetry, and this is the hidden nerve which gives vigor to the whole frame.

In aristocratic ages, each people, as well as each individual, is prone to stand separate and aloof from all others. In democratic ages, the extreme fluctuations of men, and the impatience of their desires, keep them perpetually on the move; so that the inhabitants of different countries intermingle, see, listen to, and borrow from each other. It is not only, then, the members of the same community who grow more alike; communities themselves are assimilated to one another, and the whole assemblage presents to the eye of the spectator one vast democracy, each citizen of which is a nation. This displays the aspect of mankind for the first time in the broadest light. All that belongs to the existence of the human race taken as a whole, to its vicissitudes and its future, becomes an abundant mine of poetry.

Amongst a democratic people, poetry will not be fed with legends or the memorials of old traditions. The poet will not attempt to people the universe with supernatural beings, in whom his readers and his own fancy have ceased to believe; nor will he coldly personify virtues and vices, which are better received under their own features. All these resources fail him; but Man remains, and the poet needs no more. The destinies of mankind—man himself, taken aloof from his country and his age, and standing in the presence of Nature and of God, with his passions, his doubts, his rare prosperities and inconceivable wretchedness—will become the chief, if not the sole, theme of poetry amongst these nations.

Experience may confirm this assertion, if we consider the productions of the greatest poets who have appeared since the world has been turned to democracy. The authors of our age who have so admirably delineated the features of Faust, Childe Harold, Réné, and Jocelyn, did not seek to record the actions of an individual, but to enlarge and to throw light on some of the obscurer recesses of the human heart.

Such are the poems of democracy. The principle of equality does not then destroy all the subjects of poetry: it renders them less numerous, but more vast.

CHAPTER XVIII

———————★———————

Why American Writers and Orators
Often Use an Inflated Style

I have frequently remarked that the Americans, who generally treat of business in clear, plain language, devoid of all ornament, and so extremely simple as to be often coarse, are apt to become inflated as soon as they attempt a more poetical diction. They then vent their pomposity from one end of a harangue to the other; and to hear them lavish imagery on every occasion, one might fancy that they never spoke of anything with simplicity.

The English less frequently commit a similar fault. The cause of this may be pointed out without much difficulty. In democratic communities, each citizen is habitually engaged in the contemplation of a very puny object, namely, himself. If he ever raises his looks higher, he perceives only the immense form of society at large, or the still more imposing aspect of mankind. His ideas are all either extremely minute and clear, or extremely general and vague: what lies between is a void. When he has been drawn out of his own sphere, therefore, he always expects that some amazing object will be offered to his attention; and it is on these terms alone that he consents to tear himself for a moment from the petty, complicated cares which form the charm and the excitement of his life.

This appears to me sufficiently to explain why men in democracies, whose concerns are in general so paltry, call upon their poets for conceptions so vast and descriptions so unlimited.

The authors, on their part, do not fail to obey a propensity of which they themselves partake; they perpetually inflate their imaginations, and, expanding them beyond all bounds, they not infrequently abandon the great in order to reach the gigantic. By these means, they hope to attract the observation of the multitude, and to fix it easily upon themselves: nor are their hopes disappointed; for, as the multitude seeks for nothing in poetry but objects of vast dimensions, it has neither the time to measure with accuracy the proportions of all the objects set before it, nor a taste sufficiently correct to perceive at once in what respect they are out of proportion. The author and the public at once vitiate one another.

We have also seen, that, amongst democratic nations, the sources of poetry are grand, but not abundant. They are soon exhausted: and poets, not finding the elements of the ideal in what is real and true, abandon them entirely and create monsters. I do not fear that the poetry of democratic nations will prove insipid, or that it will fly too near the ground; I rather apprehend that it will be forever losing itself in the clouds, and that it will range at last to purely imaginary regions. I fear that the productions of democratic poets may often be surcharged with immense and incoherent imagery, with exaggerated descriptions and strange creations; and that the fantastic beings of their brain may sometimes make us regret the world of reality.

CHAPTER XIX

———★———

Some Observations on the Drama amongst Democratic Nations

When the revolution which has changed the social and political state of an aristocratic people begins to penetrate into literature, it generally first manifests itself in the drama, and it always remains conspicuous there.

———

The drama brings out most of the good qualities, and almost all the defects, inherent in democratic literature. Democratic communities hold erudition very cheap, and care but little for what occurred at Rome and Athens; they want to hear something which concerns themselves, and the delineation of the present age is what they demand. When the heroes and the manners of antiquity are frequently brought upon the stage, and dramatic authors faithfully observe the rules of antiquated precedent, that is enough to warrant a conclusion that the democratic classes have not yet got the upper hand in the theatres.

———

In democracies, dramatic pieces are listened to, but not read. Most of those who frequent the amusements of the stage do not go there to seek the pleasures of mind, but the keen emotions of the heart. They do not expect to hear a fine literary work, but to see a play; and provided the author writes the language of his country correctly enough to be understood, and that his characters excite curiosity and awaken sympathy, the audience are satisfied. They ask no more of fiction, and immediately return to real life. Accuracy of style is therefore less

required, because the attentive observance of its rules is less perceptible on the stage.

As for the probability of the plot, it is incompatible with perpetual
novelty, surprise, and rapidity of invention. It is therefore neglected,
and the public excuses the neglect. You may be sure that, if you succeed in bringing your audience into the presence of something that
affects them, they will not care by what road you brought them there:
and they will never reproach you for having excited their emotions in
spite of dramatic rules.

The Americans, when they go to the theatres, very broadly display all the different propensities which I have here described; but it
must be acknowledged that, as yet, very few of them go to theatres
at all. Although playgoers and plays have prodigiously increased in
the United States in the last forty years, the population indulge in this
kind of amusement only with the greatest reserve. This is attributable
to peculiar causes, which the reader is already acquainted with, and
of which a few words will suffice to remind him.

The Puritans who founded the American republics were not only
enemies to amusements, but they professed an especial abhorrence
for the stage. They considered it as an abominable pastime; and as
long as their principles prevailed with undivided sway, scenic performances were wholly unknown amongst them. These opinions of the
first fathers of the colony have left very deep traces on the minds of
their descendants.

The extreme regularity of habits and the great strictness of morals which are observable in the United States, have as yet been little
favorable to the growth of dramatic art. There are no dramatic subjects in a country which has witnessed no great political catastrophes,
and in which love invariably leads by a straight and easy road to matrimony. People who spend every day in the week in making money,
and the Sunday in going to church, have nothing to invite the Muse
of Comedy.

A single fact suffices to show that the stage is not very popular in the
United States. The Americans, whose laws allow of the utmost freedom,
and even license of language in all other respects, have nevertheless
subjected their dramatic authors to a sort of censorship. Theatrical
performances can only take place by permission of the municipal
authorities. This may serve to show how much communities are like

individuals; they surrender themselves unscrupulously to their ruling passions, and afterwards take the greatest care not to yield too much to the vehemence of tastes which they do not possess.

CHAPTER XX

---★---

Some Characteristics of Historians in Democratic Times

Historians who write in aristocratic ages are wont to refer all occurrences to the particular will and character of certain individuals; and they are apt to attribute the most important revolutions to slight accidents. They trace out the smallest causes with sagacity, and frequently leave the greatest unperceived.

Historians who live in democratic ages exhibit precisely opposite characteristics. Most of them attribute hardly any influence to the individual over the destiny of the race, or to citizens over the fate of a people; but, on the other hand, they assign great general causes to all petty incidents. These contrary tendencies explain each other.

When the historian of aristocratic ages surveys the theatre of the world, he at once perceives a very small number of prominent actors, who manage the whole piece. These great personages, who occupy the front of the stage, arrest attention, and fix it on themselves; and whilst the historian is bent on penetrating the secret motives which make these persons speak and act, the others escape his memory. The importance of the things which some men are seen to do, gives him an exaggerated estimate of the influence which one man may possess; and naturally leads him to think, that, in order to explain the impulses of the multitude, it is necessary to refer them to the particular influence of some one individual.

When, on the contrary, all the citizens are independent of one another, and each of them is individually weak, no one is seen to exert a great, or still less a lasting, power over the community. At first sight, individuals appear to be absolutely devoid of any influence over it; and society would seem to advance alone by the free and voluntary action of all the men who compose it. This naturally prompts the mind to search for that general reason which operates upon so many men's faculties at once, and turns them simultaneously in the same direction.

I am very well convinced that, even amongst democratic nations, the genius, the vices, or the virtues of certain individuals retard or accelerate the natural current of a people's history; but causes of this secondary and fortuitous nature are infinitely more various, more concealed, more complex, less powerful, and consequently less easy to trace, in periods of equality than in ages of aristocracy, when the task of the historian is simply to detach from the mass of general events the particular influence of one man or of a few men. In the former case, the historian is soon wearied by the toil; his mind loses itself in this labyrinth; and, in his inability clearly to discern or conspicuously to point out the influence of individuals, he denies that they have any. He prefers talking about the characteristics of race, the physical conformation of the country, or the genius of civilization,—which abridges his own labors, and satisfies his reader better at less cost.

The historians who seek to describe what occurs in democratic societies are right, therefore, in assigning much to general causes, and in devoting their chief attention to discover them; but they are wrong in wholly denying the special influence of individuals, because they cannot easily trace or follow it.

The historians who live in democratic ages are not only prone to assign a great cause to every incident, but they are also given to connect incidents together so as to deduce a system from them. In aristocratic ages, as the attention of historians is constantly drawn to individuals, the connection of events escapes them; or, rather, they do not believe in any such connection. To them, the clew of history seems every instant crossed and broken by the step of man. In democratic ages, on the contrary, as the historian sees much more of actions than of actors, he may easily establish some kind of sequence and methodical order amongst the former.

Ancient literature, which is so rich in fine historical compositions, does not contain a single great historical system, whilst the poorest of modern literatures abound with them. It would appear that the ancient historians did not make sufficient use of those general theories which our historical writers are ever ready to carry to excess.

Those who write in democratic ages have another more dangerous tendency. When the traces of individual action upon nations are lost, it often happens that the world goes on to move, though the moving agent is no longer discoverable. As it becomes extremely difficult to discern and analyze the reasons which, acting separately on the will of each member of the community, concur in the end to produce movement in the whole mass, men are led to believe that this movement is involuntary, and that societies unconsciously obey some superior force ruling over them. But even when the general fact which governs the private volition of all individuals is supposed to be discovered upon the earth, the principle of human free-will is not secured. A cause sufficiently extensive to affect millions of men at once, and sufficiently strong to bend them all together in the same direction, may well seem irresistible: having seen that mankind do yield to it, the mind is close upon the inference that mankind cannot resist it.

Historians who live in democratic ages, then, not only deny that the few have any power of acting upon the destiny of a people, but they deprive the people themselves of the power of modifying their own condition, and they subject them either to an inflexible Providence or to some blind necessity. According to them, each nation is indissolubly bound by its position, its origin, its antecedents, and its character, to a certain lot which no efforts can ever change. They involve generation in generation, and thus, going back from age to age, and from necessity to necessity, up to the origin of the world, they forge a close and enormous chain, which girds and binds the human race. To their minds it is not enough to show what events have occurred: they would fain show that events could not have occurred otherwise. They take a nation arrived at a certain stage of its history, and they affirm that it could not but follow the track which brought it thither. It is easier to make such an assertion than to show how the nation might have adopted a better course.

In reading the historians of aristocratic ages, and especially those of antiquity, it would seem that, to be master of his lot and to govern his fellow-creatures, man requires only to be master of himself. In perusing the historical volumes which our age has produced, it would seem that man is utterly powerless over himself and over all around him. The historians of antiquity taught how to command: those of our time teach only how to obey; in their writings the author often appears great, but humanity is always diminutive.

If this doctrine of necessity, which is so attractive to those who write history in democratic ages, passes from authors to their readers, till it infects the whole mass of the community and gets possession of the public mind, it will soon paralyze the activity of modern society, and reduce Christians to the level of the Turks.

I would moreover observe, that such doctrines are peculiarly dangerous at the period at which we are arrived. Our contemporaries are but too prone to doubt of human free-will, because each of them feels himself confined on every side by his own weakness; but they are still willing to acknowledge the strength and independence of men united in society. Let not this principle be lost sight of; for the great object in our time is to raise the faculties of men, not to complete their prostration.

CHAPTER XXI

★

Of Parliamentary Eloquence
in the United States

Amongst aristocratic nations, all the members of the community are connected with, and dependent upon, each other; the graduated scale of different ranks acts as a tie, which keeps every one in his proper place, and the whole body in subordination. Something of the same kind always occurs in the political assemblies of these nations. Parties naturally range themselves under certain leaders, whom they obey by a sort of instinct, which is only the result of habits contracted elsewhere. They carry the manners of general society into the lesser assemblage.

In democratic countries, it often happens that a great number of citizens are tending to the same point; but each one only moves thither, or at least flatters himself that he moves, of his own accord. Accustomed to regulate his doings by personal impulse alone, he does not willingly submit to dictation from without. This taste and habit of independence accompany him into the councils of the nation. If he consents to connect himself with other men in the prosecution of the same purpose, at least he chooses to remain free to contribute to the common success after his own fashion. Hence it is that, in democratic countries, parties are so impatient of control, and are never manageable except in moments of great public danger. Even then, the authority of leaders, which under such circumstances may be able to make men act or speak, hardly ever reaches the extent of making them keep silence.

Amongst aristocratic nations, the members of political assemblies are at the same time members of the aristocracy. Each of them enjoys high established rank in his own right, and the position which he occupies in the assembly is often less important in his eyes than that which he fills in the country. This consoles him for playing no part in the discussion of public affairs, and restrains him from too eagerly attempting to play an insignificant one.

In America, it generally happens that a representative only becomes somebody from his position in the assembly. He is therefore perpetually haunted by a craving to acquire importance there, and he feels a petulant desire to be constantly obtruding his opinions upon his fellow-members. His own vanity is not the only stimulant which urges him on in this course, but that of his constituents, and the continual necessity of propitiating them. Amongst aristocratic nations, a member of the legislature is rarely in strict dependence upon his constituents: he is frequently to them a sort of unavoidable representative; sometimes they are themselves strictly dependent upon him; and if, at length, they reject him, he may easily get elected elsewhere, or, retiring from public life, he may still enjoy the pleasures of splendid idleness. In a democratic country, like the United States, a representative has hardly ever a lasting hold on the minds of his constituents. However small an electoral body may be, the fluctuations of democracy are constantly changing its aspect: it must therefore be courted unceasingly. One is never sure of his supporters, and, if they forsake him, he is left without a resource; for his natural position is not sufficiently elevated for him to be easily known to those not close to him; and, with the complete state of independence prevailing among the people, he cannot hope that his friends or the government will send him down to be returned by an electoral body unacquainted with him. The seeds of his fortune are, therefore, sown in his own neighborhood: from that nook of earth he must start, to raise himself to command the people and to influence the destinies of the world. Thus it is natural that, in democratic countries, the members of political assemblies should think more of their constituents than of their party, whilst, in aristocracies, they think more of their party than of their constituents.

But what ought to be said to gratify constituents is not always what ought to be said in order to serve the party to which representatives profess to belong. The general interest of a party frequently demands that members belonging to it should not speak on great questions which they understand imperfectly; that they should speak but little on those minor questions which impede the great ones; lastly, and for the most part, that they should not speak at all. To keep silence is the most useful service that an indifferent spokesman can render to the commonwealth.

Constituents, however, do not think so. The population of a district send a representative to take a part in the government of a country, because they entertain a very high notion of his merits. As men appear greater in proportion to the littleness of the objects by which they are surrounded, it may be assumed that the opinion entertained of the delegate will be so much the higher, as talents are more rare among his constituents. It will therefore frequently happen, that, the less constituents ought to expect from their representative, the more they will anticipate from him; and, however incompetent he may be, they will not fail to call upon him for signal exertions, corresponding to the rank they have conferred upon him.

Independently of his position as a legislator of the State, electors also regard their representative as the natural patron of the constituency in the legislature; they almost consider him as the proxy of each of his supporters, and they flatter themselves that he will not be less zealous in defence of their private interests than of those of the country. Thus electors are well assured beforehand that the representative of their choice will be an orator; that he will speak often if he can, and that, in case he is forced to refrain, he will strive at any rate to compress into his less frequent orations an inquiry into all the great questions of state, combined with a statement of all the petty grievances they have themselves to complain of; so that, though he be not able to come forward frequently, he should on each occasion prove what he is capable of doing; and that, instead of perpetually lavishing his powers, he should occasionally condense them in a small compass, so as to furnish a sort of complete and brilliant epitome of his constituents and of himself. On these terms, they will vote for him at the next election.

These conditions drive worthy men of humble abilities to despair; who, knowing their own powers, would never voluntarily have come forward. But thus urged on, the representative begins to speak, to the great alarm of his friends; and, rushing imprudently into the midst of the most celebrated orators, he perplexes the debate and wearies the House.

VOLUME II

———★———

SECOND BOOK

Influence of Democracy on the Feelings of the Americans

CHAPTER I

★

Why Democratic Nations Show a More Ardent and Enduring Love of Equality Than of Liberty

The first and most intense passion which is produced by equality of condition is, I need hardly say, the love of that equality. My readers will therefore not be surprised that I speak of this feeling before all others.

Everybody has remarked that, in our time, and especially in France, this passion for equality is every day gaining ground in the human heart. It has been said a hundred times, that our contemporaries are far more ardently and tenaciously attached to equality than to freedom; but, as I do not find that the causes of the fact have been sufficiently analyzed, I shall endeavor to point them out.

It is possible to imagine an extreme point at which freedom and equality would meet and be confounded together. Let us suppose that all the people take a part in the government, and that each one of them has an equal right to take a part in it. As no one is different from his fellows, none can exercise a tyrannical power; men will be perfectly free, because they are all entirely equal; and they will all be perfectly equal, because they are entirely free. To this ideal state democratic nations tend. This is the only complete form that equality can assume upon earth; but there are a thousand others which, without being equally perfect, are not less cherished by those nations.

The principle of equality may be established in civil society, without prevailing in the political world. Equal rights may exist of indulging in the same pleasures, of entering the same professions, of frequenting the same places; in a word, of living in the same manner and seeking wealth by the same means,—although all men do not take an equal share in the government. A kind of equality may even be established in the political world, though there should be no political freedom there. A man may be the equal of all his countrymen save one, who is the master of all without distinction, and who selects equally from among them all the agents of his power. Several other combinations might be easily imagined, by which very great equality would be united to institutions more or less free, or even to institutions wholly without freedom.

Although men cannot become absolutely equal unless they are entirely free; and consequently equality, pushed to its furthest extent, may be confounded with freedom, yet there is good reason for distinguishing the one from the other. The taste which men have for liberty, and that which they feel for equality, are, in fact, two different things; and I am not afraid to add, that, amongst democratic nations, they are two unequal things.

Upon close inspection, it will be seen that there is in every age some peculiar and preponderating fact with which all others are connected; this fact almost always gives birth to some pregnant idea or some ruling passion, which attracts to itself and bears away in its course all the feelings and opinions of the time: it is like a great stream, towards which each of the neighboring rivulets seems to flow.

Freedom has appeared in the world at different times and under various forms; it has not been exclusively bound to any social condition, and it is not confined to democracies. Freedom cannot, therefore, form the distinguishing characteristic of democratic ages. The peculiar and preponderating fact which marks those ages as its own is the equality of condition; the ruling passion of men in those periods is the love of this equality. Ask not what singular charm the men of democratic ages find in being equal, or what special reasons they may have for clinging so tenaciously to equality rather than to the other advantages which society holds but to them: equality is the distinguishing characteristic of the age they live in; that, of itself, is enough to explain that they prefer it to all the rest.

But independently of this reason, there are several others, which will at all times habitually lead men to prefer equality to freedom.

If a people could ever succeed in destroying, or even in diminishing, the equality which prevails in its own body, they could do so only by long and laborious efforts. Their social condition must be modified, their laws abolished, their opinions superseded, their habits changed, their manners corrupted. But political liberty is more easily lost; to neglect to hold it fast, is to allow it to escape. Men therefore cling to equality not only because it is dear to them; they also adhere to it because they think it will last forever.

That political freedom may compromise in its excesses the tranquility, the property, the lives of individuals, is obvious even to narrow and unthinking minds. On the contrary, none but attentive and clearsighted men perceive the perils with which equality threatens us, and they commonly avoid pointing them out. They know that the calamities they apprehend are remote, and flatter themselves that they will only fall upon future generations, for which the present generation takes but little thought. The evils which freedom sometimes brings with it are immediate; they are apparent to all, and all are more or less affected by them. The evils which extreme equality may produce are slowly disclosed; they creep gradually into the social frame; they are seen only at intervals; and at the moment at which they become most violent, habit already causes them to be no longer felt.

The advantages which freedom brings are only shown by the lapse of time; and it is always easy to mistake the cause in which they originate. The advantages of equality are immediate, and they may always be traced from their source.

Political liberty bestows exalted pleasures, from time to time, upon a certain number of citizens. Equality every day confers a number of small enjoyments on every man. The charms of equality are every instant felt, and are within the reach of all; the noblest hearts are not insensible to them, and the most vulgar souls exult in them. The passion which equality creates must therefore be at once strong and general. Men cannot enjoy political liberty unpurchased by some sacrifices, and they never obtain it without great exertions. But the pleasures of equality are self-proffered: each of the petty incidents of life seems to occasion them; and in order to taste them, nothing is required but to live.

Democratic nations are at all times fond of equality, but there are certain epochs at which the passion they entertain for it swells to the height of fury. This occurs at the moment when the old social system, long menaced, is overthrown after a severe intestine struggle, and the barriers of rank are at length thrown down. At such times, men pounce upon equality as their booty, and they cling to it as to some precious treasure which they fear to lose. The passion for equality penetrates on every side into men's hearts, expands there, and fills them entirely. Tell them not that, by this blind surrender of themselves to an exclusive passion, they risk their dearest interests: they are deaf. Show them not freedom escaping from their grasp, whilst they are looking another way: they are blind, or, rather, they can discern but one object to be desired in the universe.

What I have said is applicable to all democratic nations; what I am about to say concerns the French alone. Amongst most modern nations, and especially amongst all those of the continent of Europe, the taste and the idea of freedom only began to exist and to be developed at the time when social conditions were tending to equality, and as a consequence of that very equality. Absolute kings were the most efficient levellers of ranks amongst their subjects. Amongst these nations, equality preceded freedom: equality was therefore a fact of some standing when freedom was still a novelty; the one had already created customs, opinions, and laws belonging to it, when the other, alone and for the first time, came into actual existence. Thus the latter was still only an affair of opinion and of taste, whilst the former had already crept into the habits of the people, possessed itself of their manners, and given a particular turn to the smallest actions in their lives. Can it be wondered at that the men of our own time prefer the one to the other?

I think that democratic communities have a natural taste for freedom: left to themselves, they will seek it, cherish it, and view any privation of it with regret. But for equality, their passion is ardent, insatiable, incessant, invincible: they call for equality in freedom; and if they cannot obtain that, they still call for equality in slavery. They will endure poverty, servitude, barbarism; but they will not endure aristocracy.

This is true at all times, and especially in our own day. All men and all powers seeking to cope with this irresistible passion will be overthrown and destroyed by it. In our age, freedom cannot be established without it, and despotism itself cannot reign without its support.

CHAPTER II

———— ★ ————

Of Individualism in Democratic Countries

I have shown how it is that, in ages of equality, every man seeks for his opinions within himself: I am now to show how it is that, in the same ages, all his feelings are turned towards himself alone. *Individualism* is a novel expression, to which a novel idea has given birth. Our fathers were only acquainted with *égoïsme* (selfishness). Selfishness is a passionate and exaggerated love of self, which leads a man to connect everything with himself, and to prefer himself to everything in the world. Individualism is a mature and calm feeling, which disposes each member of the community to sever himself from the mass of his fellows, and to draw apart with his family and his friends; so that, after he has thus formed a little circle of his own, he willingly leaves society at large to itself. Selfishness originates in blind instinct: individualism proceeds from erroneous judgment more than from depraved feelings; it originates as much in deficiencies of mind as in perversity of heart.

Selfishness blights the germ of all virtue: individualism, at first, only saps the virtues of public life; but, in the long run, it attacks and destroys all others, and is at length absorbed in downright selfishness. Selfishness is a vice as old as the world, which does not belong to one form of society more than to another: individualism is of democratic origin, and it threatens to spread in the same ratio as the equality of condition.

Amongst aristocratic nations, as families remain for centuries in the same condition, often on the same spot, all generations become, as it were, contemporaneous. A man almost always knows his forefathers, and respects them: he thinks he already sees his remote descendants, and he loves them. He willingly imposes duties on himself towards the former and the latter; and he will frequently sacrifice his personal gratifications to those who went before and to those who will come after him. Aristocratic institutions have, moreover, the effect of closely binding every man to several of his fellow-citizens. As the classes of an aristocratic people are strongly marked and permanent, each of them is regarded by its own members as a sort of lesser country, more tangible and more cherished than the country at large. As, in aristocratic communities, all the citizens occupy fixed positions, one above the other, the result is, that each of them always sees a man above himself whose patronage is necessary to him, and, below himself, another man whose co-operation he may claim. Men living in aristocratic ages are therefore almost always closely attached to something placed out of their own sphere, and they are often disposed to forget themselves. It is true that, in these ages, the notion of human fellowship is faint, and that men seldom think of sacrificing themselves for mankind; but they often sacrifice themselves for other men. In democratic times, on the contrary, when the duties of each individual to the race are much more clear, devoted service to any one man becomes more rare; the bond of human affection is extended, but it is relaxed.

Amongst democratic nations, new families are constantly springing up, others are constantly falling away, and all that remain change their condition; the woof of time is every instant broken, and the track of generations effaced. Those who went before are soon forgotten; of those who will come after, no one has any idea: the interest of man is confined to those in close propinquity to himself. As each class approximates to other classes, and intermingles with them, its members become indifferent, and as strangers to one another. Aristocracy had made a chain of all the members of the community, from the peasant to the king: democracy breaks that chain, and severs every link of it.

As social conditions become more equal, the number of persons increases who, although they are neither rich nor powerful enough to exercise any great influence over their fellows, have nevertheless acquired or retained sufficient education and fortune to satisfy their own wants. They owe nothing to any man, they expect nothing from any man; they acquire the habit of always considering themselves as standing alone, and they are apt to imagine that their whole destiny is in their own hands.

Thus, not only does democracy make every man forget his ancestors, but it hides his descendants and separates his contemporaries from him; it throws him back forever upon himself alone, and threatens in the end to confine him entirely within the solitude of his own heart.

CHAPTER III

———————————— ★ ————————————

Individualism Stronger at the Close of a Democratic Revolution Than at Other Periods

The period when the construction of democratic society upon the ruins of an aristocracy has just been completed is especially that at which this isolation of men from one another, and the selfishness resulting from it, most forcibly strike the observation. Democratic communities not only contain a large number of independent citizens, but they are constantly filled with men who, having entered but yesterday upon their independent condition, are intoxicated with their new power. They entertain a presumptuous confidence in their own strength, and, as they do not suppose that they can henceforward ever have occasion to claim the assistance of their fellow-creatures, they do not scruple to show that they care for nobody but themselves.

An aristocracy seldom yields without a protracted struggle, in the course of which implacable animosities are kindled between the different classes of society. These passions survive the victory, and traces of them may be observed in the midst of the democratic confusion which ensues. Those members of the community who were at the top of the late gradations of rank cannot immediately forget their former greatness; they will long regard themselves as aliens in the midst of the newly-composed society. They look upon all those whom this state of society has made their equals as oppressors, whose destiny can excite no sympathy; they have lost sight of their former equals, and feel no longer bound by a common interest to their fate: each of them, standing aloof, thinks that he is reduced to care for himself alone. Those, on the contrary, who were formerly at the foot of the social scale, and who have been brought up to the common level by a sudden revolution, cannot enjoy their newly-acquired independence without secret uneasiness; and if they meet with some of their former superiors on the same footing as themselves, they stand aloof from them with an expression of triumph and fear.

It is, then, commonly at the outset of democratic society that citizens are most disposed to live apart. Democracy leads men not to draw near to their fellow-creatures; but democratic revolutions lead them to shun each other, and perpetuate in a state of equality the animosities which the state of inequality created.

The great advantage of the Americans is, that they have arrived at a state of democracy without having to endure a democratic revolution; and that they are born equal, instead of becoming so.

CHAPTER IV

———————— ★ ————————

That the Americans Combat the Effects of Individualism by Free Institutions

Despotism, which is of a very timorous nature, is never more secure of continuance than when it can keep men asunder; and all its influence is commonly exerted for that purpose. No vice of the human heart is so acceptable to it as selfishness: a despot easily forgives his subjects for not loving him, provided they do not love each other. He does not ask them to assist him in governing the state; it is enough that they do not aspire to govern it themselves. He stigmatizes as turbulent and unruly spirits those who would combine their exertions to promote the prosperity of the community; and, perverting the natural meaning of words, he applauds as good citizens those who have no sympathy for any but themselves.

Thus the vices which despotism produces are precisely those which equality fosters. These two things mutually and perniciously complete and assist each other. Equality places men side by side, unconnected by any common tie; despotism raises barriers to keep them asunder: the former predisposes them not to consider their fellow-creatures, the latter makes general indifference a sort of public virtue.

Despotism, then, which is at all times dangerous, is more particularly to be feared in democratic ages. It is easy to see that in those same ages men stand most in need of freedom. When the members of a community are forced to attend to public affairs, they are necessarily drawn from the circle of their own interests, and snatched at times from self-observation. As soon as a man begins to treat of public affairs in public, he begins to perceive that he is not so independent of his fellow-men as he had at first imagined, and that, in order to obtain their support, he must often lend them his co-operation.

When the public govern, there is no man who does not feel the value of public good-will, or who does not endeavor to court it by drawing to himself the esteem and affection of those amongst whom he is to live. Many of the passions which congeal and keep asunder human hearts, are then obliged to retire and hide below the surface. Pride must be dissembled; disdain dares not break out; selfishness fears its own self. Under a free government, as most public offices are elective, the men whose elevated minds or aspiring hopes are too closely circumscribed in private life constantly feel that they cannot do without the people who surround them. Men learn at such times to think of their fellow-men from ambitious motives; and they frequently find it, in a manner, their interest to forget themselves.

I may here be met by an objection derived from electioneering intrigues, the meanness of candidates, and the calumnies of their opponents. These are occasions of enmity which occur the oftener, the more frequent elections become. Such evils are doubtless great, but they are transient; whereas the benefits which attend them remain. The desire of being elected may lead some men for a time to violent hostility; but this same desire leads all men in the long run mutually to support each other; and, if it happens that an election accidentally severs two friends, the electoral system brings a multitude of citizens permanently together, who would otherwise always have remained unknown to each other. Freedom produces private animosities, but despotism gives birth to general indifference.

The Americans have combated by free institutions the tendency of equality to keep men asunder, and they have subdued it. The legislators of America did not suppose that a general representation of the whole nation would suffice to ward off a disorder at once so natural to the frame of democratic society, and so fatal: they also thought that it would be well to infuse political life into each portion of the territory, in order to multiply to an infinite extent opportunities of acting in concert for all the members of the community, and to make them constantly feel their mutual dependence on each other. The plan was a wise one. The general affairs of a country only engage the attention of leading politicians, who assemble from time to time in the same places; and, as they often lose sight of each other afterwards, no lasting ties are established between them. But if the object be to have the local affairs of a district conducted by the men who reside there, the same persons are always in contact, and they are, in a manner, forced to be acquainted, and to adapt themselves to one another.

It is difficult to draw a man out of his own circle to interest him in the destiny of the state, because he does not clearly understand what influence the destiny of the state can have upon his own lot. But if it be proposed to make a road cross the end of his estate, he will see at a glance that there is a connection between this small public affair and his greatest private affairs; and he will discover, without its being shown to him, the close tie which unites private to general interest. Thus, far more may be done by entrusting to the citizens the administration of minor affairs than by surrendering to them the control of important ones, towards interesting them in the public welfare, and convincing them that they constantly stand in need one of another in order to provide for it. A brilliant achievement may win for you the favor of a people at one stroke; but to earn the love and respect of the population which surrounds you, a long succession of little services rendered and of obscure good deeds,—a constant habit of kindness, and an established reputation for disinterestedness,—will be required. Local freedom, then, which leads a great number of citizens to value the affection of their neighbors and of their kindred, perpetually brings men together, and forces them to help one another, in spite of the propensities which sever them.

CHAPTER V

---★---

Of The Use Which The Americans Make Of Public Associations In Civil Life

I do not propose to speak of those political associations by the aid of which men endeavor to defend themselves against the despotic action of a majority, or against the aggressions of regal power. That subject I have already treated. If each citizen did not learn, in proportion as he individually becomes more feeble, and consequently more incapable of preserving his freedom single-handed, to combine with his fellow-citizens for the purpose of defending it, it is clear that tyranny would unavoidably increase together with equality.

Those associations only which are formed in civil life, without reference to political objects, are here adverted to. The political associations which exist in the United States are only a single feature in the midst of the immense assemblage of associations in that country. Americans of all ages, all conditions, and all dispositions, constantly form associations. They have not only commercial and manufacturing companies, in which all take part, but associations of a thousand other kinds,—religious, moral, serious, futile, general or restricted, enormous or diminutive. The Americans make associations to give entertainments, to found seminaries, to build inns, to construct churches, to diffuse books, to send missionaries to the antipodes; they found in this manner hospitals, prisons, and schools. If it be proposed to inculcate some truth, or to foster some feeling, by the encouragement of a great example, they form a society. Wherever, at the head of some new undertaking, you see the government in France, or a man of rank in England, in the United States you will be sure to find an association.

I met with several kinds of associations in America of which I confess I had no previous notion; and I have often admired the extreme skill with which the inhabitants of the United States succeed in proposing a common object to the exertions of a great many men, and in inducing them voluntarily to pursue it.

I have since travelled over England, whence the Americans have taken some of their laws and many of their customs; and it seemed to me that the principle of association was by no means so constantly or adroitly used in that country. The English often perform great things singly, whereas the Americans form associations for the smallest undertakings. It is evident that the former people consider association as a powerful means of action, but the latter seem to regard it as the only means they have of acting.

Thus, the most democratic country on the face of the earth is that in which men have, in our time, carried to the highest perfection the art of pursuing in common the object of their common desires, and have applied this new science to the greatest number of purposes. Is this the result of accident? or is there in reality any necessary connection between the principle of association and that of equality?

Aristocratic communities always contain, amongst a multitude of persons who by themselves are powerless, a small number of powerful and wealthy citizens, each of whom can achieve great undertakings single-handed. In aristocratic societies, men do not need to combine in order to act, because they are strongly held together. Every wealthy and powerful citizen constitutes the head of a permanent and compulsory association, composed of all those who are dependent upon him, or whom he makes subservient to the execution of his designs.

Amongst democratic nations, on the contrary, all the citizens are independent and feeble; they can do hardly anything by themselves, and none of them can oblige his fellow-men to lend him their assistance. They all, therefore, become powerless, if they do not learn voluntarily to help each other. If men living in democratic countries had no right and no inclination to associate for political purposes, their independence would be in great jeopardy; but they might long preserve their wealth and their cultivation: whereas, if they never acquired the habit of forming associations in ordinary life, civilization itself would be endangered. A people amongst whom individuals should lose the power of achieving great things single-handed, without acquiring the means of producing them by united exertions, would soon relapse into barbarism.

Nothing, in my opinion, is more deserving of our attention than the intellectual and moral associations of America. The political and industrial associations of that country strike us forcibly; but the others elude our observation, or, if we discover them, we understand them imperfectly, because we have hardly ever seen anything of the kind. It must, however, be acknowledged, that they are as necessary to the American people as the former, and perhaps more so. In democratic countries, the science of association is the mother of science; the progress of all the rest depends upon the progress it has made.

Amongst the laws which rule human societies, there is one which seems to be more precise and clear than all others. If men are to remain civilized, or to become so, the art of associating together must grow and improve in the same ratio in which the equality of conditions is increased.

CHAPTER VI

———————★———————

Of the Relation Between Public Associations and the Newspapers

When men are no longer united amongst themselves by firm and lasting ties, it is impossible to obtain the co-operation of any great number of them, unless you can persuade every man whose help you require that his private interest obliges him voluntarily to unite his exertions to the exertions of all the others. This can be habitually and conveniently effected only by means of a newspaper: nothing but a newspaper can drop the same thought into a thousand minds at the same moment. A newspaper is an adviser who does not require to be sought, but who comes of his own accord, and talks to you briefly every day of the common weal, without distracting you from your private affairs.

Newspapers therefore become more necessary in proportion as men become more equal, and individualism more to be feared. To suppose that they only serve to protect freedom would be to diminish their importance: they maintain civilization. I shall not deny that, in democratic countries, newspapers frequently lead the citizens to launch together into very ill-digested schemes; but if there were no newspapers, there would be no common activity. The evil which they produce is therefore much less than that which they cure.

———————————————

I am of opinion that a democratic people, without any national representative assemblies, but with a great number of small local powers, would have in the end more newspapers than another people governed by a centralized administration and an elective legislature. What best explains to me the enormous circulation of the daily press in the United States is, that, amongst the Americans, I find the utmost national freedom combined with local freedom of every kind.

CHAPTER VII

---★---

Relation of Civil to Political Associations

There is only one country on the face of the earth where the citizens enjoy unlimited freedom of association for political purposes. This same country is the only one in the world where the continual exercise of the right of association has been introduced into civil life, and where all the advantages which civilization can confer are procured by means of it.

In all the countries where political associations are prohibited, civil associations are rare. It is hardly probable that this is the result of accident; but the inference should rather be, that there is a natural, and perhaps a necessary, connection between these two kinds of associations.

Civil associations, therefore, facilitate political association; but, on the other hand, political association singularly strengthens and improves associations for civil purposes. In civil life, every man may, strictly speaking, fancy that he can provide for his own wants; in politics, he can fancy no such thing. When a people, then, have any knowledge of public life, the notion of association, and the wish to coalesce, present themselves every day to the minds of the whole community: whatever natural repugnance may restrain men from acting in concert, they will always be ready to combine for the sake of a party. Thus political life makes the love and practice of association more general; it imparts a desire of union, and teaches the means of combination to numbers of men who otherwise would have always lived apart.

I do not say that there can be no civil associations in a country where political association is prohibited; for men can never live in society without embarking in some common undertakings: but I maintain that, in such a country, civil associations will always be few in number, feebly planned, unskilfully managed, that they will never form any vast designs, or that they will fail in the execution of them.

This naturally leads me to think that freedom of association in political matters is not so dangerous to public tranquility as is supposed; and that possibly, after having agitated society for some time, it may strengthen the state in the end. In democratic countries, political associations are, so to speak, the only powerful persons who aspire to rule the state. Accordingly, the governments of our time look upon associations of this kind just as sovereigns in the Middle Ages regarded the great vassals of the crown: they entertain a sort of instinctive abhorrence of them, and combat them on all occasions. They bear, on the contrary, a natural good-will to civil associations, because they readily discover that, instead of directing the minds of the community to public affairs, these institutions serve to divert them from such reflections; and that, by engaging them more and more in the pursuit of objects which cannot be attained without public tranquility, they deter them from revolutions. But these governments do not attend to the fact, that political associations tend amazingly to multiply and facilitate those of a civil character, and that, in avoiding a dangerous evil, they deprive themselves of an efficacious remedy.

When you see the Americans freely and constantly forming associations for the purpose of promoting some political principle, of raising one man to the head of affairs, or of wresting power from another, you have some difficulty in understanding how men so independent do not constantly fall into the abuse of freedom. If, on the other hand, you survey the infinite number of trading companies which are in operation in the United States, and perceive that the Americans are on every side unceasingly engaged in the execution of important and difficult plans, which the slightest revolution would throw into confusion, you will readily comprehend why people so well employed are by no means tempted to perturb the state, nor to destroy that public tranquility by which they all profit.

Is it enough to observe these things separately, or should we not discover the hidden tie which connects them? In their political associations, the Americans, of all conditions, minds, and ages, daily acquire a general taste for association, and grow accustomed to the use of it. There they meet together in large numbers,—they converse, they listen to each other, and they are mutually stimulated to all sorts of undertakings. They afterwards transfer to civil life the notions they have thus acquired, and make them subservient to a thousand purposes. Thus it is by the enjoyment of a dangerous freedom that the Americans learn the art of rendering the dangers of freedom less formidable.

If a certain moment in the existence of a nation be selected, it is easy to prove that political associations perturb the state and paralyze productive industry; but take the whole life of a people, and it may perhaps be easy to demonstrate, that freedom of association in political matters is favorable to the prosperity, and even to the tranquility, of the community.

I said in the former part of this work: "The unrestrained liberty of political association cannot be entirely assimilated to the liberty of the press. The one is at the same time less necessary and more dangerous than the other. A nation may confine it within certain limits, without ceasing to be mistress of itself; and it may sometimes be obliged to do so, in order to maintain its own authority." And, further on, I added: "It cannot be denied that the unrestrained liberty of association for political purposes is the last degree of liberty which a people is fit for. If it does not throw them into anarchy, it perpetually brings them, as it were, to the verge of it." Thus, I do not think that a nation is always at liberty to invest its citizens with an absolute right of association for political purposes; and I doubt whether, in any country or in any age, it be wise to set no limits to freedom of association.

A certain nation, it is said, could not maintain tranquility in the community, cause the laws to be respected, or establish a lasting government, if the right of association were not confined within narrow limits. These blessings are doubtless invaluable; and I can imagine that, to acquire or to preserve them, a nation may impose upon itself severe temporary restrictions: but still it is well that the nation should know at what price these blessings are purchased. I can understand that it may be advisable to cut off a man's arm in order to save his life; but it would be ridiculous to assert that he will be as dexterous as he was before he lost it.

CHAPTER VIII

───────── ★ ─────────

How the Americans Combat Individualism by the Principle of Interest Rightly Understood

W hen the world was managed by a few rich and powerful individuals, these persons loved to entertain a lofty idea of the duties of man. They were fond of professing that it is praiseworthy to forget one's self, and that good should be done without hope of reward, as it is by the Deity himself. Such were the standard opinions of that time in morals.

I doubt whether men were more virtuous in aristocratic ages than in others; but they were incessantly talking of the beauties of virtue, and its utility was only studied in secret. But since the imagination takes less lofty flights, and every man's thoughts are centered in himself, moralists are alarmed by this idea of self-sacrifice, and they no longer venture to present it to the human mind. They therefore content themselves with inquiring, whether the personal advantage of each member of the community does not consist in working for the good of all; and when they have hit upon some point on which private interest and public interest meet and amalgamate, they are eager to bring it into notice. Observations of this kind are gradually multiplied: what was only a single remark becomes a general principle; and it is held as a truth, that man serves himself in serving his fellow-creatures, and that his private interest is to do good.

I have already shown, in several parts of this work, by what means the inhabitants of the United States almost always manage to combine their own advantage with that of their fellow-citizens: my present purpose is to point out the general rule which enables them to do so. In the United States, hardly anybody talks of the beauty of virtue; but they maintain that virtue is useful, and prove it every day. The American moralists do not profess that men ought to sacrifice themselves for their fellow-creatures *because* it is noble to make such sacrifices; but they boldly aver that such sacrifices are as necessary to him who imposes them upon himself, as to him for whose sake they are made.

They have found out that, in their country and their age, man is brought home to himself by an irresistible force; and, losing all hope of stopping that force, they turn all their thoughts to the direction of it. They therefore do not deny that every man may follow his own interest; but they endeavor to prove that it is the interest of every man to be virtuous. I shall not here enter into the reasons they allege, which would divert me from my subject: suffice it to say, that they have convinced their fellow-countrymen.

Montaigne said long ago, "Were I not to follow the straight road for its straightness, I should follow it for having found by experience that, in the end, it is commonly the happiest and most useful track." The doctrine of interest rightly understood is not then new, but amongst the Americans of our time it finds universal acceptance: it has become popular there; you may trace it at the bottom of all their actions, you will remark it in all they say. It is as often asserted by the poor man as by the rich. In Europe, the principle of interest is much grosser than it is in America, but it is also less common, and especially it is less avowed; amongst us, men still constantly feign great abnegation which they no longer feel.

The Americans, on the contrary, are fond of explaining almost all the actions of their lives by the principle of interest rightly understood; they show with complacency how an enlightened regard for themselves constantly prompts them to assist each other, and inclines them willingly to sacrifice a portion of their time and property to the welfare of the state. In this respect, I think they frequently fail to do themselves justice; for, in the United States, as well as elsewhere, people are sometimes seen to give way to those disinterested and spontaneous impulses which are natural to man: but the Americans seldom allow that they yield to emotions of this kind; they are more anxious to do honor to their philosophy than to themselves.

I might here pause, without attempting to pass a judgment on what I have described. The extreme difficulty of the subject would be my excuse, but I shall not avail myself of it; and I had rather that my readers, clearly perceiving my object, should refuse to follow me, than that I should leave them in suspense.

The principle of interest rightly understood is not a lofty one, but it is clear and sure. It does not aim at mighty objects, but it attains without excessive exertion all those at which it aims. As it lies within the reach of all capacities, every one can without difficulty apprehend and retain it. By its admirable conformity to human weaknesses, it easily obtains great dominion; nor is that dominion precarious, since the principle checks one personal interest by another, and uses, to direct the passions, the very same instrument which excites them.

The principle of interest rightly understood produces no great acts of self-sacrifice, but it suggests daily small acts of self-denial. By itself, it cannot suffice to make a man virtuous; but it disciplines a number of persons in habits of regularity, temperance, moderation, foresight, self-command; and, if it does not lead men straight to virtue by the will, it gradually draws them in that direction by their habits. If the principle of interest rightly understood were to sway the whole moral world, extraordinary virtues would doubtless be more rare; but I think that gross depravity would then also be less common. The principle of interest rightly understood perhaps prevents men from rising far above the level of mankind; but a great number of other men, who were falling far below it, are caught and restrained by it. Observe some few individuals, they are lowered by it; survey mankind, they are raised.

I am not afraid to say, that the principle of interest rightly understood appears to me the best suited of all philosophical theories to the wants of the men of our time, and that I regard it as their chief remaining security against themselves. Towards it, therefore, the minds of the moralists of our age should turn; even should they judge it to be incomplete, it must nevertheless be adopted as necessary.

I do not think, upon the whole, that there is more selfishness amongst us than in America; the only difference is, that there it is enlightened, here it is not. Every American will sacrifice a portion of his private interests to preserve the rest; we would fain preserve the whole, and oftentimes the whole is lost. Everybody I see about me seems bent on teaching his contemporaries, by precept and example, that what is useful is never wrong. Will nobody undertake to make them understand how what is right may be useful?

No power upon earth can prevent the increasing equality of conditions from inclining the human mind to seek out what is useful, or from leading every member of the community to be wrapped up in himself. It must therefore be expected that personal interest will become more than ever the principal, if not the sole, spring of men's actions; but it remains to be seen how each man will understand his personal interest. If the members of a community, as they become more equal, become more ignorant and coarse, it is difficult to foresee to what pitch of stupid excesses their selfishness may lead them; and no one can foretell into what disgrace and wretchedness they would plunge themselves, lest they should have to sacrifice something of their own well-being to the prosperity of their fellow-creatures.

I do not think that the system of interest, as it is professed in America, is, in all its parts, self-evident; but it contains a great number of truths so evident, that men, if they are but educated, cannot fail to see them. Educate, then, at any rate; for the age of implicit self-sacrifice and instinctive virtues is already flitting far away from us, and the time is fast approaching when freedom, public peace, and social order itself will not be able to exist without education.

CHAPTER IX

―――――★―――――

That the Americans Apply the Principle of Interest Rightly Understood to Religious Matters

If the principle of interest rightly understood had nothing but the present world in view, it would be very insufficient, for there are many sacrifices which can only find their recompense in another; and whatever ingenuity may be put forth to demonstrate the utility of virtue, it will never be an easy task to make that man live aright who has no thought of dying.

It is therefore necessary to ascertain whether the principle of interest rightly understood can be easily reconciled with religious belief. The philosophers who inculcate this system of morals tell men that, to be happy in this life, they must watch their own passions, and steadily control their excess; that lasting happiness can be secured only by renouncing a thousand transient gratifications; and that a man must perpetually triumph over himself in order to secure his own advantage. The founders of almost all religions have held the same language. The track they point out to man is the same, onl'y the goal is more remote; instead of placing in this world the reward of the sacrifices they impose, they transport it to another.

Nevertheless, I cannot believe that all those who practise virtue from religious motives are actuated only by the hope of a recompense. I have known zealous Christians who constantly forgot themselves, to work with greater ardor for the happiness of their fellow-men; and I have heard them declare that all they did was only to earn the blessings of a future state. I cannot but think that they deceive themselves: I respect them too much to believe them.

Christianity, indeed, teaches that a man must prefer his neighbor to himself, in order to gain eternal life; but Christianity also teaches that men ought to benefit their fellow-creatures for the love of God. A sublime expression! Man searches by his intellect into the Divine conception, and sees that order is the purpose of God; he freely gives his own efforts to aid in prosecuting this great design, and, whilst he sacrifices his personal interests to this consummate order of all created things, expects no other recompense than the pleasure of contemplating it.

I do not believe that interest is the sole motive of religious men: but I believe that interest is the principal means which religions themselves employ to govern men, and I do not question that in this way they strike the multitude and become popular. I do not see clearly why the principle of interest rightly understood should undermine the religious opinions of men; it seems to me more easy to show why it should strengthen them. Let it be supposed that, in order to attain happiness in this world, a man combats his instincts on all occasions, and deliberately calculates every action of his life; that, instead of yielding blindly to the impetuosity of first desires, he has learned the art of resisting them, and that he has accustomed himself to sacrifice without an effort the pleasure of a moment to the lasting interest of his whole life. If such a man believes in the religion which he professes, it will cost him but little to submit to the restrictions it may impose. Reason herself counsels him to obey, and habit has prepared him to endure these limitations. If he should have conceived any doubts as to the object of his hopes, still he will not easily allow himself to be stopped by them; and he will decide that it is wise to risk some of the advantages of this world, in order to preserve his rights to the great inheritance promised him in another. "To be mistaken in believing that the Christian religion is true," says Pascal, "is no great loss to any one; but how dreadful to be mistaken in believing it to be false!"

The Americans do not affect a brutal indifference to a future state; they affect no puerile pride in despising perils which they hope to escape from. They therefore profess their religion without shame and without weakness; but there generally is, even in their zeal, something so indescribably tranquil, methodical, and deliberate, that it would seem as if the head, far more than the heart, brought them to the foot of the altar.

The Americans not only follow their religion from interest, but they often place in this world the interest which makes them follow it. In the Middle Ages, the clergy spoke of nothing but a future state; they hardly cared to prove that a sincere Christian may be a happy man here below. But the American preachers are constantly referring to the earth; and it is only with great difficulty that they can divert their attention from it. To touch their congregations, they always show them how favorable religious opinions are to freedom and public tranquility; and it is often difficult to ascertain from their discourses whether the principal object of religion is to procure eternal felicity in the other world, or prosperity in this.

CHAPTER X

---★---

Of the Taste for Physical Well-Being in America

In America, the passion for physical well-being is not always exclusive, but it is general; and if all do not feel it in the same manner, yet it is felt by all. Carefully to satisfy even the least wants of the body, and to provide the little conveniences of life, is uppermost in every mind. Something of an analogous character is more and more apparent in Europe.

CHAPTER XI

━━━━★━━━━

Peculiar Effects of the Love of Physical Gratifications in Democratic Times

It may be supposed, from what has just been said, that the love of physical gratifications must constantly urge the Americans to irregularities in morals, disturb the peace of families, and threaten the security of society at large. But it is not so: the passion for physical gratifications produces in democracies effects very different from those which it occasions in aristocratic nations.

It sometimes happens that, wearied with public affairs and sated with opulence, amidst the ruin of religious belief and the decline of the state, the heart of an aristocracy may by degrees be seduced to the pursuit of sensual enjoyments alone. At other times, the power of the monarch or the weakness of the people, without stripping the nobility of their fortune, compels them to stand aloof from the administration of affairs, and, whilst the road to mighty enterprise is closed, abandons them to the inquietude of their own desires; they then fall back heavily upon themselves, and seek in the pleasures of the body oblivion of their former greatness.

When the members of an aristocratic body are thus exclusively devoted to the pursuit of physical gratifications, they commonly turn in that direction all the energy which they derive from their long experience of power. Such men are not satisfied with the pursuit of comfort; they require sumptuous depravity and splendid corruption. The worship they pay the senses is a gorgeous one; and they seem to vie with each other in the art of degrading their own natures. The stronger, the more famous, and the more free an aristocracy has been, the more depraved will it then become; and, however brilliant may have been the lustre of its virtues, I dare predict that they will always be surpassed by the splendor of its vices.

The taste for physical gratifications leads a democratic people into no such excesses. The love of well-being is there displayed as a tenacious, exclusive, universal passion; but its range is confined. To build enormous palaces, to conquer or to mimic nature, to ransack the world in order to gratify the passions of a man, is not thought of: but to add a few roods of land to your field, to plant an orchard, to enlarge a dwelling, to be always making life more comfortable and convenient, to avoid trouble, and to satisfy the smallest wants without effort and almost without cost. These are small objects, but the soul clings to them; it dwells upon them closely and day by day, till they at last shut out the rest of the world, and sometimes intervene between itself and Heaven.

This, it may be said, can only be applicable to those members of the community who are in humble circumstances; wealthier individuals will display tastes akin to those which belonged to them in aristocratic ages. I contest the proposition: in point of physical gratifications, the most opulent members of a democracy will not display tastes very different from those of the people; whether it be that, springing from the people, they really share those tastes, or that they esteem it a duty to submit to them. In democratic society, the sensuality of the public has taken a moderate and tranquil course, to which all are bound to conform: it is as difficult to depart from the common rule by one's vices as by one's virtues. Rich men who live amidst democratic nations are therefore more intent on providing for their smallest wants, than for their extraordinary enjoyments; they gratify a number of petty desires, without indulging in any great irregularities of passion: thus, they are more apt to become enervated than debauched.

The special taste which the men of democratic times entertain for physical enjoyments is not naturally opposed to the principles of public order; nay, it often stands in need of order, that it may be gratified. Nor is it adverse to regularity of morals, for good morals contribute to public tranquility and are favorable to industry. It may even be frequently combined with a species of religious morality: men wish to be as well off as they can in this world, without foregoing their chance of another. Some physical gratifications cannot be indulged in without crime; from such they strictly abstain. The enjoyment of others is sanctioned by religion and morality; to these the heart, the imagination, and life itself, are unreservedly given up; till, in snatching at these lesser gifts, men lose sight of those more precious possessions which constitute the glory and the greatness of mankind.

The reproach I address to the principle of equality is not that it leads men away in the pursuit of forbidden enjoyments, but that it absorbs them wholly in quest of those which are allowed. By these means, a kind of virtuous materialism may ultimately be established in the world, which would not corrupt, but enervate, the soul, and noiselessly unbend its springs of action.

CHAPTER XII

---★---

Why Some Americans Manifest a
Sort of Fanatical Spiritualism

Although the desire of acquiring the good things of this world is the prevailing passion of the American people, certain momentary outbreaks occur, when their souls seem suddenly to burst the bonds of matter by which they are restrained, and to soar impetuously towards Heaven. In all the States of the Union, but especially in the half-peopled country of the Far West, itinerant preachers may be met with, who hawk about the word of God from place to place. Whole families, old men, women, and children, cross rough passes and untrodden wilds, coming from a great distance, to join a camp-meeting, where they totally forget, for several days and nights, in listening to these discourses, the cares of business and even the most urgent wants of the body.

Here and there, in the midst of American society, you meet with men full of a fanatical and almost wild spiritualism, which hardly exists in Europe. From time to time, strange sects arise, which endeavor to strike out extraordinary paths to eternal happiness. Religious insanity is very common in the United States.

Nor ought these facts to surprise us. It was not man who implanted in himself the taste for what is infinite, and the love of what is immortal: these lofty instincts are not the offspring of his capricious will; their steadfast foundation is fixed in human nature, and they exist in spite of his efforts. He may cross and distort them; destroy them he cannot.

The soul has wants which must be satisfied; and whatever pains be taken to divert it from itself, it soon grows weary, restless, and disquieted amidst the enjoyments of sense. If ever the faculties of the great majority of mankind were exclusively bent upon the pursuit of material objects, it might be anticipated that an amazing reaction would take place in the souls of some men. They would drift at large in the world of spirits, for fear of remaining shackled by the close bondage of the body.

It is not, then, wonderful, if, in the midst of a community whose thoughts tend earthward, a small number of individuals are to be found who turn their looks to Heaven. I should be surprised if mysticism did not soon make some advance amongst a people solely engaged in promoting their own worldly welfare.

—————————————#

---★---

CHAPTER XIII

Why the Americans Are So Restless
in the Midst of Their Prosperity

In certain remote corners of the Old World, you may still sometimes stumble upon a small district which seems to have been forgotten amidst the general tumult, and to have remained stationary whilst everything around it was in motion. The inhabitants are, for the most part, extremely ignorant and poor; they take no part in the business of the country, and are frequently oppressed by the government; yet their countenances are generally placid, and their spirits light.

In America, I saw the freest and most enlightened men placed in the happiest circumstances which the world affords: it seemed to me as if a cloud habitually hung upon their brow, and I thought them serious, and almost sad, even in their pleasures.

The chief reason of this contrast is, that the former do not think of the ills they endure, while the latter are forever brooding over advantages they do not possess. It is strange to see with what feverish ardor the Americans pursue their own welfare; and to watch the vague dread that constantly torments them, lest they should not have chosen the shortest path which may lead to it.

A native of the United States clings to this world's goods as if he were certain never to die; and he is so hasty in grasping at all within his reach, that one would suppose he was constantly afraid of not living long enough to enjoy them. He clutches everything, he holds nothing fast, but soon loosens his grasp to pursue fresh gratifications.

In the United States, a man builds a house in which to spend his old age, and he sells it before the roof is on; he plants a garden, and lets it just as the trees are coming into bearing; he brings a field into tillage, and leaves other men to gather the crops; he embraces a profession, and gives it up; he settles in a place, which he soon afterwards leaves, to carry his changeable longings elsewhere. If his private affairs leave him any leisure, he instantly plunges into the vortex of politics; and if, at the end of a year of unremitting labor, he finds he has a few days' vacation, his eager curiosity whirls him over the vast extent of the United States, and he will travel fifteen hundred miles in a few days, to shake off his happiness. Death at length overtakes him, but it is before he is weary of his bootless chase of that complete felicity which forever escapes him.

At first sight, there is something surprising in this strange unrest of so many happy men, restless in the midst of abundance. The spectacle itself is, however, as old as the world; the novelty is, to see a whole people furnish an exemplification of it.

Their taste for physical gratifications must be regarded as the original source of that secret inquietude which the actions of the Americans betray, and of that inconstancy of which they daily afford fresh examples. He who has set his heart exclusively upon the pursuit of worldly welfare is always in a hurry, for he has but a limited time at his disposal to reach, to grasp, and to enjoy it. The recollection of the shortness of life is a constant spur to him. Besides the good things which he possesses, he every instant fancies a thousand others, which death will prevent him from trying if he does not try them soon. This thought fills him with anxiety, fear, and regret, and keeps his mind in ceaseless trepidation, which leads him perpetually to change his plans and his abode.

In democratic times, enjoyments are more intense than in the ages of aristocracy, and the number of those who partake in them is vastly larger: but, on the other hand, it must be admitted that man's hopes and desires are oftener blasted, the soul is more stricken and perturbed, and care itself more keen.

———————★———————

CHAPTER XIV

How the Taste for Physical Gratifications Is United in America to Love of Freedom and Attention to Public Affairs

When a democratic state turns to absolute monarchy, the activity which was before directed to public and to private affairs is all at once centered upon the latter: the immediate consequence is, for some time, great physical prosperity; but this impulse soon slackens, and the amount of productive industry is checked. I know not if a single trading or manufacturing people can be cited, from the Tyrians down to the Florentines and the English, who were not a free people also. There is therefore a close bond and necessary relation between these two elements,—freedom and productive industry.

This proposition is generally true of all nations, but especially of democratic nations. I have already shown that men who live in ages of equality continually require to form associations in order to procure the things they covet; and, on the other hand, I have shown how great political freedom improves and diffuses the art of association. Freedom in these ages is therefore especially favorable to the production of wealth; nor is it difficult to perceive, that despotism is especially adverse to the same result.

The nature of despotic power in democratic ages is not to be fierce or cruel, but minute and meddling. Despotism of this kind, though it does not trample on humanity, is directly opposed to the genius of commerce and the pursuits of industry.

Thus, the men of democratic times require to be free in order more readily to procure those physical enjoyments for which they are always longing. It sometimes happens, however, that the excessive taste they conceive for these same enjoyments makes them surrender to the first master who appears. The passion for worldly welfare then defeats itself, and, without their perceiving it, throws the object of their desires to a greater distance.

There is, indeed, a most dangerous passage in the history of a democratic people. When the taste for physical gratifications amongst them has grown more rapidly than their education and their experience of free institutions, the time will come when men are carried away, and lose all self-restraint, at the sight of the new possessions they are about to obtain. In their intense and exclusive anxiety to make a fortune, they lose sight of the close connection which exists between the private fortune of each and the prosperity of all. It is not necessary to do violence to such a people in order to strip them of the rights they enjoy; they themselves willingly loosen their hold. The discharge of political duties appears to them to be a troublesome impediment, which diverts them from their occupations and business. If they be required to elect representatives, to support the government by personal service, to meet on public business, they think they have no time,—they cannot waste their precious hours in useless engagements: such idle amusements are unsuited to serious men, who are engaged with the more important interests of life. These people think they are following the principle of self-interest, but the idea they entertain of that principle is a very rude one; and the better to look after what they call their own business, they neglect their chief business, which is to remain their own masters.

As the citizens who labor do not care to attend to public affairs, and as the class which might devote its leisure to these duties has ceased to exist, the place of the government is, as it were, unfilled. If, at that critical moment, some able and ambitious man grasps the supreme power, he will find the road to every kind of usurpation open before him. If he does but attend for some time to the material prosperity of the country, no more will be demanded of him. Above all, he must insure public tranquility: men who are possessed by the passion for physical gratification generally find out that the turmoil of freedom disturbs their welfare, before they discover how freedom itself serves to promote it. If the slightest rumor of public commotion intrudes into the petty pleasures of private life, they are aroused and alarmed by it. The fear of anarchy perpetually haunts them, and they are always ready to fling away their freedom at the first disturbance.

I readily admit that public tranquility is a great good; but at the same time, I cannot forget that all nations have been enslaved by being kept in good order. Certainly, it is not to be inferred that nations ought to despise public tranquility; but that state ought not to content them. A nation which asks nothing of its government but the maintenance of order is already a slave at heart,—the slave of its own well-being, awaiting but the hand that will bind it.

By such a nation, the despotism of faction is not less to be dreaded than the despotism of an individual. When the bulk of the community are engrossed by private concerns, the smallest parties need not despair of getting the upper hand in public affairs. At such times, it is not rare to see upon the great stage of the world, as we see at our theatres, a multitude represented by a few players, who alone speak in the name of an absent or inattentive crowd: they alone are in action, whilst all others are stationary; they regulate everything by their own caprice; they change the laws, and tyrannize at will over the manners of the country; and then men wonder to see into how small a number of weak and worthless hands a great people may fall.

Hitherto, the Americans have fortunately escaped all the perils which I have just pointed out; and in this respect they are really deserving of admiration. Perhaps there is no country in the world where fewer idle men are to be met with than in America, or where all who work are more eager to promote their own welfare. But if the passion of the Americans for physical gratifications is vehement, at least it is not indiscriminate; and reason, though unable to restrain it, still directs its course.

An American attends to his private concerns as if he were alone in the world, and the next minute he gives himself up to the common weal as if he had forgotten them. At one time, he seems animated by the most selfish cupidity; at another, by the most lively patriotism. The human heart cannot be thus divided. The inhabitants of the United States alternately display so strong and so similar a passion for their own welfare and for their freedom, that it may be supposed that these passions are united and mingled in some part of their character. And indeed, the Americans believe their freedom to be the best instrument and surest safeguard of their welfare: they are attached to the one by the other. They by no means think that they are not called upon to take a part in public affairs; they believe, on the contrary, that their chief business is to secure for themselves a government which will allow them to acquire the things they covet, and which will not debar them from the peaceful enjoyment of those possessions which they have already acquired.

———————★———————

How Religious Belief Sometimes Turns the Thoughts of the Americans to Immaterial Pleasures

In the United States, on the seventh day of every week, the trading and working life of the nation seems suspended; all noises cease; a deep tranquility, say rather the solemn calm of meditation, succeeds the turmoil of the week, and the soul resumes possession and contemplation of itself. Upon this day, the marts of traffic are deserted; every member of the community, accompanied by his children, goes to church, where he listens to strange language, which would seem unsuited to his ear. He is told of the countless evils caused by pride and covetousness; he is reminded of the necessity of checking his desires, of the finer pleasures which belong to virtue alone, and of the true happiness which attends it. On his return home, he does not turn to the ledgers of his business, but he opens the book of Holy Scripture; there he meets with sublime and affecting descriptions of the greatness and goodness of the Creator, of the infinite magnificence of the handiwork of God, and of the lofty destinies of man, his duties, and his immortal privileges.

Thus it is, that the American at times steals an hour from himself; and, laying aside for a while the petty passions which agitate his life, and the ephemeral interests which engross it, he strays at once into an ideal world, where all is great, eternal, and pure.

I have endeavored to point out, in another part of this work, the causes to which the maintenance of the political institutions of the Americans is attributable, and religion appeared to be one of the most prominent amongst them. I am now treating of the Americans in an individual capacity, and I again observe, that religion is not less useful to each citizen than to the whole state. The Americans show, by their practice, that they feel the high necessity of imparting morality to democratic communities by means of religion. What they think of themselves in this respect is a truth of which every democratic nation ought to be thoroughly persuaded.

I do not doubt that the social and political constitution of a people predisposes them to adopt certain doctrines and tastes, which afterwards flourish without difficulty amongst them; whilst the same causes may divert them from certain other opinions and propensities, without any voluntary effort, and, as it were, without any distinct consciousness, on their part. The whole art of the legislator is correctly to discern beforehand these natural inclinations of communities of men, in order to know whether they should be fostered, or whether it may not be necessary to check them. For the duties incumbent on the legislator differ at different times; only the goal towards which the human race ought ever to be tending is stationary: the means of reaching it are perpetually varied.

If I had been born in an aristocratic age, in the midst of a nation where the hereditary wealth of some, and the irremediable penury of others, equally diverted men from the idea of bettering their condition, and held the soul, as it were, in a state of torpor, fixed on the contemplation of another world, I should then wish that it were possible for me to rouse that people to a sense of their wants; I should seek to discover more rapid and easy means for satisfying the fresh desires which I might have awakened; and, directing the most strenuous efforts of the citizens to physical pursuits, I should endeavor to stimulate them to promote their own well-being. If it happened that some men were thus immoderately incited to the pursuit of riches, and caused to display an excessive liking for physical gratifications, I should not be alarmed; these peculiar cases would soon disappear in the general aspect of the whole community.

The attention of the legislators of democracies is called to other cares. Give democratic nations education and freedom, and leave them alone. They will soon learn to draw from this world all the benefits which it can afford; they will improve each of the useful arts, and will day by day render life more comfortable, more convenient, and more easy. Their social condition naturally urges them in this direction; I do not fear that they will slacken their course.

But whilst man takes delight in this honest and lawful pursuit of his own well-being, it is to be apprehended that he may, in the end, lose the use of his sublimest faculties; and that, whilst he is busied in improving all around him, he may at length degrade himself. Here, and here only, does the peril lie. It should therefore be the unceasing object of the legislators of democracies, and of all the virtuous and enlightened men who live there, to raise the souls of their fellow-citizens, and keep them lifted up towards Heaven. It is necessary that all who feel an interest in the future destinies of democratic society should unite, and that all should make joint and continual efforts to diffuse the love of the infinite, lofty aspirations, and a love of pleasures not of earth. If, amongst the opinions of a democratic people, any of those pernicious theories exist which tend to inculcate that all perishes with the body, let men by whom such theories are professed be marked as the natural foes of the whole people.

Most religions are only general, simple, and practical means of teaching men the doctrine of the immortality of the soul. That is the greatest benefit which a democratic people derives from its belief, and hence belief is more necessary to such a people than to all others. When, therefore, any religion has struck its roots deep into a democracy, beware that you do not disturb it; but rather watch it carefully, as the most precious bequest of aristocratic ages. Seek not to supersede the old religious opinions of men by new ones, lest in the passage from one faith to another, the soul being left for a while stripped of all belief the love of physical gratifications should grow upon it, and fill it wholly.

If it be easy to see that it is more particularly important in democratic ages that spiritual opinions should prevail, it is not easy to say by what means those who govern democratic nations may make them predominate. I am no believer in the prosperity, any more than in the durability, of official philosophies; and as to state religions, I have always held that, if they be sometimes of momentary service to the interests of political power, they always, sooner or later, become fatal to the Church. Nor do I agree with those who think that, to raise religion in the eyes of the people, and to make them do honor to her spiritual doctrines, it is desirable indirectly to give her ministers a political influence which the laws deny them. I am so much alive to the almost inevitable dangers which beset religious belief whenever the clergy take part in public affairs, and I am so convinced that Christianity must be maintained at any cost in the bosom of modern democracies, that I had rather shut up the priesthood within the sanctuary, than allow them to step beyond it.

What means then remain in the hands of constituted authorities to bring men back to spiritual opinions, or to hold them fast to the religion by which those opinions are suggested?

My answer will do me harm in the eyes of politicians. I believe that the sole effectual means which governments can employ, in order to have the doctrine of the immortality of the soul duly respected, is ever to act as if they believed in it themselves; and I think that it is only by scrupulous conformity to religious morality in great affairs, that they can hope to teach the community at large to know, to love, and to observe it in the lesser concerns of life.

CHAPTER XVI

————— ★ —————

How Excessive Care for Worldly Welfare May Impair That Welfare

There is a closer tie than is commonly supposed between the improvement of the soul and the amelioration of what belongs to the body. Man may leave these two things apart, and consider each of them alternately; but he cannot sever them entirely without at last losing sight of both.

The beasts have the same senses as ourselves, and very nearly the same appetites. We have no sensual passions which are not common to our race and theirs, and which are not to be found, at least in the germ, in a dog as well as in a man. Whence is it, then, that the animals can only provide for their first and lowest wants, whereas we can infinitely vary and endlessly increase our enjoyments?

We are superior to the beasts in this, that we use our souls to find out those material benefits to which they are only led by instinct. In man, the angel teaches the brute the art of satisfying its desires. It is because man is capable of rising above the things of the body, and of contemning life itself, of which the beasts have not the least notion, that he can multiply these same goods of the body to a degree which the inferior races cannot conceive of.

Whatever elevates, enlarges, and expands the soul, renders it more capable of succeeding in those very undertakings which concern it not. Whatever, on the other hand, enervates or lowers it, weakens it for all purposes, the chief as well as the least, and threatens to render it almost equally impotent for both. Hence the soul must remain great and strong, though it were only to devote its strength and greatness from time to time to the service of the body. If men were ever to content themselves with material objects, it is probable that they would lose by degrees the art of producing them; and they would enjoy them in the end, like the brutes, without discernment and without improvement.

How, When Conditions Are Equal and Skepticism is Rife, it is Important to Direct Human Actions to Distant Objects

I n ages of faith, the final aim of life is placed beyond life. The men of those ages, therefore, naturally and almost involuntarily, accustom themselves to fix their gaze for many years on some immovable object, towards which they are constantly tending; and they learn by insensible degrees to repress a multitude of petty passing desires, in order to be the better able to content that great and lasting desire which possesses them. When these same men engage in the affairs of this world, the same habits may be traced in their conduct. They are apt to set up some general and certain aim and end to their actions here below, towards which all their efforts are directed: they do not turn from day to day to chase some novel object of desire, but they have settled designs which they are never weary of pursuing.

This explains why religious nations have so often achieved such lasting results: for whilst they were thinking only of the other world, they had found out the great secret of success in this. Religions give men a general habit of conducting themselves with a view to futurity: in this respect, they are not less useful to happiness in this life than to felicity hereafter; and this is one of their chief political characteristics.

But in proportion as the light of faith grows dim, the range of man's sight is circumscribed, as if the end and aim of human actions appeared every day to be more within his reach. When men have once allowed themselves to think no more of what is to befall them after life, they readily lapse into that complete and brutal indifference to futurity which is but too conformable to some propensities of mankind. As soon as they have lost the habit of placing their chief hopes upon remote events, they naturally seek to gratify without delay their smallest desires; and no sooner do they despair of living forever, than they are disposed to act as if they were to exist but for a single day. In skeptical ages, it is always therefore to be feared, that men may perpetually give way to their daily casual desires; and that, wholly renouncing whatever cannot be acquired without protracted effort, they may establish nothing great, permanent, and calm.

If the social condition of a people, under these circumstances, becomes democratic, the danger which I here point out is thereby increased. When every one is constantly striving to change his position; when an immense field for competition is thrown open to all; when wealth is amassed or dissipated in the shortest possible space of time amidst the turmoil of democracy,—visions of sudden and easy fortunes, of great possessions easily won and lost, of chance under all its forms, haunt the mind. The instability of society itself fosters the natural instability of man's desires. In the midst of these perpetual fluctuations of his lot, the present grows upon his mind, until it conceals futurity from his sight, and his looks go no further than the morrow.

In those countries in which, unhappily, irreligion and democracy coexist, philosophers and those in power ought to be always striving to place the objects of human actions far beyond man's immediate range. Adapting himself to the spirit of his country and his age, the moralist must learn to vindicate his principles in that position. He must constantly endeavor to show his contemporaries, that, even in the midst of the perpetual commotion around them, it is easier than they think to conceive and to execute protracted undertakings. He must teach them that, although the aspect of mankind may have changed, the methods by which men may provide for their prosperity in this world are still the same; and that, amongst democratic nations, as well as elsewhere, it is only by resisting a thousand petty selfish passions of the hour, that the general and unquenchable passion for happiness can be satisfied.

The task of those in power is not less clearly marked out. At all times it is important that those who govern nations should act with a view to the future: but this is even more necessary in democratic and skeptical ages than in any others. By acting thus, the leading men of democracies not only make public affairs prosperous, but they also teach private individuals, by their example, the art of managing their private concerns.

Above all, they must strive as much as possible to banish chance from the sphere of politics. The sudden and undeserved promotion of a courtier produces only a transient impression in an aristocratic country, because the aggregate institutions and opinions of the nation habitually compel men to advance slowly in tracks which they cannot get out of. But nothing is more pernicious than similar instances of favor exhibited to a democratic people: they give the last impulse to the public mind in a direction where everything hurries it onwards. At times of skepticism and equality more especially, the favor of the people or of the prince, which chance may confer or chance withhold, ought never to stand in lieu of attainments or services. It is desirable that every advancement should there appear to be the result of some effort; so that no greatness should be of too easy acquirement, and that ambition should be obliged to fix its gaze long upon an object before it is gratified.

Governments must apply themselves to restore to men that love of the future with which religion and the state of society no longer inspire them; and, without saying so, they must practically teach the community day by day that wealth, fame, and power are the rewards of labor; that great success stands at the utmost range of long desires, and that there is nothing lasting but what is obtained by toil.

When men have accustomed themselves to foresee from afar what is likely to befall them in the world, and to feed upon hopes, they can hardly confine their minds within the precise limits of life, and they are ready to break the boundary, and cast their looks beyond. I do not doubt that, by training the members of a community to think of their future condition in this world, they would be gradually and unconsciously brought nearer to religious convictions. Thus, the means which allow men, up to a certain point, to go without religion, are perhaps, after all, the only means we still possess for bringing mankind back, by a long and roundabout path, to a state of faith.

CHAPTER XVIII

———————★———————

Why Amongst the Americans All Honest Callings Are Considered Honorable

Amongst a democratic people, where there is no hereditary wealth, every man works to earn a living, or has worked, or is born of parents who have worked. The notion of labor is therefore presented to the mind, on every side, as the necessary, natural, and honest condition of human existence. Not only is labor not dishonorable amongst such a people, but it is held in honor: the prejudice is not against it, but in its favor. In the United States, a wealthy man thinks that he owes it to public opinion to devote his leisure to some kind of industrial or commercial pursuit, or to public business. He would think himself in bad repute if he employed his life solely in living. It is for the purpose of escaping this obligation to work, that so many rich Americans come to Europe, where they find some scattered remains of aristocratic society, amongst whom idleness is still held in honor.

Equality of conditions not only ennobles the notion of labor, but it raises the notion of labor as a source of profit.

In aristocracies, it is not exactly labor that is despised, but labor with a view to profit. Labor is honorable in itself, when it is undertaken at the bidding of ambition or virtue. Yet, in aristocratic society, it constantly happens that he who works for honor is not insensible to the attractions of profit. But these two desires only intermingle in the depths of his soul: he carefully hides from every eye the point at which they join; he would fain conceal it from himself. In aristocratic countries there are few public officers who do not affect to serve their country without interested motives. Their salary is an incident of which they think but little, and of which they always affect not to think at all. Thus the notion of profit is kept distinct from that of labor; however they may be united in point of fact, they are not thought of together.

In democratic communities these two notions are, on the contrary, always palpably united. As the desire of well-being is universal, as fortunes are slender or fluctuating, as every one wants either to increase his own resources or to provide fresh ones for his progeny, men clearly see that it is profit which, if not wholly, at least partially, leads them to work. Even those who are principally actuated by the love of fame are necessarily made familiar with the thought that they are not exclusively actuated by that motive; and they discover that the desire of getting a living is mingled in their minds with the desire of making life illustrious.

As soon as, on the one hand, labor is held by the whole community to be an honorable necessity of man's condition,—and, on the other, as soon as labor is always ostensibly performed, wholly or in part, for the purpose of earning remuneration,—the immense interval which separated different callings in aristocratic societies disappears. If all are not alike, all at least have one feature in common. No profession exists in which men do not work for money; and the remuneration which is common to them all gives them all an air of resemblance.

This serves to explain the opinions which the Americans entertain with respect to different callings. In America, no one is degraded because he works, for every one about him works also; nor is any one humiliated by the notion of receiving pay, for the President of the United States also works for pay. He is paid for commanding, other men for obeying orders. In the United States, professions are more or less laborious, more or less profitable; but they are never either high or low: every honest calling is honorable.

CHAPTER XIX

———————★———————

What Causes Almost All Americans to Follow Industrial Callings

Agriculture is, perhaps, of all the useful arts that which improves most slowly amongst democratic nations. Frequently, indeed, it would seem to be stationary, because other arts are making rapid strides towards perfection. On the other hand, almost all the tastes and habits which the equality of condition produces naturally lead men to commercial and industrial occupations.

————————————

In aristocracies, the rich are at the same time the governing power. The attention which they unceasingly devote to important public affairs diverts them from the lesser cares which trade and manufactures demand. But if an individual happens to turn his attention to business, the will of the body to which he belongs will immediately prevent him from pursuing it; for, however men may declaim against the rule of numbers, they cannot wholly escape it; and even amongst those aristocratic bodies which most obstinately refuse to acknowledge the rights of the national majority, a private majority is formed which governs the rest.

In democratic countries, where money does not lead those who possess it to political power, but often removes them from it, the rich do not know how to spend their leisure. They are driven into active life by the inquietude and the greatness of their desires, by the extent of their resources, and by the taste for what is extraordinary, which is almost always felt by those who rise, by whatsoever means, above the crowd. Trade is the only road open to them. In democracies, nothing is more great or more brilliant than commerce: it attracts the attention of the public, and fills the imagination of the multitude; all energetic passions are directed towards it. Neither their own prejudices nor those of anybody else can prevent the rich from devoting themselves to it. The wealthy members of democracies never form a body which has manners and regulations of its own; the opinions peculiar to their class do not restrain them, and the common opinions of their country urge them on. Moreover, as all the large fortunes which are found in a democratic community are of commercial growth, many generations must succeed each other before their possessors can have entirely laid aside their habits of business.

Circumscribed within the narrow space which politics leave them, rich men in democracies eagerly embark in commercial enterprise: there they can extend and employ their natural advantages; and indeed, it is even by the boldness and the magnitude of their industrial speculations that we may measure the slight esteem in which productive industry would have been held by them, if they had been born amidst an aristocracy.

A similar observation is likewise applicable to all men living in democracies, whether they be poor or rich. Those who live in the midst of democratic fluctuations have always before their eyes the image of chance; and they end by liking all undertakings in which chance plays a part. They are therefore all led to engage in commerce, not only for the sake of the profit it holds out to them, but for the love of the constant excitement occasioned by that pursuit.

The United States of America have only been emancipated for half a century from the state of colonial dependence in which they stood to Great Britain: the number of large fortunes there is small, and capital is still scarce. Yet no people in the world have made such rapid progress in trade and manufactures as the Americans: they constitute at the present day the second maritime nation in the world; and although their manufactures have to struggle with almost insurmountable natural impediments, they are not prevented from making great and daily advances.

In the United States, the greatest undertakings and speculations are executed without difficulty, because the whole population are engaged in productive industry, and because the poorest as well as the most opulent members of the commonwealth are ready to combine their efforts for these purposes. The consequence is, that a stranger is constantly amazed by the immense public works executed by a nation which contains, so to speak, no rich men. The Americans arrived but as yesterday on the territory which they inhabit, and they have already changed the whole order of nature for their own advantage. They have joined the Hudson to the Mississippi, and made the Atlantic Ocean communicate with the Gulf of Mexico, across a continent of more than five hundred leagues in extent which separates the two seas. The longest railroads which have been constructed, up to the present time, are in America.

But what most astonishes me in the United States is not so much the marvellous grandeur of some undertakings, as the innumerable multitude of small ones. Almost all the farmers of the United States combine some trade with agriculture; most of them make agriculture itself a trade. It seldom happens that an American farmer settles for good upon the land which he occupies: especially in the districts of the Far West, he brings land into tillage in order to sell it again, and not to farm it: he builds a farm-house on the speculation, that, as the state of the country will soon be changed by the increase of population, a good price may be obtained for it.

CHAPTER XX

★

How an Aristocracy May Be Created by Manufactures

I have shown how democracy favors the growth of manufactures, and increases without limit the numbers of the manufacturing classes: we shall now see by what side-road manufacturers may possibly, in their turn, bring men back to aristocracy.

While the workman concentrates his faculties more and more upon the study of a single detail, the master surveys an extensive whole, and the mind of the latter is enlarged in proportion as that of the former is narrowed. In a short time, the one will require nothing but physical strength without intelligence; the other stands in need of science, and almost of genius, to insure success. This man resembles more and more the administrator of a vast empire,—that man, a brute.

The master and the workman have then here no similarity, and their differences increase every day. They are only connected as the two rings at the extremities of a long chain. Each of them fills the station which is made for him, and which he does not leave: the one is continually, closely, and necessarily dependent upon the other, and seems as much born to obey, as that other is to command. What is this but aristocracy?

As the conditions of men constituting the nation become more and more equal, the demand for manufactured commodities becomes more general and extensive; and the cheapness which places these objects within the reach of slender fortunes becomes a great element of success. Hence, there are every day more men of great opulence and education who devote their wealth and knowledge to manufactures; and who seek, by opening large establishments, and by a strict division of labor, to meet the fresh demands which are made on all sides. Thus, in proportion as the mass of the nation turns to democracy, that particular class which is engaged in manufactures becomes more aristocratic. Men grow more alike in the one, more different in the other; and inequality increases in the less numerous class, in the same ratio in which it decreases in the community. Hence it would appear, on searching to the bottom, that aristocracy should naturally spring out of the bosom of democracy.

But this kind of aristocracy by no means resembles those kinds which preceded it. It will be observed at once, that, as it applies exclusively to manufactures and to some manufacturing callings, it is a monstrous exception in the general aspect of society. The small aristocratic societies, which are formed by some manufacturers in the midst of the immense democracy of our age, contain, like the great aristocratic societies of former ages, some men who are very opulent, and a multitude who are wretchedly poor. The poor have few means of escaping from their condition and becoming rich; but the rich are constantly becoming poor, or they give up business when they have realized a fortune. Thus the elements of which the class of the poor is composed are fixed; but the elements of which the class of the rich is composed are not so. To say the truth, though there are rich men, the class of rich men does not exist; for these rich individuals have no feelings or purposes in common, no mutual traditions or mutual hopes; there are individuals, therefore, but no definite class.

Not only are the rich not compactly united amongst themselves, but there is no real bond between them and the poor. Their relative position is not a permanent one; they are constantly drawn together or separated by their interests. The workman is generally dependent on the master, but not on any particular master: these two men meet in the factory, but know not each other elsewhere; and whilst they come into contact on one point, they stand very wide apart on all others. The manufacturer asks nothing of the workman but his labor; the workman expects nothing from him but his wages. The one contracts no obligation to protect, nor the other to defend; and they are not permanently connected either by habit or duty. The aristocracy created by business rarely settles in the midst of the manufacturing population which it directs: the object is not to govern that population, but to use it. An aristocracy thus constituted can have no great hold upon those whom it employs; and, even if it succeed in retaining them at one moment, they escape the next: it knows not how to will, and it cannot act.

The territorial aristocracy of former ages was either bound by law, or thought itself bound by usage, to come to the relief of its serving-men, and to succor their distresses. But the manufacturing aristocracy of our age first impoverishes and debases the men who serve it, and then abandons them to be supported by the charity of the public. This is a natural consequence of what has been said before. Between the workman and the master there are frequent relations, but no real association.

I am of opinion, upon the whole, that the manufacturing aristocracy which is growing up under our eyes is one of the harshest which ever existed in the world; but, at the same time, it is one of the most confined and least dangerous. Nevertheless, the friends of democracy should keep their eyes anxiously fixed in this direction; for if ever a permanent inequality of conditions and aristocracy again penetrate into the world, it may be predicted that this is the gate by which they will enter.

VOLUME II

$\bigstar$

THIRD BOOK

Influence of Democracy on Manners Properly So Called

———————★———————

How Manners Are Softened as Social Conditions Become More Equal

W e perceive that, for several centuries, social conditions have tended to equality, and we discover that at the same time the manners of society have been softened. Are these two things merely contemporaneous, or does any secret link exist between them, so that the one cannot advance without the other? Several causes may concur to render the manners of a people less rude; but, of all these causes, the most powerful appears to me to be the equality of conditions. Equality of conditions and greater mildness in manners are then, in my eyes, not only contemporaneous occurrences, but correlative facts.

———————————————

Amongst an aristocratic people, each caste has its own opinions, feelings, rights, manners, and modes of living. Thus, the men who compose it do not resemble the mass of their fellow-citizens; they do not think or feel in the same manner, and they scarcely believe that they belong to the same race. They cannot therefore thoroughly understand what others feel, nor judge of others by themselves. Yet they are sometimes eager to lend each other aid; but this is not contrary to my previous observation.

These aristocratic institutions, which made the beings of one and the same race so different, nevertheless bound them to each other by close political ties. Although the serf had no natural interest in the fate of the nobles, he did not the less think himself obliged to devote his person to the service of that noble who happened to be his lord: and although the noble held himself to be of a different nature from that of his serfs, he nevertheless held that his duty and his honor constrained him to defend, at the risk of his own life, those who dwelt upon his domains.

It is evident that these mutual obligations did not originate in the law of nature, but in the law of society; and that the claim of social duty was more stringent than that of mere humanity. These services were not supposed to be due from man to man, but to the vassal or to the lord. Feudal institutions awakened a lively sympathy for the sufferings of certain men, but none at all for the miseries of mankind. They infused generosity rather than mildness into the manners of the time; and although they prompted men to great acts of self-devotion, they created no real sympathies, for real sympathies can only exist between those who are alike; and, in aristocratic ages, men acknowledge none but the members of their own caste to be like themselves.

In democratic ages, men rarely sacrifice themselves for one another; but they display general compassion for the members of the human race. They inflict no useless ills; and they are happy to relieve the griefs of others, when they can do so without much hurting themselves; they are not disinterested, but they are humane.

Although the Americans have in a manner reduced selfishness to a social and philosophical theory, they are nevertheless extremely open to compassion. In no country is criminal justice administered with more mildness than in the United States. Whilst the English seem disposed carefully to retain the bloody traces of the Middle Ages in their penal legislation, the Americans have almost expunged capital punishment from their codes. North America is, I think, the only country upon earth in which the life of no one citizen has been taken for a political offence in the course of the last fifty years.

The circumstance which conclusively shows that this singular mildness of the Americans arises chiefly from their social condition, is the manner in which they treat their slaves. Perhaps there is not, upon the whole, a single European colony in the New World, in which the physical condition of the blacks is less severe than in the United States; yet the slaves still endure frightful misery there, and are constantly exposed to very cruel punishments. It is easy to perceive that the lot of these unhappy beings inspires their masters with but little compassion, and that they look upon slavery not only as an institution which is profitable to them, but as an evil which does not affect them. Thus, the same man who is full of humanity towards his fellow-creatures, when they are at the same time his equals, becomes insensible to their afflictions as soon as that equality ceases. His mildness should therefore be attributed to the equality of conditions, rather than to civilization and education.

What I have here remarked of individuals is to a certain extent applicable to nations. When each nation has its distinct opinions, belief, laws, and customs, it looks upon itself as the whole of mankind, and is moved by no sorrows but its own. Should war break out between two nations animated by this feeling, it is sure to be waged with great cruelty.

At the time of their highest culture, the Romans slaughtered the generals of their enemies, after having dragged them in triumph behind a car; and they flung their prisoners to the beasts of the Circus for the amusement of the people. Cicero, who declaimed so vehemently at the notion of crucifying a Roman citizen, had not a word to say against these horrible abuses of victory. It is evident that, in his eyes, a barbarian did not belong to the same human race as a Roman.

On the contrary, in proportion as nations become more like each other, they become reciprocally more compassionate, and the law of nations is mitigated.

CHAPTER II

---★---

How Democracy Renders the Habitual Intercourse of the Americans Simple and Easy

D emocracy does not attach men strongly to each other; but it places their habitual intercourse upon an easier footing.

In America, where the privileges of birth never existed, and where riches confer no peculiar rights on their possessors, men unacquainted with each other are very ready to frequent the same places, and find neither peril nor advantage in the free interchange of their thoughts. If they meet by accident, they neither seek nor avoid intercourse; their manner is therefore natural, frank, and open: it is easy to see that they hardly expect or apprehend anything from each other, and that they do not care to display, any more than to conceal, their position in the world. If their demeanor is often cold and serious, it is never haughty or constrained; and if they do not converse, it is because they are not in a humor to talk, not because they think it their interest to be silent.

In a foreign country two Americans are at once friends, simply because they are Americans. They are repulsed by no prejudice; they are attracted by their common country. For two Englishmen, the same blood is not enough; they must be brought together by the same rank. The Americans remark this unsociable mood of the English as much as the French do, and are not less astonished by it. Yet the Americans are connected with England by their origin, their religion, their language, and partially by their manners: they only differ in their social condition. It may therefore be inferred, that the reserve of the English proceeds from the constitution of their country, much more than from that of its inhabitants.

CHAPTER III

———★———

Why the Americans Show So Little Sensitiveness in Their Own Country, and are So Sensitive in Europe

The temper of the Americans is vindictive, like that of all serious and reflecting nations. They hardly ever forget an offence, but it is not easy to offend them; and their resentment is as slow to kindle as it is to abate.

In aristocratic communities, where a small number of persons manage everything, the outward intercourse of men is subject to settled conventional rules. Every one then thinks he knows exactly what marks of respect or of condescension he ought to display, and none are presumed to be ignorant of the science of etiquette. These usages of the first class in society afterwards serve as a model to all the others; besides which, each of the latter lays down a code of its own, to which all its members are bound to conform. Thus the rules of politeness form a complex system of legislation, which it is difficult to be perfectly master of, but from which it is dangerous for any one to deviate; so that men are constantly exposed involuntarily to inflict or to receive bitter affronts.

But as the distinctions of rank are obliterated, as men differing in education and in birth meet and mingle in the same places of resort, it is almost impossible to agree upon the rules of good breeding. As its laws are uncertain, to disobey them is not a crime, even in the eyes of those who know what they are: men attach more importance to intentions than to forms, and they grow less civil, but at the same time less quarrelsome.

There are many little attentions which an American does not care about; he thinks they are not due to him, or he presumes that they are not known to be due: he therefore either does not perceive a rudeness, or he forgives it; his manners become less courteous, and his character more plain and masculine.

The mutual indulgence which the Americans display, and the manly confidence with which they treat each other, also result from another deeper and more general cause, which I have already adverted to in the preceding chapter. In the United States, the distinctions of rank in civil society are slight, in political society they are null; an American, therefore, does not think himself bound to pay particular attentions to any of his fellow-citizens, nor does he require such attentions from them towards himself. As he does not see that it is his interest eagerly to seek the company of any of his countrymen, he is slow to fancy that his own company is declined: despising no one on account of his station, he does not imagine that any one can despise him for that cause; and until he has clearly perceived an insult, he does not suppose that an affront was intended. The social condition of the Americans naturally accustoms them not to take offence in small matters; and, on the other hand, the democratic freedom which they enjoy transfuses this same mildness of temper into the character of the nation.

The political institutions of the United States constantly bring citizens of all ranks into contact, and compel them to pursue great undertakings in concert. People thus engaged have scarcely time to attend to the details of etiquette, and they are besides too strongly interested in living harmoniously for them to stick at such things. They therefore soon acquire a habit of considering the feelings and opinions of those whom they meet more than their manners, and they do not allow themselves to be annoyed by trifles.

I have often remarked, in the United States, that it is not easy to make a man understand that his presence may be dispensed with; hints will not always suffice to shake him off. I contradict an American at every word he says, to show him that his conversation bores me; he instantly labors with fresh pertinacity to convince me: I preserve a dogged silence, and he thinks I am meditating deeply on the truths which he is uttering: at last, I rush from his company, and he supposes that some urgent business hurries me elsewhere. This man will never understand that he wearies me to death, unless I tell him so; and the only way to get rid of him is to make him my enemy for life.

It appears surprising, at first sight, that the same man, transported to Europe, suddenly becomes so sensitive and captious, that I often find it as difficult to avoid offending him here, as it was there to put him out of countenance. These two opposite effects proceed from the same cause. Democratic institutions generally give men a lofty notion of their country and of themselves. An American leaves his country with a heart swollen with pride: on arriving in Europe, he at once finds out that we are not so engrossed by the United States and the great people who inhabit them as he had supposed; and this begins to annoy him. He has been informed that the conditions of society are not equal in our part of the globe; and he observes that, among the nations of Europe, the traces of rank are not wholly obliterated,—that wealth and birth still retain some indeterminate privileges, which force themselves upon his notice whilst they elude definition. He is therefore profoundly ignorant of the place which he ought to occupy in this half-ruined scale of classes, which are sufficiently distinct to hate and despise each other, yet sufficiently alike for him to be always confounding them. He is afraid of ranging himself too high, still more is he afraid of being ranged too low: this twofold peril keeps his mind constantly on the stretch, and embarrasses all he says and does.

He learns from tradition that in Europe ceremonial observances were infinitely varied according to different ranks; this recollection of former times completes his perplexity, and he is the more afraid of not obtaining those marks of respect which are due to him, as he does not exactly know in what they consist. He is like a man surrounded by traps: society is not a recreation for him, but a serious toil: he weighs your least actions, interrogates your looks, and scrutinizes all you say, lest there should be some hidden allusion to affront him. I doubt whether there was ever a provincial man of quality so punctilious in breeding as he is: he endeavors to attend to the slightest rules of etiquette, and does not allow one of them to be waived towards himself: he is full of scruples, and at the same time of pretensions; he wishes to do enough, but fears to do too much; and as he does not very well know the limits of the one or of the other, he keeps up a haughty and embarrassed air of reserve.

But this is not all: here is yet another double of the human heart. An American is forever talking of the admirable equality which prevails in the United States: aloud, he makes it the boast of his country, but in secret, he deplores it for himself; and he aspires to show that, for his part, he is an exception to the general state of things which he vaunts. There is hardly an American to be met with who does not claim some remote kindred with the first founders of the Colonies; and as for the scions of the noble families of England, America seemed to me to be covered with them. When an opulent American arrives in Europe, his first care is to surround himself with all the luxuries of wealth: he is so afraid of being taken for the plain citizen of a democracy, that he adopts a hundred distorted ways of bringing some new instance of his wealth before you every day. His house will be in the most fashionable part of the town: he will always be surrounded by a host of servants. I have heard an American complain that, in the best houses of Paris, the society was rather mixed; the taste which prevails there was not pure enough for him; and he ventured to hint that, in his opinion, there was a want of elegance of manner; he could not accustom himself to see wit concealed under such unpretending forms.

These contrasts ought not to surprise us. If the vestiges of former aristocratic distinctions were not so completely effaced in the United States, the Americans would be less simple and less tolerant in their own country; they would require less, and be less fond of borrowed manners, in ours.

CHAPTER IV

———★———

Consequences of the Three
Preceding Chapters

When men feel a natural compassion for the sufferings of each other,—when they are brought together by easy and frequent intercourse, and no sensitive feelings keep them asunder,—it may readily be supposed that they will lend assistance to one another whenever it is needed. When an American asks for the co-operation of his fellow-citizens, it is seldom refused; and I have often seen it afforded spontaneously, and with great good-will. If an accident happens on the highway, everybody hastens to help the sufferer; if some great and sudden calamity befalls a family, the purses of a thousand strangers are at once willingly opened, and small but numerous donations pour in to relieve their distress.

It often happens, amongst the most civilized nations of the globe, that a poor wretch is as friendless in the midst of a crowd as the savage in his wilds: this is hardly ever the case in the United States. The Americans, who are always cold and often coarse in their manners, seldom show insensibility; and if they do not proffer services eagerly, yet they do not refuse to render them.

All this is not in contradiction to what I have said before on the subject of individualism. The two things are so far from combating each other, that I can see how they agree. Equality of conditions, whilst it makes men feel their independence, shows them their own weakness: they are free, but exposed to a thousand accidents; and experience soon teaches them that, although they do not habitually require the assistance of others, a time almost always comes when they cannot do without it.

We constantly see, in Europe, that men of the same profession are ever ready to assist each other; they are all exposed to the same ills, and that is enough to teach them to seek mutual preservatives, however hard-hearted and selfish they may otherwise be. When one of them falls into danger, from which the others may save him by a slight transient sacrifice or a sudden effort, they do not fail to make the attempt. Not that they are deeply interested in his fate,—for if, by chance, their exertions are unavailing, they immediately forget the object of them, and return to their own business,—but a sort of tacit and almost involuntary agreement has been passed between them, by which each one owes to the others a temporary support, which he may claim for himself in turn.

Extend to a people the remark here applied to a class, and you will understand my meaning. A similar covenant exists, in fact, between all the citizens of a democracy: they all feel themselves subject to the same weakness and the same dangers; and their interest, as well as their sympathy, makes it a rule with them to lend each other mutual assistance when required. The more equal social conditions become, the more do men display this reciprocal disposition to oblige each other. In democracies, no great benefits are conferred, but good offices are constantly rendered; a man seldom displays self-devotion, but all men are ready to be of service to one another.

★

CHAPTER V

How Democracy Affects the Relations of Masters and Servants

An American who had travelled for a long time in Europe once said to me: "The English treat their servants with a stiffness and imperiousness of manner which surprise us; but, on the other hand, the French sometimes treat their attendants with a degree of familiarity or of politeness which we cannot understand. It looks as if they were afraid to give orders; the posture of the superior and the inferior is ill maintained." The remark was a just one, and I have often made it myself. I have always considered England as the country of all the world where, in our time, the bond of domestic service is drawn most tightly, and France as the country where it is most relaxed. Nowhere have I seen masters stand so high or so low as in these two countries. Between these two extremes the Americans are to be placed. Such is the fact, as it appears upon the surface of things: to discover the causes of that fact, it is necessary to search the matter thoroughly.

No communities have ever yet existed in which social conditions have been so equal that there were neither rich nor poor, and, consequently, neither masters nor servants. Democracy does not prevent the existence of these two classes, but it changes their dispositions, and modifies their mutual relations.

Equality of conditions turns servants and masters into new beings, and places them in new relative positions. When social conditions are nearly equal, men are constantly changing their situations in life: there is still a class of menials and a class of masters, but these classes are not always composed of the same individuals, still less of the same families; and those who command are not more secure of perpetuity than those who obey. As servants do not form a separate people, they have no habits, prejudices, or manners peculiar to themselves: they are not remarkable for any particular turn of mind or moods of feeling. They know no vices or virtues of their condition, but they partake of the education, the opinions, the feelings, the virtues and the vices of their contemporaries; and they are honest men or scoundrels in the same way as their masters are.

The conditions of servants are not less equal than those of masters. As no marked ranks or fixed subordination are to be found amongst them, they will not display either the meanness or the greatness which characterize the aristocracy of menials, as well as all other aristocracies. I never saw a man in the United States who reminded me of that class of confidential servants of which we still retain a reminiscence in Europe, neither did I ever meet with such a thing as a *lackey*: all traces of the one and the other have disappeared.

In democracies, servants are not only equal amongst themselves, but it may be said that they are, in some sort, the equals of their masters. This requires explanation in order to be rightly understood. At any moment, a servant may become a master, and he aspires to rise to that condition: the servant is therefore not a different man from the master. Why then has the former a right to command, and what compels the latter to obey?—the free and temporary consent of both their wills. Neither of them is, by nature, inferior to the other; they only become so for a time, by covenant. Within the terms of this covenant, the one is a servant, the other a master; beyond it, they are two citizens of the commonwealth,—two men.

I beg the reader particularly to observe, that this is not only the notion which servants themselves entertain of their own condition; domestic service is looked upon by masters in the same light; and the precise limits of authority and obedience are as clearly settled in the mind of the one as in that of the other.

When the greater part of the community have long attained a condition nearly alike, and when equality is an old and acknowledged fact, the public mind, which is never affected by exceptions, assigns certain general limits to the value of man, above or below which no man can long remain placed. It is in vain that wealth and poverty, authority and obedience, accidentally interpose great distances between two men; public opinion, founded upon the usual order of things, draws them to a common level, and creates a species of imaginary equality between them, in spite of the real inequality of their conditions. This all-powerful opinion penetrates at length even into the hearts of those whose interest might arm them to resist it; it affects their judgment, whilst it subdues their will.

In their inmost convictions the master and the servant no longer perceive any deep-seated difference between them, and they neither hope nor fear to meet with any such at any time. They are therefore neither subject to disdain nor to anger, and they discern in each other neither humility nor pride. The master holds the contract of service to be the only source of his power, and the servant regards it as the only cause of his obedience. They do not quarrel about their reciprocal situations, but each knows his own and keeps it.

In the French army, the common soldier is taken from nearly the same class as the officer, and may hold the same commissions: out of the ranks, he considers himself entirely equal to his military superiors, and, in point of fact, he is so; but when under arms, he does not hesitate to obey, and his obedience is not the less prompt, precise, and ready, for being voluntary and defined. This example may give a notion of what takes place between masters and servants in democratic communities.

It would be preposterous to suppose that those warm and deepseated affections which are sometimes kindled in the domestic service of aristocracy will ever spring up between these two men, or that they will exhibit strong instances of self-sacrifice. In aristocracies, masters and servants live apart, and frequently their only intercourse is through a third person; yet they commonly stand firmly by one another. In democratic countries, the master and the servant are close together: they are in daily personal contact, but their minds do not intermingle; they have common occupations, hardly ever common interests.

Amongst such a people, the servant always considers himself as a sojourner in the dwelling of his masters. He knew nothing of their forefathers; he will see nothing of their descendants; he has nothing lasting to expect from them. Why, then, should he confound his life with theirs, and whence should so strange a surrender of himself proceed? The reciprocal position of the two men is changed; their mutual relations must be so, too.

I would fain illustrate all these reflections by the example of the Americans; but, for this purpose, the distinctions of persons and places must be accurately traced. In the South of the Union, slavery exists; all that I have just said is consequently inapplicable there. In the North, the majority of servants are either freedmen, or the children of freedmen: these persons occupy a contested position in the public estimation; by the laws, they are brought up to the level of their masters; by the manners of the country, they are obstinately detruded from it. They do not themselves clearly know their proper place, and are almost always either insolent or craven.

But in the Northern States, especially in New England, there are a certain number of whites who agree, for wages, to yield a temporary obedience to the will of their fellow-citizens. I have heard that these servants commonly perform the duties of their situations with punctuality and intelligence; and that, without thinking themselves naturally inferior to the person who orders them, they submit without reluctance to obey him. They appeared to me to carry into service some of those manly habits which independence and equality create. Having once selected a hard way of life, they do not seek to escape from it by indirect means; and they have sufficient respect for themselves not to refuse to their masters that obedience which they have freely promised. On their part, masters require nothing of their servants but the faithful and rigorous performance of the covenant: they do not ask for marks of respect, they do not claim their love, or devoted attachment; it is enough that, as servants, they are exact and honest.

It would not, then, be true to assert that, in democratic society, the relation of servants and masters is disorganized: it is organized on another footing; the rule is different, but there is a rule.

It is not my purpose to inquire whether the new state of things which I have just described is inferior to that which preceded it, or simply different. Enough for me that it is fixed and determined; for what is most important to meet with among men is not any given ordering, but order.

But what shall I say of those sad and troubled times at which equality is established in the midst of the tumult of revolution,—when democracy, after having been introduced into the state of society, still struggles with difficulty against the prejudices and manners of the country? The laws, and partially public opinion, already declare that no natural or permanent inferiority exists between the servant and the master. But this new belief has not yet reached the innermost convictions of the latter, or rather his heart rejects it: in the secret persuasion of his mind, the master thinks that he belongs to a peculiar and superior race; he dares not say so, but he shudders at allowing himself to be dragged to the same level. His authority over his servants becomes timid, and at the same time harsh; he has already ceased to entertain for them the feelings of patronizing kindness which long uncontested power always produces, and he is surprised that, being changed himself, his servant changes also. He wants his attendants to form regular and permanent habits, in a condition of domestic service which is only temporary; he requires that they should appear contented with and proud of a servile condition, which they will one day shake off,—that they should sacrifice themselves to a man who can neither protect nor ruin them; and, in short, that they should contract an indissoluble engagement to a being like themselves, and one who will last no longer than they will.

Amongst aristocratic nations, it often happens that the condition of domestic service does not degrade the character of those who enter upon it, because they neither know nor imagine any other; and the amazing inequality which is manifest between them and their master appears to be the necessary and unavoidable consequence of some hidden law of Providence.

In democracies, the condition of domestic service does not degrade the character of those who enter upon it, because it is freely chosen, and adopted for a time only,—because it is not stigmatized by public opinion, and creates no permanent inequality between the servant and the master.

But whilst the transition from one social condition to another is going on, there is almost always a time when men's minds fluctuate between the aristocratic notion of subjection and the democratic notion of obedience. Obedience then loses its moral importance in the eyes of him who obeys; he no longer considers it as a species of divine obligation, and he does not yet view it under its purely human aspect; it has to him no character of sanctity or of justice, and he submits to it as to a degrading but profitable condition.

At that period, a confused and imperfect phantom of equality haunts the minds of servants; they do not at once perceive whether the equality to which they are entitled is to be found within or without the pale of domestic service; and they rebel in their hearts against a subordination to which they have subjected themselves, and from which they derive actual profit. They consent to serve, and they blush to obey: they like the advantages of service, but not the master; or, rather, they are not sure that they ought not themselves to be masters, and they are inclined to consider him who orders them as an unjust usurper of their own rights.

CHAPTER VI

─────────★─────────

How Democratic Institutions and Manners Tend to Raise Rents and Shorten the Terms of Leases

What has been said of servants and masters is applicable, to a certain extent, to land-owners and farming tenants; but this subject deserves to be considered by itself.

In America there are, properly speaking, no farming tenants; every man owns the ground he tills. It must be admitted that democratic laws tend greatly to increase the number of land-owners, and to diminish that of farming tenants. Yet what takes place in the United States is much less attributable to the institutions of the country, than to the country itself. In America land is cheap, and any one may easily become a land-owner; its returns are small, and its produce cannot well be divided between a land-owner and a farmer. America therefore stands alone in this respect, as well as in many others, and it would be a mistake to take it as an example.

I believe that, in democratic as well as in aristocratic countries, there will be land-owners and tenants, but the connection existing between them will be of a different kind. In aristocracies, the hire of a farm is paid to the landlord, not only in rent, but in respect, regard, and duty; in democracies, the whole is paid in cash. When estates are divided and passed from hand to hand, and the permanent connection which existed between families and the soil is dissolved, the land-owner and the tenant are only casually brought into contact. They meet for a moment to settle the conditions of the agreement, and then lose sight of each other; they are two strangers brought together by a common interest, and who keenly talk over a matter of business, the sole object of which is to make money.

In proportion as property is subdivided and wealth distributed over the country, the community is filled with people whose former opulence is declining, and with others whose fortunes are of recent growth, and whose wants increase more rapidly than their resources. For all such persons the smallest pecuniary profit is a matter of importance, and none of them feel disposed to waive any of their claims, or to lose any portion of their income.

As ranks are intermingled, and as very large as well as very scanty fortunes become more rare, every day brings the social condition of the land-owner nearer to that of the farmer: the one has not naturally any uncontested superiority over the other; between two men who are equal, and not at ease in their circumstances, the contract of hire is exclusively an affair of money.

A man whose estate extends over a whole district, and who owns a hundred farms, is well aware of the importance of gaining at the same time the affections of some thousands of men; this object appears to call for his exertions, and to attain it he will readily make considerable sacrifices. But he who owns a hundred acres is insensible to similar considerations, and cares but little to win the private regard of his tenant.

CHAPTER VII

———————★———————

Influence of Democracy on Wages

M ost of the remarks which I have already made in speaking of masters and servants may be applied to masters and workmen. As the gradations of the social scale come to be less observed, whilst the great sink and the humble rise, and poverty as well as opulence ceases to be hereditary, the distance, both in reality and in opinion, which heretofore separated the workman from the master, is lessened every day. The workman conceives a more lofty opinion of his rights, of his future, of himself; he is filled with new ambition and new desires, he is harassed by new wants. Every instant he views with longing eyes the profits of his employer; and in order to share them, he strives to dispose of his labor at a higher rate, and he generally succeeds at length in the attempt.

In democratic countries, as well as elsewhere, most of the branches of productive industry are carried on at a small cost, by men little removed by their wealth or education above the level of those whom they employ. These manufacturing speculators are extremely numerous; their interests differ; they cannot therefore easily concert or combine their exertions. On the other hand, the workmen have always some sure resources, which enable them to refuse to work when they cannot get what they conceive to be the fair price of their labor. In the constant struggle for wages which is going on between these two classes, their strength is divided, and success alternates from one to the other.

It is even probable that, in the end, the interest of the working class will prevail; for the high wages which they have already obtained make them every day less dependent on their masters; and as they grow more independent, they have greater facilities for obtaining a farther increase of wages.

I shall take for example that branch of productive industry which is still, at the present day, the most generally followed in France, and in almost all the countries of the world;—I mean the cultivation of the soil. In France, most of those who labor for hire in agriculture are themselves owners of certain plots of ground, which just enable them to subsist without working for any one else. When these laborers come to offer their services to a neighboring land-owner or farmer, if he refuses them a certain rate of wages, they retire to their own small property and await another opportunity.

I think that, upon the whole, it may be asserted that a slow and gradual rise of wages is one of the general laws of democratic communities. In proportion as social conditions become more equal, wages rise; and as wages are higher, social conditions become more equal.

CHAPTER VIII

---★---

Influence of Democracy on the Family

I have just examined the changes which the equality of conditions produces in the mutual relations of the several members of the community amongst democratic nations, and amongst the Americans in particular. I would now go deeper, and inquire into the closer ties of family: my object here is not to seek for new truths, but to show in what manner facts already known are connected with my subject.

It has been universally remarked, that, in our time, the several members of a family stand upon an entirely new footing towards each other; that the distance which formerly separated a father from his sons has been lessened; and that paternal authority, if not destroyed, is at least impaired.

Something analogous to this, but even more striking, may be observed in the United States. In America, the family, in the Roman and aristocratic signification of the word, does not exist. All that remains of it are a few vestiges in the first years of childhood, when the father exercises, without opposition, that absolute domestic authority which the feebleness of his children renders necessary, and which their interest, as well as his own incontestable superiority, warrants. But as soon as the young American approaches manhood, the ties of filial obedience are relaxed day by day: master of his thoughts, he is soon master of his conduct. In America, there is, strictly speaking, no adolescence: at the close of boyhood, the man appears, and begins to trace out his own path.

In a democratic family, the father exercises no other power than that which is granted to the affection and the experience of age; his orders would perhaps be disobeyed, but his advice is for the most part authoritative. Though he be not hedged in with ceremonial respect, his sons at least accost him with confidence; they have no settled form of addressing him, but they speak to him constantly, and are ready to consult him every day: the master and the constituted ruler have vanished; the father remains.

Nothing more is needed in order to judge of the difference between the two states of society in this respect, than to peruse the family correspondence of aristocratic ages. The style is always correct, ceremonious, stiff, and so cold that the natural warmth of the heart can hardly be felt in the language. In democratic countries, on the contrary, the language addressed by a son to his father is always marked by mingled freedom, familiarity, and affection, which at once show that new relations have sprung up in the bosom of the family.

A similar revolution takes place in the mutual relations of children. In aristocratic families, as well as in aristocratic society, every place is marked out beforehand. Not only does the father occupy a separate rank, in which he enjoys extensive privileges, but even the children are not equal amongst themselves. The age and sex of each irrevocably determine his rank, and secure to him certain privileges: most of these distinctions are abolished or diminished by democracy.

In aristocratic families, the eldest son, inheriting the greater part of the property, and almost all the rights of the family, becomes the chief, and, to a certain extent, the master, of his brothers. Greatness and power are for him; for them, mediocrity and dependence. But it would be wrong to suppose that, amongst aristocratic nations, the privileges of the eldest son are advantageous to himself alone, or that they excite nothing but envy and hatred around him. The eldest son commonly endeavors to procure wealth and power for his brothers, because the general splendor of the house is reflected back on him who represents it; the younger sons seek to back the elder brother in all his undertakings, because the greatness and power of the head of the family better enable him to provide for all its branches. The different members of an aristocratic family are therefore very closely bound together; their interests are connected, their minds agree, but their hearts are seldom in harmony.

Democracy also binds brothers to each other, but by very different means. Under democratic laws, all the children are perfectly

equal, and consequently independent: nothing brings them forcibly together, but nothing keeps them apart; and as they have the same origin, as they are trained under the same roof, as they are treated with the same care, and as no peculiar privilege distinguishes or divides, them, the affectionate and frank intimacy of early years easily springs up between them. Scarcely anything can occur to break the tie thus formed at the outset of life, for brotherhood brings them daily together, without embarrassing them. It is not then by interest, but by common associations and by the free sympathy of opinion and of taste, that democracy unites brothers to each other. It divides their inheritance, but allows their hearts and minds to unite.

Such is the charm of these democratic manners, that even the partisans of aristocracy are attracted by it; and after having experienced it for some time, they are by no means tempted to revert to the respectful and frigid observances of aristocratic families. They would be glad to retain the domestic habits of democracy, if they might throw off its social conditions and its laws; but these elements are indissolubly united, and it is impossible to enjoy the former without enduring the latter.

The remarks I have made on filial love and fraternal affection are applicable to all the passions which emanate spontaneously from human nature itself.

If a certain mode of thought or feeling is the result of some peculiar condition of life, when that condition is altered nothing whatever remains of the thought or feeling. Thus, a law may bind two members of the community very closely to one another; but that law being abolished, they stand asunder. Nothing was more strict than the tie which united the vassal to the lord under the feudal system: at the present day, the two men know not each other; the fear, the gratitude, and the affection which formerly connected them have vanished, and not a vestige of the tie remains.

Such, however, is not the case with those feelings which are natural to mankind. Whenever a law attempts to tutor these feelings in any particular manner, it seldom fails to weaken them; by attempting to add to their intensity, it robs them of some of their elements, for they are never stronger than when left to themselves.

Democracy, which destroys or obscures almost all the old conventional rules of society, and which prevents men from readily assenting to new ones, entirely effaces most of the feelings to which these conventional rules have given rise; but it only modifies some others, and frequently imparts to them a degree of energy and sweetness unknown before.

Perhaps it is not impossible to condense into a single proposition the whole purport of this chapter, and of several others that preceded it. Democracy loosens social ties, but tightens natural ones; it brings kindred more closely together, whilst it throws citizens more apart.

———————

─────── ★ ───────

Education of Young Women
in the United States

No free communities ever existed without morals; and, as I observed in the former part of this work, morals are the work of woman. Consequently, whatever affects the condition of women, their habits and their opinions, has great political importance in my eyes.

Amongst almost all Protestant nations, young women are far more the mistresses of their own actions than they are in Catholic countries. This independence is still greater in Protestant countries like England, which have retained or acquired the right of self-government; freedom is then infused into the domestic circle by political habits and by religious opinions. In the United States, the doctrines of Protestantism are combined with great political liberty and a most democratic state of society; and nowhere are young women surrendered so early or so completely to their own guidance.

Long before an American girl arrives at the marriageable age, her emancipation from maternal control begins: she has scarcely ceased to be a child, when she already thinks for herself, speaks with freedom, and acts on her own impulse. The great scene of the world is constantly open to her view: far from seeking to conceal it from her, it is every day disclosed more completely, and she is taught to survey it with a firm and calm gaze. Thus the vices and dangers of society are early revealed to her; as she sees them clearly, she views them without illusion, and braves them without fear; for she is full of reliance on her own strength, and her confidence seems to be shared by all around her.

An American girl scarcely ever displays that virginal softness in the midst of young desires, or that innocent and ingenuous grace, which usually attend the European woman in the transition from girlhood to youth. It is rare that an American woman, at any age, displays child-ish timidity or ignorance. Like the young women of Europe, she seeks to please, but she knows precisely the cost of pleasing. If she does not abandon herself to evil, at least she knows that it exists; and she is remarkable rather for purity of manners than for chastity of mind.

I have been frequently surprised, and almost frightened, at the singular address and happy boldness with which young women in America contrive to manage their thoughts and their language, amidst all the difficulties of free conversation; a philosopher would have stumbled at every step along the narrow path which they trod without accident and without effort. It is easy, indeed, to perceive that, even amidst the independence of early youth, an American woman is always mistress of herself: she indulges in all permitted pleasures, without yielding herself up to any of them; and her reason never allows the reins of self-guidance to drop, though it often seems to hold them loosely.

In France, where traditions of every age are still so strangely mingled in the opinions and tastes of the people, women commonly receive a reserved, retired, and almost conventual education, as they did in aristocratic times; and then they are suddenly abandoned, without a guide and without assistance, in the midst of all the irregu-larities inseparable from democratic society.

The Americans are more consistent. They have found out that, in a democracy, the independence of individuals cannot fail to be very great, youth premature, tastes ill-restrained, customs fleeting, public opinion often unsettled and powerless, paternal authority weak, and marital authority contested. Under these circumstances, believing that they had little chance of repressing in woman the most vehement passions of the human heart, they held that the surer way was to teach her the art of combating those passions for herself. As they could not prevent her virtue from being exposed to frequent danger, they deter-mined that she should know how best to defend it; and more reliance was placed on the free vigor of her will than on safeguards which have been shaken or overthrown. Instead then of inculcating mistrust of herself, they constantly seek to enhance her confidence in her own strength of character. As it is neither possible nor desirable to keep a young woman in perpetual and complete ignorance, they hasten to give her a precocious knowledge on all subjects. Far from hiding the corruptions of the world from her, they prefer that she should see them at once, and train herself to shun them; and they hold it of more importance to protect her conduct, than to be over-scrupulous of the innocence of her thoughts.

Although the Americans are a very religious people, they do not rely on religion alone to defend the virtue of woman; they seek to arm her reason also. In this respect they have followed the same method as in several others: they first make vigorous efforts to cause individual independence to control itself, and they do not call in the aid of religion until they have reached the utmost limits of human strength.

I am aware that an education of this kind is not without danger; I am sensible that it tends to invigorate the judgment at the expense of the imagination, and to make cold and virtuous women instead of affectionate wives and agreeable companions to man. Society may be more tranquil and better regulated, but domestic life has often fewer charms. These, however, are secondary evils, which may be braved for the sake of higher interests. At the stage at which we are now arrived, the choice is no longer left to us; a democratic education is indispensable to protect women from the dangers with which democratic institutions and manners surround them.

CHAPTER X

★

The Young Woman in the Character of a Wife

In America, the independence of woman is irrecoverably lost in the bonds of matrimony. If an unmarried woman is less constrained there than elsewhere, a wife is subjected to stricter obligations. The former makes her father's house an abode of freedom and of pleasure; the latter lives in the home of her husband as if it were a cloister. Yet these two different conditions of life are perhaps not so contrary as may be supposed, and it is natural that the American women should pass through the one to arrive at the other.

Religious communities and trading nations entertain peculiarly serious notions of marriage: the former consider the regularity of woman's life as the best pledge and most certain sign of the purity of her morals; the latter regard it as the highest security for the order and prosperity of the household. The Americans are, at the same time, a puritanical people and a commercial nation; their religious opinions, as well as their trading habits, consequently lead them to require much abnegation on the part of women, and a constant sacrifice of her pleasures to her duties, which is seldom demanded of her in Europe. Thus, in the United States, the inexorable opinion of the public carefully circumscribes woman within the narrow circle of domestic interests and duties, and forbids her to step beyond it.

Upon her entrance into the world, a young American woman finds these notions firmly established; she sees the rules which are derived from them; she is not slow to perceive that she cannot depart for an instant from the established usages of her contemporaries, without putting in jeopardy her peace of mind, her honor, nay, even her social existence; and she finds the energy required for such an act of submission in the firmness of her understanding, and in the virile habits which her education has given her. It may be said that she has learned, by the use of her independence, to surrender it without a struggle and without a murmur when the time comes for making the sacrifice.

But no American woman falls into the toils of matrimony as into a snare held out to her simplicity and ignorance. She has been taught beforehand what is expected of her, and voluntarily and freely enters upon this engagement. She supports her new condition with courage, because she chose it. As, in America, paternal discipline is very relaxed and the conjugal tie very strict, a young woman does not contract the latter without considerable circumspection and apprehension. Precocious marriages are rare. American women do not marry until their understandings are exercised and ripened; whereas, in other countries, most women generally only begin to exercise and ripen their understandings after marriage.

I by no means suppose, however, that the great change which takes place in all the habits of women in the United States, as soon as they are married, ought solely to be attributed to the constraint of public opinion; it is frequently imposed upon themselves by the sole effort of their own will. When the time for choosing a husband is arrived, that cold and stern reasoning power which has been educated and invigorated by the free observation of the world teaches an American woman that a spirit of levity and independence in the bonds of marriage is a constant subject of annoyance, not of pleasure; it tells her that the amusements of the girl cannot become the recreations of the wife, and that the sources of a married woman's happiness are in the home of her husband. As she clearly discerns beforehand the only road which can lead to domestic happiness, she enters upon it at once, and follows it to the end without seeking to turn back.

The same strength of purpose which the young wives of America display, in bending themselves at once and without repining to the austere duties of their new condition, is no less manifest in all the great trials of their lives. In no country in the world are private fortunes more precarious than in the United States. It is not uncommon for the same man, in the course of his life, to rise and sink again through all the grades which lead from opulence to poverty. American women support these vicissitudes with calm and unquenchable energy: it would seem that their desires contract as easily as they expand with their fortunes.

The greater part of the adventurers who migrate every year to people the Western wilds belong, as I observed in the former part of this work, to the old Anglo-American race of the Northern States. Many of these men, who rush so boldly onwards in pursuit of wealth, were already in the enjoyment of a competency in their own part of the country. They take their wives along with them, and make them share the countless perils and privations which always attend the commencement of these expeditions. I have often met, even on the verge of the wilderness, with young women who, after having been brought up amidst all the comforts of the large towns of New England, had passed, almost without any intermediate stage, from the wealthy abode of their parents to a comfortless hovel in a forest. Fever, solitude, and a tedious life had not broken the springs of their courage. Their features were impaired and faded, but their looks were firm; they appeared to be at once sad and resolute. I do not doubt that these young American women had amassed, in the education of their early years, that inward strength which they displayed under these circumstances. The early culture of the girl may still, therefore, be traced, in the United States, under the aspect of marriage; her part is changed, her habits are different, but her character is the same.

CHAPTER XI

───────★───────

How Equality of Condition Contributes to Maintain Good Morals in America

Some philosophers and historians have said or hinted that the strictness of female morality was increased or diminished simply by the distance of a country from the equator. This solution of the difficulty was an easy one; and nothing was required but a globe and a pair of compasses to settle in an instant one of the most difficult problems in the condition of mankind. But I am not sure that this principle of the materialists is supported by facts. The same nations have been chaste or dissolute, at different periods of their history; the strictness or the laxity of their morals depended, therefore, on some variable cause, and not alone on the natural qualities of their country, which were invariable. I do not deny that, in certain climates, the passions which are occasioned by the mutual attraction of the sexes are peculiarly intense; but I believe that this natural intensity may always be excited or restrained by the condition of society, and by political institutions.

Although the travellers who have visited North America differ on many points, they all agree in remarking that morals are far more strict there than elsewhere. It is evident that, on this point, the Americans are very superior to their progenitors, the English. A superficial glance at the two nations will establish the fact.

In England, as in all other countries of Europe, public malice is constantly attacking the frailties of women. Philosophers and statesmen are heard to deplore that morals are not sufficiently strict, and the literary productions of the country constantly lead one to suppose so. In America, all books, novels not excepted, suppose women to be chaste, and no one thinks of relating affairs of gallantry.

No doubt, this great regularity of American morals is due in part to qualities of country, race, and religion; but all these causes, which operate elsewhere, do not suffice to account for it: recourse must be had to some special reason. This reason appears to me to be the principle of equality, and the institutions derived from it. Equality of condition does not of itself produce regularity of morals, but it unquestionably facilitates and increases it.

Amongst aristocratic nations, birth and fortune frequently make two such different beings of man and woman, that they can never be united to each other. Their passions draw them together, but the condition of society, and the notions suggested by it, prevent them from contracting a permanent and ostensible tie. The necessary consequence is a great number of transient and clandestine connections. Nature secretly avenges herself for the constraint imposed upon her by the laws of man.

This is not so much the case when the equality of conditions has swept away all the imaginary or the real barriers which separated man from woman. No girl then believes that she cannot become the wife of the man who loves her; and this renders all breaches of morality before marriage very uncommon: for, whatever be the credulity of the passions, a woman will hardly be able to persuade herself that she is beloved, when her lover is perfectly free to marry her and does not.

The same cause operates, though more indirectly, on married life. Nothing better serves to justify an illicit passion, either to the minds of those who have conceived it or to the world which looks on, than marriages made by compulsion or chance.

In a country in which a woman is always free to exercise her choice, and where education has prepared her to choose rightly, public opinion is inexorable to her faults. The rigor of the Americans arises in part from this cause. They consider marriages as a covenant which is often onerous, but every condition of which the parties are strictly bound to fulfil, because they knew all those conditions beforehand, and were perfectly free not to have contracted them.

The very circumstances which render matrimonial fidelity more obligatory, also render it more easy.

In aristocratic countries, the object of marriage is rather to unite property than persons; hence the husband is sometimes at school and the wife at nurse when they are betrothed. It cannot be wondered at if the conjugal tie which holds the fortunes of the pair united allows their hearts to rove; this is the result of the nature of the contract. When, on the contrary, a man always chooses a wife for himself, without any external coercion, or even guidance, it is generally a conformity of tastes and opinions which brings a man and a woman together, and this same conformity keeps and fixes them in close habits of intimacy.

Our forefathers had conceived a strange opinion on the subject of marriage; as they had remarked that the small number of love-matches which occurred in their time almost always turned out ill, they resolutely inferred that it was dangerous to listen to the dictates of the heart on the subject. Accident appeared to them a better guide than choice.

Yet it was not difficult to perceive that the examples which they witnessed in fact proved nothing at all. For, in the first place, if democratic nations leave a woman at liberty to choose her husband, they take care to give her mind sufficient knowledge, and her will sufficient strength, to make so important a choice; whereas the young women who, amongst aristocratic nations, furtively elope from the authority of their parents to throw themselves of their own accord into the arms of men whom they have had neither time to know, nor ability to judge of, are totally without those securities. It is not surprising that they make a bad use of their freedom of action the first time they avail themselves of it; nor that they fall into such cruel mistakes when, not having received a democratic education, they choose to marry in conformity to democratic customs. But this is not all. When a man and woman are bent upon marriage in spite of the differences of an aristocratic state of society, the difficulties to be overcome are enormous. Having broken or relaxed the bonds of filial obedience, they have then to emancipate themselves by a final effort from the sway of custom and the tyranny of opinion; and when at length they have succeeded in this arduous task, they stand estranged from their natural friends and kinsmen: the prejudice they have crossed separates them from all, and places them in a situation which soon breaks their courage and sours their hearts.

If, then, a couple married in this manner are first unhappy and afterwards criminal, it ought not to be attributed to the freedom of their choice, but rather to their living in a community in which this freedom of choice is not admitted.

Moreover, it should not be forgotten that the same effort which makes a man violently shake off a prevailing error, commonly impels him beyond the bounds of reason; that, to dare to declare war, in however just a cause, against the opinion of one's age and country, a violent and adventurous spirit is required, and that men of this character seldom arrive at happiness or virtue, whatever be the path they follow. And this, it may be observed by the way, is the reason why, in the most necessary and righteous revolutions, it is so rare to meet with virtuous or moderate revolutionary characters. There is, then, no just ground for surprise if a man who, in an age of aristocracy, chooses to consult nothing but his own opinion and his own taste in the choice of a wife, soon finds that infractions of morality and domestic wretchedness invade his household; but when this same line of action is in the natural and ordinary course of things,—when it is sanctioned by parental authority, and backed by public opinion,—it cannot be doubted that the internal peace of families will be increased by it, and conjugal fidelity more rigidly observed.

Almost all men in democracies are engaged in public or professional life; and on the other hand, the limited income obliges a wife to confine herself to the house, in order to watch in person, and very closely, over the details of domestic economy. All these distinct and compulsory occupations are so many natural barriers, which, by keeping the two sexes asunder, render the solicitations of the one less frequent and less ardent, the resistance of the other more easy.

The equality of conditions cannot, it is true, ever succeed in making men chaste, but it may impart a less dangerous character to their breaches of morality. As no one has then either sufficient time or opportunity to assail a virtue armed in self-defence, there will be at the same time a great number of courtesans and a great number of virtuous women. This state of things causes lamentable cases of individual hardship, but it does not prevent the body of society from being strong and alert: it does not destroy family ties, or enervate the morals of the nation. Society is endangered, not by the great profligacy of a few, but by laxity of morals amongst all. In the eyes of a legislator, prostitution is less to be dreaded than intrigue.

The tumultuous and constantly harassed life which equality makes men lead, not only distracts them from the passion of love, by denying them time to indulge it, but it diverts them from it by another more secret but more certain road. All men who live in democratic times more or less contract the ways of thinking of the manufacturing and trading classes; their minds take a serious, deliberate, and positive turn; they are apt to relinquish the ideal, in order to pursue some visible and proximate object, which appears to be the natural and necessary aim of their desires. Thus, the principle of equality does not destroy the imagination, but lowers its flight to the level of the earth.

CHAPTER XII

———★———

How the Americans Understand
the Equality of the Sexes

I have shown how democracy destroys or modifies the different inequalities which originate in society; but is this all? or does it not ultimately affect that great inequality of man and woman which has seemed, up to the present day, to be eternally based in human nature? I believe that the social changes which bring nearer to the same level the father and son, the master and servant, and, in general, superiors and inferiors, will raise woman, and make her more and more the equal of man. But here, more than ever, I feel the necessity of making myself clearly understood; for there is no subject on which the coarse and lawless fancies of our age have taken a freer range.

There are people in Europe who, confounding together the different characteristics of the sexes, would make man and woman into beings not only equal, but alike. They would give to both the same functions, impose on both the same duties, and grant to both the same rights; they would mix them in all things,—their occupations, their pleasures, their business. It may readily be conceived, that, by thus attempting to make one sex equal to the other, both are degraded; and from so preposterous a medley of the works of nature, nothing could ever result but weak men and disorderly women.

It is not thus that the Americans understand that species of democratic equality which may be established between the sexes. They admit that, as nature has appointed such wide differences between the physical and moral constitution of man and woman, her manifest design was to give a distinct employment to their various faculties; and they hold that improvement does not consist in making beings so dissimilar do pretty nearly the same things, but in causing each of them to fulfil their respective tasks in the best possible manner.

The Americans have applied to the sexes the great principle of political economy which governs the manufactures of our age, by carefully dividing the duties of man from those of woman, in order that the great work of society may be the better carried on.

In no country has such constant care been taken as in America to trace two clearly distinct lines of action for the two sexes, and to make them keep pace one with the other, but in two pathways which are always different. American women never manage the outward concerns of the family, or conduct a business, or take a part in political life; nor are they, on the other hand, ever compelled to perform the rough labor of the fields, or to make any of those laborious exertions which demand the exertion of physical strength. No families are so poor as to form an exception to this rule. If, on the one hand, an American woman cannot escape from the quiet circle of domestic employments, she is never forced, on the other, to go beyond it. Hence it is, that the women of America, who often exhibit a masculine strength of understanding and a manly energy, generally preserve great delicacy of personal appearance, and always retain the manners of women, although they sometimes show that they have the hearts and minds of men.

Nor have the Americans ever supposed that one consequence of democratic principles is the subversion of marital power, or the confusion of the natural authorities in families. They hold that every association must have a head in order to accomplish its object, and that the natural head of the conjugal association is man. They do not therefore deny him the right of directing his partner; and they maintain that, in the smaller association of husband and wife, as well as in the great social community, the object of democracy is to regulate and legalize the powers which are necessary, and not to subvert all power.

This opinion is not peculiar to one sex, and contested by the other: I never observed that the women of America consider conjugal authority as a fortunate usurpation of their rights, nor that they thought themselves degraded by submitting to it. It appeared to me, on the contrary, that they attach a sort of pride to the voluntary surrender of their own will, and make it their boast to bend themselves to the yoke,—not to shake it off. Such, at least, is the feeling expressed by the most virtuous of their sex; the others are silent; and, in the United States, it is not the practice for a guilty wife to clamor for the rights of women, whilst she is trampling on her own holiest duties.

Thus, the Americans do not think that man and woman have either, the duty or the right to perform the same offices, but they show an equal regard for both their respective parts; and though their lot is different, they consider both of them as beings of equal value. They do not give to the courage of woman the same form or the same direction as to that of man; but they never doubt her courage: and if they hold that man and his partner ought not always to exercise their intellect and understanding in the same manner, they at least believe the understanding of the one to be as sound as that of the other, and her intellect to be as clear. Thus, then, whilst they have allowed the social inferiority of woman to subsist, they have done all they could to raise her morally and intellectually to the level of man; and in this respect they appear to me to have excellently understood the true principle of democratic improvement.

As for myself, I do not hesitate to avow, that, although the women of the United States are confined within the narrow circle of domestic life, and their situation is, in some respects, one of extreme dependence, I have nowhere seen woman occupying a loftier position; and if I were asked, now that I am drawing to the close of this work, in which I have spoken of so many important things done by the Americans, to what the singular prosperity and growing strength of that people ought mainly to be attributed, I should reply, To the superiority of their women.

CHAPTER XIII

———————— ★ ————————

How the Principle of Equality
Naturally Divides the Americans into
a Multitude of Small Private Circles

It might be supposed that the final and necessary effect of democratic institutions would be to confound together all the members of the community in private as well as in public life, and to compel them all to live alike; but this would be to ascribe a very coarse and oppressive form to the equality which originates in democracy. No state of society or laws can render men so much alike, but that education, fortune, and tastes will interpose some differences between them; and, though different men may sometimes find it their interest to combine for the same purposes, they will never make it their pleasure. They will therefore always tend to evade the provisions of law, whatever they may be; and, escaping in some respect from the circle in which the legislator sought to confine them, they will set up, close by the great political community, small private societies, united together by similitude of conditions, habits, and manners.

In the United States, the citizens have no sort of preeminence over each other; they owe each other no mutual obedience or respect; they all meet for the administration of justice, for the government of the state, and, in general, to treat of the affairs which concern their common welfare; but I never heard that attempts have been made to bring them all to follow the same diversions, or to amuse themselves promiscuously in the same places of recreation.

The Americans, who mingle so readily in their political assemblies and courts of justice, are wont carefully to separate into small distinct circles, in order to indulge by themselves in the enjoyments of private life. Each of them willingly acknowledges all his fellow-citizens as his equals, but will only receive a very limited number of them as his friends or his guests. This appears to me to be very natural. In proportion as the circle of public society is extended, it may be anticipated that the sphere of private intercourse will be contracted; far from supposing that the members of modern society will ultimately live in common, I am afraid they will end by forming only small coteries.

Amongst aristocratic nations, the different classes are like vast enclosures, out of which it is impossible to get, into which it is impossible to enter. These classes have no communication with each other, but within them men necessarily live in daily contact; even though they would not naturally suit, the general conformity of a similar condition brings them near together.

But when neither law nor custom professes to establish frequent and habitual relations between certain men, their intercourse originates in the accidental similarity of opinions and tastes; hence private society is infinitely varied. In democracies, where the members of the community never differ much from each other, and naturally stand so near that they may all at any time be confounded in one general mass, numerous artificial and arbitrary distinctions spring up, by means of which every man hopes to keep himself aloof, lest he should be carried away against his will in the crowd.

This can never fail to be the case; for human institutions can be changed, but man cannot: whatever may be the general endeavor of a community to render its members equal and alike, the personal pride of individuals will always seek to rise above the line, and to form somewhere an inequality to their own advantage.

In aristocracies, men are separated from each other by lofty stationary barriers: in democracies, they are divided by many small and almost invisible threads, which are constantly broken or moved from place to place. Thus, whatever may be the progress of equality, in democratic nations a great number of small private associations will always be formed within the general pale of political society; but none of them will bear any resemblance in its manners to the higher class in aristocracies.

CHAPTER XIV

———————★———————

Some Reflections on American Manners

Nothing seems at first sight less important than the outward form of human actions, yet there is nothing upon which men set more store: they grow used to everything except to living in a society which has not their own manners. The influence of the social and political state of a country upon manners is therefore deserving of serious examination.

Manners are generally the product of the very basis of character, but they are also sometimes the result of an arbitrary convention between certain men; thus they are at once natural and acquired.

When some men perceive that they are the foremost persons in society, without contest and without effort,—when they are constantly engaged on large objects, leaving the more minute details to others,—and when they live in the enjoyment of wealth which they did not amass and do not fear to lose,—it may be supposed that they feel a kind of haughty disdain of the petty interests and practical cares of life, and that their thoughts assume a natural greatness, which their language and their manners denote. In democratic countries, manners are generally devoid of dignity, because private life is there extremely petty in its character; and they are frequently low, because the mind has few opportunities of rising above the engrossing cares of domestic interests.

True dignity in manners consists in always taking one's proper station, neither too high nor too low; and this is as much within the reach of a peasant as of a prince. In democracies, all stations appear doubtful; hence it is that the manners of democracies, though often full of arrogance, are commonly wanting in dignity, and, moreover, they are never either well-trained or accomplished.

The men who live in democracies are too fluctuating for a certain number of them ever to succeed in laying down a code of good breeding, and in forcing people to follow it. Every man therefore behaves after his own fashion, and there is always a certain incoherence in the manners of such times, because they are moulded upon the feelings and notions of each individual, rather than upon an ideal model proposed for general imitation. This, however, is much more perceptible when an aristocracy has just been overthrown, than after it has long been destroyed. New political institutions and new social elements then bring to the same places of resort, and frequently compel to live in common, men whose education and habits are still amazingly dissimilar, and this renders the motley composition of society peculiarly visible. The existence of a former strict code of good breeding is still remembered, but what it contained, or where it is to be found, is already forgotten. Men have lost the common law of manners, and they have not yet made up their minds to do without it; but every one endeavors to make to himself some sort of arbitrary and variable rule, from the remnant of former usages; so that manners have neither the regularity and the dignity which they often display amongst aristocratic nations, nor the simplicity and freedom which they sometimes assume in democracies; they are at once constrained and without constraint.

This, however, is not the normal state of things. When the equality of conditions is long established and complete, as all men entertain nearly the same notions and do nearly the same things, they do not require to agree, or to copy from one another, in order to speak or act in the same manner; their manners are constantly characterized by a number of lesser diversities, but not by any great differences. They are never perfectly alike, because they do not copy from the same pattern; they are never very unlike, because their social condition is the same. At first sight, a traveller would say that the manners of all Americans are exactly similar; it is only upon close examination that the peculiarities in which they differ may be detected.

The English make game of the manners of the Americans; but it is singular that most of the writers who have drawn these ludicrous delineations belonged themselves to the middle classes in England, to whom the same delineations are exceedingly applicable; so that these pitiless censors furnish, for the most part, an example of the very thing they blame in the United States: they do not perceive that they are deriding themselves, to the great amusement of the aristocracy of their own country.

Nothing is more prejudicial to democracy than its outward forms of behavior; many men would willingly endure its vices, who cannot support its manners. I cannot, however, admit that there is nothing commendable in the manners of a democratic people.

———— ★ ————

Of the Gravity of the Americans, and Why it Does Not Prevent Them from Often Doing Inconsiderate Things

M en who live in democratic countries do not value the simple, turbulent, or coarse diversions in which the people in aristocratic communities indulge: such diversions are thought by them to be puerile or insipid. Nor have they a greater inclination for the intellectual and refined amusements of the aristocratic classes. They want something productive and substantial in their pleasures; they want to mix actual fruition with their joy.

In aristocratic communities, the people readily give themselves up to bursts of tumultuous and boisterous gayety, which shake off at once the recollection of their privations: the inhabitants of democracies are not fond of being thus violently broken in upon, and they never lose sight of themselves without regret. Instead of these frivolous delights, they prefer those more serious and silent amusements which are like business, and which do not drive business wholly out of their minds.

An American, instead of going in a leisure hour to dance merrily at some place of public resort, as the fellows of his class continue to do throughout the greater part of Europe, shuts himself up at home to drink. He thus enjoys two pleasures; he can go on thinking of his business, and can get drunk decently by his own fireside.

I thought that the English constituted the most serious nation on the face of the earth; but I have since seen the Americans and have changed my opinion. I do not mean to say that temperament has not a great deal to do with the character of the inhabitants of the United

States, but I think that their political institutions are a still more influential cause.

I believe the seriousness of the Americans arises partly from their pride. In democratic countries, even poor men entertain a lofty notion of their personal importance: they look upon themselves with complacency, and are apt to suppose that others are looking at them too. With this disposition, they watch their language and their actions with care, and do not lay themselves open so as to betray their deficiencies; to preserve their dignity, they think it necessary to retain their gravity.

But I detect another more deep-seated and powerful cause, which instinctively produces amongst the Americans this astonishing gravity. Under a despotism, communities give way at times to bursts of vehement joy; but they are generally gloomy and moody, because they are afraid. Under absolute monarchies tempered by the customs and manners of the country, their spirits are often cheerful and even, because, as they have some freedom and a good deal of security, they are exempted from the most important cares of life; but all free nations are serious, because their minds are habitually absorbed by the contemplation of some dangerous or difficult purpose. This is more especially the case amongst those free nations which form democratic communities. Then there are, in all classes, a large number of men constantly occupied with the serious affairs of the government; and those whose thoughts are not engaged in the matters of the commonwealth, are wholly engrossed by the acquisition of a private fortune. Amongst such a people, a serious demeanor ceases to be peculiar to certain men, and becomes a habit of the nation.

When the inhabitant of a democracy is not urged by his wants, he is so at least by his desires; for of all the possessions which he sees around him, none are wholly beyond his reach. He therefore does everything in a hurry, he is always satisfied with "pretty well," and never pauses more than an instant to consider what he has been doing. His curiosity is at once insatiable and cheaply satisfied; for he cares more to know a great deal quickly, than to know anything well: he has no time and but little taste to search things to the bottom.

Thus, then, a democratic people are grave, because their social and political condition constantly leads them to engage in serious occupations; and they act inconsiderately, because they give but little time and attention to each of these occupations. The habit of inattention must be considered as the greatest defect of the democratic character.

CHAPTER XVI

──────★──────

Why the National Vanity of the Americans Is More Restless and Captious Than That of the English

All free nations are vainglorious, but national pride is not displayed by all in the same manner. The Americans, in their intercourse with strangers, appear impatient of the smallest censure, and insatiable of praise. The most slender eulogium is acceptable to them, the most exalted seldom contents them; they unceasingly harass you to extort praise, and if you resist their entreaties, they fall to praising themselves. It would seem as if, doubting their own merit, they wished to have it constantly exhibited before their eyes. Their vanity is not only greedy, but restless and jealous; it will grant nothing, whilst it demands everything, but is ready to beg and to quarrel at the same time.

If I say to an American that the country he lives in is a fine one, "Ay," he replies, "there is not its equal in the world." If I applaud the freedom which its inhabitants enjoy, he answers, "Freedom is a fine thing, but few nations are worthy to enjoy it." If I remark the purity of morals which distinguishes the United States, "I can imagine," says he, "that a stranger, who has witnessed the corruption that prevails in other nations, should be astonished at the difference." At length, I leave him to the contemplation of himself; but he returns to the charge, and does not desist till he has got me to repeat all I had just been saying. It is impossible to conceive a more troublesome or more garrulous patriotism; it wearies even those who are disposed to respect it.

──────────────

How the Aspect of Society in the United States Is at Once Excited and Monotonous

In an orderly and peaceable democracy like the United States, where men cannot enrich themselves by war, by public office, or by political confiscation, the love of wealth mainly drives them into business and manufactures. Although these pursuits often bring about great commotions and disasters, they cannot prosper without strictly regular habits and a long routine of petty uniform acts. The stronger the passion is, the more regular are these habits, and the more uniform are these acts. It may be said that it is the vehemence of their desires which makes the Americans so methodical; it perturbs their minds, but it disciplines their lives.

The remark I here apply to America may indeed be addressed to almost all our contemporaries. Variety is disappearing from the human race; the same ways of acting, thinking, and feeling are to be met with all over the world. This is not only because nations work more upon each other, and copy each other more faithfully; but as the men of each country relinquish more and more the peculiar opinions and feelings of a caste, a profession, or a family, they simultaneously arrive at something nearer to the constitution of man, which is everywhere the same. Thus they become more alike, even without having imitated each other. Like travellers scattered about some large wood, intersected by paths converging to one point, if all of them keep their eyes fixed upon that point, and advance towards it, they insensibly draw nearer together,—though they seek not, though they see not and know not each other; and they will be surprised at length to find themselves all collected on the same spot. All the nations which take, not any particular man, but Man himself, as the object of their researches and their imitations, are tending in the end to a similar state of society, like these travellers converging to the central plot of the forest.

CHAPTER XVIII

---★---

Of Honor in the United States and in Democratic Communities

It would seem that men employ two very distinct methods in the judgment which they pass upon the actions of their fellow-men; at one time, they judge them by those simple notions of right and wrong which are diffused all over the world; at another, they appreciate them by a few very special rules which belong exclusively to some particular age and country. It often happens that these two standards differ; they sometimes conflict: but they are never either entirely identified or entirely annulled by one another.

Honor, at the periods of its greatest power, sways the will more than the belief of men; and even whilst they yield without hesitation and without a murmur to its dictates, they feel notwithstanding, by a dim but mighty instinct, the existence of a more general, more ancient, and more holy law, which they sometimes disobey, although they cease not to acknowledge it. Some actions have been held to be at the same time virtuous and dishonorable;—a refusal to fight a duel is an instance.

I think these peculiarities may be otherwise explained than by the mere caprices of certain individuals and nations, as has hitherto been customary. Mankind are subject to general and permanent wants that have created moral laws, to the neglect of which men have ever and in all places attached the notion of censure and shame: to infringe them was *to do ill,—to do well* was to conform to them.

Within this vast association of the human race, lesser associations have been formed, which are called nations; and amidst these nations, further subdivisions have assumed the names of classes or castes. Each of these associations forms, as it were, a separate species of the human race; and though it has no essential difference from the mass of mankind, to a certain extent it stands apart, and has certain wants peculiar to itself. To these special wants must be attributed the modifications which affect, in various degrees and in different countries, the mode of considering human actions, and the estimate which is formed of them. It is the general and permanent interest of mankind that men should not kill each other; but it may happen to be the peculiar and temporary interest of a people or a class to justify, or even to honor, homicide.

Honor is simply that peculiar rule founded upon a peculiar state of society, by the application of which a people or a class allot praise or blame.

Any nation would furnish us with similar grounds of observation; for, as I have already remarked, whenever men collect together as a distinct community, the notion of honor instantly grows up amongst them; that is to say, a system of opinions peculiar to themselves as to what is blamable or commendable; and these peculiar rules always originate in the special habits and special interests of the community.

This is applicable to a certain extent to democratic communities as well as to others, as we shall now proceed to prove by the example of the Americans.

Some loose notions of the old aristocratic honor of Europe are still to be found scattered amongst the opinions of the Americans; but these traditional opinions are few in number, they have but little root in the country, and but little power. They are like a religion which has still some temples left standing, though men have ceased to believe in it. But amidst these half-obliterated notions of exotic honor some new opinions have sprung up, which constitute what may be termed in our days American honor.

I have shown how the Americans are constantly driven to engage in commerce and industry. Their origin, their social condition, their political institutions, and even the region they inhabit, urge them irresistibly in this direction. Their present condition, then, is that of an almost exclusively manufacturing and commercial association, placed in the midst of a new and boundless country, which their principal object is to explore for purposes of profit. This is the characteristic which most distinguishes the American people from all others at the present time.

All those quiet virtues which tend to give a regular movement to the community, and to encourage business, will therefore be held in peculiar honor by that people, and to neglect those virtues will be to incur public contempt. All the more turbulent virtues, which often dazzle, but more frequently disturb society, will, on the contrary, occupy a subordinate rank in the estimation of this same people; they may be neglected without forfeiting the esteem of the community; to acquire them would perhaps be to run a risk of losing it.

The Americans make a no less arbitrary classification of men's vices. There are certain propensities which appear censurable to the general reason and the universal conscience of mankind, but which happen to agree with the peculiar and temporary wants of the American community: these propensities are lightly reproved, sometimes even encouraged; for instance, the love of wealth and the secondary propensities connected with it may be more particularly cited. To clear, to till, and to transform the vast uninhabited continent which is his domain, the American requires the daily support of an energetic passion; that passion can only be the love of wealth; the passion for wealth is therefore not reprobated in America, and, provided it does not go beyond the bounds assigned to it for public security, it is held in honor. The American lauds as a noble and praiseworthy ambition what our own forefathers, in the Middle Ages, stigmatized as servile cupidity, just as he treats as a blind and barbarous frenzy that ardor of conquest and martial temper which bore them to battle.

In the United States, fortunes are lost and regained without difficulty; the country is boundless, and its resources inexhaustible. The people have all the wants and cravings of a growing creature; and, whatever be their efforts, they are always surrounded by more than they can appropriate. It is not the ruin of a few individuals, which may be soon repaired, but the inactivity and sloth of the community at large, which would be fatal to such a people. Boldness of enterprise is the foremost cause of its rapid progress, its strength, and its greatness. Commercial business is there like a vast lottery, by which a small number of men continually lose, but the state is always a gainer; such a people ought therefore to encourage and do honor to boldness in commercial speculations. But any bold speculation risks the fortune of the speculator and of all those who put their trust in him. The Americans, who make a virtue of commercial temerity, have no right in any case to brand with disgrace those who practise it. Hence arises the strange indulgence which is shown to bankrupts in the United States; their honor does not suffer by such an accident. In this respect the Americans differ, not only from the nations of Europe, but from all the commercial nations of our time; and accordingly they resemble none of them in their position or their wants.

In America, all those vices which tend to impair the purity of morals, and to destroy the conjugal tie, are treated with a degree of severity which is unknown in the rest of the world. At first sight, this seems strangely at variance with the tolerance shown there on other subjects, and one is surprised to meet with a morality so relaxed and also so austere amongst the self-same people. But these things are less incoherent than they seem to be. Public opinion in the United States very gently represses that love of wealth which promotes the commercial greatness and the prosperity of the nation, and it especially condemns that laxity of morals which diverts the human mind from the pursuit of well-being, and disturbs the internal order of domestic life which is so necessary to success in business. To earn the esteem of their countrymen, the Americans are therefore constrained to adapt themselves to orderly habits; and it may be said in this sense that they make it a matter of honor to live chastely.

On one point, American honor accords with the notions of honor acknowledged in Europe; it places courage as the highest virtue, and treats it as the greatest of the moral necessities of man; but the notion of courage itself assumes a different aspect. In the United States, martial valor is but little prized; the courage which is best known and most esteemed is that which emboldens men to brave the dangers of the ocean, in order to arrive earlier in port,—to support the privations of the wilderness without complaint, and solitude more cruel than privations,—the courage which renders them almost insensible to the loss of a fortune laboriously acquired, and instantly prompts to fresh exertions to make another. Courage of this kind is peculiarly necessary to the maintenance and prosperity of the American communities, and it is held by them in peculiar honor and estimation; to betray a want of it is to incur certain disgrace.

Thus the laws of honor will be less peculiar and less multifarious amongst a democratic people than in an aristocracy. They will also be more obscure; and this is a necessary consequence of what goes before; for as the distinguishing marks of honor are less numerous and less peculiar, it must often be difficult to distinguish them. To this other reasons may be added. Amongst the aristocratic nations of the Middle Ages, generation succeeded generation in vain; each family was like a never-dying, ever-stationary man, and the state of opinions was hardly more changeable than that of conditions. Every one then had the same objects always before his eyes, which he contemplated from the same point; his eyes gradually detected the smallest details, and his discernment could not fail to become in the end clear and accurate. Thus, not only had the men of feudal times very extraordinary opinions in matters of honor, but each of those opinions was present to their minds under a clear and precise form.

This can never be the case in America, where all men are in constant motion, and where society, transformed daily by its own operations, changes its opinions together with its wants. In such a country, men have glimpses of the rules of honor, but they seldom have time to fix attention upon them.

When ranks are commingled and privileges abolished, the men of whom a nation is composed being once more equal and alike, their interests and wants become identical, and all the peculiar notions which each caste styled honor successively disappear: the notion of honor no longer proceeds from any other source than the wants peculiar to the nation at large, and it denotes the individual character of that nation to the world.

Lastly, if it were allowable to suppose that all the races of mankind should be commingled, and that all the nations of earth should ultimately come to have the same interests, the same wants, undistinguished from each other by any characteristic peculiarities, no conventional value whatever would then be attached to men's actions; they would all be regarded by all in the same light; the general necessities of mankind, revealed by conscience to every man, would become the common standard. The simple and general notions of right and wrong only would then be recognized in the world, to which, by a natural and necessary tie, the idea of censure or approbation would be attached.

Thus, to comprise all my meaning in a single proposition, the dissimilarities and inequalities of men gave rise to the notion of honor; that notion is weakened in proportion as these differences are obliterated, and with them it would disappear.

CHAPTER XIX

———— ★ ————

Why So Many Ambitious Men and So Little Lofty Ambition Are To Be Found in the United States

The first thing which strikes a traveller in the United States is the innumerable multitude of those who seek to emerge from their original condition; and the second is the rarity of lofty ambition to be observed in the midst of the universally ambitious stir of society. No Americans are devoid of a yearning desire to rise; but hardly any appear to entertain hopes of great magnitude, or to pursue very lofty aims. All are constantly seeking to acquire property, power, and reputation; few contemplate these things upon a great scale; and this is the more surprising, as nothing is to be discerned in the manners or laws of America to limit desire, or to prevent it from spreading its impulses in every direction. It seems difficult to attribute this singular state of things to the equality of social condition; for as soon as that same equality was established in France, the flight of ambition became unbounded. Nevertheless, I think that we may find the principal cause of this fact in the social condition and democratic manners of the Americans.

All revolutions enlarge the ambition of men: this is more peculiarly true of those revolutions which overthrow an aristocracy. When the former barriers which kept back the multitude from fame and power are suddenly thrown down, a violent and universal movement takes place towards that eminence so long coveted and at length to be enjoyed. In this first burst of triumph, nothing seems impossible to any one: not only are desires boundless, but the power of satisfying them seems almost boundless too. Amidst the general and sudden change of laws and customs, in this vast confusion of all men and all ordinances, the various members of the community rise and sink again with excessive rapidity, and power passes so quickly from hand to hand that none need despair of catching it in turn.

It must be recollected, moreover, that the people who destroy an aristocracy have lived under its laws; they have witnessed its splendor, and they have unconsciously imbibed the feelings and notions which it entertained. Thus, at the moment when an aristocracy is dissolved, its spirit still pervades the mass of the community, and its tendencies are retained long after it has been defeated. Ambition is therefore always extremely great as long as a democratic revolution lasts, and it will remain so for some time after the revolution is consummated.

The reminiscence of the extraordinary events which men have witnessed is not obliterated from their memory in a day. The passions which a revolution has roused do not disappear at its close. A sense of instability remains in the midst of re-established order; a notion of easy success survives the strange vicissitudes which gave it birth; desires still remain extremely enlarged, while the means of satisfying them are diminished day by day. The taste for large fortunes subsists, though large fortunes are rare; and on every side we trace the ravages of inordinate and unsuccessful ambition kindled in hearts which it consumes in secret and in vain.

At length, however, the last vestiges of the struggle are effaced; the remains of aristocracy completely disappear; the great events by which its fall was attended are forgotten; peace succeeds to war, and the sway of order is restored in the new realm; desires are again adapted to the means by which they may be fulfilled; the wants, the opinions, and the feelings of men cohere once more; the level of the community is permanently determined, and democratic society established.

A democratic nation, arrived at this permanent and regular state of things, will present a very different spectacle from that which we have just described; and we may readily conclude that, if ambition becomes great whilst the conditions of society are growing equal, it loses that quality when they have grown so.

As wealth is subdivided and knowledge diffused, no one is entirely destitute of education or of property; the privileges and disqualifications of caste being abolished, and men having shattered the bonds which once held them fixed, the notion of advancement suggests itself to every mind, the desire to rise swells in every heart, and all men want to mount above their station; ambition is the universal feeling.

But if the equality of conditions gives some resources to all the members of the community, it also prevents any of them from having resources of great extent, which necessarily circumscribes their desires within somewhat narrow limits. Thus, amongst democratic nations, ambition is ardent and continual, but its aim is not habitually lofty; and life is generally spent in eagerly coveting small objects which are within reach.

What chiefly diverts the men of democracies from lofty ambition is not the scantiness of their fortunes, but the vehemence of the exertions they daily make to improve them. They strain their faculties to the utmost to achieve paltry results, and this cannot fail speedily to limit their range of view, and to circumscribe their powers. They might be much poorer, and still be greater.

In a democratic society, as well as elsewhere, there are only a certain number of great fortunes to be made; and as the paths which lead to them are indiscriminately open to all, the progress of all must necessarily be slackened. As the candidates appear to be nearly alike, and as it is difficult to make a selection without infringing the principle of equality, which is the supreme law of democratic societies, the first idea which suggests itself is to make them all advance at the same rate, and submit to the same trials. Thus, in proportion as men become more alike, and the principle of equality is more peaceably and deeply infused into the institutions and manners of the country, the rules for advancement become more inflexible, advancement itself slower, the difficulty of arriving quickly at a certain height far greater. From hatred of privilege and from the embarrassment of choosing, all men are at last constrained, whatever may be their standard, to pass the same ordeal; all are indiscriminately subjected to a multitude of petty preliminary exercises, in which their youth is wasted and their imagination quenched, so that they despair of ever fully attaining what is held out to them; and when at length they are in a condition to perform any extraordinary acts, the taste for such things has forsaken them.

I believe that ambitious men in democracies are less engrossed than any others with the interests and the judgment of posterity; the present moment alone engages and absorbs them. They are more apt to complete a number of undertakings with rapidity, than to raise lasting monuments of their achievements; and they care much more for success than for fame. What they most ask of men is obedience, what they most covet is empire. Their manners have, in almost all cases, remained below their station; the consequence is, that they frequently carry very low tastes into their extraordinary fortunes, and that they seem to have acquired the supreme power only to minister to their coarse or paltry pleasures.

I think that, in our time, it is very necessary to purify, to regulate, and to proportion the feeling of ambition, but that it would be extremely dangerous to seek to impoverish and to repress it over much. We should attempt to lay down certain extreme limits, which it should never be allowed to outstep; but its range within those established limits should not be too much checked.

I confess that I apprehend much less for democratic society from the boldness than from the mediocrity of desires. What appears to me most to be dreaded is, that, in the midst of the small, incessant occupations of private life, ambition should lose its vigor and its greatness; that the passions of man should abate, but at the same time be lowered; so that the march of society should every day become more tranquil and less aspiring.

I think, then, that the leaders of modern society would be wrong to seek to lull the community by a state of too uniform and too peaceful happiness; and that it is well to expose it from time to time to matters of difficulty and danger, in order to raise ambition, and to give it a field of action.

Moralists are constantly complaining that the ruling vice of the present time is pride. This is true in one sense, for indeed every one thinks that he is better than his neighbor, or refuses to obey his superior; but it is extremely false in another, for the same man who cannot endure subordination or equality, has so contemptible an opinion of himself that he thinks he is born only to indulge in vulgar pleasures.

He willingly takes up with low desires, without daring to embark in lofty enterprises, of which he scarcely dreams.

Thus, far from thinking that humility ought to be preached to our contemporaries, I would have endeavors made to give them a more enlarged idea of themselves and of their kind. Humility is unwholesome to them; what they most want is, in my opinion, pride. I would willingly exchange several of our small virtues for this one vice.

CHAPTER XX

───────★───────

The Trade of Place-Hunting in Certain Democratic Countries

In the United States, as soon as a man has acquired some education and pecuniary resources, he either endeavors to get rich by commerce or industry, or he buys land in the bush and turns pioneer. All that he asks of the state is, not to be disturbed in his toil, and to be secure of his earnings. Amongst most European nations, when a man begins to feel his strength and to extend his desires, the first thing that occurs to him is to get some public employment. These opposite effects, originating in the same cause, deserve our passing notice.

When public employments are few in number, ill-paid, and precarious, whilst the different kinds of business are numerous and lucrative, it is to business, and not to official duties, that the new and eager desires created by the principle of equality turn from every side. But if, whilst the ranks of society are becoming more equal, the education of the people remains incomplete, or their spirit the reverse of bold,— if commerce and industry, checked in their growth, afford only slow and arduous means of making a fortune,—the various members of the community, despairing of ameliorating their own condition, rush to the head of the state and demand its assistance. To relieve their own necessities at the cost of the public treasury appears to them the easiest and most open, if not the only, way of rising above a condition which no longer contents them; place-hunting becomes the most generally followed of all trades.

This must especially be the case in those great centralized monarchies, in which the number of paid offices is immense, and the tenure of them tolerably secure, so that no one despairs of obtaining a place, and of enjoying it as undisturbedly as an hereditary fortune.

I shall not remark that the universal and inordinate desire for place is a great social evil; that it destroys the spirit of independence in the citizen, and diffuses a venal and servile humor throughout the frame of society; that it stifles the manlier virtues: nor shall I be at the pains to demonstrate that this kind of traffic only creates an unproductive activity, which agitates the country without adding to its resources: all these things are obvious. But I would observe, that a government which encourages this tendency risks its own tranquility, and places its very existence in great jeopardy.

I am aware that, at a time like our own, when the love and respect which formerly clung to authority are seen gradually to decline, it may appear necessary to those in power to lay a closer hold on every man by his own interest, and it may seem convenient to use his own passions to keep him in order and in silence; but this cannot be so long, and what may appear to be a source of strength for a certain time will assuredly become, in the end, a great cause of embarrassment and weakness.

Amongst democratic nations, as well as elsewhere, the number of official appointments has, in the end, some limits; but amongst those nations, the number of aspirants is unlimited; it perpetually increases, with a gradual and irresistible rise, in proportion as social conditions become more equal, and is only checked by the limits of the population.

Thus, when public employments afford the only outlet for ambition, the government necessarily meets with a permanent opposition at last; for it is tasked to satisfy with limited means unlimited desires. It is very certain that, of all people in the world, the most difficult to restrain and to manage are a people of office-hunters. Whatever endeavors are made by rulers, such a people can never be contented; and it is always to be apprehended that they will ultimately overturn the constitution of the country, and change the aspect of the state, for the sole purpose of making a clearance of places.

The sovereigns of the present age, who strive to fix upon themselves alone all those novel desires which are aroused by equality, and to satisfy them, will repent in the end, if I am not mistaken, that ever they embarked in this policy: they will one day discover that they have hazarded their own power by making it so necessary, and that the more safe and honest course would have been to teach their subjects the art of providing for themselves.

CHAPTER XXI

———————★———————

Why Great Revolutions Will
Become More Rare

A people who have existed for centuries under a system of castes and classes, can only arrive at a democratic state of society by passing through a long series of more or less critical transformations, accomplished by violent efforts, and after numerous vicissitudes; in the course of which, property, opinions, and power are rapidly transferred from one to another. Even after this great revolution is consummated, the revolutionary habits produced by it may long be traced, and it will be followed by deep commotion. As all this takes place at the very time when social conditions are becoming more equal, it is inferred that some concealed relation and secret tie exists between the principle of equality itself and revolution, insomuch that the one cannot exist without giving rise to the other.

On this point, reasoning may seem to lead to the same result as experience. Amongst a people whose ranks are nearly equal, no ostensible bond connects men together, or keeps them settled in their station. None of them have either a permanent right or power to command, none are forced by their condition to obey; but every man, finding himself possessed of some education and some resources, may choose his own path, and proceed apart from all his fellow-men. The same causes which make the members of the community independent of each other, continually impel them to new and restless desires, and constantly spur them onwards. It therefore seems natural that, in a democratic community, men, things, and opinions should be forever changing their form and place, and that democratic ages should be times of rapid and incessant transformation.

But is this really the case? Does the equality of social conditions habitually and permanently lead men to revolution? Does that state of society contain some perturbing principle, which prevents the community from ever subsiding into calm, and disposes the citizens to alter incessantly their laws, their principles, and their manners? I do not believe it; and as the subject is important, I beg for the reader's close attention.

Almost all the revolutions which have changed the aspect of nations have been made to consolidate or to destroy social inequality. Remove the secondary causes which have produced the great convulsions of the world, and you will almost always find the principle of inequality at the bottom. Either the poor have attempted to plunder the rich, or the rich to enslave the poor. If, then, a state of society can ever be founded in which every man shall have something to keep, and little to take from others, much will have been done for the peace of the world.

I am aware that, amongst a great democratic people, there will always be some members of the community in great poverty, and others in great opulence; but the poor, instead of forming the immense majority of the nation, as is always the case in aristocratic communities, are comparatively few in number, and the laws do not bind them together by the ties of irremediable and hereditary penury.

The wealthy, on their side, are few and powerless; they have no privileges which attract public observation; even their wealth, as it is no longer incorporated and bound up with the soil, is impalpable, and, as it were, invisible. As there is no longer a race of poor men, so there is no longer a race of rich men; the latter spring up daily from the multitude, and relapse into it again. Hence they do not form a distinct class, which may be easily marked out and plundered; and, moreover, as they are connected with the mass of their fellow-citizens by a thousand secret ties, the people cannot assail them without inflicting an injury upon themselves.

Between these two extremes of democratic communities stand an innumerable multitude of men almost alike, who, without being exactly either rich or poor, are possessed of sufficient property to desire the maintenance of order, yet not enough to excite envy. Such men are the natural enemies of violent commotions; their stillness keeps all beneath them and above them still, and secures the balance of the fabric of society.

Not, indeed, that even these men are contented with what they have gotten, or that they feel a natural abhorrence for a revolution in which they might share the spoil without sharing the calamity; on the contrary, they desire, with unexampled ardor, to get rich, but the difficulty is to know from whom riches can be taken. The same state of society which constantly prompts desires, restrains these desires within necessary limits; it gives men more liberty of changing, and less interest in change.

Not only are the men of democracies not naturally desirous of revolutions, but they are afraid of them. All revolutions more or less threaten the tenure of property: but most of those who live in democratic countries are possessed of property; not only are they possessed of property, but they live in the condition where men set the greatest store upon their property.

If we attentively consider each of the classes of which society is composed, it is easy to see that the passions created by property are keenest and most tenacious amongst the middle classes. The poor often care but little for what they possess, because they suffer much more from the want of what they have not, than they enjoy the little they have. The rich have many other passions besides that of riches to satisfy; and, besides, the long and arduous enjoyment of a great fortune sometimes makes them in the end insensible to its charms. But the men who have a competency, alike removed from opulence and from penury, attach an enormous value to their possessions. As they are still almost within the reach of poverty, they see its privations near at hand, and dread them; between poverty and themselves there is nothing but a scanty fortune, upon which they immediately fix their apprehensions and their hopes. Every day increases the interest they take in it, by the constant cares which it occasions; and they are the more attached to it by their continual exertions to increase the amount. The notion of surrendering the smallest part of it is insupportable to them, and they consider its total loss as the worst of misfortunes.

Now, these eager and apprehensive men of small property constitute the class which is constantly increased by the equality of conditions. Hence, in democratic communities, the majority of the people do not clearly see what they have to gain by a revolution, but they continually and in a thousand ways feel that they might lose by one.

Moreover, whatever profession men may embrace, and whatever species of property they may possess, one characteristic is common to them all. No one is fully contented with his present fortune; all are perpetually striving, in a thousand ways, to improve it. Consider any one of them at any period of his life, and he will be found engaged with some new project for the purpose of increasing what he has; talk not to him of the interests and the rights of mankind, this small domestic concern absorbs for the time all his thoughts, and inclines him to defer political agitations to some other season. This not only prevents men from making revolutions, but deters men from desiring them. Violent political passions have but little hold on those who have devoted all their faculties to the pursuit of their wellbeing. The ardor which they display in small matters calms their zeal for momentous undertakings.

If ever America undergoes great revolutions, they will be brought about by the presence of the black race on the soil of the United States; that is to say, they will owe their origin, not to the equality, but to the inequality of condition.

When social conditions are equal, every man is apt to live apart, centered in himself and forgetful of the public. If the rulers of democratic nations were either to neglect to correct this fatal tendency, or to encourage it from a notion that it weans men from political passions and thus wards off revolutions, they might eventually produce the evil they seek to avoid, and a time might come when the inordinate passions of a few men, aided by the unintelligent selfishness or the pusillanimity of the greater number, would ultimately compel society to pass through strange vicissitudes. In democratic communities, revolutions are seldom desired except by a minority; but a minority may sometimes effect them.

I do not assert that democratic nations are secure from revolutions; I merely say that the state of society in those nations does not lead to revolutions, but rather wards them off. A democratic people left to itself will not easily embark in great hazards; it is only led to revolutions unawares; it may sometimes undergo them, but it does not make them: and I will add, that, when such a people has been allowed to acquire sufficient knowledge and experience, it will not suffer them to be made.

I am well aware that, in this respect, public institutions may themselves do much; they may encourage or repress the tendencies which originate in the state of society. I therefore do not maintain, I repeat, that a people is secure from revolutions simply because conditions are equal in the community; but I think that, whatever the institutions of such a people may be, great revolutions will always be far less violent and less frequent than is supposed; and I can easily discern a state of polity which, when combined with the principle of equality, would render society more stationary than it has ever been in our western part of the world.

The observations I have here made on events may also be applied in part to opinions. Two things are surprising in the United States,— the mutability of the greater part of human actions, and the singular stability of certain principles. Men are in constant motion; the mind of man appears almost unmoved. When once an opinion has spread over the country and struck root there, it would seem that no power on earth is strong enough to eradicate it. In the United States, general principles in religion, philosophy, morality, and even politics, do not vary, or at least are only modified by a hidden and often an imperceptible process: even the grossest prejudices are obliterated with incredible slowness, amidst the continual friction of men and things.

We live at a time which has witnessed the most rapid changes of opinion in the minds of men; nevertheless it may be that the leading opinions of society will erelong be more settled than they have been for several centuries in our history: that time is not yet come, but it may perhaps be approaching. As I examine more closely the natural wants and tendencies of democratic nations, I grow persuaded that, if ever social equality is generally and permanently established in the world, great intellectual and political revolutions will become more difficult and less frequent than is supposed. Because the men of democracies appear always excited, uncertain, eager, changeable in their wills and in their positions, it is imagined that they are suddenly to abrogate their laws, to adopt new opinions, and to assume new manners. But if the principle of equality predisposes men to change, it also suggests to them certain interests and tastes which cannot be satisfied without a settled order of things; equality urges them on, but at the same time it holds them back; it spurs them, but fastens them to earth; it kindles their desires, but limits their powers.

This, however, is not perceived at first; the passions which tend to sever the citizens of a democracy are obvious enough; but the hidden force which restrains and unites them is not discernible at a glance.

Amidst the ruins which surround me, shall I dare to say that revolutions are not what I most fear for coming generations? If men continue to shut themselves more closely within the narrow circle of domestic interests, and to live upon that kind of excitement, it is to be apprehended that they may ultimately become inaccessible to those great and powerful public emotions which perturb nations, but which develop them and recruit them. When property becomes so fluctuating, and the love of property so restless and so ardent, I cannot but fear that men may arrive at such a state as to regard every new theory as a peril, every innovation as an irksome toil, every social improvement as a stepping-stone to revolution, and so refuse to move altogether for fear of being moved too far. I dread, and I confess it, lest they should at last so entirely give way to a cowardly love of present enjoyment, as to lose sight of the interests of their future selves and those of their descendants; and prefer to glide along the easy current of life, rather than to make, when it is necessary, a strong and sudden effort to a higher purpose.

It is believed by some that modern society will be ever changing its aspect; for myself, I fear that it will ultimately be too invariably fixed in the same institutions, the same prejudices, the same manners, so that mankind will be stopped and circumscribed; that the mind will swing backwards and forwards forever, without begetting fresh ideas; that man will waste his strength in bootless and solitary trifling; and, though in continual motion, that humanity will cease to advance.

———★———

CHAPTER XXII

Why Democratic Nations Are Naturally Desirous of Peace, and Democratic Armies of War

The same interests, the same fears, the same passions, which deter democratic nations from revolutions, deter them also from war; the spirit of military glory and the spirit of revolution are weakened at the same time and by the same causes. The ever-increasing numbers of men of property who are lovers of peace, the growth of personal wealth which war so rapidly consumes, the mildness of manners, the gentleness of heart, those tendencies to pity which are produced by the equality of conditions, that coolness of understanding which renders men comparatively insensible to the violent and poetical excitement of arms,—all these causes concur to quench the military spirit. I think it may be admitted as a general and constant rule, that, amongst civilized nations, the warlike passions will become more rare and less intense in proportion as social conditions shall be more equal.

War is nevertheless an occurrence to which all nations are subject, democratic nations as well as others. Whatever taste they may have for peace, they must hold themselves in readiness to repel aggression, or, in other words, they must have an army. Fortune, which has conferred so many peculiar benefits upon the inhabitants of the United States, has placed them in the midst of a wilderness, where they have, so to speak, no neighbors: a few thousand soldiers are sufficient for their wants; but this is peculiar to America, not to democracy.

The equality of conditions, and the manners as well as the institutions resulting from it, do not exempt a democratic people from the necessity of standing armies, and their armies always exercise a powerful influence over their fate. It is therefore of singular importance to inquire what are the natural propensities of the men of whom these armies are composed.

In democratic armies, all the soldiers may become officers, which makes the desire of promotion general, and immeasurably extends the bounds of military ambition. The officer, on his part, sees nothing which naturally and necessarily stops him at one grade more than at another; and each grade has immense importance in his eyes, because his rank in society almost always depends on his rank in the army. Amongst democratic nations, it often happens that an officer has no property but his pay, and no distinction but that of military honors: consequently, as often as his duties change his fortune changes, and he becomes, as it were, a new man. What was only an appendage to his position in aristocratic armies, has thus become the main point, the basis of his whole condition.

Under the old French monarchy, officers were always called by their titles of nobility; they are now always called by the title of their military rank. This little change in the forms of language suffices to show that a great revolution has taken place in the constitution of society and in that of the army.

In democratic armies, the desire of advancement is almost universal: it is ardent, tenacious, perpetual; it is strengthened by all other desires, and only extinguished with life itself. But it is easy to see, that, of all armies in the world, those in which advancement must be slowest in time of peace are the armies of democratic countries. As the number of commissions is naturally limited, whilst the number of competitors is almost unlimited, and as the strict law of equality is over all alike, none can make rapid progress,—many can make no progress at all. Thus, the desire of advancement is greater, and the opportunities of advancement fewer there than elsewhere. All the ambitious spirits of a democratic army are consequently ardently desirous of war, because war makes vacancies, and warrants the violation of that law of seniority which is the sole privilege natural to democracy.

We thus arrive at this singular consequence, that, of all armies, those most ardently desirous of war are democratic armies, and of all nations, those most fond of peace are democratic nations; and what makes these facts still more extraordinary is, that these contrary effects are produced at the same time by the principle of equality.

All the members of the community, being alike, constantly harbor the wish and discover the possibility of changing their condition and improving their welfare: this makes them fond of peace, which is favorable to industry, and allows every man to pursue his own little undertakings to their completion. On the other hand, this same equality makes soldiers dream of fields of battle, by increasing the value of military honors in the eyes of those who follow the profession of arms, and by rendering those honors accessible to all. In either case, the inquietude of the heart is the same, the taste for enjoyment as insatiable, the ambition of success as great,—the means of gratifying it alone are different.

These opposite tendencies of the nation and the army expose democratic communities to great dangers. When a military spirit forsakes a people, the profession of arms immediately ceases to be held in honor, and military men fall to the lowest rank of the public servants: they are little esteemed, and no longer understood. The reverse of what takes place in aristocratic ages then occurs; the men who enter the army are no longer those of the highest, but of the lowest rank. Military ambition is only indulged when no other is possible. Hence arises a circle of cause and consequence from which it is difficult to escape: the best part of the nation shuns the military profession because that profession is not honored, and the profession is not honored because the best part of the nation has ceased to follow it.

It is then no matter of surprise that democratic armies are often restless, ill-tempered, and dissatisfied with their lot, although their physical condition is commonly far better, and their discipline less strict, than in other countries. The soldier feels that he occupies an inferior position, and his wounded pride either stimulates his taste for hostilities which would render his services necessary, or gives him a desire for revolution, during which he may hope to win by force of arms the political influence and personal importance now denied him.

The composition of democratic armies makes this last-mentioned danger much to be feared. In democratic communities, almost every man has some property to preserve; but democratic armies are generally led by men without property, most of whom have little to lose in civil broils. The bulk of the nation is naturally much more afraid of revolutions than in the ages of aristocracy, but the leaders of the army much less so.

Moreover, as amongst democratic nations (to repeat what I have just remarked) the wealthiest, best educated, and ablest men seldom adopt the military profession, the army, taken collectively, eventually forms a small nation by itself, where the mind is less enlarged, and habits are more rude, than in the nation at large. Now, this small uncivilized nation has arms in its possession, and alone knows how to use them; for, indeed, the pacific temper of the community increases the danger to which a democratic people is exposed from the military and turbulent spirit of the army. Nothing is so dangerous as an army amidst an unwarlike nation; the excessive love of the whole community for quiet continually puts the constitution at the mercy of the soldiery.

It may therefore be asserted, generally speaking, that, if democratic nations are naturally prone to peace from their interests and their propensities, they are constantly drawn to war and revolutions by their armies. Military revolutions, which are scarcely ever to be apprehended in aristocracies, are always to be dreaded amongst democratic nations. These perils must be reckoned amongst the most formidable which beset their future fate, and the attention of statesmen should be sedulously applied to find a remedy for the evil.

When a nation perceives that it is inwardly affected by the restless ambition of its army, the first thought which occurs is to give this inconvenient ambition an object by going to war. I do not wish to speak ill of war: war almost always enlarges the mind of a people, and raises their character. In some cases, it is the only check to the excessive growth of certain propensities which naturally spring out of the equality of conditions, and it must be considered as a necessary corrective to certain inveterate diseases to which democratic communities are liable.

War has great advantages, but we must not flatter ourselves that it can diminish the danger I have just pointed out. That peril is only suspended by it, to return more fiercely when the war is over; for armies are much more impatient of peace after having tasted military exploits. War could only be a remedy for a people who should always be athirst for military glory.

I foresee that all the military rulers who may rise up in great democratic nations will find it easier to conquer with their armies, than to make their armies live at peace after conquest. There are two things which a democratic people will always find very difficult,—to begin a war and to end it.

The remedy for the vices of the army is not to be found in the army itself, but in the country. Democratic nations are naturally afraid of disturbance and of despotism; the object is to turn these natural instincts into intelligent, deliberate, and lasting tastes. When men have at last learned to make a peaceful and profitable use of freedom, and have felt its blessings,—when they have conceived a manly love of order, and have freely submitted themselves to discipline,—these same men, if they follow the profession of arms, bring into it, unconsciously and almost against their will, these same habits and manners. The general spirit of the nation being infused into the spirit peculiar to the army, tempers the opinions and desires engendered by military life, or represses them by the mighty force of public opinion. Teach but the citizens to be educated, orderly, firm, and free, and the soldiers will be disciplined and obedient.

Any law which, in repressing the turbulent spirit of the army, should tend to diminish the spirit of freedom in the nation, and to overshadow the notion of law and right, would defeat its object: it would do much more to favor, than to defeat the establishment of military tyranny.

After all, and in spite of all precautions, a large army amidst a democratic people will always be a source of great danger; the most effectual means of diminishing that danger would be to reduce the army, but this is a remedy which all nations are not able to apply.

CHAPTER XXIII

---★---

Which Is the Most Warlike and Most Revolutionary Class in Democratic Armies

I t is of the essence of a democratic army to be very numerous in proportion to the people to which it belongs, as I shall hereafter show. On the other hand, men living in democratic times seldom choose a military life. Democratic nations are therefore soon led to give up the system of voluntary recruiting for that of compulsory enlistment. The necessity of their social condition compels them to resort to the latter means, and it may easily be foreseen that they will all eventually adopt it.

In aristocratic armies, the officers are the conservative element, because the officers alone have retained a strict connection with civil society, and never forego their purpose of resuming their place in it sooner or later: in democratic armies, the private soldiers stand in this position, and from the same cause.

It often happens, on the contrary, that, in these same democratic armies, the officers contract tastes and wants wholly distinct from those of the nation,—a fact which may be thus accounted for. Amongst democratic nations, the man who becomes an officer severs all the ties which bound him to civil life; he leaves it forever, and no interest urges him to return to it. His true country is the army, since he owes all he has to the rank he has attained in it; he therefore follows the fortunes of the army, rises or sinks with it, and henceforward directs all his hopes to that quarter only. As the wants of an officer are distinct from those of the country, he may, perhaps, ardently desire war, or labor to bring about a revolution, at the very moment when the nation is most desirous of stability and peace.

There are, nevertheless, some causes which allay this restless and warlike spirit. Though ambition is universal and continual amongst democratic nations, we have seen that it is seldom great. A man who, being born in the lower classes of the community, has risen from the ranks to be an officer, has already taken a prodigious step. He has gained a footing in a sphere above that which he filled in civil life, and has acquired rights which most democratic nations will ever consider as inalienable. He is willing to pause after so great an effort, and to enjoy what he has won. The fear of risking what he has already obtained damps the desire of acquiring what he has not got. Having conquered the first and greatest impediment which opposed his advancement, he resigns himself with less impatience to the slowness of his progress. His ambition will be more and more cooled in proportion as the increasing distinction of his rank teaches him that he has more to put in jeopardy. If I am not mistaken, the least warlike, and also the least revolutionary, part of a democratic army will always be its chief commanders.

But the remarks I have just made on officers and soldiers are not applicable to a numerous class which, in all armies, fills the intermediate space between them; I mean the class of non-commissioned officers. This class of non-commissioned officers, which had never acted a part in history until the present century, is henceforward destined, I think, to play one of some importance. Like the officers, non-commissioned officers have broken, in their minds, all the ties which bound them to civil life; like the former, they devote themselves permanently to the service, and perhaps make it even more exclusively the object of all their desires; but non-commissioned officers are men who have not yet reached a firm and lofty post, at which they may pause and breathe more freely, ere they can attain further promotion.

By the very nature of his duties, which are invariable, a non-commissioned officer is doomed to lead an obscure, confined, comfortless, and precarious existence; as yet, he sees nothing of military life but its dangers; he knows nothing but its privations and its discipline,— more difficult to support than dangers: he suffers the more from his present miseries, from knowing that the constitution of society and of the army allow him to rise above them; he may, indeed, at any time, obtain his commission, and enter at once upon command, honors, independence, rights, and enjoyments. Not only does this object of his hopes appear to him of immense importance, but he is never sure of reaching it till it is actually his own; the grade he fills is by no means irrevocable; he is always entirely abandoned to the arbitrary pleasure of his commanding officer, for this is imperiously required by the necessity of discipline: a slight fault, a whim, may always deprive him in an instant of the fruits of many years of toil and endeavor; until he has reached the grade to which he aspires, he has accomplished nothing; not till he reaches that grade does his career seem to begin. A desperate ambition cannot fail to be kindled in a man thus incessantly goaded on by his youth, his wants, his passions, the spirit of his age, his hopes, and his fears.

Non-commissioned officers are therefore bent on war,—on war always, and at any cost; but if war be denied them, then they desire revolutions, to suspend the authority of established regulations, and to enable them, aided by the general confusion and the political passions of the time, to get rid of their superior officers, and to take their places. Nor is it impossible for them to bring about such a crisis, because their common origin and habits give them much influence over the soldiers, however different may be their passions and their desires.

It would be an error to suppose that these various characteristics of officers, non-commissioned officers, and men belong to any particular time or country; they will always occur at all times, and amongst all democratic nations. In every democratic army the non-commissioned officers will be the worst representatives of the pacific and orderly spirit of the country, and the private soldiers will be the best. The latter will carry with them into military life the strength or weakness of the manners of the nation; they will display a faithful reflection of the community: if that community is ignorant and weak, they will allow themselves to be drawn by their leaders into disturbances, either unconsciously or against their will; if it is enlightened and energetic, the community will itself keep them within the bounds of order.

CHAPTER XXIV

★

Causes Which Render Democratic Armies Weaker Than Other Armies at the Outset of a Campaign, and More Formidable in Protracted Warfare

A ny army is in danger of being conquered at the outset of a campaign, after a long peace; any army which has long been engaged in warfare has strong chances of victory: this truth is peculiarly applicable to democratic armies. In aristocracies, the military profession, being a privileged career, is held in honor even in time of peace. Men of great talents, great attainments, and great ambition embrace it; the army is in all respects on a level with the nation, and frequently above it.

When the officers of an aristocratic army have lost their warlike spirit and the desire of raising themselves by service, they still retain a certain respect for the honor of their class, and an old habit of being foremost to set an example. But when the officers of a democratic army have no longer the love of war and the ambition of arms, nothing whatever remains to them.

I am therefore of opinion, that, when a democratic people engages in a war after a long peace, it incurs much more risk of defeat than any other nation; but it ought not easily to be cast down by its reverses, for the chances of success for such an army are increased by the duration of the war. When a war has at length, by its long continuance, roused the whole community from their peaceful occupations, and ruined their minor undertakings, the same passions which made them attach so much importance to the maintenance of peace will be turned to arms. War, after it has destroyed all modes of speculation, becomes itself the great and sole speculation, to which all the ardent and ambitious desires that equality engenders are exclusively directed. Hence it is, that the selfsame democratic nations which are so reluctant to engage in hostilities, sometimes perform prodigious achievements when once they have taken the field.

As the war attracts more and more of public attention, and is seen to create high reputations and great fortunes in a short space of time, the choicest spirits of the nation enter the military profession: all the enterprising, proud, and martial minds, no longer of the aristocracy solely, but of the whole country, are drawn in this direction. As the number of competitors for military honors is immense, and war drives every man to his proper level, great generals are always sure to spring up. A long war produces upon a democratic army the same effects that a revolution produces upon a people; it breaks through regulations, and allows extraordinary men to rise above the common level. Those officers whose bodies and minds have grown old in peace, are removed, or superannuated, or they die. In their stead, a host of young men are pressing on, whose frames are already hardened, whose desires are extended and inflamed by active service. They are bent on advancement at all hazards, and perpetual advancement; they are followed by others with the same passions and desires, and after these are others, yet unlimited by aught but the size of the army. The principle of equality opens the door of ambition to all, and death provides chances for ambition. Death is constantly thinning the ranks, making vacancies, closing and opening the career of arms.

There is, moreover, a secret connection between the military character and the character of democracies, which war brings to light. The men of democracies are naturally passionately eager to acquire what they covet, and to enjoy it on easy conditions. They for the most part worship chance, and are much less afraid of death than of difficulty. This is the spirit which they bring to commerce and manufactures; and this same spirit, carried with them to the field of battle, induces them willingly to expose their lives in order to secure in a moment the rewards of victory. No kind of greatness is more pleasing to the imagination of a democratic people than military greatness,—a greatness of vivid and sudden lustre, obtained without toil, by nothing but the risk of life.

Thus, whilst the interest and the tastes of the members of a democratic community divert them from war, their habits of mind fit them for carrying on war well: they soon make good soldiers, when they are aroused from their business and their enjoyments.

If peace is peculiarly hurtful to democratic armies, war secures to them advantages which no other armies ever possess; and these advantages, however little felt at first, cannot fail in the end to give them the victory. An aristocratic nation, which, in a contest with a democratic people, does not succeed in ruining the latter at the outset of the war, always runs a great risk of being conquered by it.

CHAPTER XXV

★

Of Discipline in Democratic Armies

It is a very common opinion, especially in aristocratic countries, that the great social equality which prevails in democracies ultimately renders the private soldier independent of the officer, and thus destroys the bond of discipline. This is a mistake, for there are two kinds of discipline, which it is important not to confound.

A democratic people must despair of ever obtaining from soldiers that blind, minute, submissive, and invariable obedience, which an aristocratic people may impose on them without difficulty. The state of society does not prepare them for it, and the nation might be in danger of losing its natural advantages, if it sought artificially to acquire advantages of this particular kind. Amongst democratic communities, military discipline ought not to attempt to annihilate the free action of the faculties; all that can be done by discipline is to direct it; the obedience thus inculcated is less exact, but it is more eager and more intelligent. It has its root in the will of him who obeys: it rests not only on his instinct, but on his reason; and consequently, it will often spontaneously become more strict as danger requires. The discipline of an aristocratic army is apt to be relaxed in war, because that discipline is founded upon habits, and war disturbs those habits. The discipline of a democratic army, on the contrary, is strengthened in sight of the enemy, because every soldier then clearly perceives that he must be silent and obedient in order to conquer.

The nations which have performed the greatest warlike achievements knew no other discipline than that which I speak of. Amongst the ancients, none were admitted into the armies but freemen and citizens, who differed but little from one another, and were accustomed to treat each other as equals. In this respect, it may be said that the armies of antiquity were democratic, although they came out of the bosom of aristocracy; the consequence was, that in those armies a sort of fraternal familiarity prevailed between the officers and the men. Plutarch's lives of great commanders furnish convincing instances of the fact: the soldiers were in the constant habit of freely addressing their general, and the general listened to and answered whatever the soldiers had to say; they were kept in order by language and by example, far more than by constraint or punishment; the general was as much their companion as their chief. I know not whether the soldiers of Greece and Rome ever carried the minutiæ of military discipline to the same degree of perfection as the Russians have done; but this did not prevent Alexander from conquering Asia,—and Rome, the world.

CHAPTER XXVI

---★---

Some Considerations on War in Democratic Communities

When the principle of equality is spreading, not only amongst a single nation, but amongst several neighboring nations at the same time, as is now the case in Europe, the inhabitants of these different countries, notwithstanding the dissimilarity of language, of customs, and of laws, still resemble each other in their equal dread of war and their common love of peace. It is in vain that ambition or anger puts arms in the hands of princes; they are appeased in spite of themselves by a species of general apathy and good-will, which makes the sword drop from their grasp, and wars become more rare.

As the spread of equality, taking place in several countries at once, simultaneously impels their various inhabitants to follow manufactures and commerce, not only do their tastes become similar, but their interests are so mixed and entangled with one another, that no nation can inflict evils on other nations without those evils falling back upon itself; and all nations ultimately regard war as a calamity almost as severe to the conqueror as to the conquered.

Thus, on the one hand, it is extremely difficult in democratic times to draw nations into hostilities; but, on the other, it is almost impossible that any two of them should go to war without embroiling the rest. The interests of all are so interlaced, their opinions and their wants so much alike, that none can remain quiet when the others stir. Wars therefore become more rare, but when they break out, they spread over a larger field.

In democratic countries, the moral power of the majority is immense, and the physical resources which it has at its command are out of all proportion to the physical resources which may be combined against it. Therefore, the party which occupies the seat of the majority, which speaks in its name and wields its power, triumphs instantaneously and irresistibly over all private resistance; it does not even give such opposition time to exist, but nips it in the bud.

VOLUME II

FOURTH BOOK

Influence of Democratic Ideas and Feelings on Political Society

I should imperfectly fulfil the purpose of this book, if, after having shown what ideas and feelings are suggested by the principle of equality, I did not point out, ere I conclude, the general influence which these same ideas and feelings may exercise upon the government of human societies. To succeed in this object, I shall frequently have to retrace my steps; but I trust the reader will not refuse to follow me through paths already known to him, which may lead to some new truth.

CHAPTER I

---★---

Equality Naturally Gives Men a Taste for Free Institutions

The principle of equality, which makes men independent of each other, gives them a habit and a taste for following, in their private actions, no other guide than their own will. This complete independence, which they constantly enjoy in regard to their equals and in the intercourse of private life, tends to make them look upon all authority with a jealous eye, and speedily suggests to them the notion and the love of political freedom. Men living at such times have a natural bias to free institutions. Take any one of them at a venture, and search if you can his most deep-seated instincts; and you will find that, of all governments, he will soonest conceive and most highly value that government whose head he has himself elected, and whose administration he may control.

Of all the political effects produced by the equality of conditions, this love of independence is the first to strike the observing, and to alarm the timid; nor can it be said that their alarm is wholly misplaced, for anarchy has a more formidable aspect in democratic countries than elsewhere. As the citizens have no direct influence on each other, as soon as the supreme power of the nation fails, which kept them all in their several stations, it would seem that disorder must instantly reach its utmost pitch, and that, every man drawing aside in a different direction, the fabric of society must at once crumble away.

I am persuaded, however, that anarchy is not the principal evil which democratic ages have to fear, but the least. For the principle of equality begets two tendencies: the one leads men straight to independence, and may suddenly drive them into anarchy; the other conducts them by a longer, more secret, but more certain road, to servitude. Nations readily discern the former tendency, and are prepared to resist it; they are led away by the latter, without perceiving its drift; hence it is peculiarly important to point it out.

For myself, I am so far from urging it as a reproach to the principle of equality that it renders men intractable, that this very circumstance principally calls forth my approbation. I admire to see how it deposits in the mind and heart of man the dim conception and instinctive love of political independence, thus preparing the remedy for the evil which it produces: it is on this very account that I am attached to it.

CHAPTER II

———— ★ ————

That the Opinions of Democratic Nations about Government Are Naturally Favorable to the Concentration Of Power

The notion of secondary powers, placed between the sovereign and his subjects, occurred naturally to the imagination of aristocratic nations, because those communities contained individuals or families raised above the common level, and apparently destined to command by their birth, their education, and their wealth. This same notion is naturally wanting in the minds of men in democratic ages, for converse reasons; it can only be introduced artificially, it can only be kept there with difficulty; whereas they conceive, as it were without thinking upon the subject, the notion of a single and central power, which governs the whole community by its direct influence. Moreover, in politics as well as in philosophy and in religion, the intellect of democratic nations is peculiarly open to simple and general notions. Complicated systems are repugnant to it, and its favorite conception is that of a great nation composed of citizens all formed upon one pattern, and all governed by a single power.

The very next notion to that of a single and central power, which presents itself to the minds of men in the ages of equality, is the notion of uniformity of legislation. As every man sees that he differs but little from those about him, he cannot understand why a rule which is applicable to one man should not be equally applicable to all others. Hence the slightest privileges are repugnant to his reason; the faintest dissimilarities in the political institutions of the same people offend him, and uniformity of legislation appears to him to be the first condition of good government.

I find, on the contrary, that this notion of a uniform rule, equally binding on all the members of the community, was almost unknown to the human mind in aristocratic ages; it was either never broached, or it was rejected.

These contrary tendencies of opinion ultimately turn on both sides to such blind instincts and ungovernable habits, that they still direct the actions of men, in spite of particular exceptions. Notwithstanding the immense variety of conditions in the Middle Ages, a certain number of persons existed at that period in precisely similar circumstances; but this did not prevent the laws then in force from assigning to each of them distinct duties and different rights. On the contrary, at the present time, all the powers of government are exerted to impose the same customs and the same laws on populations which have as yet but few points of resemblance.

As the conditions of men become equal amongst a people, individuals seem of less, and society of greater importance; or rather, every citizen, being assimilated to all the rest, is lost in the crowd, and nothing stands conspicuous but the great and imposing image of the people at large. This naturally gives the men of democratic periods a lofty opinion of the privileges of society, and a very humble notion of the rights of individuals; they are ready to admit that the interests of the former are everything, and those of the latter nothing. They are willing to acknowledge that the power which represents the community has far more information and wisdom than any of the members of that community; and that it is the duty, as well as the right, of that power, to guide as well as govern each private citizen.

If we closely scrutinize our contemporaries, and penetrate to the root of their political opinions, we shall detect some of the notions which I have just pointed out, and we shall perhaps be surprised to find so much accordance between men who are so often at variance.

The Americans hold, that, in every state, the supreme power ought to emanate from the people; but when once that power is constituted, they can conceive, as it were, no limits to it, and they are ready to admit that it has the right to do whatever it pleases. They have not the slightest notion of peculiar privileges granted to cities, families, or persons: their minds appear never to have foreseen that it might be possible not to apply with strict uniformity the same laws to every part of the state, and to all its inhabitants.

These same opinions are more and more diffused in Europe; they even insinuate themselves amongst those nations which most vehemently reject the principle of the sovereignty of the people. Such nations assign a different origin to the supreme power, but they ascribe to that power the same characteristics. Amongst them all, the idea of intermediate powers is weakened and obliterated; the idea of rights inherent in certain individuals is rapidly disappearing from the minds of men; the idea of the omnipotence and sole authority of society at large rises to fill its place. These ideas take root and spread in proportion as social conditions become more equal, and men more alike; they are produced by equality, and in turn they hasten the progress of equality.

In France, where the revolution of which I am speaking has gone further than in any other European country, these opinions have got complete hold of the public mind. If we listen attentively to the language of the various parties in France, we shall find that there is not one which has not adopted them. Most of these parties censure the conduct of the government, but they all hold that the government ought perpetually to act and interfere in everything that is done. Even those which are most at variance are nevertheless agreed upon this head. The unity, the ubiquity, the omnipotence of the supreme power, and the uniformity of its rules, constitute the principal characteristics of all the political systems which have been put forward in our age. They recur even in the wildest visions of political regeneration: the human mind pursues them in its dreams.

If these notions spontaneously arise in the minds of private individuals, they suggest themselves still more forcibly to the minds of princes. Whilst the ancient fabric of European society is altered and dissolved, sovereigns acquire new conceptions of their opportunities and their duties; they learn for the first time that the central power which they represent may and ought to administer, by its own agency and on a uniform plan, all the concerns of the whole community. This opinion, which, I will venture to say, was never conceived before our time by the monarchs of Europe, now sinks deeply into the minds of kings, and abides there amidst all the agitation of more unsettled thoughts.

Our contemporaries are therefore much less divided than is commonly supposed; they are constantly disputing as to the hands in which supremacy is to be vested, but they readily agree upon the duties and the rights of that supremacy. The notion they all form of government is that of a sole, simple, providential, and creative power.

All secondary opinions in politics are unsettled; this one remains fixed, invariable, and consistent. It is adopted by statesmen and political philosophers; it is eagerly laid hold of by the multitude; those who govern and those who are governed agree to pursue it with equal ardor; it is the earliest notion of their minds, it seems innate. It originates, therefore, in no caprice of the human intellect, but it is a necessary condition of the present state of mankind.

─────────★─────────

That the Sentiments of Democratic Nations Accord with Their Opinions in Leading Them to Concentrate Political Power

I f it be true that, in ages of equality, men readily adopt the notion of a great central power, it cannot be doubted, on the other hand, that their habits and sentiments predispose them to recognize such a power, and to give it their support. This may be demonstrated in a few words, as the greater part of the reasons to which the fact may be attributed have been previously stated.

As the men who inhabit democratic countries have no superiors, no inferiors, and no habitual or necessary partners in their undertakings, they readily fall back upon themselves, and consider themselves as beings apart. I had occasion to point this out at considerable length in treating of individualism. Hence such men can never, without an effort, tear themselves from their private affairs to engage in public business; their natural bias leads them to abandon the latter to the sole visible and permanent representative of the interests of the community, that is to say, to the state. Not only are they naturally wanting in a taste for public business, but they have frequently no time to attend to it. Private life in democratic times is so busy, so excited, so full of wishes and of work, that hardly any energy or leisure remains to each individual for public life. I am the last man to contend that these propensities are unconquerable, since my chief object in writing this book has been to combat them. I only maintain that, at the present day, a secret power is fostering them in the human heart, and that, if they are not checked, they will wholly overgrow it.

I have also had occasion to show how the increasing love of well-being and the fluctuating character of property cause democratic nations to dread all violent disturbances. The love of public tranquility is frequently the only passion which these nations retain, and it becomes more active and powerful amongst them in proportion as all other passions droop and die. This naturally disposes the members of the community constantly to give or to surrender additional rights to the central power, which alone seems to be interested in defending them by the same means that it uses to defend itself.

As in periods of equality, no man is compelled to lend his assistance to his fellow-men, and none has any right to expect much support from them, every one is at once independent and powerless. These two conditions, which must never be either separately considered or confounded together, inspire the citizen of a democratic country with very contrary propensities. His independence fills him with self-reliance and pride amongst his equals; his debility makes him feel from time to time the want of some outward assistance, which he cannot expect from any of them, because they are all impotent and unsympathizing. In this predicament, he naturally turns his eyes to that imposing power which alone rises above the level of universal depression. Of that power his wants and especially his desires continually remind him, until he ultimately views it as the sole and necessary support of his own weakness.

This may more completely explain what frequently takes place in democratic countries, where the very men who are so impatient of superiors patiently submit to a master, exhibiting at once their pride and their servility.

The hatred which men bear to privilege increases in proportion as privileges become fewer and less considerable, so that democratic passions would seem to burn most fiercely just when they have least fuel. I have already given the reason of this phenomenon. When all conditions are unequal, no inequality is so great as to offend the eye; whereas the slightest dissimilarity is odious in the midst of general uniformity: the more complete this uniformity is, the more insupportable does the sight of such a difference become. Hence it is natural that the love of equality should constantly increase together with equality itself, and that it should grow by what it feeds on.

This never-dying, ever-kindling hatred, which sets a democratic people against the smallest privileges, is peculiarly favorable to the gradual concentration of all political rights in the hands of the representative of the state alone. The sovereign, being necessarily and incontestably above all the citizens, excites not their envy, and each of them thinks that he strips his equals of the prerogative which he concedes to the crown. The man of a democratic age is extremely reluctant to obey his neighbor who is his equal; he refuses to acknowledge superior ability in such a person; he mistrusts his justice, and is jealous of his power; he fears and he contemns him; and he loves continually to remind him of the common dependence in which both of them stand to the same master.

Every central power, which follows its natural tendencies, courts and encourages the principle of equality; for equality singularly facilitates, extends, and secures the influence of a central power.

In like manner, it may be said that every central government worships uniformity: uniformity relieves it from inquiry into an infinity of details, which must be attended to if rules have to be adapted to different men, instead of indiscriminately subjecting all men to the same rule: thus the government likes what the citizens like, and naturally hates what they hate. These common sentiments, which, in democratic nations, constantly unite the sovereign and every member of the community in one and the same conviction, establish a secret and lasting sympathy between them. The faults of the government are pardoned for the sake of its tastes; public confidence is only reluctantly withdrawn in the midst even of its excesses and its errors; and it is restored at the first call. Democratic nations often hate those in whose hands the central power is vested; but they always love that power itself.

Thus, by two separate paths, I have reached the same conclusion. I have shown that the principle of equality suggests to men the notion of a sole, uniform, and strong government: I have now shown that the principle of equality imparts to them a taste for it. To governments of this kind the nations of our age are therefore tending. They are drawn thither by the natural inclination of mind and heart; and in order to reach that result, it is enough that they do not check themselves in their course.

I am of opinion, that, in the democratic ages which are opening upon us, individual independence and local liberties will ever be the products of art; that centralization will be the natural government.

———————★———————

Of Certain Peculiar and Accidental Causes, Which Either Lead a People to Complete the Centralization of Government, or Which Divert Them from It

I f all democratic nations are instinctively led to the centralization of government, they tend to this result in an unequal manner.
This depends on the particular circumstances which may promote or
prevent the natural consequences of that state of society,—circumstances which are exceedingly numerous, but of which I shall mention only a few.

Amongst men who have lived free long before they became equal,
the tendencies derived from free institutions combat, to a certain
extent, the propensities superinduced by the principle of equality;
and although the central power may increase its privileges amongst
such a people, the private members of such a community will never
entirely forfeit their independence. But when the equality of conditions grows up amongst a people who have never known, or have
long ceased to know, what freedom is, (and such is the case upon the
continent of Europe,) as the former habits of the nation are suddenly
combined, by some sort of natural attraction, with the new habits and
principles engendered by the state of society, all powers seem spontaneously to rush to the center. These powers accumulate there with
astonishing rapidity, and the state instantly attains the utmost limits
of its strength, whilst private persons allow themselves to sink as suddenly to the lowest degree of weakness.

The English who emigrated three hundred years ago to found a
democratic commonwealth on the shores of the New World had all
learned to take a part in public affairs in their mother country; they

were conversant with trial by jury; they were accustomed to liberty of speech and of the press,—to personal freedom, to the notion of rights and the practice of asserting them. They carried with them to America these free institutions and manly customs, and these institutions preserved them against the encroachments of the state. Thus, amongst the Americans, it is freedom which is old,—equality is of comparatively modern date. The reverse is occurring in Europe, where equality, introduced by absolute power and under the rule of kings, was already infused into the habits of nations long before freedom had entered into their thoughts.

I have said that, amongst democratic nations, the notion of government naturally presents itself to the mind under the form of a sole and central power, and that the notion of intermediate powers is not familiar to them. This is peculiarly applicable to the democratic nations which have witnessed the triumph of the principle of equality by means of a violent revolution. As the classes which managed local affairs have been suddenly swept away by the storm, and as the confused mass which remains has as yet neither the organization nor the habits which fit it to assume the administration of these affairs, the state alone seems capable of taking upon itself all the details of government, and centralization becomes, as it were, the unavoidable state of the country.

Napoleon deserves neither praise nor censure for having center in his own hands almost all the administrative power of France; for, after the abrupt disappearance of the nobility and the higher rank of the middle classes, these powers devolved on him of course: it would have been almost as difficult for him to reject as to assume them. But a similar necessity has never been felt by the Americans, who, having passed through no revolution, and having governed themselves from the first, never had to call upon the state to act for a time as their guardian. Thus, the progress of centralization amongst a democratic people depends not only on the progress of equality, but on the manner in which this equality has been established.

At the commencement of a great democratic revolution, when hostilities have but just broken out between the different classes of society, the people endeavor to centralize the public administration in the hands of the government, in order to wrest the management of local affairs from the aristocracy. Towards the close of such a revolution, on the contrary, it is usually the conquered aristocracy who endeavor to make over the management of all affairs to the state, because such an aristocracy dread the tyranny of a people who have become their equal, and not infrequently their master. Thus, it is not always the same class of the community which strives to increase the prerogative of the government; but as long as the democratic revolution lasts, there is always one class in the nation, powerful in numbers or in wealth, who are induced, by peculiar passions or interests, to centralize the public administration, independently of that hatred of being governed by one's neighbor which is a general and permanent feeling amongst democratic nations.

It may be remarked, that, at the present day, the lower orders in England are striving with all their might to destroy local independence, and to transfer the administration from all the points of the circumference to the center; whereas the higher classes are endeavoring to retain this administration within its ancient boundaries. I venture to predict that a time will come when the very reverse will happen.

These observations explain why the supreme power is always stronger, and private individuals weaker, amongst a democratic people, who have passed through a long and arduous struggle to reach a state of equality, than amongst a democratic community in which the citizens have been equal from the first. The example of the Americans completely demonstrates the fact. The inhabitants of the United States were never divided by any privileges; they have never known the mutual relation of master and inferior; and as they neither dread nor hate each other, they have never known the necessity of calling in the supreme power to manage their affairs. The lot of the Americans is singular: they have derived from the aristocracy of England the notion of private rights and the taste for local freedom; and they have been able to retain both, because they have had no aristocracy to combat.

If education enables men at all times to defend their independence, this is most especially true in democratic times. When all men are alike, it is easy to found a sole and all-powerful government by the aid of mere instinct. But men require much intelligence, knowledge, and art to organize and to maintain secondary powers under similar circumstances, and to create, amidst the independence and individual weakness of the citizens, such free associations as may be able to struggle against tyranny without destroying public order.

Hence the concentration of power and the subjection of individuals will increase amongst democratic nations, not only in the same proportion as their equality, but in the same proportion as their ignorance. It is true that, in ages of imperfect civilization, the government is frequently as wanting in the knowledge required to impose a despotism upon the people, as the people are wanting in the knowledge required to shake it off; but the effect is not the same on both sides. However rude a democratic people may be, the central power which rules them is never completely devoid of cultivation, because it readily draws to its own uses what little cultivation is to be found in the country, and, if necessary, may seek assistance elsewhere. Hence, amongst a nation which is ignorant as well as democratic, an amazing difference cannot fail speedily to arise between the intellectual capacity of the ruler and that of each of his subjects. This completes the easy concentration of all power in his hands: the administrative function of the state is perpetually extended, because the state alone is competent to administer the affairs of the country.

The foremost, or indeed the sole condition, which is required in order to succeed in centralizing the supreme power in a democratic community, is to love equality, or to get men to believe you love it. Thus, the science of despotism, which was once so complex, is simplified, and reduced, as it were, to a single principle.

CHAPTER V

———— ★ ————

That amongst the European Nations of Our Time the Sovereign Power Is Increasing, although the Sovereigns Are Less Stable

On reflecting upon what has already been said, the reader will be startled and alarmed to find that in Europe everything seems to conduce to the indefinite extension of the prerogatives of government, and to render every day private independence more weak, more subordinate, and more precarious.

The democratic nations of Europe have all the general and permanent tendencies which urge the Americans to the centralization of government, and they are moreover exposed to a number of secondary and incidental causes with which the Americans are unacquainted. It would seem as if every step they make towards equality brings them nearer to despotism.

And, indeed, if we do but cast our looks around, we shall be convinced that such is the fact. During the aristocratic ages which preceded the present time, the sovereigns of Europe had been deprived of, or had relinquished, many of the rights inherent in their power. Not a hundred years ago, amongst the greater part of European nations, numerous private persons and corporations were sufficiently independent to administer justice, to raise and maintain troops, to levy taxes, and frequently even to make or interpret the law. The state has everywhere resumed to itself alone these natural attributes of sovereign power; in all matters of government, the state tolerates no intermediate agent between itself and the people, and it directs them by itself in general affairs. I am far from blaming this concentration of power,—I simply point it out.

At the same period a great number of secondary powers existed in Europe, which represented local interests and administered local affairs. Most of these local authorities have already disappeared; all are speedily tending to disappear, or to fall into the most complete dependence. From one end of Europe to the other the privileges of the nobility, the liberties of cities, and the powers of provincial bodies are either destroyed or are upon the verge of destruction.

Europe has endured, in the course of the last half-century, many revolutions and counter revolutions, which have agitated it in opposite directions; but all these perturbations resemble each other in one respect,—they have all shaken or destroyed the secondary powers of government. The local privileges which the French did not abolish in the countries they conquered, have finally succumbed to the policy of the princes who conquered the French. Those princes rejected all the innovations of the French Revolution except centralization: that is the only principle they consented to receive from such a source.

My object is to remark, that all these various rights, which have been successively wrested, in our time, from classes, corporations, and individuals, have not served to raise new secondary powers on a more democratic basis, but have uniformly been concentrated in the hands of the sovereign. Everywhere the state acquires more and more direct control over the humblest members of the community, and a more exclusive power of governing each of them in his smallest concerns.

CHAPTER VI

★

What Sort of Despotism Democratic Nations Have to Fear

I had remarked during my stay in the United States, that a democratic state of society, similar to that of the Americans, might offer singular facilities for the establishment of despotism; and I perceived, upon my return to Europe, how much use had already been made, by most of our rulers, of the notions, the sentiments, and the wants created by this same social condition, for the purpose of extending the circle of their power. This led me to think that the nations of Christendom would perhaps eventually undergo some oppression like that which hung over several of the nations of the ancient world.

A more accurate examination of the subject, and five years of further meditation, have not diminished my fears, but have changed the object of them.

No sovereign ever lived in former ages so absolute or so powerful as to undertake to administer by his own agency, and without the assistance of intermediate powers, all the parts of a great empire: none ever attempted to subject all his subjects indiscriminately to strict uniformity of regulation, and personally to tutor and direct every member of the community. The notion of such an undertaking never occurred to the human mind; and if any man had conceived it, the want of information, the imperfection of the administrative system, and, above all, the natural obstacles caused by the inequality of conditions, would speedily have checked the execution of so vast a design.

When the Roman Emperors were at the height of their power, the different nations of the empire still preserved manners and customs of great diversity; although they were subject to the same monarch, most of the provinces were separately administered; they abounded in powerful and active municipalities; and although the whole government of the empire was centered in the hands of the Emperor alone, and he always remained, in case of need, the supreme arbiter in all matters, yet the details of social life and private occupations lay for the most part beyond his control. The Emperors possessed, it is true, an immense and unchecked power, which allowed them to gratify all their whimsical tastes, and to employ for that purpose the whole strength of the state. They frequently abused that power arbitrarily to deprive their subjects of property or of life: their tyranny was extremely onerous to the few, but it did not reach the many; it was fixed to some few main objects, and neglected the rest; it was violent, but its range was limited.

It would seem that, if despotism were to be established amongst the democratic nations of our days, it might assume a different character; it would be more extensive and more mild; it would degrade men without tormenting them. I do not question, that, in an age of instruction and equality like our own, sovereigns might more easily succeed in collecting all political power into their own hands, and might interfere more habitually and decidedly with the circle of private interests, than any sovereign of antiquity could ever do. But this same principle of equality which facilitates despotism, tempers its rigor. We have seen how the manners of society become more humane and gentle, in proportion as men become more equal and alike. When no member of the community has much power or much wealth, tyranny is, as it were, without opportunities and a field of action. As all fortunes are scanty, the passions of men are naturally circumscribed, their imagination limited, their pleasures simple. This universal moderation moderates the sovereign himself, and checks within certain limits the inordinate stretch of his desires.

Independently of these reasons, drawn from the nature of the state of society itself, I might add many others arising from causes beyond my subject; but I shall keep within the limits I have laid down.

Democratic governments may become violent, and even cruel, at certain periods of extreme effervescence or of great danger; but these crises will be rare and brief. When I consider the petty passions of our contemporaries, the mildness of their manners, the extent of their education, the purity of their religion, the gentleness of their morality, their regular and industrious habits, and the restraint which they almost all observe in their vices no less than in their virtues, I have no fear that they will meet with tyrants in their rulers, but rather with guardians.

I think, then, that the species of oppression by which democratic nations are menaced is unlike anything which ever before existed in the world: our contemporaries will find no prototype of it in their memories. I seek in vain for an expression which will accurately convey the whole of the idea I have formed of it; the old words despotism and tyranny are inappropriate: the thing itself is new, and since I cannot name, I must attempt to define it.

I seek to trace the novel features under which despotism may appear in the world. The first thing that strikes the observation is an innumerable multitude of men, all equal and alike, incessantly endeavoring to procure the petty and paltry pleasures with which they glut their lives. Each of them, living apart, is as a stranger to the fate of all the rest,—his children and his private friends constitute to him the whole of mankind; as for the rest of his fellow-citizens, he is close to them, but he sees them not;—he touches them, but he feels them not; he exists but in himself and for himself alone; and if his kindred still remain to him, he may be said at any rate to have lost his country.

Above this race of men stands an immense and tutelary power, which takes upon itself alone to secure their gratifications, and to watch over their fate. That power is absolute, minute, regular, provident, and mild. It would be like the authority of a parent, if, like that authority, its object was to prepare men for manhood; but it seeks, on the contrary, to keep them in perpetual childhood: it is well content that the people should rejoice, provided they think of nothing but rejoicing. For their happiness such a government willingly labors, but it chooses to be the sole agent and the only arbiter of that happiness; it provides for their security, foresees and supplies their necessities, facilitates their pleasures, manages their principal concerns, directs their industry, regulates the descent of property, and subdivides their inheritances: what remains, but to spare them all the care of thinking and all the trouble of living?

Thus, it every day renders the exercise of the free agency of man less useful and less frequent; it circumscribes the will within a narrower range, and gradually robs a man of all the uses of himself. The principle of equality has prepared men for these things; it has predisposed men to endure them, and oftentimes to look on them as benefits.

After having thus successively taken each member of the community in its powerful grasp, and fashioned him at will, the supreme power then extends its arm over the whole community. It covers the surface of society with a network of small complicated rules, minute and uniform, through which the most original minds and the most energetic characters cannot penetrate, to rise above the crowd. The will of man is not shattered, but softened, bent, and guided; men are seldom forced by it to act, but they are constantly restrained from acting: such a power does not destroy, but it prevents existence; it does not tyrannize, but it compresses, enervates, extinguishes, and stupefies a people, till each nation is reduced to be nothing better than a flock of timid and industrious animals, of which the government is the shepherd.

I have always thought that servitude of the regular, quiet, and gentle kind which I have just described might be combined more easily than is commonly believed with some of the outward forms of freedom, and that it might even establish itself under the wing of the sovereignty of the people.

Our contemporaries are constantly excited by two conflicting passions; they want to be led, and they wish to remain free: as they cannot destroy either the one or the other of these contrary propensities, they strive to satisfy them both at once. They devise a sole, tutelary, and all-powerful form of government, but elected by the people. They combine the principle of centralization and that of popular sovereignty; this gives them a respite: they console themselves for being in tutelage by the reflection that they have chosen their own guardians. Every man allows himself to be put in leading-strings, because he sees that it is not a person or a class of persons, but the people at large, who hold the end of his chain.

By this system, the people shake off their state of dependence just long enough to select their master, and then relapse into it again. A great many persons at the present day are quite contented with this sort of compromise between administrative despotism and the sovereignty of the people; and they think they have done enough for the protection of individual freedom when they have surrendered it to the power of the nation at large. This does not satisfy me:

the nature of him I am to obey signifies less to me than the fact of extorted obedience.

I do not, however, deny that a constitution of this kind appears to me to be infinitely preferable to one which, after having concentrated all the powers of government, should vest them in the hands of an irresponsible person or body of persons. Of all the forms which democratic despotism could assume, the latter would assuredly be the worst.

When the sovereign is elective, or narrowly watched by a legislature which is really elective and independent, the oppression which he exercises over individuals is sometimes greater, but it is always less degrading; because every man, when he is oppressed and disarmed, may still imagine that, whilst he yields obedience, it is to himself he yields it, and that it is to one of his own inclinations that all the rest give way. In like manner, I can understand that, when the sovereign represents the nation, and is dependent upon the people, the rights and the power of which every citizen is deprived not only serve the head of the state, but the state itself; and that private persons derive some return from the sacrifice of their independence which they have made to the public. To create a representation of the people in every centralized country is, therefore, to diminish the evil which extreme centralization may produce, but not to get rid of it.

I admit that, by this means, room is left for the intervention of individuals in the more important affairs; but it is not the less suppressed in the smaller and more private ones. It must not be forgotten that it is especially dangerous to enslave men in the minor details of life. For my own part, I should be inclined to think freedom less necessary in great things than in little ones, if it were possible to be secure of the one without possessing the other.

Subjection in minor affairs breaks out every day, and is felt by the whole community indiscriminately. It does not drive men to resistance, but it crosses them at every turn, till they are led to surrender the exercise of their own will. Thus their spirit is gradually broken and their character enervated; whereas that obedience which is exacted on a few important but rare occasions, only exhibits servitude at certain intervals, and throws the burden of it upon a small number of men. It is in vain to summon a people, who have been rendered so dependent on the central power, to choose from time to time the representatives of that power; this rare and brief exercise of their free choice, however important it may be, will not prevent them from gradually losing the faculties of thinking, feeling, and acting for themselves, and thus gradually falling below the level of humanity.

I add, that they will soon become incapable of exercising the great and only privilege which remains to them. The democratic nations which have introduced freedom into their political constitution, at the very time when they were augmenting the despotism of their administrative constitution, have been led into strange paradoxes. To manage those minor affairs in which good sense is all that is wanted,—the people are held to be unequal to the task; but when the government of the country is at stake, the people are invested with immense powers; they are alternately made the playthings of their ruler, and his masters,—more than kings, and less than men. After having exhausted all the different modes of election, without finding one to suit their purpose, they are still amazed, and still bent on seeking further; as if the evil they remark did not originate in the constitution of the country, far more than in that of the electoral body.

It is, indeed, difficult to conceive how men who have entirely given up the habit of self-government should succeed in making a proper choice of those by whom they are to be governed; and no one will ever believe that a liberal, wise, and energetic government can spring from the suffrages of a subservient people.

A constitution which should be republican in its head, and ultra-monarchical in all its other parts, has ever appeared to me to be a short-lived monster. The vices of rulers and the inaptitude of the people would speedily bring about its ruin; and the nation, weary of its representatives and of itself, would create freer institutions, or soon return to stretch itself at the feet of a single master.

CHAPTER VII

---★---

Continuation of the Preceding Chapters

I believe that it is easier to establish an absolute and despotic government amongst a people in which the conditions of society are equal, than amongst any other; and I think that, if such a government were once established amongst such a people, it would not only oppress men, but would eventually strip each of them of several of the highest qualities of humanity. Despotism, therefore, appears to me peculiarly to be dreaded in democratic times. I should have loved freedom, I believe, at all times, but in the time in which we live I am ready to worship it.

On the other hand, I am persuaded that all who shall attempt, in the ages upon which we are entering, to base freedom upon aristocratic privilege, will fail; that all who shall attempt to draw and to retain authority within a single class, will fail. At the present day, no ruler is skilful or strong enough to found a despotism by re-establishing permanent distinctions of rank amongst his subjects: no legislator is wise or powerful enough to preserve free institutions, if he does not take equality for his first principle and his watchword. All of our contemporaries who would establish or secure the independence and the dignity of their fellow-men, must show themselves the friends of equality; and the only worthy means of showing themselves as such is to be so: upon this depends the success of their holy enterprise. Thus, the question is not how to reconstruct aristocratic society, but how to make liberty proceed out of that democratic state of society in which God has placed us.

I shall conclude by one general idea, which comprises not only all the particular ideas which have been expressed in the present chapter, but also most of those which it is the object of this book to treat of. In the ages of aristocracy which preceded our own, there were private persons of great power, and a social authority of extreme weakness. The outline of society itself was not easily discernible, and constantly confounded with the different powers by which the community was ruled. The principal efforts of the men of those times were required to strengthen, aggrandize, and secure the supreme power; and, on the other hand, to circumscribe individual independence within narrower limits, and to subject private interests to the interests of the public. Other perils and other cares await the men of our age. Amongst the greater part of modern nations, the government, whatever may be its origin, its constitution, or its name, has become almost omnipotent, and private persons are falling, more and more, into the lowest stage of weakness and dependence.

In olden society, everything was different; unity and uniformity were nowhere to be met with. In modern society, everything threatens to become so much alike, that the peculiar characteristics of each individual will soon be entirely lost in the general aspect of the world. Our forefathers were ever prone to make an improper use of the notion that private rights ought to be respected; and we are naturally prone, on the other hand, to exaggerate the idea that the interest of a private individual ought always to bend to the interest of the many.

The political world is metamorphosed: new remedies must henceforth be sought for new disorders. To lay down extensive but distinct and settled limits to the action of the government; to confer certain rights on private persons, and to secure to them the undisputed enjoyment of those rights; to enable individual man to maintain whatever independence, strength, and original power he still possesses; to raise him by the side of society at large, and uphold him in that position,— these appear to me the main objects of legislators in the ages upon which we are now entering.

It would seem as if the rulers of our time sought only to use men in order to make things great; I wish that they would try a little more to make great men; that they would set less value on the work, and more upon the workman; that they would never forget that a nation cannot long remain strong when every man belonging to it is individually weak; and that no form or combination of social polity has yet been devised to make an energetic people out of a community of pusillanimous and enfeebled citizens.

CHAPTER VIII

———★———

General Survey of the Subject

Before closing forever the subject that I have now discussed, I would fain take a parting survey of all the different characteristics of modern society, and appreciate at last the general influence to be exercised by the principle of equality upon the fate of mankind; but I am stopped by the difficulty of the task, and, in presence of so great a theme, my sight is troubled, and my reason fails.

The society of the modern world, which I have sought to delineate, and which I seek to judge, has but just come into existence. Time has not yet shaped it into perfect form; the great revolution by which it has been created is not yet over; and, amidst the occurrences of our time, it is almost impossible to discern what will pass away with the revolution itself, and what will survive its close. The world which is rising into existence is still half encumbered by the remains of the world which is waning into decay; and, amidst the vast perplexity of human affairs, none can say how much of ancient institutions and former manners will remain, or how much will completely disappear.

Although the revolution which is taking place in the social condition, the laws, the opinions, and the feelings of men is still very far from being terminated, yet its results already admit of no comparison with anything that the world has ever before witnessed. I go back from age to age up to the remotest antiquity, but I find no parallel to what is occurring before my eyes: as the past has ceased to throw its light upon the future, the mind of man wanders in obscurity.

Nevertheless, in the midst of a prospect so wide, so novel, and so confused, some of the more prominent characteristics may already be discerned and pointed out. The good things and the evils of life are more equally distributed in the world: great wealth tends to disappear, the number of small fortunes to increase; desires and gratifications are multiplied, but extraordinary prosperity and irremediable penury are alike unknown. The sentiment of ambition is universal, but the scope of ambition is seldom vast. Each individual stands apart in solitary weakness; but society at large is active, provident, and powerful: the performances of private persons are insignificant, those of the state immense.

There is little energy of character, but manners are mild, and laws humane. If there be few instances of exalted heroism or of virtues of the highest, brightest, and purest temper, men's habits are regular, violence is rare, and cruelty almost unknown. Human existence becomes longer, and property more secure: life is not adorned with brilliant trophies, but it is extremely easy and tranquil. Few pleasures are either very refined or very coarse; and highly polished manners are as uncommon as great brutality of tastes. Neither men of great learning, nor extremely ignorant communities, are to be met with; genius becomes more rare, information more diffused. The human mind is impelled by the small efforts of all mankind combined together, not by the strenuous activity of a few men. There is less perfection, but more abundance, in all the productions of the arts. The ties of race, of rank, and of country are relaxed; the great bond of humanity is strengthened.

If I endeavor to find out the most general and most prominent of all these different characteristics, I perceive that what is taking place in men's fortunes manifests itself under a thousand other forms. Almost all extremes are softened or blunted: all that was most prominent is superseded by some middle term, at once less lofty and less low, less brilliant and less obscure, than what before existed in the world.

When I survey this countless multitude of beings, shaped in each other's likeness, amidst whom nothing rises and nothing falls, the sight of such universal uniformity saddens and chills me, and I am tempted to regret that state of society which has ceased to be. When the world was full of men of great importance and extreme insignificance, of great wealth and extreme poverty, of great learning and extreme ignorance, I turned aside from the latter to fix my observation on the former alone, who gratified my sympathies. But I admit that this gratification arose from my own weakness: it is because I am unable to see at once all that is around me, that I am allowed thus to select and separate the objects of my predilection from among so many others. Such is not the case with that Almighty and Eternal Being, whose gaze necessarily includes the whole of created things, and who surveys distinctly, though at once, mankind and man.

We may naturally believe that it is not the singular prosperity of the few, but the greater well-being of all, which is most pleasing in the sight of the Creator and Preserver of men. What appears to me to be man's decline is, to His eye, advancement; what afflicts me is acceptable to Him. A state of equality is perhaps less elevated, but it is more just: and its justice constitutes its greatness and its beauty. I would strive, then, to raise myself to this point of the Divine contemplation, and thence to view and to judge the concerns of men.

No man, upon the earth, can as yet affirm, absolutely and generally, that the new state of the world is better than its former one; but it is already easy to perceive that this state is different. Some vices and some virtues were so inherent in the constitution of an aristocratic nation, and are so opposite to the character of a modern people, that they can never be infused into it; some good tendencies and some bad propensities which were unknown to the former, are natural to the latter; some ideas suggest themselves spontaneously to the imagination of the one, which are utterly repugnant to the mind of the other. They are like two distinct orders of human beings, each of which has its own merits and defects, its own advantages and its own evils. Care must therefore be taken not to judge the state of society which is now coming into existence, by notions derived from a state of society which no longer exists; for, as these states of society are exceedingly different in their structure, they cannot be submitted to a just or fair comparison. It would be scarcely more reasonable to require of our contemporaries the peculiar virtues which originated in the social condition of their forefathers, since that social condition is itself fallen, and has drawn into one promiscuous ruin the good and evil which belonged to it.

But as yet these things are imperfectly understood. I find that a great number of my contemporaries undertake to make a selection from amongst the institutions, the opinions, and the ideas which originated in the aristocratic constitution of society as it was: a portion of these elements they would willingly relinquish, but they would keep the remainder and transplant them into their new world. I apprehend that such men are wasting their time and their strength in virtuous but unprofitable efforts. The object is, not to retain the peculiar advantages which the inequality of conditions bestows upon mankind, but to secure the new benefits which equality may supply. We have not to seek to make ourselves like our progenitors, but to strive to work out that species of greatness and happiness which is our own.

For myself, who now look back from this extreme limit of my task, and discover from afar, but at once, the various objects which have attracted my more attentive investigation upon my way, I am full of apprehensions and of hopes. I perceive mighty dangers which it is possible to ward off,—mighty evils which may be avoided or alleviated; and I cling with a firmer hold to the belief, that, for democratic nations to be virtuous and prosperous, they require but to will it.

I am aware that many of my contemporaries maintain that nations are never their own masters here below, and that they necessarily obey some insurmountable and unintelligent power, arising from anterior events, from their race, or from the soil and climate of their country. Such principles are false and cowardly; such principles can never produce aught but feeble men and pusillanimous nations. Providence has not created mankind entirely independent or entirely free. It is true, that around every man a fatal circle is traced, beyond which he cannot pass; but within the wide verge of that circle he is powerful and free: as it is with man, so with communities. The nations of our time cannot prevent the conditions of men from becoming equal; but it depends upon themselves whether the principle of equality is to lead them to servitude or freedom, to knowledge or barbarism, to prosperity or wretchedness.

SUBJECT INDEX

———————— ★ ————————

labor and, 350–52, 353–55,
375–76, 377–78
peace and, 329, 422
See also business;
manufacturing.
inequality, 13, 190–91, 204, 261,
398
revolution and, 422, 424
inheritance law, 31, 67–69, 197–98
innovation, 153, 159, 162
lawyers, lack of, 137–38, 141–43
New England, 58, 64
intelligence, 31, 36, 47, 53–54, 66,
70
Christianity and, 152–53
convictions, 111–12
doubt, 111–12, 161, 244–45
gifts of, 70, 175
imagination, 153, 221–22,
283–85, 287–88
improvement of, 118, 240–41,
259
meditation, 263–64
pleasures of the mind, 258–59
religion and, 152–53
interest rightly understood:
individualism and, 320–23
liberty and, 20–21, 220, 227–28
religion and, 324–26
self-interest and, 20–21, 321–23
Ireland, 149

Jackson, Andrew, 11, 22, 146
Jacksonian America, 2, 10–11
Jefferson, Thomas, 134, 227
judges, 9, 129, 142–43, 154
judicial power, 89–92, 148
over executive government,
92–94, 95–96
juries, 127–28, 143, 454
majority and, 129, 143

trial by, 61, 108
justice, 23, 134, 204, 214, 359
courts of, 142–43, 148
rights and, 127–28

Kentucky, 11, 23, 194–96, 231

labor, 118, 167, 195–96, 240–41,
348–49
free, 198–99, 200, 201
honor of, 348–49
industry, 350–52, 353–55,
375–76, 377–78
Native Americans, 182–83, 184
prejudice against, 198–99,
200–202, 203–4, 221–22
rewards / profits of, 195–96,
269, 347–49, 374, 376
wages, 377–78
workmen, 353–55, 369–74,
375–76, 377–78
land, 16, 32, 67–69, 375–76
inheritance of, 31, 67–69,
197–98
Native Americans and, 178–79,
185–88
language, 280–81
American, 287–88
business, 278–79, 287
English, 277–78
French, 278–79
laws, American, 80–81, 122, 165
of aristocracy, 122, 280–81
critique of, 167–68, 170–71
of democracy, 42, 121–22, 148,
168–71
manners and, 18, 170–71
municipal, 170
morality and, 16, 59–60
penal, 59–60, 359
political, 60–61, 72–73, 143